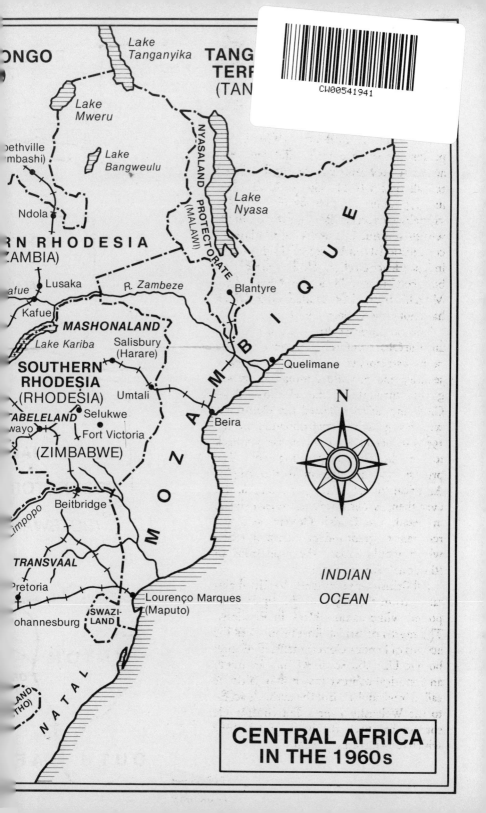

CENTRAL AFRICA
IN THE 1960s

The Road to Zimbabwe
1890-1980

The Road to
ZIMBABWE
1890–1980

Anthony Verrier

JONATHAN CAPE
THIRTY-TWO BEDFORD SQUARE LONDON

First published 1986
Copyright © 1986 by Anthony Verrier
Jonathan Cape Ltd, 32 Bedford Square, London WC1B 3EL

British Library Cataloguing in Publication Data

Verrier, Anthony
The road to Zimbabwe: 1890-1980.
1. Zimbabwe—History
I. Title
968.91   DT962.5

ISBN 0-224-02161-3

Printed by Butler & Tanner Ltd, Frome and London

For Mary Bagot
in friendship

Contents

Contents

Illustrations

Illustrations

Map

Acknowledgments

Many participants in and commentators on the events narrated in the following pages have discussed them with the writer during the past three years. A complete list would be invidious and, in some cases, inappropriate for serving officials and others. But particular thanks are due to: Major-General Sir John Acland, Julian Amery, Frank Barber, Patricia Battye, Walter Bell, Sir Arthur Benson, Mary Benson, William Bernard, Arthur Bottomley, Sir James Bottomley, John Bruce Lockhart, Lord Cledwyn, Susan Crosland, Denzil Dunnett, Sir Nigel Fisher, Malcolm Fraser, Professor Margaret Gowing, Ewen Greenfield, Lord Greenhill, E. R. Hooton, Sir John Johnston, Sir Glyn Jones, Sir Martin Le Quesne, Major-General J. M. McNeill, Dr David Owen, Sir Michael Palliser, Sir Hugh Parry, Sir Ronald Prain, Sir David Scott, Roger Sibley, Sir Harold Smedley, Arnold Smith, Sir Robert Taylor, Lord Thomson of Monifieth, Ewen Thomson, Lord Walston, Sir Duncan Watson, Sir Roy Welensky, Professor F. M. G. Willson.

In the United States George Ball, Wayne Fredericks, Donald McHenry and Garrick Utley, with others, provided much guidance.

A special debt of gratitude is owed to Sir Roy Welensky, Lord Blake and the Rhodes Trustees for permission to examine and quote from the Welensky Papers in the Bodleian Library; and to the National Archives in connection with the Mennen Williams Papers. Lord Blake, apart from providing encouragement and help, allowed me to quote from his magisterial *A History of Rhodesia* (Eyre Methuen, 1977). Thanks are also due to the staff of the Public Record Office for permission to cite material which is Crown copyright, to the Commonwealth Secretariat for permission similarly accorded; and to the London Library, the Brookings Institute, the School of Oriental and African Studies, the Royal Geographical Society, the Royal United Services Institute, and the International Institute for Strategic Studies.

My friends at Cape have been unwearying in help; Joan Barber, as always, produced a masterly typescript. I am also grateful to Mrs Alison Rogers of Times Photographic Sales.

Picture credits

For permission to reproduce photographs the author and publishers are grateful to the following: Argus South African Newspapers Ltd for no. 11; Associated Press for nos 3, 7, 8, 9 and 10; BBC Hulton Picture Library for nos 2, 4 and 12; Camera Press Ltd for no 5; Nicholas Harman for no. 14; The National Archives of Zimbabwe for no. 1; The Photo Source for no. 6; Popperfoto for no. 15; Times Newspapers Ltd for no. 13.

Abbreviations

ANC	African National Congress
AP	Assembly Place, Point
BBC	British Broadcasting Corporation
BG	British Government
`BMATT	British Military Advisory Training Team
BOSS	Bureau of State Security
BSA	British South Africa Company
BSAP	British South Africa Police (originally British South Africa Company Police)
CAF	Central African Federation
CIA	Central Intelligence Agency
CIO	Central Intelligence Organisation
CMF	Commonwealth Monitoring Force
COG/R	Commonwealth Observer Group/Report
COH/COMOPS	Combined Operations Headquarters
COIN	Counter-Insurgency Unit/operations
DMO	Director of Military Operations
FISB	Federal Intelligence and Security Bureau
FRELIMO	Mozambique Liberation Front
FROLIZI	Front for the Liberation of Zimbabwe
FSIO	Field Service Intelligence Officer
GATT	General Agreement on Tariffs and Trade
GPMG	General purpose machine-gun
MI5	British Security Service
NATO	North Atlantic Treaty Organisation

NDP	National Democratic Party
NED	National Election Directorate
NIBMAR	No Independence (for Southern Rhodesia) Before Majority African Rule
NSC	National Security Council
OAU	Organisation of African Unity
PATU	Police Anti-Terrorist Unit
PF/LO	Patriotic Front/Liaison Officer
PLAN	People's Liberation Army of Namibia
RAF	Royal Air Force
RLI	Rhodesian Light Infantry
RRAF	Royal Rhodesian Air Force
RSF	Rhodesian Security Forces
RST	Rhodesian Selection Trust
RV	Rendezvous
SADF	South African Defence Forces
SAS	Special Air Service Regiment (British, Rhodesian)
SIS	Secret Intelligence Service
SLO	Security Liaison Officer
SWAPO	South-West Africa People's Organisation
TTT	Tribal Trust Territories
UANC	United African National Council
UDI	Unilateral Declaration of Independence
UFP	United Federal Party
UNHCR	United Nations High Commission for Refugees
UNIP	United National Independence Party
UN/O	United Nations Organisation
UNTAG	United Nations Transitional Assistance Group
ZAF	Zimbabwe Air Force
ZANLA	Zimbabwe African National Liberation Army
ZANU	Zimbabwe African National Union
ZAPU	Zimbabwe African People's Union
ZIPRA	Zimbabwe People's Revolutionary Army

The white man's heaven is the black man's hell.

James Baldwin, *The Fire Next Time*

Introduction

One may as well state clearly at the outset what this book does
not set out to do. *The Road to Zimbabwe* is not another account
of black nationalism or white racialism (as those phrases tend to
be used by zealots), or of the armed struggle for an independent
Zimbabwe which was waged in and beyond Southern Rhodesia
between April 1972 and December 1979. Of course, something
must be said on these issues. Nationalism, racialism and guerrilla
war will be described and analysed. In particular, the war is given
a fair amount of attention for the years between early 1976 and
late 1979. During those years what was, in all essentials, a civil
war moved steadily in favour of Robert Mugabe's Zimbabwe
African National Liberation Army (ZANLA). As a result,
Mugabe's political movement, the Zimbabwe African National
Union (ZANU), became the dominant element in Rhodesia's
tribal conflict.

But many accounts, both objective and partisan, are available
for those who want to study black and white racial objectives. By
contrast, relatively little attention has been given to the wider
background – political, diplomatic, strategic and economic – in
which the participants were Britain, South Africa and, belatedly,
the United States. The writer had the good fortune to observe
the activities of these participants at rather close quarters during
the final stages of Zimbabwe's fight for independence, and as it
became the key element in a wider, Southern African, racial
struggle. During the 1979 Commonwealth Heads of Government

meeting in Lusaka and the subsequent Lancaster House conference, the writer also experienced, and throughout a four-month
period, another struggle – of a British Government determined
at almost all costs to deny Zimbabwe genuine independence. In
Lusaka he encountered Mrs Thatcher; at Lancaster House he
witnessed Lord Carrington's loyal but disillusioned attempt to
compensate for the defeat inflicted on his Prime Minister a month
before.

There is, perhaps, a natural tendency to assume that the
African struggle to become independent of white control in
Southern Rhodesia reflected an awakening nationalism which can
be studied in isolation from this wider background. Such an
assumption would place Harold Macmillan's February 1960
'wind of change' speech in a context where white politicians
responded to African pressure, and accepted that the imperial era
was coming to an end. This is a picturesque view of history,
where the African comes into his own, and his rights are acknowledged by the world at large. This view is fortified by the belief
that Britain always backed African rights. Alas, for far too long,
too many Africans also believed this, and waited patiently for the
day when might would be replaced by right.

But the assumption is false, because it not only ignores the
wider background but gives black nationalism a far greater vigour
and consistency of purpose than was, in fact, the case. Southern
Rhodesia's Africans were, for long, neither vigorous nor consistent in their attitudes, let alone their opposition, to white rule.
Between the first 'Chimurenga' (revolution) of the late 1890s and
the second of the 1970s, virtually no African who aspired to
influence in and beyond his tribe believed that an independent
Zimbabwe in the absolute sense was possible. The idea that
Africans could rule Zimbabwe – and thus rule over white men,
not merely govern with their consent, advice and power – was
not so much repudiated as forsworn. Even Ian Smith's Unilateral
Declaration of Independence on 11 November 1965, by which
white Southern Rhodesia rebelled from Britain because an Afrikaner South African Government rallied to its support, did not
transform conciliatory Africans into militant nationalists.

UDI was more of a challenge to African nationalism than it
was to British authority. But nearly a decade was to pass before

an African identity in Rhodesia – sensed by the Monckton Commission in 1960, established by the Pearce Commission in 1972 – was given meaning by the collapse of Portuguese rule in Mozambique. An independent Mozambique became certain, not merely probable. Sanctuary was provided in this embryo state from which ZANLA and ZANU could threaten the security of Rhodesia's eastern provinces. From the early 1970s, although no die was cast, opportunity was given to militant Africans, nationalists by circumstance rather than ideology, to plan and execute guerrilla campaigns. The war which thus began did not, alone, cast the die, but the attrition of white Rhodesia which followed forced Britain, South Africa and the United States to move into the foreground. British Governments which, for many years, had sought to remove Rhodesia from the Cabinet agenda, were compelled to reflect on the dangers rather than the merits of black rule in the rebel colony. United States Administrations extolled the black man's case but took care not to alienate South African Governments. These Governments put the utmost pressure on London and Washington with the objective of limiting black rights in Rhodesia to the shibboleth of 'responsible majority rule'.

London, Washington – and Pretoria – had cause not only to oppose African nationalism but were confident that it could be limited. Militant nationalism seemed a matter of words rather than deeds. Fabian nationalism, by contrast, was well established – and also amenable to further, but white, persuasion. Even as the final collapse of Portuguese authority in Mozambique occurred, influential Africans, notably Kenneth Kaunda and Joshua Nkomo, were actively, often ardently seeking compromise with Ian Smith and the South African Prime Minister, John Vorster. Kaunda, Nkomo and others thought that compromise would give their fellow Africans 'black majority rule' in Rhodesia. Kaunda and Nkomo cannot be blamed for seeking compromise. Kaunda was – and is – vulnerable to white pressure between the Zambeze and the Cape, to the power of multi-national business, to Wall Street and the London Metal Exchange. Nkomo's committed belief that the African should be content to accept some place at the white man's table reflects a background and experience unknown to, or derided by, the militant younger generation. Mugabe is the exemplar of that generation. Militancy, and the fortunes of war, are why Mugabe, not Nkomo, is Zimbabwe's Prime Minister. Kaunda and Nkomo did more than speak for, or negotiate on behalf of, millions of acquiescent Africans who resented the nature rather than the fact of white power. The two leaders represented an African capacity to be grateful for small mercies.

This prolonged African acquiescence in white military and economic power reflects two complementary factors. The man with the sjambok usually dominates the helot. Southern Rhodesia was not actually governed by methods familiar to Boer farmers, but a figurative sjambok was always in reserve should Africans 'get out of hand'. From its inception Southern Rhodesia was virtually self-governed; no British Government, let alone Britain's imperial representatives in South Africa – who had a vaguely defined role concerning the colony – chose to interfere. But elsewhere in Africa, Britain's colonial Governments, whose officials rarely cracked whips, evolved a doctrine of 'paramountcy' for the natives which convinced many Africans who acquired the white man's education that they would eventually attain a white man's status. Here and there, an exceptional African had the vision, or the ambition, to foresee the day when he and his people would be 'free' – of white rule. In East Africa perhaps only Jomo Kenyatta can be so described. In West Africa, where white settlement was precluded by climate, political progress for Africans had reached a stage by the eve of the Second World War where young men could not only see visions and dream dreams but actually contemplate something more positive than 'self-government'.

By contrast, both Northern and Southern Rhodesia remained in a colonial limbo. 'Paramountcy', when applied to Northern Rhodesia by a Labour Colonial Secretary, Lord Passfield, in 1930, was immediately rejected by a settler community which, although subject to some restraints by a British colonial Government, made up in racial intolerance what it lacked in political power. Despite two 'Boer' wars during the last quarter of the nineteenth century – or because of them – followed by the nominal assertion of British authority from the Cape to the Limpopo, British Governments throughout the years culminating in the Second World War left the two Rhodesias almost entirely to their

4

own devices; Downing Street, Whitehall and Westminster tacitly accepted that the Protectorate of Northern Rhodesia and the Colony of Southern Rhodesia formed part of a South African orbit. In this orbit the pull of Afrikaner beliefs and practices was only resisted when Salisbury's politicians became avid for outright independence, or when South African influence conflicted with great events and imperial priorities like World War or the place of gold in the sterling currency system.

This surrender of authority reflected Realpolitik. From at least the 1850s and the gradual 'opening up' of territory north of the Vaal and the Limpopo, British Governments had conceded, in official dispatch rather than in Parliament, that these expanding territories could not be governed by methods or on principles applicable to India, Canada, the Antipodes or elsewhere in the Empire. The Boer proved more resistant to British rule than the French Canadians. He fought, decamped, settled elsewhere. The imperial lines of communication beyond rather than to the Cape were long, and appeared to vanish into the unknown, where conditions were not conducive either to the health or the credibility of always inadequate garrisons. British Governments, Tory and Whig, Conservative and Liberal, evolved a policy which inevitably led to Boer paramountcy in the interior. Provided the Cape was securely held, as one of Palmerston's imperial 'inns on the way' - to India, where else? - colonial policy, even in Cape Colony and Natal, was based on the premise that if the Boer accepted nominal British sovereignty, he could do pretty much as he liked with the 'native'.

There were individual exceptions amongst governors and their subordinates to approval - and execution - of this policy. Enlightened soldiers sometimes murmured. Missionaries intermittently, not invariably, reported the cruelties and even discerned the dangers of relying on a policy not markedly different from that once practised by Spain in the New World - and followed by Portugal in Angola and Mozambique. Travellers and hunters, wise from endurance and close contact with these otherwise despised and neglected 'natives', aware of their culture, responsive to their courage, enlightened audiences at the Royal Geographical Society and in liberal circles with accounts of a land from the Cape to the Zambeze, from sea to shining sea, where there was room for black and white to live at peace. But as the Boer pushed north, and as the Southern African map was redrawn in the Chancelleries of Europe, the Bantu lost whatever friends he might have possessed. White men, had they the vision of a Jason, might have pointed out that the Red Indian could be defeated, the Aborigine all but exterminated, and the Maori reduced, but the Bantu of Southern Africa were a virile people, whose numbers would grow and whose ascendancy might make a bitter ending to white rule. No such prophecy, in the Victorian age, was made.

Diamonds and gold completed the ring round an African race and its many tribes. Cecil Rhodes, Starr Jameson and other shareholders in the British South Africa Company were beneficiaries of a system where Whitehall proposed and the men on the spot disposed. The adventurers, remittance men and 'gentlemen rankers' who left Kimberley for Salisbury on 6 May 1890 were heirs to a *laissez-faire* colonial policy which, in Rhodes's words, 'preferred land to niggers'. Rhodes had a vision – red on the map. But Rhodes and his kind observed 'the good old rule', and took what was neither theirs to take nor expressly sanctioned by imperial writ. Part One covers these years, and beyond, in rather summary fashion, because the record is now pretty well open to view. But the years of Rhodes's domination are mentioned here in order to focus attention on the situation which obtained in 1945, when the story as such begins.

During 1922 and 1923 Southern Rhodesia's whites, hitherto governed – lightly but not well – by the British South Africa Company, came under nominal British rule. The settlers also voted against incorporation with the Union of South Africa, but further consolidated an economic and, in the last resort, a cultural relationship with South Africa. This relationship had both British and Boer elements, but it was the latter which proved more acceptable to a white minority whose older members could remember the Matabele and Mashona on the rampage. Between 1923 and the middle 1950s Southern Rhodesia's whites succeeded in being British by precept, Boer by practice. The Colony's politics were dominated by those of British descent, but 'Pioneer Day' (13 September) was a more important date in the calendar than the Sovereign's official birthday. When the Bledisloe Royal Commission came to report on 'Rhodesia and Nyasaland' in

March 1939 amalgamation between the two larger territories – a process which was intended to prepare them for full Dominion status – was opposed by the Commission on the grounds that this would be tantamount to abandonment of the Protectorate's native races to the rule of a white-led Southern Rhodesia. These whites took their sentiments from the 'Mother country', but their racial practices came from a South Africa where Afrikaner beliefs were more potent than liberal principles.

These introductory notes are given because a strangely surviving myth of modern history is that British Labour Governments between 1945 and 1951 were committed to 'de-colonisation', to a new deal for native races everywhere. The myth must be exploded. The members of Clement Attlee's two Governments were, almost without exception, able, experienced and, as the word was then construed, patriotic. None, whatever their liberal, Fabian, imperial paternalism – or, in the case of John Strachey, his continued adherence to a Marxist interpretation of Empire – had the slightest intention of Britain voluntarily relinquishing power in any territory where the Union flag flew over Government House. Even independence for West African territories was to be balanced by a continued British role, above all in economic and commercial terms.

By extension, a Dominion like South Africa, where imperial burdens were shouldered, but adapted to white racial belief, was assured of understanding and what passed for co-operation in Downing Street and Whitehall. The record of this continued, if adapted, imperialism can be found in Cabinet Papers and other, less readily available, material. What these often tired and worried British Ministers were forced to do was concede power, retreat, abandon when no other choice remained. India and Palestine witnessed the first stages of what has aptly been called 'the long retreat from Empire'; the Indian Empire could not be held nor the Palestine Mandate sustained by the numbers of troops required. But this retreat did not begin because imperial sentiment had declined or political will had collapsed.

The retreat also reflected Realpolitik, economic in the twentieth century, not, as in Victoria's days, strategic. Between the end of the Second World War and the early 1950s Britain was flat broke. This was the national sacrifice of the Second World

War, the price for defeating Hitler, for fighting him during a year of absolute peril with none but the Empire's loyal subjects in support. The India and Palestine garrisons were needed in Britain. The men were needed in the factories and shipyards, on the land, down the mine. Given these realities, we must appreciate that such attention as Attlee's Cabinets gave to Southern Rhodesia during their years of office and travail reflected not only continued acquiescence in the imperial policies and Afrikaner practices summarised to this point but, as with virtually all the issues they tackled, an almost desperate search for ways of maintaining Britain's international status whilst simultaneously trying to alleviate the country's parlous economic situation. Therefore, at this point one must introduce the singular fact that Attlee and Bevin compounded Britain's subjection to South Africa by secretly embarking on the production of atom bombs.

Despite the virtual extinction of foreign exchange reserves (which enhanced the importance of South African gold in the international currency system), widespread material destruction in Britain caused by Hitler's bombs, and an industrial structure weakened by pre-war slump and wartime effort, Attlee and Bevin in 1947 determined that the country should have an 'independent nuclear deterrent'. The determination to embark on this grandiose folly was governed by belief in national prestige and international status, coupled with a marked, if veiled, distrust of the United States. Britain's atom bombs were not built primarily to deter the Soviet Union, but to reinsure against an American failure to do so. During the Second World War, Churchill had been satisfied by collaboration with the United States in producing the first two atom bombs. Balked of American collaboration in the postwar years, Attlee and Bevin decided to build a national, nominally independent nuclear deterrent – but one whose explosive source would come from South Africa.

By this act Britain finally placed itself in South Africa's hands. The Cabinet Papers for these fateful years are understandably silent on the nuclear factor, although almost eloquent on the grip which South Africa exerted on British policies because of the dependence of sterling on gold. But it must be emphasised here that, as a result of the decision by Attlee and Bevin to build a nuclear deterrent, South Africa acquired a power to determine what Britain would or, more usually, would not do concerning Southern Africa in general and Southern Rhodesia in particular which, directly or indirectly, was the biggest single if least readily appreciated element in the course of events between 1947 and 1980. Moreover, as the Cabinet Papers and other sources reveal, Britain's international trading position was largely governed by the role of sterling as a 'reserve' currency, that is, one against which the exchange value of many other currencies was measured. By wartime agreement with the United States (whose dollar was not so restricted), sterling was not freely 'convertible' into other currencies. Moreover, despite Britain's abandonment of the 'gold standard' in 1931, the trading value of sterling was assessed, if not precisely measured, in terms of gold reserves.

Thus, with gold and uranium as twin symbols of Britain's international status, South Africa acquired a role in British policy concerning Southern Africa which was almost embarrassingly potent. But the singular fact remains that Attlee's Cabinets did not wait for South Africa to show its hand in matters where pressure could be applied: these Cabinets proceeded to make plans for the future of the two Rhodesias which were designed to remove them from limbo, and bring them securely within the Afrikaner concept of race relations. Thus these Cabinets deliberately, although not expressly, repudiated the notion that Africans in these territories could ever acquire real power. By the late 1940s Colonial Secretaries in Attlee's Cabinets had begun to accept, indeed to argue, that self-government, possibly outright independence, for some West African territories could be contemplated, even planned. East Africa was thought too backward for full independence. Whatever solution might be devised for West and East Africa, territories there would not only remain in the 'sterling area', they would remain politically bound to and strategically valuable to Britain. But Southern Africa was a different affair altogether. The strategic – and economic – value was unquestionable, but it would remain so by continued, enforced, abandonment of imperial authority to South Africa.

This is the story told in Parts Two and Three, and it is given there in sufficient detail for the origins, life and death of the 'Federation of Rhodesia and Nyasaland' to be put in a correct historical context. The Federation – widely known, for misleading convenience, as the Central African Federation (CAF) – was nothing more or less than a device to absolve Britain from the responsibility of deciding the future of territories which British subjects had seized or otherwise acquired. In this process of propitiating white interests, Attlee's Cabinets in general and responsible Ministers in particular gave lip service to such formulae as 'multi-racialism', but were determined never to say what, if anything, they meant in practice. In practice, concessions were made to a South Africa which moved rapidly in the direction of apartheid after the Nationalist victory in the 1948 General Election. The British Government seemingly convinced itself that apartheid could be 'contained' by establishing the Federation. It is doubtful if even the conviction was long sustained. The true story, as shown in Part Two, is that, as before, Britain proposed and South Africa disposed – from the Cape to the Zambeze. Nothing reveals this truth more clearly than the episode of Seretse Khama, to which some attention is given because the critical sources are, at last, available – and because the tale is a cautionary one.

In writing these words no stone is flung at men who laboured hard to reconcile Britain's perceived imperial and international roles with the realities of power. But the Federation established in 1953 set in train a course of events which culminated in Zimbabwe's independence twenty-seven years later. There was no historic inevitability about this process. Southern Rhodesia's whites formed a tribe which lost its head, destroying itself in pursuit of racial supremacy. But, as we trace events for these years in some detail, the wider background of Britain's impotence, South Africa's power and the always equivocal roles of American Administrations – rhetorically devoted to Africans' 'rights' yet much more concerned with their supposed vulnerability to Soviet lures – becomes one in which the fate of black and white in Southern Rhodesia are subordinate to power politics, never pure nor simple.

A Labour Government in 1965 neither actively sought to deter UDI nor did it effectively oppose the act. Sanctions were a gesture, not a policy. United States Administrations progressively came to support Ian Smith, under the rose where necessary, by importing the rebels' chrome when the market deemed it favourable.

To the end of UDI, strenuous efforts were made by Labour and Conservative Governments alike to devise a 'settlement' in and for Southern Rhodesia which would give Africans the appearance of power, retaining for whites its reality. The 1979 Commonwealth Heads of Government meeting in Lusaka and the subsequent Lancaster House conference in London were genuinely dramatic examples of what power, and its loss, is about. Robert Mugabe won an independence Election in February 1980 not only because he was the tougher man, or because he was shrewd, but also because he came from the bigger tribe. But he won against all the odds which a British Government and Southern Rhodesia's whites could lay against him.

The United States was also, and for many years, governed by the uranium factor in its relations with South Africa. Unlike British Governments which, whatever their other shortcomings, remained sceptical of Soviet influence in Africa, United States Administrations could never square their opposition to apartheid with convictions that the Afrikaner republic was a bulwark against communism. In consequence, South African Governments were able to deflect or ignore criticism from Presidents and Congress. UDI and the 'Second Chimurenga' were thus years of further propitiation by Britain and the United States to a South Africa which not only supported Ian Smith as necessary but strengthened its grip on a territory also scheduled for independence – Namibia. Relationships between Britain, the United States and South Africa became increasingly complex as the Southern Rhodesian and Namibian issues interlocked. Part Four devotes some attention to another contemporary myth: that Henry Kissinger wrung concessions from Ian Smith and, indirectly, John Vorster when he met them in September 1976. Kissinger, with Namibia – and Angola – on his mind sought only to make a deal over Rhodesia, and did so. Smith lived to fight another day. Africans in Namibia – and Rhodesia – remained in bondage.

Yet neither Britain nor the United States wholly abandoned the struggle to achieve some kind of compromise over Southern Rhodesia. Africans there were not quite forgotten. Some principles remained, fortified, it is true, by British detestation of Ian Smith and American desire to 'stabilise' Southern Africa by something a little more positive than ritual gestures towards 'self-government' or 'African majority rule'. In the final event, however, Southern Rhodesia's Africans won their own battle. In doing so they defeated a South African-backed counter-revolution in which, throughout, Britain and the United States played critical but subordinate roles. But, as the Postscript shows, the counter-revolution has been thwarted, not defeated.

PART ONE
1890–1945

'We must always remember', he said again, harping on his one perennial string, 'that the gist of the South African question lies in the extension of the Cape Colony to the Zambezi.'

William Plomer, *Cecil Rhodes* (1933)

I

Raising the Flag

Frederick Selous, who led the Pioneer Column most of the way into what is now Zimbabwe's capital Harare, was a representative late Victorian figure. Often regarded by his contemporaries as the model for Rider Haggard's Allan Quartermain, Selous was, in fact, an adventurer more keen on gold than trekking the Mashonaland bush. Selous was an ideal choice from Rhodes's point of view to lead a 200-strong column of British South Africa Police and freebooters into Shona territory, and seize it – for the British South Africa (BSA), or 'Chartered' Company, but only by the widest constitutional latitude for the Crown. Selous not only knew the way better than any other white man; he grasped that the key to seizing the territory known briefly as Zambesia, subsequently as Southern Rhodesia, lay in outwitting the once powerful but for long docile Shona rather than encountering the still warlike Matabele.*

Rhodes's objective, as the dominant influence in the Chartered Company, was gold. King of the Kimberley diamond mines as principal shareholder in De Beers, he was influential but not omnipotent on the Rand. Rhodes's imperial vision of red on the map from Cairo to the Cape certainly required that territory north of the Bechuanaland Protectorate be seized so that Lord Salisbury's Conservative Government would approve, if but

---

*Usage of Mashonaland and Shona, Matabeleland and Matabele (Ndebele) cannot be completely consistent.

tacitly, the frustration of German, Boer and Portuguese ambitions. Occupation of Barotseland, or much of what later became known as Northern Rhodesia, presented no problems. In September 1889 Rhodes simply bought the land from the paramount Chief, Lewanika – for £19,000. Rhodes then left the territory in balk, abandoned even more grandiose plans for a financial deal over Katanga, and concentrated his mind on outflanking Lobengula, ruler of Matabeleland. Rhodes knew that no column of imperial troops would be spared for this purpose. But Rhodes also knew that no column of 'pioneers', even if largely composed of high-spirited emigrant Englishmen, would march into virtually unknown territory without the promise of well-lined pockets as a reward. The late Victorian was no longer a disciple of Tennyson. 'To strive, to seek, to find, and not to yield' had become by 1890 a sentiment which, for adventurers, only operated at the level of material benefits.

Selous, in the 1880s, had explored north of the Bechuanaland Protectorate; he had believed that gold lay in Mashonaland and Matabeleland, although he had need neither of King Solomon's Mines nor Rhodes's Ophir to finance imperial ventures. Nevertheless, for Selous, his contemporaries and the young men of the Pioneer Column 'the ruling passion was gold',[1] as an end in itself. Like others, Selous had a company, of sorts, and an ambition to obtain concessions over likely gold-bearing areas from Shona – or Ndebele – Chiefs who were prepared to barter, or could be bamboozled into surrendering, tribal rights for breech-loaders, armed steam boats, and hard liquor. But, by the turn of the decade, Selous and his kind knew that there was but one real contender for mastery of Lobengula, the Chief who counted. Lobengula's domination of the Ndebele and his claim to homage from the Shona made him a victim worthy of Rhodes's endeavours. Rhodes outmanœuvred all his rivals, and fortified with a piece of paper on which Lobengula had put his mark, was ready to march, opening the road by persuasion or force, as appropriate.

The history of Rhodes's defeat of rivals and deception of Lobengula has been told often enough for even the most financially discreditable episodes to be well known. The so-called Rudd Concession of 30 October 1888, which Lobengula later questioned in an eloquent, fruitless appeal to Queen Victoria, is of less importance to history as an example of a bewildered, greedy Chief bartering what was not his to give than as the first step whereby an enormous tract of territory was handed over to a purely commercial concern. The Royal Charter of 29 October 1889, which ostensibly transformed the British South Africa Company from a clutch of speculators into a species of latter-day Clives and Hastings, was, in reality, a device for extending Empire on the cheap. The Charter gave the Company *carte blanche* north of the Limpopo, other than in the Bechuanaland Protectorate. As Lord Blake says of the Charter, with urbane meiosis, 'Its scope was immense ... no northern frontier was placed on the Company's operations ...'[2] Two Dukes, one of them related to the royal family, joined the Chartered Board.

This was a kind of imperial apotheosis by proxy. By contrast, Rhodes had an imperial vision but – a factor all too rarely appreciated – none of his compatriots actually shared it. Rhodes might, perhaps, have felt a twinge for Lobengula's insistence that there should be no white settlement in his territories, but he was adamant that, by hook or by crook, 'Zambesia' must come into being. The Pioneer Column, hoisting the Union Flag in 'Fort Salisbury', gave the Chartered Company potential mastery over a territory the size of France. Rhodes's vision was in a fair way to being satisfied.

At once, however, the vision was transformed by the need to satisfy disappointed pioneers. If we are to believe Whitehall – using information 'kindly supplied by the British South Africa Company'[3] – occupation of Mashonaland and sanction by the Crown was speedily transformed into land settlement: 'The pioneers were disbanded, and, in accordance with the agreement made with them, were allowed to peg off auriferous claims and farms.' Here, and at once, we come to the heart of the matter. There is gold in Zimbabwe, but no King Solomon's Mines, no Ophir, no El Dorado. Rhodes may have had a suspicion that such was the case – his sixth sense over sources of wealth was only matched by sensitivity to where it was not – and although farms for gold may have struck the 'stranded gentry' of the Pioneer Column as poor compensation when proposed in Kimberley, a reward of 3,000 acres per head was not to be despised. With eighty million acres at its command, the Chartered

Company could afford to appear generous to adventurers who had nowhere else to go. One authority rightly says of this second stage in a rather extreme case of land theft: 'The BSA Company officials had not come to dig a hole but to make a colonial state.'[4] To make such a state, with all its potential for varieties of commercial exploitation, the Company needed settlers, men willing to connive at theft of land – and cattle.

In coming to the heart of the matter – the history of Southern Rhodesia is the history of land seizure and settlement, alienation and anger, helpless resentment followed at the last by a sanguinary harvest – we must note that the men of the Pioneer Column did not establish a *volk*. There were Afrikaners amongst them, but the spirit of the *voortrekker* was entirely absent. This difference can be partly explained by the fact that the men who crossed the Vaal found an all but empty land. Indirectly – and despite Majuba and its aftermath – the Boer pushed the imperial frontier north, establishing a presence by the threat of force. But the Boer established his Transvaal, as he had his Free State, not so much on the basis of racial superiority – he looked to the Old Testament to assure himself that the children of Ham would be his servants – as by virtue of unencumbered occupation.

The white settler in Southern Rhodesia, in rather stark contrast, displaced the Shona and Ndebele. When, at intervals throughout the 1890s, these tribes rebelled against the loss of land and cattle, they were driven away, killed, broken up. The pioneers, whose real or fictitious descendants made such a parade of settler virtues during the years of UDI, came to see themselves as defending a culture against outright attack or constant menace. A racial psychosis developed as a result, all the more dangerous from lack of compensating values and standards in white Southern Rhodesia as a whole. The white farmer in the new territory developed qualities of independence and hardihood in wringing what was for long – and for many, always – a bare living from the hard red soil stretching to the hills under those enormous skies. For many, and for long, a tin shack was home, not the cool rooms and spreading lawns of a picture-postcard colonial ranch. The racial infection was always worse in Salisbury and Bulawayo than Gwelo or Umtali. But theft of land bred what was basically a fear of the consequences throughout the territory so deliberately and so callously acquired.

Thus the birth of this most philistine of white societies should be recorded not in terms of the Matabele wars but in references to the Chartered Company's early reports and other reliable sources. One can well see in accounts of those three uprisings between 1893 and 1896 – two Ndebele, one Shona – all the causes of subsequent racial conflict, culminating in the second 'Chimurenga' between 1972 and 1980. Black tribesmen and white settlers shared murder, pillage and rape about equally, always bearing in mind that the former were driven to violence by the Chartered Company's deliberate policy of provoking it in order to entrench authority – and consolidate its fortunes.[5] 'We have the excuse for a row over murdered women and children,' Jameson reported from Mashonaland on 17 July 1893, 'and getting Matabeleland opened would give us a tremendous lift in shares and everything else.'[6]

Later, Lord Grey, the Government-appointed 'Administrator' of the territory, wrote that the BSA Company forces – a privately recruited gendarmerie – were 'crumpling up' the Ndebele: 'Once the black cloud at Bulawayo is cleared away the development of Mashonaland will proceed apace.'[7] In Kruger's words, 'Rhodes had his way and his war.'[8] The British Government made Rhodes a Privy Councillor after Lobengula had blown up his kraal and surrendered on 4 November 1893. The Chartered Company had, after all, borne the costs of the war. Thereafter, all cattle in Matabeleland were branded 'C.C.' 'Rhodes is a great jingo,' said Sir William Harcourt, Rosebery's Chancellor of the Exchequer, who was *not* a 'liberal imperialist', 'but he is a cheap jingo.'[9]

The purpose of the war was to drive desperate men into reserves. The tribes were not vanquished like Red Indians, or exterminated like the Aborigine. They were penned in areas of poor, overcrowded land none the less which increasingly denied them economic independence. Even at the turn of the century, European agriculture in Southern Rhodesia accounted for less than 10 per cent of output for the market, but thereafter the percentages moved inexorably in reverse order. Rhodes's 'equal rights for all civilised men' was always a shibboleth; land 'apportionment' – that useful euphemism – ensured that the African in

Southern Rhodesia would always be denied rights. As Professor A. P. Thornton, our most perceptive historian of the imperial idea, has written, 'A civilised man is one who is not a loafer.' Life in the reserves was a denial of civilisation on these terms. But civilisation is a curious affair. As the first Matabele war was set in train, the white man's God was mustered. The *Mashonaland Times* of 20 July 1893 reported: 'Sunday – Rev. Sylvester, as military chaplain, holds service after parade for inspection of arms. The rev. gentleman stood on- ammunition cases and said that the sons of Ham would all be cleared out.'[10] The Ndebele and Shona were doubly denied the white man's civilisation: they could not thrive and they were not of the elect.

Ironically, the reverend gentleman's sentiments are quoted in a Colonial Office Report which reflected much unease in Whitehall at the methods which the Chartered Company employed to add dominion to the Crown. But the report, like others of the time, also reflected impotence. The 1898 Southern Rhodesia Order in Council prescribed that 'the Company shall from time to time assign to the natives inhabiting Southern Rhodesia land sufficient for their occupation, whether as tribes or as portions of tribes, and suitable for their agricultural and pastoral requirements'. This was a prescription for peonage, sanctioned by the Crown, made in an Order which also authorised the Chartered Company to establish courts of justice and provide for native administration. A Resident Commissioner represented the Crown; the Company provided an Executive Council to govern the Colony. The laws of Cape Colony (of which Rhodes was Premier when Zambesia was established) applied; appeals from Southern Rhodesia's courts were heard in Cape Town. The flag had been raised in Salisbury; it was already bloodstained, and the device on it should have been the mailed fist – of the Chartered Company.

2

The South African War – and After

Before we consider Southern Rhodesia further, some aspects of imperial policy regarding Southern Africa need review. The Chartered Company was the extreme nineteenth-century expression of surrender by the imperial Government to commercial dictates. Nevertheless, the establishment of Zambesia differed from commercial ventures elsewhere – the Royal Niger Company in West Africa or the British North Borneo Company in an area of what is now Malaysia – because the Chartered Company was invested with a strategic role. Rhodes's vision died with his death on 26 March 1902. The 1895 Jameson Raid, whereby Rhodes sought to overthrow Kruger in the Transvaal and thus see the territories of both Boer republics again painted red, was an humiliating failure, eclipsing Rhodes from the Southern African scene despite an inquiry in London aptly described as 'lying in state'.

But although the British Government officially repudiated the Raid, few could deny that this only failed to do crudely what imperial policy sought to achieve by stealth: accept Boer autonomy up to the point where it did not encroach on the British 'sphere of influence' in Central and Southern Africa. By the eve of the second South African War this sphere extended to Lake Nyasa in the north, Barotseland in the west, Manicaland in the east. For all practical purposes, the map was red from Cairo to the Cape – save for those occasionally fractious but curiously useful republics of the Transvaal and the Orange Free State.

Rhodes's vision was that the map should be painted a British red. The reality turned out to be rather different.

Southern Rhodesia, the Chartered Company's self-governing Colony, was important in Whitehall because neither Kruger nor any successor could pose a threat to British interests within the sphere of influence. Not only was prospective Boer expansion blocked, but Germany was penned in South-West Africa, Portugal in Mozambique. As Afrikaner racial ideas spread north, as the Rand's wealth came to dominate much of Southern and Central Africa, Whitehall came increasingly to draw a distinction between an accommodation with the republics south of the Limpopo but, if necessary, a showdown with them beyond it. The establishment of a Protectorate over the Bechuana in 1888 was partly a compensation for Majuba in 1881 but was primarily a reflection of a policy which planned to contain the Boers territorially. There was not much to choose between Briton and Boer when it came to extinguishing the Bantu as a military force - or, as with the Zulu, a nation - between the Limpopo and the Cape.

Despite the strategic realities summarised in the Introduction, the imperatives of imperial expansion - emigration, markets, rivalries amongst the 'Powers', jingoism in various forms - were such that no British Government could allow the Boer republics to become strategically and economically influential beyond their own frontiers. In the 1890s Kruger and Marthinus Steyn (President of the Orange Free State) could maintain a *volk* culture but were denied a role in the arbitration of great affairs. The second South African War, whoever provoked it, and despite the emotions which suffering and injustice aroused, was fought to reaffirm this principle when certain events - or an excited reading of those events in some quarters - seemed to suggest that Kruger and Steyn were not satisfied with a status for the republics which hardly accorded with full sovereignty.

There would be little point in recapitulating these factors here were it not that the war's aftermath bore so directly both on Southern Rhodesia's fortunes and on the whole course of British policy for the region. Within only three years of about the most humiliatingly expensive victory in modern history - measured in military terms - a British Government certainly dedicated to imperial objectives had begun a process of propitiating the beaten enemy which was to culminate in the Act of Union, 1910. By that Act, passed through Houses of Parliament grown somewhat weary of the imperial burden, an Afrikaner 'Dominion' was not only given independence but the prospective right to incorporate territories over which Britain exercised real authority. These territories were Basutoland, Bechuanaland and Swaziland. But in 1910 few doubted that this was but a first step to a wider dominion. 'At about the time when Union was established, General Louis Botha, its first Prime Minister [and formerly Kruger's army commander] stated repeatedly his conviction that it would never be complete until Rhodesia and the [three] High Commission Territories had been included.'[1] The second South African War thus appeared to reverse a British policy of containing the Boers; in doing so, Southern Rhodesia's relationship to a new, greatly enlarged Afrikaner state fundamentally changed.

These reversals and changes occurred because the South African War was a Pyrrhic victory for Britain. The strategic realities had, as it were, reasserted themselves. If the Boer proved stronger on his home ground than an imperial Britain whose overall resources were diminishing, then eventually South Africa would be an Afrikaner state with 'extraterritorial' roles. British Governments, in order to retain some imperial role in Southern Africa, were forced to dance to the Boer tune, not vice versa. The Boers, in more senses than one, gained the sovereignty which they had sought before the war. The reversals and changes were welcomed, nay encouraged, by Conservative and Liberal Governments because both believed that an independent Afrikaner Dominion would effectively represent British interests in Southern Africa, would indeed enhance and not thwart them.

The reason why the reversals and changes became part of the fabric of white Southern African politics is because British Governments, Conservative *and* Liberal, shared the Boer outlook on race, the 'native', the sjambok, brandished or hidden. Thus Southern Rhodesia could enter the Boer racial orbit without awkward questions being asked, then or later, about whether Rhodes's vision and his rhetoric had not become somewhat tarnished. In granting a charter to the British South Africa Company one British Government handed the Shona and Ndebele over to speculators. By the Act of Union, another British Government gave the nod to racial policies in Southern Africa which differed only in degree between the Zambeze and the Cape. As a result of these changes, South Africa gained a position in the region which made the issue of its wider frontiers almost academic.

There is abundant evidence that Arthur Balfour's Conservative Government and his Liberal Party successor Sir Henry Campbell-Bannerman shared much the same racial outlook. Chinese 'indentured' coolies were employed on the Rand immediately after the war, in order to block British immigrants, and for acquiring labour on the cheap through operating a system of what one Liberal leader (Lord Ripon) accurately called 'semi-slavery'. The Conservative Government openly confessed it could not see what all the fuss was about; when the Liberals achieved office in 1906, Campbell-Bannerman and his colleagues made plain that 'The great thing was to hold the Empire together in South Africa, and this could only be done by placating the Boers.'[2]

The Union of South Africa Bill, when debated in 1909, merely carried racial prejudices and strategic necessities to a logical conclusion, one which was to have a direct bearing on Southern Rhodesia and Britain's purported role there. ' "The whole scheme of Union in South Africa would be wrecked," Asquith as Prime Minister now declared, "were interference by the imperial Government to take place in native affairs." '[3] This Liberal Government allowed no amendments to the Bill, forcing it through a Parliament in which a handful of members were prepared to oppose restricting the franchise to men 'of European descent'. Coloured voters in Cape Colony retained limited electoral rights; elsewhere a white, predominantly Boer, *herrenvolk* was expressly sanctioned by the Crown. Arthur Balfour supported this new concept of imperial responsibility when he said, 'You cannot give the natives in South Africa equal rights with the whites without threatening the whole fabric of white civilisation.'

Thus coming events cast their shadows before. Balfour's words were to be parroted down the decades by white men in Southern Rhodesia, not only by the champions of apartheid in the Afrikaner state created by a liberal British Government. Yet even in placating the Boers this Government and its successors took a risk. Giving Botha and his old comrade in arms Jan Smuts more power than they could have ever aspired to before the war did not guarantee that the new Afrikaner state would necessarily remain loyal to the Crown. It was all very well for Smuts, 'slim Janie', about equally mistrusted by Englishmen and fellow Boers, to say: 'I do not like the natives at all and I wish we had no black men in South Africa. But there they are, our lot is cast with them by an overriding Providence, and the only question is now to shape our course so as to maintain the supremacy of our race and at the same time to do our duty.'[4]

That was all very well, especially if one concentrated on supremacy and forgot about duty. In the event, throughout two World Wars, Smuts kept to his side of the bargain with the Pyrrhic victor. But, as events were to show, in those two wars and especially after the latter intermittent Afrikaner 'disloyalty' to Britain was really beside the point. Boer memories were long, and the appalling suffering inflicted by the British – during the second South African War – above all, on women and children – bred attitudes to Britain which were bound to dominate the Southern African scene eventually. There was, perhaps, more than symbolism in the flag of the new Dominion when it flew for the first time after the Act of Union was passed on 31 May 1910. The British Union flag was there – it is there today – but was surrounded by and lost in the tricolour of the old Boer republics.

3

Southern Rhodesia:
Quis Custodiet?

Whatever might be the future course of Anglo-South African relations, Southern Rhodesia by 1910 was a flourishing commercial concern - for the Chartered Company. With capital based on the Johannesburg stock market and authority to rule specifically granted by the Crown, the Company was able to proceed upon a deliberate, wholesale, cruel policy of exploitation which continued unchecked throughout the next two decades. The settler did not necessarily do so well - Southern Rhodesia was strewn with poor whites in the early years, and it was discontent with the Company and a desire for a larger share of the spoils which led to constitutional change in 1923 - but shareholders were satisfied men. The basis of their satisfaction was pillage, and one cannot understand the legacy of land ownership and use which the new Colony inherited in 1923, and by which its whites prospered thereafter, without glancing at the sheer scale of the Company exactions in the early years. These established a white political and economic structure which could only be broken by force of black reaction. White sentiment, however liberal, would never do so.

It would be easy, but profitless, to quote from early critics of the Company's policy. Lord Olivier's *Anatomy of African Misery* (1927) and John Harris's *The Chartered Millions* (1920) are admirable, genuinely liberal and solidly documented accounts of Southern Rhodesia's first thirty years, all the more impressive for evidence of consistent refusal by the British establishment to interfere with a policy of well-organised theft. The Judicial Committee of the Privy Council proved as deaf to justice as the British Government. In July 1918, the Judicial Committee ruled that land in Southern Rhodesia was vested in the Crown and not the Company, but ignored the central issue that the land in question should not have been first 'alienated' and then 'apportioned'. That Africans had rights was an idea quite beyond the Judicial Committee's comprehension. Native law and custom as to land holding was conceded, but the Empire's final court of appeal ruled that 'the land did not belong to the natives, having been lost to the Crown through conquest ...'

The conqueror, of course, was the Company, whose Charter was not invalidated in 1918, although some claims subsequent to 1889 were rejected. The 1918 ruling may have hastened constitutional change in the Colony – to the benefit of white settlers – but the Judicial Committee made no demur at Africans being forced into Reserves or 'unalienated land', there to pay rent, thereafter to be at the whim of lessees (of the Company) or urban freeholders. The complex arguments deployed before the Court and most of the caustic comments on commercial practices made by the judges do no more than remind us that the issue was essentially between white men. The African case was only heard before the Judicial Committee to the degree that it bore on the extents and limits of the Company's powers – and its share of the profits. So much for contemporary liberal sentiment and special pleading. For reality we must turn to modern writers, whose accounts, strengthened by historical perspective, explain much of the reason for a second 'Chimurenga'. And it is in the careful defence which Lord Blake offers of white men cutting a swathe through the African bush that one finds reality.

Lord Blake begins his account of the period from 1893 to the end of Company rule in 1923 by stating, 'The least defensible feature of the new regime was in its treatment of land. Within a few months of the victory over Lobengula almost all the traditional grazing grounds of the Ndebele had been given away.'[1] Lord Blake then proceeds to recount precisely who benefited from the theft. With the exception of a few specially favoured *conquistadores* – an aptly named Sir John Willoughby received 600,000 acres and over 8,000 cattle – most of the whites who fought the Ndebele merely doubled the Pioneer Column's stake to 6,000 acres. But the figures Lord Blake quotes thereafter reveal that alienation in Matabeleland and Mashonaland was on a scale which, perforce, made the Company principal owner. Moreover, the Company was always willing to buy land from whites who found bush farming beyond them: 'By 1899 more than two-thirds of the original volunteers had sold out.'[2]

Thus, from the outset, two features of the land issue predominated. Whether it was the Chartered Company or, in later decades, other large concerns, land was regarded as valuable for its extent, for potential, not utilisation. This approach not only pushed the African off his land, but strengthened the equally cruel but logically complementary policy of 'reserves'. These developments took place slowly but inexorably, creating in Southern Rhodesia's whites during those first thirty years a conviction that if they were eventually to replace the Chartered Company and govern the Colony themselves (as Rhodes had always envisaged and for which the Charter made implied provision) it would be on the same basis of alienation and apportionment, *not* on one which gave the African a place in the sun. The Company stole and operated on a scale which not only destroyed a viable African economy but bred such envy amongst the settlers that liberal sentiments became a luxury which only missionaries and eccentrics could afford.

For land, read cattle. The whites simply looted them. Indeed, the Company was so sure of its power that it actually established a 'loot committee' for the purpose. Theft of cattle was doubly evil. For the Ndebele in particular, cattle represented subsistence, economic assets, family ties. Loss of cattle was not consciously designed to break up an African society which, in any case, proved amazingly resistant to white exactions through all the years of domination and repression. But loss of cattle rendered the tribes economically impotent. After the second Matabele war the processes summarised here were accelerated: 'The crushing of the rebellions reaffirmed the white man's conquest.'[3] The Ndebele had been 'smashed' – a word then much in vogue; the Shona had been crippled. The difference was forgotten at the time.

This assumption that both tribes, let alone lesser clans, had learned their lesson is understandable. The opening years of the present century saw Southern Rhodesia get down to white man's business. Roads were made; railways built; coal was discovered near Wankie. Coal is unromantic stuff by comparison with gold, but its discovery and use symbolised a Southern Rhodesia of rich speculators and modest industrialists. The First World War stimulated this nascent economy. Minerals like copper, tungsten, chrome, zinc, antimony and asbestos were in demand. Even gold mining looked to have some future. Agriculture settled into a pattern dominated by large ranches. The African became a commodity, the settler – of whom there were some 25,000 by 1914 – a question mark. Was the Colony to remain a purely commercial property, or did it have a political future? The question could not be divorced from the future of Southern Africa as a whole, and its importance was emphasised by the 1910 Act and the expectations of 'wider union' which were then aroused. But although it is tempting to look at these years in terms of settler political ambitions, of men yearning to replace the Company's rule with their own, the truth is prosaic. The Company sold out in 1923 because it got a good deal – the equivalent of nearly £7 million in cash for assets which had been developed. The Company retained all its other Southern Rhodesian assets, mineral, commercial and ranching.[4]

There was, of course, a settler lobby, movement in the years before 1922 for greater representation on the Legislative and Executive Councils and, above all, much debate about relations, possibly incorporation, with South Africa. But what gave the lobby strength and cohesion was a growing conviction that Company rule was not fit for free men and a partly justified suspicion that the Colonial Office in London might extend British authority by insidious means. Although, as we have seen, the Company ran Southern Rhodesia to suit its shareholders, sheer necessity imposed on the Colonial Office certain responsibilities for law and order, administration and justice. The Company was not only uninterested in the Colony's development, except in crudely commercial terms: it was unable to rule, except as conqueror. Neither bureaucracy nor police, a magistracy or armed forces lay within the Company's competence except on a basis which the Matabele wars had shown to be inadequate even when punitive.

By 1914 the 1898 Order in Council was palpably defective in several important respects. On 9 October 1914 the British Government gave notice (revealingly in the press, thus avoiding firm commitments) that attention must be given to Southern Rhodesia's constitutional future, and posed the question of the Chartered Company's roles and authority. A way had been opened for the settler to rule himself. But the settler call for 'responsible government' was, in reality, an insistence that the Colonial Office, indeed the whole apparatus of Whitehall, could aid the Colony (although most officials and similar elements in Southern Rhodesia came from South Africa) but it must not attempt to rule it. Effective rule was beyond the Company's scope. The Colonial Office might advise, but rule from that distant source was unwelcome. Union with South Africa appealed to many white Southern Rhodesians after the First World War because of shared experience and a common stock of ideas, not least about 'natives'. But the dominant emotion of those who had lived through the early years and prospered thereby was to go one better than the Company, to govern a Colony without either the grasp of the shareholder or the grip of the Colonial Office impeding them on the road which they were determined to follow.

The Constitution which was granted to Southern Rhodesia on 24 September 1923 was thus bred by settler opportunism out of Colonial Office expediency. A referendum in Southern Rhodesia on 27 October 1922 had rejected incorporation in the Union by 8,774 to 5,989. Smuts, as Prime Minister of the Union, lobbied relentlessly for incorporation, but majority settler opinion in the Colony opted for self-government on the basis of a racial accord with big brother to the south, and an economic association which merely reaffirmed that the Chartered Company and its associates on the Rand would continue to arbitrate much of the future. The Colonial Office – Ministers of the Crown are irrelevant in this connection even although Winston Churchill was Colonial Secretary – realised that Company rule could not continue in Southern Rhodesia indefinitely, but in fact had no desire to replace speculators by paternal imperialists on West or East African lines. In going through the constitutional motions of replacing the Company by settlers deemed competent to rule themselves the

British Government of the day gave more power to a minority than almost anywhere else in the Dominions. Whatever its sins of omission and commission, the Chartered Company had injected capital into Southern Rhodesia – financing the railways, for example. The settler Government of 1923 acquired a leasehold from the Crown of actual, not merely potential value. But the Crown imposed few restrictions on what these sunburned provincials would do with their legacies. The African was left in bondage; the land remained alienated and apportioned.

4

The Self-Governing Colony

When the result of the 'Union' referendum was announced at the Bulawayo Court House on 6 November 1922, Charles Coghlan, leader of the 'Unofficials' in the legislative Council and chief proponent of self-government, made a speech which ended rousingly: 'For King and Empire; that is our motto.'[1] Whites in Southern Rhodesia were always to wear their patriotism and imperialism with a difference; Ian Smith all but echoed Coghlan's words when he rebelled against the Crown forty-three years later. But the Duke of Devonshire, who replaced Churchill as Colonial Secretary on 15 November, seems to have shared with his official advisers a simple conviction that provided the new Colony succeeded in managing its affairs without making financial demands on a British Government, the settlers there could say, and do, pretty much as they pleased. Both union and federation with South Africa had been rejected. Amalgamation with Northern Rhodesia, briefly considered by some, was even more decisively and effectively opposed there. Northern Rhodesia, in which no more than 3,000 whites lived rather meagrely, was thus left in a state of nature. In April 1924, it was designated a Protectorate, like Nyasaland to the east, where the Colonial Office hand, although light, was at all times felt. The self-governing Colony, in sharp contrast, was left to carve out a future free from political intervention by Westminster or bureaucratic interference by Whitehall.

This is the only possible interpretation which can be put

on the constitution which the Crown gave to the new Colony. Coghlan, who was knighted when he became Premier of Southern Rhodesia on 1 October 1923, was, in fact, monarch of all he surveyed. Southern Rhodesia was not, strictly speaking, a 'Dominion', and the British Government was constitutionally responsible for its relations with foreign Governments. As these relations were, in practice, confined to South African Governments whose members accepted rejection of Union because they knew where Salisbury stood on all important issues, Britain's responsibility was purely nominal. Southern Rhodesia gradually acquired a quasi-Dominion status – appointing High Commissioners, for example, for diplomatic representation in London – because it was constitutionally unique, a fact of which its governments took full advantage.

The governmental system was Westminster in miniature, apart from the absence of a second Chamber. Thirty members of the Legislative Assembly constituted Parliament: the dry words of the 1939 Bledisloe Royal Commission summarise how they got there:

> The Assembly is an elected body, the franchise being granted to all adult British subjects who have resided for not less than six months in the Colony, provided that they possess one of the three requisite qualifications, viz., the occupation of premises of the value of £150, an income of not less than £100 a year, or the ownership of a registered mining location. Natives who can satisfy these conditions are entitled to be placed on the voter's roll, but the property and income qualifications have so far excluded the vast majority of them. There are at present 24,626 electors on the roll, of whom only 39 [in an African population estimated in 1936 at 1,243,000] are natives.[2]

The only limitations which the Crown placed on self-government was that some categories of legislation affecting Africans were 'reserved' for the Colonial Secretary's imprimatur; he could also 'disallow' such measures. The Governor-General (also High Commissioner) for South Africa between 1923 and 1937 retained some discretionary powers concerning native Reserves in Southern Rhodesia. These powers were then, 'At the instance of the

Government of Southern Rhodesia',[3] withdrawn and vested, constitutionally in the Secretary of State. Throughout its entire existence as a self-governing Colony neither Colonial, Dominions Secretary nor High Commissioner ever intervened in the exercise of these so-called powers. Nor did the Colonial or Dominions Office ever exercise powers, of an even wider nature, concerning legislation which required a two-thirds majority in the Legislative Assembly. Thus, in 1923 a Conservative Government which, in the same year, proclaimed the doctrine of 'paramountcy' for the African in Kenya and, by implication, elsewhere, specifically allowed Southern Rhodesia to assert the paramountcy of the white man.

After the second South African War, both Conservative and Liberal Governments had conceded the Boer's power to govern himself and his British-born or descended neighbours. This concession was made because the Boer could not be defeated, but also because Edwardian imperial sentiment had no room for paternalism towards the Bantu. Much the same attitudes explain the Bonar Law Government's decision in 1923 to give self-government to Southern Rhodesia. Logically, this Government and the Lloyd George coalition which preceded it, should have favoured Southern Rhodesia's incorporation in the Union. Smuts, however, was reckoned the man to push incorporation through. When he failed, the new Conservative Government had little choice but to devise the September 1923 constitution – or take direct responsibility. Devonshire, like Churchill before him, was adamant that the cost, in strategic no less than financial terms, was beyond Governments seeking to lighten the imperial burden on the British taxpayer.

The residual responsibilities of British Governments for Southern Rhodesia, and specifically to the African, were to return at intervals during the next half-century to haunt the minds and, occasionally, trouble the consciences of Ministers. Near the end of the road, a collective Commonwealth principle operated to remind all concerned that the Letters Patent of 24 September 1923 did not, entirely, sever Britain's responsibility for the native. But, on the day Sir Charles Coghlan was sworn in by the Colony's first Governor (Sir John Chancellor), only an odd white man here and there could have supposed the reserved and discretionary powers meant anything at all. Politically, the settler had broken free from the Chartered Company; the idea that a distant British Government would ever flex its muscles would have struck Coghlan and his colleagues as absurd.

There is, in fact, little more that need be said about the next twenty-odd years. The European population doubled; the African increased by, at best, a quarter. When the Dominions Office was set up in 1923 – a mere Post Office to many in Whitehall – Southern Rhodesia was conveniently found a place. Godfrey Huggins – who had favoured incorporation in the Union – became Premier in September 1933, and remained so for twenty years. Huggins was given the title of 'Prime Minister' – another step towards quasi-Dominion status. Of greater importance than Whitehall musical chairs or the advent and promotion of a tenacious politician was a Land Apportionment Act, passed in 1930, which confirmed the Chartered Company's policies in every particular. This Act gave legal sanction to a process initiated by the Company of forcing Africans off their land not merely by violence and theft but also by taxation and rent. By the time the Act was passed '20 million hectares had been reserved for Europeans, of which only 30 per cent was being used ... [But] in contrast the African Reserves totalled 8·7 million hectares ... Further, between 1931 and 1941 50,000 Africans were moved [to Reserves], between 1945 and 1959 85,000 were moved ...'[4] The operative word is 'moved'; it should be 'evicted'.

Doubtless there were many white British subjects in Southern Rhodesia during these years who deplored this economic and social apartheid, vicious in itself even if it had not been accompanied by a prevailing attitude to the African of contempt and dismissal. White farmers were frequently considerate employers of African labour; missionaries taught promising youth; there were men and women in the Department of Native Affairs who believed in the right of the Africans to be treated with the dignity of human beings even if sceptical of their capacity for self-government in a white man's world. African education, however limited, was a reality, not a mere gesture. But the prevailing tone was set by Huggins himself. Shortly after becoming Prime Minister, he proposed to 'export' educated Africans to Northern Rhodesia and Nyasaland, where they might not only find jobs but would cease to provoke their white betters with demands for political advance. The plan foundered because mineral companies in Northern Rhodesia and plantation owners in Nyasaland had no intention of acting as employment agencies for Huggins's cast-offs. Despite worldwide economic problems, both Protectorates showed signs of progress, and their colonial Governments were as hostile to the Huggins plan as multi-national business. The Dominions Office, normally supine, noted that 'segregation might be all right in Southern Rhodesia, but Huggins and his friends should not be supported in a policy that would only get the imperial authorities into trouble if applied elsewhere'.[5]

The Dominions Office, of course, did not actually criticise Huggins. He wielded his powers and pushed his segregationist policies in Southern Rhodesia with no more than the bleat quoted above being heard in London. Throughout the 1930s and 1940s the African in Southern Rhodesia knew his place because he was kept in it. He kept his head down because he would have been pushed off the sidewalk otherwise. Africans in Salisbury and other urban centres were denied permanent residence. *Their* place, of course, was on the 'land' which had been seized by the White man. Huggins and his kind thus created both an African rural proletariat and a shifting urban population. The white tribe began to lose its head almost from the moment it was given the power to govern itself: rootless people breed revolutionaries.

The Dominions Office did not, collectively, care what happened in Southern Rhodesia. Nevertheless, it is probably true to say that Huggins's advent as Prime Minister did coincide with a belated realisation in London that, whatever political and social imperatives might obtain, the self-governing Colony would not consider itself economically viable unless a link was forged with the potentially mineral-rich Northern Rhodesia. Huggins had been an advocate of incorporation with the Union; his premiership was to be marked by a campaign for amalgamation of the two Rhodesias. Yet being, like so many men of his type, a good tactician but a poor strategist, Huggins failed to see that such a campaign would force both the British Government and the officials whose 'advice' actually made policy to consider whether the Crown retained any responsibilities for these territories.

The Bledisloe Commission, which toured both Rhodesias and

Nyasaland between May and August 1938, was not established because the Chamberlain Government had acquired a conscience about Southern Rhodesia's Africans or as a result of direct pressure from Huggins to support amalgamation. He was so confident of success that he assumed that Bledisloe and his colleagues would simply give the nod. However, although a Labour Colonial Secretary in 1930 (Lord Passfield) had made no objection to the Land Apportionment Act, several of his fellow peers argued that African rights were being further usurped. In 1930, Ramsay MacDonald, as Prime Minister, had more pressing problems than Southern Rhodesia, but his son Malcolm, as both Colonial and Dominions Secretary at all material times in 1938, was not only interested in the Rhodesias but considered himself a Liberal on racial issues. The future of Britain's colonial Empire was beginning to occupy attention as territories in West and East Africa moved towards limited self-government. Not for the first time, the advent of a Royal Commission signified rather than symbolised an imperial concern for subject peoples which had seemed dormant concerning Southern Africa and hitherto non-existent for Southern Rhodesia. The Commission marked the first stage in the process of asking what was really meant, for Southern Rhodesia, by *Quis Custodiet?*

Yet the case for amalgamation must have seemed strong when, in leisurely imperial style, Lord Bledisloe and his fellow Commissioners embarked on the Royal Mail marine vessel *Capetown Castle* at Southampton on 29 April 1938. For all that the Commissioners had, before leaving Britain, collectively imbibed the wisdom of Lord Hailey, a retired pro-Consul, whose monumental *An African Survey* (1938) had begun to influence a whole generation of enlightened late imperialists, their overriding preoccupation was economic. Southern Rhodesia had survived the world slump of the early 1930s in reasonably good shape, but its economic base was bound to be fragile if it remained dependent on primary agricultural products and a valuable, but essentially limited mineral sector. Northern Rhodesia, by contrast, was poised for a leap into the industrialised future. Discovery of large copper reserves in the Ndola area during the 1920s would not have excited the attention of the multi-national metals industry if, at much the same time, technological developments ensured

37

the usable ores could be economically separated from the unusable 'overburden' in which they were embedded. By 1938 men were talking about Northern Rhodesia's copperbelt as their forebears once discussed Kimberley or the Rand.

But even this prospective shift in the fortunes of what had hitherto been Southern Rhodesia's poor relation depended for realisation on decisions taken in Johannesburg, the City of London and Wall Street. The British South Africa Company, whose directors had falsely complained of being sold short by the British Government in 1923, were, by 1938, in a good position to have the next laugh. Retention of the Chartered Company's assets in Northern Rhodesia and a complex series of mergers with other companies in South Africa and the United States led to a situation by 1938 where two main groups had entrenched themselves on the copperbelt. The Anglo-American Corporation and the Rhodesian Selection Trust, granted generous leases by the British South Africa Company, were prepared to invest heavily in the economy of what was also a Protectorate. Anglo-American, whose individual and corporate shareholding reflected the origins of South Africa's mineral wealth, took the view that a black industrial proletariat in Northern Rhodesia could be treated like migrant mine labour on the Rand. The Rhodesian Selection Trust (RST) dominated by Chester Beatty, a quintessential American magnate of genuinely liberal beliefs, was to benefit from a management team whose members decided to treat their new black employees like men.

This marked divergence of view between Anglo-American and RST was to have a profound, a direct effect on postwar events; on the Federation of Rhodesia and Nyasaland; on the Protectorate which became the independent state of Zambia; and on certain developments in Southern Rhodesia. In 1938, however, all that Bledisloe and his colleagues knew was that Southern Rhodesia was ruled by and for white men, whereas Northern Rhodesia was a Protectorate whose future might depend more on the metal market than the priorities of British Governments or the paternalist philosophy of Lord Hailey. The Commission was also charged to investigate conditions in and prospects for Nyasaland. Beginning their investigations in Salisbury – after a visit to Cecil Rhodes's grave in the Matopo Hills – the Commission entered on a three-month journey of which few in Southern Rhodesia could doubt the result.

And yet, plodding through the dry official prose of the Bledisloe Commission Report one discerns the growing disquiet of honest men for what they saw and heard. For the first time at any level where British Governments might conceivably take notice, the ordinary African, the non-person to Huggins and his fellow whites, spoke up without fear of retribution. This African did not want amalgamation. It was not the concept as such, of which only a handful could have seen the deeper implications. What the African feared and, given this unique chance to be heard, opposed, was *anything* which the white men in Salisbury planned to do, or did. Nor was this all. The Bledisloe Commission, in reporting these views, recorded for posterity the African capacity to think clearly and speak well. The Commission's Report, if notable for nothing else, should be known for defining and describing an African identity which the white man, so far as he thought about it at all, rejected as laughable. The Report said, in words which should have been pondered: 'The African possesses a knowledge and shrewdness, in matters affecting his welfare, with which he is not always credited. It would be wrong to assume that his opposition [to amalgamation] is based, to a very large extent on ignorance or prejudice or an instinctive dread of change.' Lord Blake remarks tersely after quoting this passage: 'It is an interesting commentary that this should have come as a slight surprise to Huggins.'[6]

The Commission's outright rejection of amalgamation despite all the perceived economic benefits which it might bring was swallowed up by the outbreak of the Second World War in September 1939. Once more, the Protectorate and the self-governing Colony were left in an imperial limbo. All three territories prospered economically during the war; but political momentum was checked. Huggins, thwarted over amalgamation, remained convinced of its inevitability, and was quite prepared to tackle the British Government again at a time and place of his choosing. The Empire Air Training Scheme sent thousands of young men from Britain to Southern Rhodesia. Many who survived campaigns over Germany or in the Middle East were determined to make this white man's land their postwar home.

Southern Rhodesians serving in units like the Long Range Desert Group seemed to their English compatriots the embodiment of qualities which suggested they had something worth fighting for. Ex-servicemen and emigrants were to provide new, postwar strength for the white laager in Southern Rhodesia. But these postwar years were to take a course which even the most perceptive reader of the Bledisloe Commission Report in 1939 or 1945 could scarcely have foreseen.

PART TWO
From World War to Federation

'The British Government in London looked to the attainment of an old dream – a great white loyalist dominion stretching all the way from the Cape to the Zambesi and possibly beyond.'

Ronald Hyam, *The Failure of South African Expansion, 1908-1948* (1972)

5

The Scene

The end of the Second World War in Europe and Asia made no immediate impact on events in Southern Africa. South African troops had fought in East and North Africa. The 6th South African Division had earned a justified reputation in the Italian campaign. Afrikaner soldiers' loyalties were divided, and occasionally suspect, matching the Nazi sympathies of the Broederbond in the Union. Nevertheless, in late 1945, as the men came home, Field-Marshal (and Prime Minister) Smuts could feel justified in assuming the continuation of an Anglo-South African relationship based on a concept of the Union as a member of the white, Western comity of nations.[1]

The wind of change which was sweeping India and Burma and before which a British Labour Government, nominally socialist, in practice resolutely paternal, reluctantly bent was not heard on the veldt or the Rand. Nor was the wind heard in the corridors of the new United Nations Organisation. At the San Francisco Conference in June 1945, Smuts rejected the notion of Trusteeship for South-West Africa, and repeated his intention of incorporating, indeed annexing, this mandated territory as part of the Union. Britain, relieved that Smuts preferred forcefully ending a Mandate to seizing the High Commission territories, gave him unqualified support. So too did the Truman Administration, which had quickly decided that territories with economic potential developed by Western capital should be excluded from the list of British Colonies otherwise entitled to independence.[2] A black American organisation, the Council on African Affairs, was vocal but ineffectual when it spoke up for the rights, in Africa, of coloured peoples. The day of Martin Luther King - and Nelson Mandela - was not yet.

Africans from Rhodesia had fought also, in East Africa, Ethiopia and Burma, returning home matured by the experience. Some of them saw no reason to accept a helot existence in civilian life when the Army had treated them like men. They found such an existence awaiting them none the less. There were District and Provincial Commissioners in Northern Rhodesia who had also fought. Some began to wonder whether the Conservative Party's doctrine of paramountcy for the native races, which a Labour Government in 1930 had extended to Northern Rhodesia, could be given meaning or would remain mere rhetoric. The imminence of industrial development for the Protectorate, on a scale capable of generating internal economic change, turned consideration of paramountcy into politics. Northern Rhodesia's whites, above all the poorish whites of the copperbelt and the railways, had no intention of sharing any kind of power, role or status with the blacks.

The Protectorate's white community would have been less determined in their opposition to rights for blacks if Southern Rhodesia had shown any sign of moderating its practices of social and economic apartheid. But Godfrey Huggins, the Colony's Prime Minister, continued to regard Africans with unamiable contempt. Moreover, despite Huggins's commitment not merely to 'closer association' between the two Rhodesias but eventually to their amalgamation as an independent white Dominion, he based his policy on acceptance of the fact that all power in Southern Africa ultimately derived from the Union. Sir Evelyn Baring, Southern Rhodesia's Governor, noted in May 1943: 'Huggins spends more time flying to Pretoria than he does to Lusaka.'[3]

Amalgamation - or, in some minds, Federation - was thus an issue for the Labour Government which, although ostensibly minor in the context of international relations, implicitly posed a challenge to the whole concept of independence for colonial peoples. This concept, going far beyond any doctrine of paramountcy, had been espoused by many members of the Labour

Party, although Clement Attlee, its leader since 1936, was luke-warm about it and ensured its exclusion from policy statements except in language so vague as to be meaningless. Attlee believed in independence for India because he saw it as inevitable. Beyond that act of imperial fate Attlee's mind did not go. Ernest Bevin, Attlee's Foreign Secretary and indisputable political henchman, did not even believe in the inevitability of Indian independence. Bevin reluctantly supported Attlee because he decided in his own mind that it was more important to demobilise the British army in order to aid economic recovery than use large numbers of troops as an Indian occupation force.

Attlee and Bevin saw the world beyond Britain exclusively in terms of power, its loss, and the means therefore necessary to maintain Britain's international roles by stratagems rather than strength. Thus Attlee and Bevin sought for 'Atlantic' allies, West European partners, Middle East satellites and, in Southern Africa, reliance on a white dominion – or dominions – character-ised by Afrikaner beliefs and racial practices. Some of Attlee's Cabinet colleagues and many of the new Labour members of Parliament saw this world in terms of morals. Attlee and Bevin, however, dominated their colleagues and, in turn, their Party, to a unique degree. During Attlee's two Governments – six years of painful British adjustment from wartime greatness to postwar penury – successive Colonial Secretaries could talk as much as they liked about native peoples and independence. But Arthur Hall, Arthur Creech Jones, and James Griffiths did what Attlee and Bevin told them to do. Successive Dominions and Common-wealth Secretaries – Addison and Pethick-Lawrence, Philip Noel-Baker, and Patrick Gordon Walker – did not demur from this assertion of Cabinet power by Prime Minister and Foreign Secretary. Enforced Cabinet preoccupation with India and Pales-tine between 1945 and 1948 – issues only transcended by the atom bomb, the economic situation, and Russian actions in East-ern Europe – relegated other imperial affairs to the foot of the agenda, and also cemented a relationship between Attlee and his colleagues of leader and led.

On the other side of the world only Smuts understood these elements of British politics. Unlike Canada, Australia and New Zealand, where politicians had a good working knowledge of how matters were ordered in the mother country, South Africans and Southern Rhodesians were not only ignorant but prejudiced. The roots of both conditions lay deep in the past, and although there were basic and striking differences in the South African and Southern Rhodesian white societies – above all between occasional cruelty to and habitual contempt for Africans – the bonds of race and a sustained fear of the supposedly liberal tendencies of British Governments were highest common factors in policy considerations, not the mere common denominators of a minority culture. Despite the virtual abdication of responsibility by British Governments since at least the 1850s for matters south of the Zambeze, and the growing dependence of the pound sterling through the 1930s and 1940s on the gold mines of the Rand, Afrikaner politicians in Pretoria remained at best wary, at worst hostile concerning every facet of British imperial policy.[4]

Smuts was no exception to these prejudices, but his long exposure to English ways and British Governments enabled him to act as an elder statesman whose vision would take all white men in Southern Africa beyond the laager and into his wider world. In 1947, a year before his electoral defeat by the committed Afrikaner Daniel François Malan and on the eve of momentous events in the Union, Bechuanaland and the Rhodesias, Smuts was host to King George VI, Queen Elizabeth and the two Princesses during a royal tour of South Africa which symbolised not only the end of an era but the further decline of British power. The royal party travelled to South Africa in HMS *Vanguard*, a battleship laid down in the closing years of the war, too late to see action, too costly for any operational role in Britain's shrunken postwar Navy. The Royal Navy's greatest ship was reduced to the role of a glorified royal yacht.

Smuts played his host's part to perfection; the final performance of a politician whose failure ever to be trusted or consistently supported by his fellow Afrikaners had, apparently, been redeemed by royal favour and international acclaim. But the South African electorate was not fooled by symbols. Towards the end of his tour, the King asked: 'Are we not one brotherhood – the greatest brotherhood in the history of man, that has been strengthened and not weakened by past differences?'[5] The answer at the South African General Election in 1948 was a resounding

'No'. Briton and Boer agreed about keeping the African in his place, but differed fundamentally on method. On the future of the Empire – or Commonwealth – there was total disagreement. Malan, a wartime internee, wanted a Boer Republic, outside the Commonwealth, free from all British influence.

Those of British stock in South Africa, one of whom had written a book with the prophetic title of *When Smuts Goes*, knew that when the Afrikaner achieved unequivocal power, at last, all would be changed. Paradoxically, an Afrikaner Government – no longer a coalition, as in the 1930s – would be less interested in seizing the High Commission territories than its predecessors, seeking instead to consolidate power in that 'German South-West' from which much of its neo-Nazi ideology derived. The real change would be internal. Whatever hope not only the Bantu, but the Indian and coloured communities might have had for some alleviation of their existence was about to be crushed, and by storm-trooper methods. The United States Embassy in Pretoria took some time to digest the implications of Malan's victory, but as the Cold War began to be conducted on an extended front, eventually decided that power was, indeed, more important than morals. 'It must be a major objective of American policy to maintain, and strengthen South Africa's support of the Western world.'[6] Evelyn Baring, since 1944 High Commissioner in Pretoria, made the same appreciation.

6

Southern Rhodesia – and London

No man was more conscious of the significance of Malan's victory on 26 May 1948 than Godfrey Huggins. Lacking storm-troopers but merely provided with a gendarmerie force in the British South Africa Police, Huggins knew that final consolidation of white power in the Rhodesias required that Britain's Labour Government be stampeded into acceptance of amalgamation or federation before the realities of racial politics in Southern Africa became too crudely apparent. Huggins needed to work a confidence trick, in which 'a multi-racial society' in the Rhodesias was the display of cards and entrenchment of apartheid the joker up the sleeve. Multi-racialism could mean anything, but apartheid as practised through the 1930 Southern Rhodesian Land Apportionment Act would, if enshrined in a federal constitution, consolidate white power from the Zambeze to the Limpopo. The African would lose his land in Northern Rhodesia as he had been robbed of it in Southern. Huggins boasted of Southern Rhodesia's franchise, which ignored colour and only demanded educational and income qualifications; but whenever Africans seemed likely to become educated and prosperous, Huggins promptly raised the minimum income qualification, excluding all but a handful from the vote.

In retrospect, it can be said that Huggins was not especially well equipped for tricking the Labour Government, and one of the ironies of Southern African history is that Federation was given its final impetus by that Government and its advisers rather than the hard men in Salisbury and Lusaka. Huggins had been Prime Minister of Southern Rhodesia for fifteen years when Malan came to power, and had found many opportunities for travelling to London, not just to Pretoria. Yet, despite a background wholly of the English bourgeois and professional class (and in manner, indeed, not unlike Attlee), Huggins never succeeded in understanding British politics or allowing for the simple fact that the imperial capital, even in decline, was still the hub of Empire.

Incurably provincial in outlook – his racialism was dismissive rather than openly vicious – Huggins was quite unable to appreciate that British Governments had their own, inexorable priorities. In April 1944, Huggins all but forced his way into Churchill's presence; the latter had the invasion of Europe, and little else, on his mind. Huggins all but demanded amalgamation for the Rhodesias. Churchill turned him off, partly because Huggins dealt a card with which British Governments were familiar. Despite rejection of incorporation in the Union in 1922, Huggins indicated that Southern Rhodesia might be 'forced' to consider this possibility again. D-Day, 6 June, successfully accomplished, Churchill minuted on 12 July: 'The United Kingdom Government consider the amalgamation of these territories under existing circumstances impracticable ...'[1] The irritation implied in the Minute was to remain a constant element in relationships between sometimes patrician Conservative politicians – also occasionally imbued with feelings of *noblesse oblige*, if no more, towards 'the native races' – and a set of Rhodesians whose proper place seemed below the salt. Huggins and Roy Welensky (a railwayman born all too literally the wrong side of the tracks, but the one Northern Rhodesian politician he favoured with his chilly friendship), remained suspicious of Attlee's Governments. But Attlee's Ministers never treated them as inferior beings.

For this, and other quirks of human behaviour we must look beneath the surface of events, examining with some care the fortunes of Labour Governments whose six years in office were dominated by Britain's struggle to recover from six years of total war. The personal domination over their colleagues which was asserted by Attlee and Bevin explains lack of disagreement on most issues – in the international, or imperial, context Palestine was the one major exception – but it is essential also to understand that Secretaries of State responsible for Colonial and Commonwealth affairs had no problem in agreeing with Huggins, Welensky and, in practice, Malan, when the future of Southern Africa was discussed, and decided. This statement substantially modifies, to some would wholly contradict, the usual interpretation of the Labour Government's imperial record. This interpretation is that the Governments began the process of 'giving' independence to the dependent Empire. As a recent American survey puts it: 'In 1946 the Labour Colonial Secretary, Arthur Creech Jones, set up a committee of officials ... to chart "a new approach" to Africa ... It was assumed that "within a generation ... the principal African territories will have attained ... full responsible government," which in effect meant independence within the Commonwealth.' But the same survey also says, and more accurately: 'The Labour Government in the late 1940s believed they were prolonging the Empire's life, not liquidating it.'[2] From 1948 onwards (following riots in the Gold Coast which coercion did not deter and only partly contained) West Africa did move towards both responsible and representative government. No such change occurred elsewhere in British Africa.

Reference has been made to the imperial view of Attlee and Bevin, which did not favour gratuitous independence for all and sundry. But, as much to the point, 'responsible government' did not automatically mean independence. In 1946 the only African dependency with such a form or denomination of government was Southern Rhodesia, but it was just because of this territory's wholly anomalous position in the Southern African context that the issue of independence for other territories in the area was virtually impossible to resolve. To grant independence to the Rhodesias would mean the abandonment of the Africans; to withhold independence would, or so it was widely thought in London, drive the whites of those two territories towards an Afrikaner South Africa. The Central African Federation, in constitutional terms largely the work of officials who had reported to Creech Jones in 1946, was the device found most convenient for perpetuating white power in a quasi-dependent status, doing so by means of that useful, meaningless, quasi-constitutional formula 'multi-racialism'.

The Cabinet Memoranda in the Public Record Office and Sir Roy Welensky's voluminous Papers provide a full account of the Federation's origins, and its constitutional establishment in 1953. Some survivors from the late 1940s and early 1950s have provided a personal gloss. The Memoranda, together with material from the United States National Archives, shows how impossible it is to separate the Federation – and all the half-formulated and half-baked ideas which in the late 1940s and early 1950s camouflaged its real structure – from the always looming power of South Africa. During this period, in fact, a Labour Cabinet still struggling to keep Britain afloat through one economic hurricane after another, spared more time to attempting to conciliate South African Governments than debating the Federation's future.

The issue of the chieftainship of the Bamangwato tribe in Bechuanaland may seem trivial in the perspective of history. The issue, argued for years in London and Pretoria, is of fundamental importance for any understanding of the times and the sub-continent. The marriage on 2 October 1948 between Seretse Khama and Ruth Williams went to the heart of every emotion about race and culture in Southern Africa. The marriage went to the root of the issue of whether a British Government retained, or was prepared to use, any power or influence in relation to a South Africa whose gold could keep Britain afloat – or sink it. Such considerations of survival did not directly affect the Truman Administration, but the National Archives do reveal an American view of South Africa which has not changed: a bastion against communism; a market for American goods.

7

Money and Measures

Given these economic and political factors, it is hardly surprising that Pretoria did not feel the necessity to intervene directly as possibilities of Federation were shifted by determined Rhodesians and self-deceiving Whitehall officials from paper plans to draft constitutions. In Johannesburg, Sir Ernest Oppenheimer, head of the Anglo-American Corporation, a man whose career was a supreme and potent symbol of international big business (also camouflaged with liberal notions about race and opportunity), let it be known in his characteristically covert way that he favoured the Federation. Northern Rhodesia's copper and Southern Rhodesia's coal were hardly of major importance to a financier whose industrial base was gold and diamonds. Nevertheless, the Federation's economic potential did not escape Oppenheimer's attention. He opposed the genuinely liberal ideas of the men in the Rhodesian Selection Trust who had done most to develop Northern Rhodesia's copper, Englishmen (and the American Hochschild brothers) untroubled by racial phobias, who not only believed in African trades unions but were prepared to negotiate with them as equals.

But Oppenheimer calculated that these liberal notions would disappear as a Federation dominated by Southern Rhodesia refashioned apartheid with an almost human face. Oppenheimer had no reason to suppose that Rhodesia's Africans, bred to accept the word of a British Government, would object to a philosophy expressed by that internationally known businessman-politician

Oliver Lyttelton who, in 1951, became Churchill's Colonial Secretary: 'Federation will give us four per cent on our copper investment.' History has proved the great financier wrong. All other factors apart, Federation, imposed on Africans, stimulated a nationalism which, although of long descent, had been vigorously suppressed in Southern Rhodesia and all but killed by paternalism in the Protectorate.[1]

In the late 1940s, however, Oppenheimer and his like could be forgiven for supposing that determination and deception would produce a federation to suit businessmen. The one essential element in the development of profitable South African industry – and, by economic extension, profits in and from a Central African Federation – was an abundant supply of cheap, docile black labour, controlled by well-paid white managers and technicians. Smuts, in his dislike of Africans, had stigmatised them above all because 'they would not work'. To work, they had to be coerced. Huggins had similar views: his notion of partnership, or 'multiracialism', was expressed as 'the rider and the horse' – white rider, black horse, the latter knowing his master, and the spur. Huggins needed Northern Rhodesia's copper, plus rail outlets to ports in South-West Africa, Angola and Mozambique, for Federation to become not just 'a great white loyalist Dominion' but remain a going concern.

By political extension, Northern Rhodesia had to be brought within this helot economy. Huggins could count on Welensky, leader of the 'Unofficials' in Northern Rhodesia's Legislative Council, and of most white farmers and artisans. The potential focus of opposition to this belated consummation of Cecil Rhodes's Zambeze El Dorado were the Governor in Lusaka and his Commissioners in the Provinces and Districts. These men represented the British Crown, in practice His Majesty's Government, theoretically committed to the 'paramount' interests of the native races. In 1930 Northern Rhodesia's whites had rejected paramountcy, although they were powerless to impose on Africans the segregation and systematic theft of land which obtained in Southern Rhodesia. By the late 1940s much was changing. A constitutional conference on Northern Rhodesia – reducing the Governor's powers, increasing those of the Unofficials – was scheduled for 1948. By final extension, therefore, Huggins and

Welensky had to convince a Labour Government which they mistrusted, indeed despised for its 'gutlessness', its supposed sympathy with, in Welensky's infelicitous words, 'the short haired women and long haired men'[2] of the Fabian Society and similar organisations, that the Federation was in Britain's interest.

Huggins's and Welensky's fears of opposition were natural, but misplaced. They were natural because the Bledisloe Commission in 1939 had found Africans totally opposed to 'amalgamation'. Lord Hailey, greatest of experts on colonial Africa, had reported to Churchill's Government in 1943 that 'Northern Rhodesia's Africans had an implacable opposition to amalgamation'. Hailey was certainly no friend of the Fabian Colonial Bureau, but he agreed with active members, notably Arthur Creech Jones, that whether one accepted the doctrine of paramountcy or not, African opposition to amalgamation – or federation – should be considered; if possible, it should be overcome by persuasion; if Africans remained opposed, amalgamation and its like should be abandoned.

But fears of opposition to federation by a British Labour Government were misplaced because the economic and strategic potential of Southern Africa was of greater importance to Britain's survival than the rights of Africans. As the biographer of that extreme Tory Lord Swinton (Commonwealth Relations Secretary in 1953, and thus nominally responsible for the Federation's establishment) fairly puts it: 'The Labour Government devised no method for sounding African opinion.'[3] Socialists in London ignored African opposition and, to paraphrase Rhodes, 'preferred gold to niggers'. But gold meant economic survival; the Rhodesias' Africans could not compete with that imperative.

Even if Attlee's supporters in the House of Commons had been vociferously pro-African, his Cabinet would have recommended Federation. In December 1947, just over a year before detailed planning for Federation began, Noel-Baker and Gordon Walker jointly wrote a memorandum for the Cabinet which stressed the necessity for the economic development of Northern and Southern Rhodesia, and for this to be undertaken with the co-operation of the South African and Portuguese Governments. By July 1948, the Colonial-Office-sponsored Central Africa Council – an informal grouping of like-minded politicians and acquiescent officials from the two Rhodesias – had reported to Huggins that 'the British Government was studying Federation'. Concern was being expressed in London about African rights – and objections to federation – but the Council report reckoned that if Northern Rhodesia retained control over native affairs a satisfactory compromise could be reached.

So sensitive was the Colonial Office to any hint that its political masters were contemplating what, in fact, Creech Jones was already calling 'the possible political destiny of the Central African territories' that the Council's Secretary, Hugh Parry, was given an official reprimand.[4] But Parry, South African born – like so many of his colleagues, and well aware of wider implications – was quickly told that the reprimand was merely a cover for active, British governmental concentration on Federation. Gradually it began to dawn on Huggins and Welensky that whilst, as the latter noted, 'a Conservative Government might prove helpful to Europeans in Central Africa',[5] the current Labour Government was proving remarkably acquiescent. By the time of the Victoria Falls conference in February 1949, the two determined proponents of Federation reckoned that they were at least half-way to success.

But the essential second stage owed more to deception than determination, and was more a reflection of what Whitehall could achieve than the pressures on Attlee's Government to find any means of keeping Britain afloat economically. Huggins, Welensky and their like, men who found the African 'without mental ability', nevertheless often faltered in pursuit of the Federation idea. They lacked, rather than possessed, the larger vision: they were parochial, as many a British Cabinet Minister, disdainfully spending time in Salisbury and Lusaka, was wont, privately, to remark. The vision, if such it can be called, came from Colonial and Commonwealth Relations Office officials in London who, somehow, convinced themselves that black could, as it were, become white, that a very small minority of educated, enfranchised Africans would accept Federation because they would have a place in it.

More to the point, Andrew Cohen and G. H. Baxter succeeded in convincing their masters Creech Jones and Noel-Baker that a formula could be devised which would have something in it for everybody: power for whites; status for enfranchised Africans, an

'African Affairs Board' for the rest, for that overwhelming majority, including the Federation's future copper miners and railwaymen. The idea that Africans might be fit, might be allowed to govern themselves was not even entertained. The most that Creech Jones would commit himself to (in 1950) was 'self-government', as meaningless a formula as 'multi-racialism'.

History should not condemn Cohen and Baxter, able, high-minded bureaucrats who exemplified, if to an extreme degree, Lord Blake's dictum that 'In all British-based systems of government the Civil Service is the most important and usually the least noticed or studied component.' But there are ironies to consider. Cohen and Baxter were men of the desk and the committee. John Buchan, reflecting on his South African experience, defined a certain type of official 'who saw the world through a mist of papers'.[6] Buchan defined Cohen and Baxter. Both men had spent their entire careers in London. Africa was *terra incognita*. They respected, as did Ministers, 'the man on the spot' – if he was a British High Commissioner or Governor. Neither had much time for Huggins or the Welenskys of Africa. Both knew the educated Indian, Jamaican or West African heirs to a generous imperial tradition, products of Oxford and the London School of Economics, habitués of a society where ideas were easy to entertain because they rarely had to be put into practice.

Cohen was a flamboyant Jew with equally flamboyant, supposedly 'left-wing' views. Baxter was a discreet Scot. These two innocents succeeded in producing a plan for Federation which bore about as much relation to reality as More's *Utopia* to Elizabethan England. The eminent American historian Professor Gifford errs on the side of charity when he writes of Cohen, 'It is said he naively believed better constitutions can improve human nature; if there is any truth in this claim, it is to be found in the bargains that his plan for federating the two Rhodesias and Nyasaland offered the settler leaders.'[7] But Cohen and Baxter did one thing for which history will remember them. Nyasaland, 'the colonial slum', acquired sixty years before by the Foreign Office, placed under the Colonial Office in 1907, was tacked on to the Federation for no better reason than nobody knew what to do with it.[8] Nyasaland was to prove the joker in the Federal pack, the proximate cause of its downfall.

8

Tribal Feelings

By early 1951 plans for the Federation were well advanced. The result of the second Victoria Falls conference in September was almost a foregone conclusion. Gordon Walker, as Commonwealth Secretary, visited Southern Africa in February and wrote for the Cabinet thereafter a report which is not only revealing in itself but should also be related to the appreciations and policies of the State Department in Washington and the United States Embassy in Pretoria. The British Minister dwelt mainly on economics; American officials, led by the formidable George McGhee, concentrated on politics and strategy. The joint, although uncoordinated, result was an emphatic endorsement of federation as a source of wealth and a barrier to communism.

Evelyn Baring, on whom Gordon Walker depended greatly, minuted at the time: 'Nationalist fanatics control a strong and important country. However unpalatable may be the political and social theories of the present rulers, it will be useless to attempt to draw a complete cordon sanitaire round South Africa and to cut ourselves and our African dependencies off from that country.'[1] Baring recommended federation in order to strengthen the Western connection. He deluded himself that Afrikaner immigration to Southern Rhodesia could be contained; 'containment', a word Gordon Walker used thereafter when advocating Federation, would prevent too obvious or odious a form of apartheid. In fact, Afrikaners, sensing that the wind of change was blowing in their

57

direction, flooded into Southern Rhodesia from 1948 onwards. These immigrants greatly outnumbered those from Britain. The latter were keen to preserve racial privilege, but loath to do so by coercive means. Afrikaners provided Huggins with his political storm-troopers. The British Government continued to hope for the best.

Gordon Walker, like Cohen and Baxter, was, above all, a man for committees and consensus. A history don at Christ Church in the 1930s, he gravitated naturally into the BBC during the war, and into a safe Labour seat after it. Three years as Noel-Baker's Parliamentary Under-Secretary brought him directly in touch with South Africa over the Seretse Khama affair, an experience which shaped his whole approach to Federation. Creech Jones, despite his unquestioning acceptance of Attlee's imperialism, knew Africans, liked, and was respected by them. His contact in 1926 with the trades unionist Clements Kadalie (General-Secretary of the South African Industrial and Commercial Workers' Union) initiated hopes for the eventual establishment of political rights, if no more, for Bantu and coloureds. 'Creech' was patently a good man, whose self-deceptions were, probably, inevitable.

By contrast, Gordon Walker saw the realities of South African power, and wholly accepted them. Hence his *rapport* with, not merely his dependence on, Baring. From the moment of Seretse Khama's marriage to Ruth Williams, Gordon Walker paid the closest attention to the views of the South African Government and the man on the spot. The views of the Bamangwato tribe (initially hostile to the marriage but, between September 1948 and June 1949, not only changing to support of Seretse's right to the Chieftainship, but increasingly warm to that remarkable Englishwoman, his wife) were wholly disregarded. Between 1948 and 1951 (during which time Seretse, Ruth and the able, far-sighted, but masterful ruling Chief Tshekedi were banished from Bechuanaland), Gordon Walker maintained a relationship with Malan, Baring and South Africa House in London which was based on two simple premises: if His Majesty's Government opposed the South African Government concerning the Bamangwato, the latter might realise Smuts's old ambition and seize Bechuanaland; if His Majesty's Government opposed the South African Government on any issue, the latter would demonstrate its power to injure Britain economically and strategically.

The details of the Seretse Khama affair need not concern us here, although the human issues involved evoked in the House of Commons and amongst the man and woman in the British street an emotional response today reserved for the victims of terror rather than simple repression. The Khamas' champion in England was Michael Scott, a gaunt, ascetic Anglican priest, whose ardent personality rather than his oratory filled halls and satisfied consciences. Here was a moral issue, said Scott, and one to be set against the *herrenvolk* philosophy of the Afrikaner. Lord Macaulay once remarked that there was nothing so ridiculous as the British public in one of its fits of morality, and it has to be said that parliamentary critics of the Labour Government in general and Gordon Walker in particular mixed genuine concern with tactical advantage.

The Times's correspondence columns debated the issues both passionately and fairly; the undue power of South Africa was compared with Gordon Walker's reiterated public assertions that his sole concern was the welfare of the Bamangwato. Yet *The Times* could refer without blush to Seretse's marriage as the likely cause of a 'half-breed succession', an insult to feeling and of language to which those natural (and hereditary) aristocrats, Tshekedi and Seretse, took the strongest exception. Conservative MPs who later ardently supported Federation and the effective suppression of African rights were less honest than their leader. Winston Churchill said at the end of the 26 June 1950 three-line-whip debate on Tshekedi's banishment, 'We are all going in the wrong direction.' That was a moral statement, in being honest.

But morality, or a version of it, stood a poor chance against a policy summarised by Gordon Walker in a Cabinet Memorandum, curiously enough, also dated 26 June 1950: 'We must do our utmost to keep the Union in the Commonwealth for strategic, economic, and other reasons ... if the Union got into a mood to defy us and the world, there is very little we could do to hold the (High Commission) territories ... economic boycott by South Africa would render us helpless.'[2] In a later Memorandum,

Gordon Walker summarised South Africa's power. The Royal Navy base at Simonstown could be closed down; South African troops, which Smuts and Malan had 'pledged', might not be available to support Britain in the Middle East in the event of another World War – which, with Korea on the boil, looked a distinct possibility; South Africa's gold (production, stockpile and price) directly affected Britain's sterling balances. Gordon Walker recommended, by no means for the first time in two years, that the Khamas should be treated as trouble-makers (he had so described them in the House of Commons); and nothing should be done to oppose or even criticise the South African Government. The latter, for example, was about to strip Indians in the Cape of their votes. So be it, whatever Pandit Nehru might say or India, as a new member of this new Commonwealth, might do.

Publicly, Gordon Walker denied South African pressure. The Cabinet and Commonwealth Relations Office papers tell another tale. Not only was Baring the all-too-receptive man on the spot when Malan attacked Seretse Khama's marriage; from July 1949 the South African Government demanded 'that His Majesty's Government refuse to recognise Seretse as the Chief of his tribe'. This Afrikaner *démarche* – in a 'Priority Secret' telegram – was accompanied by racial comment. Lief Egeland, the High Commissioner in London, 'said he would wager a large sum of money she [Ruth Williams] would not last six months'[3] if allowed into Bechuanaland. So far this prediction has been proved wrong by thirty-seven years. Ruth Khama, now a serene widow, was worthy of the Bamangwatos' trust. In similar vein, Huggins writing to Baring a coincidental few days after the latter received his copy of the *démarche* and Gordon Walker's acquiescent reactions, expressed Southern Rhodesia's view of the marriage as 'another poor result of the policy of sending native Africans out of Africa for education in a completely strange environment'. Malan congratulated Huggins on his views, at the same time predicting to Baring that unless Tshekedi and Seretse were banished, the South African Government might still find it necessary to 'move' against the High Commission territories. Huggins made no predictions, but he did reveal his usual ignorance. Tshekedi and Seretse, members of a tribe as civilised as any white community in Africa – as Baring, another aristocrat by descent and in manner, openly conceded – knew Britain, and some British ways all too well. They expected Englishmen to keep their word. Eventually, some Conservative Englishmen did so.

9

Enter America

South Africa's looming power had begun to receive the serious attention of the State Department once the Cold War really got under way. Throughout 1950 and 1951, McGhee and his colleagues conducted a lengthy seminar on an area where 'our important economic and strategic interests should be strengthened'. Except in terms of the General Agreement on Tariffs and Trade (GATT) and the open door, economics did not demand a great deal of attention. The practice of 'favouring the economic interests of the United Kingdom should be opposed', but not so much that Englishmen, and other Europeans, 'who are more willing to live under primitive conditions than Americans',[1] would be discouraged from becoming, or remaining, the technical experts in a white Southern African industrial economy increasingly financed by Wall Street. McGhee visited South Africa in March 1950, and disliked what he saw of the *herrenvolk* and their policies. But McGhee also decided South Africa must be backed. Malan and his Ministers cleverly played on Cold War fears. Did Mr McGhee not know that Michael Scott – who had lived in South Africa and whose relationship with Africans was notorious to Afrikaners – was a member of the Communist Party? The point, or the bait, was duly taken.

By October 1950 Malan's tactics – he even spoke approvingly to McGhee of NATO, in which he had no conceivable interest – had produced the dividends of solid support and status. Talks on defence were held in Washington, the South African delegation, venturing into a world beyond the laager, being received by no less a Liberal, Christian general and Secretary for Defence, than George Catlett Marshall. South African participation in the Korean War earned good marks, the promise of modern arms, the accolade of a reliable ally. By August 1951, British suscepti-bilities on South Africa and American views on Cold War led to a conference in Nairobi, at which the entire future of Africa, but particularly south of the Sahara, was debated. The State Depart-ment team had a difficult hand to play. The Truman Adminis-tration was determined to continue Roosevelt's commitment to independence for colonial Africa, provided American commercial interests were unimpaired – *and* provided African nationalism could be detached from its supposed adherence to Soviet com-munism. Nominally, the conference was a joint, Anglo-South African exercise in planning regional defence. Ostensibly the United States team was present as an observer, coeval with France, Belgium, Italy and Portugal. In reality, American pledges of economic aid and military equipment, both the product of Cold War phobias, set the scene.

Malan's Government, satisfied that it had British weaknesses to bargain with, and flattered by American approval, was able to play the role of leading a powerful, independent, Western nation, responsible for the defence not only of the sub-continent but the sea lanes around it. The Southern Rhodesian Government, which was also represented at the conference, indicated clearly that it would take no orders from London, but was responsive to leader-ship from Pretoria. Ward, the United States Consul-General in Nairobi, noted that, in consequence, it was necessary for the British delegation to seek the most active support from the South African team. In short, 'the South Africans are prime movers in the conference'.[2] In fact, Malan's Government had no intention of re-creating the Second World War spirit of co-operation which had characterised Smuts's and Churchill's relationship. What Malan and his Ministers wanted was American – and, to a degree, British – support for their internal and Southern African policies. To get such support, a Government of 'nationalist fanatics' was prepared to deal the defence co-operation, Cold War, anti-communist card.

The deal brought the trick. Huggins was an incidental bene-ficiary of American policy, dollar funds, unavailable from Britain, being provided in 1951 for copper mines, railways and trunk roads. But 'the utilization of South Africa's raw materials', in the Pretoria Embassy's words, together with the requirement of ensuring that 'Communist penetration' was forestalled, led to a major American aid and investment commitment. Indeed, through 1951, the supply of arms and equipment for the South African Army and Air Force led to speculation that something really significant was in train, namely to cite the Embassy again, 'The conclusion of a Financial Agreement for uranium production in South Africa'.[3] Anglo-American, which objected to State Department interference in what Oppenheimer regarded as private business, however much related to the production of nuclear weapons, noted nevertheless with relief that the United States Government thought 'the status of South-West Africa not entirely clear'. In the 1950s, most geologists assumed the Rand would produce uranium; the farsighted looked to South-West Africa. The status – a League of Nations Mandate transferred to the United Nations – was perfectly clear, as was the fact that the United States Administration wanted the uranium, and would raise objections neither to its source nor by what means it was secured and supplied.

Over the years which followed, United States Administrations and South African Governments came to conduct their affairs without much regard for British interests. In 1951, however, with the fanatics only three years in office, both Pretoria and Washington thought it best to go through the motions of tripartite co-operation. The initial American investment of $12 million in South African uranium (two-thirds from the Ex-Im Bank, a third 'loan finance' – from Wall Street) covered an arrangement whereby 'all the production of uranium will be delivered to the South African Atomic Energy Boards ... the Board will then make deliveries to the United States Atomic Energy Commission and the United Kingdom Ministry of Supply at prices established by the basic uranium agreement'.[4] Malan had done more than take a trick; he had won the rubber.

10

Victoria Falls, 1951

Thus, as Attlee's second, lame duck Government dragged out its final months, the map of Southern Africa was redrawn not by the European powers, as in the nineteenth century, but by the one Western Super Power and its two surrogates, Britain and South Africa. The Victoria Falls conference in September 1951 was as little the direct concern of Washington as it was of Pretoria, but the decisions taken there reflected the convictions of policy-makers and their advisers in those two capitals. Nor were the participants at the Conference particularly important in themselves. They represented the times, and the circumstances. Huggins and Welensky scented victory; Gordon Walker and Griffiths, who had organised a preliminary conference during June in London, were prepared to concede it. Andrew Cohen continued to believe in constitutions as possessing a real, not an abstract, political identity.

The June conference, Cohen's affair, recommended Federation with 'a constitutional status broadly similar to Southern Rhodesia'.[1] There was to be a Federal legislature of 35 (17 from Southern Rhodesia; 11 from Northern Rhodesia; 7 from Nyasaland), in which 3 from each territory would be 'specially chosen to represent African interests, and in each of the two Northern territories two of these would be Africans'. (In 1951, the three territories comprised six million Africans and just over 200,000 Europeans.) An African Affairs Board would consider African interests, and the Governor-General of the Federation could re-

65

serve legislation affecting them, and refer it to the Secretary of
State for Commonwealth Relations. The Colonial Office would,
in effect, lose its role as protector of the Africans, surrendering
it to a department which, in nearly thirty years, had never interfered with the actions of Southern Rhodesian Governments.
Although they attended the Victoria Falls conference, the Governors of Southern Rhodesia, Northern Rhodesia and Nyasaland
saw their day as done. Only Sir Arthur Benson, summoned from
Lusaka, was openly prepared both to condemn the Federation
for overriding African objections and to entertain sincere yet
pious hopes that British justice would continue to protect peoples
whose rights were, supposedly, paramount.[2]

Huggins had refused to allow Africans to attend the 1949
Victoria Falls conference. He grudgingly conceded the presence
of a handful in 1951, but ordered them to be accommodated in
huts and to be separated for meals from their white colleagues.
The British delegation was unaware of this treatment, but Hugh
Parry, the one Rhodesian bureaucrat at the centre of things,
spared time from paper work to arrange hostel accommodation
for the African delegates, and ensure their eating, indeed living
with whites as equals – during the conference. But all these
devices and all this temporary conciliation quite failed to overcome the widespread and vocal African objection to the imposition of Federation. The National Congresses of Northern
Rhodesia and Nyasaland were only reluctantly persuaded to send
representatives to Victoria Falls because Griffiths personally
pledged that 'the protectorate status of the two Northern territories would be accepted and preserved'. Using all the Welsh
rhetoric of which, alas, he was all too easily capable, Griffiths
pleaded for a concept of partnership in which black and white
would live 'side by side'.

The Africans were not fooled. They could not have read the
confidential material prepared for the conference, which summarised correspondence between London and Salisbury in the
preceding months, and where Gordon Walker, whilst admitting
that 'African opinion in Northern Rhodesia and Nyasaland was
almost unanimously opposed to the proposals', recommended
Federation to the Cabinet because 'Southern Rhodesia already
has practical independence ... the day is not far off when it could

defy us with impunity if we sought to interfere improperly, as its white inhabitants would think in its internal affairs.'[3] The Africans at Victoria Falls would not have read the 'confidential Minute on South Africa', which stressed the still latent danger that if Southern Rhodesia was, by the British Government, 'improperly' interfered with, Malan stood ready to welcome it.

The Congress delegates knew what they knew, and that despite – or because – of Griffiths's rhetoric and the conference's internal statement that 'the ultimate aim of (Federation) is to advance the African to a stage where he is in all respects a full partner exercising all the rights and accepting all the responsibilities of citizenship', Huggins, in April, had raised the Southern Rhodesia franchise qualification from £150 to £500. The African would not be a partner. He would not even be 'side by side'; he would remain segregated. With a franchise qualification of £500, his chance of voting simply disappeared. Huggins was hardly likely to concede to Africans in a Federation, and Federal Legislature, what he denied them in Southern Rhodesia. The Federal Legislature of thirty-five would contain *four*, nominated, African members. Rhodes's rhetoric – 'equal rights for all civilised men' – had been finally revealed as totally hypocritical, not by the Hugginses and Welenskys, but by high-minded gentlemen in London.

Rhodes had also said, 'We are going to be lords of these people and keep them in a subject position ... They should not have the franchise because we don't want them on an equality with us ... These are my politics on native affairs and these are the politics of South Africa.'[4] Gordon Walker's belief, indeed Attlee's and that of his Party, that Southern Rhodesia was 'different' from South Africa would have struck those Africans present at Victoria Falls in September 1951 as wholly bogus if, without exception, they had not been bred to accept the Englishman's word, to believe that a British Government was different from the white roughnecks in Salisbury and Lusaka. If such a Government faltered, there was always the Queen. In 1953, the Chiefs and citizens of Nyasaland sent a Petition to the Queen, with their 'respectful greetings and undying loyalty', protesting against Federation. 'We humbly pray your Majesty to protect us from it ... We have lost confidence in the wisdom and justice of the Ministers who at present advise your Majesty on Colonial

policy ...' But good Queen Elizabeth was like Queen Victoria.*
Federation went ahead.

In 1951 the Rhodesian African was neither militant nor bitter;
liberation war was in the future. The Central African Federation
sowed the seeds for that bloody struggle, the white man willing
his own destruction. Federation was still two years distant in
September 1951, but its realities could not be hidden. Lyttelton
and his kind were to get their 4 per cent, eventually, but their
compatriots in Salisbury were not slow to act. The first Federal
budget in 1953 took half a crown off a bottle of whisky – and put
five shillings on a bag of maize.

* When the recipient of letters from Lobengula.

PART THREE
The Central African Federation, 1953-63

'As I said to the PM [Huggins] only a day
or so ago, we now have the OK to go ahead
and it will be difficult to produce alibis in
five years' time if we don't do something.'

Welensky to W. M. Macmillan,
25 February 1954

I I

What the Whites Wanted

Those who made the first Federal Government were, in odd combination, theorists, cynics and idealists. These three facets of personal conviction reflected Cohen's innocence, Huggins's acceptance of Federation as a paltry alternative to amalgamation of the two Rhodesias, and Welensky's belief in a new imperium. But those in Churchill's confidence who, in October 1951, met round the Cabinet table to plan a Tory version of postwar Britain and its place in the world, found themselves in a dilemma concerning Federation which neither theory, cynicism nor idealism could solve.

The dilemma was, quite simply, a progressive decrease in Britain's military and economic strength. Although such strength had rarely been applied to, or in, Central and Southern Africa, it was believed none the less in Salisbury – and Pretoria – to be available if necessary for the maintenance of white supremacy and the suppression of black dissent. Those officials who, between 1947 and 1951, planned or urged Federation ignored the central element in Empire: coercive power. Churchill and his Cabinet, the men who brought Federation into constitutional being, could not ignore the progressive loss of such power; concerning Federation, Churchill and his colleagues hoped that white Rhodesians would muster enough coercive power of their own to deal with local difficulties. If they did not do so, South Africa could and would step in. In neither case would Britain do so. These strategic factors were never communicated to Salisbury –

71

or Pretoria – in clear and positive language. Eden, Churchill's successor in 1955, ignored Africa. Macmillan, Prime Minister between 1957 and 1963, gave Africa much of his time, but never told Welensky and his colleagues what he really thought or intended.

Thus, in considering what the whites wanted it is essential not only to distinguish between London, Salisbury and Pretoria, but between different conceptions of coercive power in those three capitals. It is not enough to say that the whites wanted, and were determined, to remain the rider, applying the spur, or the whip, when necessary. There was no dissent from this objective in any of the three capitals. Oliver Lyttelton, who, as already noted, was the one member of Churchill's inner circle with sufficient interest, experience and intellect to express views on Federation with force and clarity, minuted for the Cabinet on 9 November 1951 (Ismay, a reluctant Commonwealth Relations Secretary, silently assenting): 'We recommend that Her Majesty's Government should issue a statement endorsing the proposed Federation of Southern Rhodesia, Northern Rhodesia and Nyasaland.'

Lyttelton continued: 'White public opinion in all three territories is generally in favour. On the other hand the Africans have declared their opposition. The strength of this is partly due to the lack of a lead from the last Government, which allowed the opponents of the proposals to misrepresent them.'[1] Without troubling to analyse this alleged misrepresentation – which would have been difficult as both the constitutional proposals and African opposition to them were known – Lyttelton argued that 'there is a firm chance of winning over the African opposition by Her Majesty's Government giving a clear lead, but little or no chance otherwise'.[2] Thereafter, when not attempting to thwart 'that negro' Kwame Nkrumah in the Gold Coast by all possible means short of coercion, Lyttelton instructed officials in Northern Rhodesia and Nyasaland to urge Federation on the native population, and not to take 'No' for an answer.

A year later Swinton (as Ismay's successor) and Lyttelton jointly minuted: 'In South Africa a decision not to impose Federation would be regarded as an act of deplorable weakness by Her Majesty's Government.' Yet African opposition to Federation had not decreased. Neither blandishments nor veiled threats had prevailed. So Federation would be imposed, not least because as Swinton had noted on 24 September 1952 (in a paper which was mainly concerned with approving Pretoria's case for 'incorporating' South-West Africa into the Union in order to increase Malan's parliamentary majority): 'We must do all we can to preserve and strengthen our relations with South Africa ... economically, the stability of the sterling area is dependent on the United Kingdom obtaining a substantial part of South Africa's gold output.'[3]

This was the South Africa which was entrenching apartheid and stripping Indians and coloureds of the vote. But, as Milner wrote to Asquith in 1897: 'You have only to sacrifice the "nigger" absolutely and the game is easy.'[4] Although relations between British and South African Governments cooled after 1948 – primarily because the latter began to doubt Britain's capacity for coercive action, thus forcing South Africa to contemplate, or take it – one historian of the period accurately remarks, 'Among Western States, South Africa's relationship with the United Kingdom remained the most important ... the British Imperial factor was still a firm reality in Southern Africa.'[5]

Thus London, Salisbury – and Pretoria – were of the same political mind once Cohen's formula had been turned into a device for imposing Federation behind a façade of constitutional innovation and advance. But the fundamental difference between the politicians in the three capitals was that London hoped that the African would tamely submit, and that no British Government would be asked to make him do so; Salisbury was determined that the African would submit, or take the consequences; Pretoria assumed, on the basis of recent events, notably the British Government's acquiescence in Malan's apartheid, that London and Salisbury would cow the African into submission without the necessity for active South African intervention. Submission would complete the white ring against Pan-African, 'communist-inspired' nationalism. It would be the African, not the Afrikaner, who would be 'contained'.

The ten years of Federation were marked by much that is strange, ironic, unpleasant, or equivocal, but perhaps the most striking if least consciously recognised factor in this bogus political experiment was the lack of communication between the three capitals, above all between London and Salisbury, and most notably on coercive power, or its absence in terms of will and capacity. This lack of communication, indeed virtual silence during the time of the 1960 Monckton Commission and from thence until the Federation's demise in 1963, was most notable from London, reflecting decisions taken but not communicated in 1957, when Macmillan decided to reduce drastically and covertly Britain's overseas commitments – and Sir Roy Welensky, a good man fallen among political hustlers in Salisbury and *fainéants* in London became, fortuitously and, for him, unfortunately, Federal Prime Minister.

Even in 1960, some time after Macmillan had decided that the 1953 Federation was doomed, Welensky, most of his colleagues, and many of his advisers were still assuming not only its modified continuance but expecting increased British support for the business of keeping Africans in their place. As late as January 1962 and as Welensky put together a plan for 'a new Central Africa', an independent state of the copperbelt and Southern Rhodesia, the Federal Ministry of Defence wrote a paper which argued that Royal Air Force squadrons should be stationed in the latter territory. Although Macmillan had just ordered a 10 per cent cut in all overseas military expenditure – an act which the paper noted – its authors assumed that 'the United Kingdom must be established in Africa'. Limited liaison between the British and Federal intelligence services over the former Belgian Congo – where civil war had broken out at independence in July 1960 – helped to delude Welensky that the Macmillan Government would not only support him politically at all times but do so coercively in a crisis in or on the borders of the Federation.

The delusion was perhaps natural, because although intelligence liaison between London and Salisbury had been in existence for many years, it became important to Welensky concerning the Congo because of his conviction that white interests there were being damaged by the United Nations and the United States in unholy combination. Few facts supported this conviction; the emotional factor was uppermost. Welensky had no objection to independence for the Congo provided, as Parry (the Federal Cabinet Secretary) put it: 'The blacks had a government but the whites told it what to do.'[6] Macmillan would not have put the case so crudely, but throughout 1960 and 1961 his allusive ambiguities appeared to indicate sympathy for Welensky and support for his policy of undermining the Congo Government by various overt and covert means.

Unfortunately for Welensky, he quite failed to grasp that Macmillan's foreign policy was based on maintaining the closest possible relations with the United States, although the illusion was also preserved of a Britain well able to make up its mind and equally well able to coerce lesser powers. Welensky also failed to grasp, despite being on a British intelligence 'distribution' which provided him with an adequate summary of events in different parts of the world, that American policy objectives for and in the Congo were not substantially different from those sought in Salisbury and concocted in London. Indeed, Welensky ignored the voluntarily tendered advice – some of it quite good – from the Federal Intelligence and Security Bureau (FISB), whose Director and staff knew which way the British wind was blowing.

But even in Huggins's day, and throughout his four years as Federal Prime Minister, London and Salisbury spoke different versions of the Queen's English and differed profoundly if unconsciously on the meaning, purpose – and survival – of Empire, let alone the sources of coercive power. Churchill, his colleagues and their successors supported Huggins's determination to keep Africans in their place. Men like Lyttelton would have had no objection to Huggins's eve of Federation plan to remove the franchise entirely from Africans.[7] But Lyttelton and his kind lived in the world and were affected by it. Lyttelton, who called himself 'case-hardened', was to be indirectly responsible for Kenya's independence in 1964 because throughout the early 1950s he bluntly told whites there that their day was done. Even in 1955 increased African representation on Northern Rhodesia's Legislative Council was being considered, a move which owed something to Lyttelton's determination that the copperbelt should be peaceful, and hence prosperous.

But white Rhodesians were imperialists stuck in a time warp, living in a world which for Britain had started to come apart on the Somme and had finally disintegrated over Hiroshima. Salisbury in the early 1950s was a provincial town whose politicians, as Gordon Walker remarked, had the mentality and outlook of

County Councillors. But the Councillors saw themselves as superior beings none the less. The Rhodesian imperial ethos was based exclusively on assumed racial superiority. Whites went to Rhodesia to *feel* superior; the feeling, over generations, bred racialists, many of whom were personally decent in their handling of Africans but very few of whom actually had any real working or personal relationship with them.

This white culture, in short, was remarkably similar not only to that of South Africa but also to that of the southern states in America, a factor which Ian Smith exploited with some skill during his years as leader of a rebel regime. Yet the white Rhodesian culture, despite Afrikaner immigration, was fundamentally different from South Africa's in one crucial respect. Afrikaners were also neurotic – in the clinical sense of the word – about the Bantu. But Afrikaners, during three centuries, had built a nation, of sorts; they neither could nor desired to live anywhere else. Despite Welensky's claims as Federation crumbled for 'third and fourth generation Rhodesians', he and his compatriots were really transients in Central Africa. South African Governments saw them as such, and hedged their bets accordingly about Southern Rhodesia's capacity to survive as an independent state.

In considering, therefore, the eve of Federation and the pattern of government which characterised its short life, far more attention should be paid to contradictions in relationship between London, Salisbury and Pretoria than to details of constitutions or commissions which reviewed and revised them, let alone the fairly bitter arguments in Lusaka and Salisbury as to which territory should have the biggest slice of the economic cake. These details have been discussed exhaustively in many accounts, particularly those concerning the Federation's final years, when Macmillan's 'wind of change' had become a gale even threatening to destroy what was left of a British neo-Colonial Empire in Africa based on covert support for 'reliable' black rulers.

Yet some attention must be given to the details because the federal and territorial constitutions were the ostensible basis of common policies between London and Salisbury, and the commissions the force which destroyed them. The fundamental difference between constitutions and commissions was that the former fudged the issue of independence; if granted this meant majority rule, which could only be opposed by those denied it with violence or subversion. Various inquiries, above all the 1960 Monckton Commission, faced the issue, and concluded that the African, no less than the European, saw independence and majority rule as synonymous. 'Self-government', like 'partnership' and 'multi-racialism', was thus exposed as no more than a shibboleth. The Monckton Commission finally broke the Federation, because it recommended ways, albeit veiled in euphemistic language, whereby the territories could, at independence, secede. Once Monckton had pronounced, African opposition to Federation became transmuted into an essentially nationalist movement, not 'Pan-African' as Welensky asserted, nor communist-backed, as Smith and his supporters shouted into Pretoria's ear – but Zimbabwean. The Monckton Commission legitimised hitherto nervous if vocal African opinion, and put the Uncle Toms on notice to declare where they stood.

The 1953 Constitution was an ingenious piece of political carpentry, whose solid appearance belied a rickety edifice built on the foundations of one federal and three territorial legislatures. The federal constitution was based on a conference held at Lancaster House in April 1952 which Africans refused to attend, and differed only from the proposals summarised on page 65 to the extent that the nine members of Parliament representing African interests were to comprise six elected Africans and three nominated whites. This apparent concession to democratic principles made no practical difference to political realities nor to prejudices expressed by Welensky on 23 July 1952 in Ndola: 'If there is going to be domination it is going to be my race that will dominate.'[8] But, in any case, with white domination clearly established, Huggins and Welensky were primarily concerned to urge other provisions on an acquiescent Conservative Government (the Commonwealth Relations Office was supine, the Colonial Office muzzled by Lyttelton), which would ensure that Southern Rhodesia's virtual independence from the Crown concerning defence and foreign relations was extended to the Federation as such.

The Labour Party in the House of Commons opposed the Bill and Order which gave constitutional life to Federation, but did so ineffectually. To condemn in Opposition what you have advocated in office rarely commands respect. Africans in the territories may have come to believe that the Labour Party supported their aspirations (it is part of the mythology of Federation that it did), but in 1953 the political centre of gravity concerning Federations shifted from London to Salisbury, and criticism by the Labour Party fell on deaf white ears.

A momentarily euphoric white caucus in Salisbury – chosen, without much discussion, to be the Federal capital – thus arrogated to itself the power to control and deploy the forces of law and order throughout and indeed beyond Federal territory. In 1952 and 1953 British Ministers were keen to push Federation, and ignored the fine print of constitutions. But, in retrospect, it can be seen that Huggins and Welensky made their first serious error of judgment in assuming that Her Majesty's Governments would always accept without demur a situation in which their Protectorate role in Northern Rhodesia and Nyasaland could be usurped during security crises by a Federal Government which was, in constitutional law, a dependency of the Crown. Lyttelton's conviction that 'self-government' was a catchphrase which the Federation's Africans would accept as a truth may have led the caucus to believe that he gave them a free hand to prepare for a new white dominion.

The County Councillors were not entirely wrong, but they miscalculated. Lyttelton returned to the City in 1954, and never again was there to be a Conservative Cabinet Minister so well able to support white political and economic interests. Lyttelton's successor, Alan Lennox-Boyd, a genial brewer with liberal tendencies, held office for five years, during which British policies in Africa were fundamentally changed by 'Suez', and hence by a belated realisation that power had gone and only influence remained. In 1959 Lennox-Boyd was replaced by Macmillan's protégé, Iain Macleod, who actually believed that Africans should rule – or misrule – themselves. That Macleod believed this because a large part of the Conservative Parliamentary Party did is neither here nor there.

On 23 October 1953, however, when Federation was formally inaugurated, Huggins and Welensky could feel reasonably sure that, at last, they were on their way. Benson opposed the Federal

Government's intention to commit the British South Africa Police (BSAP) in Northern Rhodesia if Protectorate forces proved inadequate to maintain internal security – or, which was the more likely hypothesis, if the Colonial Government in Lusaka defined subversion in different terms from Salisbury – but, with his colleague, Sir Robert Armitage, in Nyasaland's centre of Government (Zomba), clung to the belief that the Crown's authority, which meant that it alone could amend the Federal constitution, was understood by the new Government. But Huggins was already contemplating an approach to London which was designed to produce constitutional independence for the Federation. Huggins succeeded at Lancaster House in 1952, and after an eve of Federation conference in January 1953, in acquiring power over economic development in the three territories, thus consolidating in every sense the gains made concerning security and external relations. But Huggins's real goal was independence, as soon as possible. All the lengthy analyses which have been published about the 'pledges' the British Government gave in 1952 and 1953 to the effect that no Federation constitutional changes would be made without Salisbury's agreement overlook the fact that Huggins was not prepared to wait for the independence prize to be given. He intended to ask for it, confident that he would not be rejected.

Lord Blake is quite right to characterise the first four years of Federation as a honeymoon between a Conservative Government in London and the Federal Government in Salisbury. What the whites in both Governments wanted was not only 4 per cent on the copper investments but a black population in the Federation which would docilely accept denial of political rights in return for a slowly rising standard of living. For many years Lyttelton had worked for the establishment of a system whereby the 'Empire' would provide Britain with raw materials. Federation appeared to do that concerning copper and chrome. Lyttelton – an able, witty, but conceited entrepreneur – then turned to other matters; Swinton reckoned that Federation had consolidated white interests in Central Africa without humiliating Africans in the process. But not for nothing had Huggins's sole contribution to medical science been a work on amputation. Amalgamation of the two Rhodesias remained his aim; to achieve it, Federal independence from the Crown required amputation, not a messy constitutional operation which continued to 'reserve' powers to the Government in London. Once independence was achieved, amalgamation could take place. Both Huggins and Welensky realised that their Conservative friends in London would, in the nature of British, democratic politics, lose a General Election eventually, and that a Labour Government might actually honour a belated pledge to stand up for the African. Time was not on the Federation's side.

These factors underline the irony that it was a Conservative, not a Labour Government which, on 31 December 1963, finally and formally dissolved the Federation. In 1956, however, it would have taken a more perceptive man than Huggins to realise that Britain and the Conservatives who governed it were already being forced by inexorable circumstance into making the most painful adjustments in their international role. Huggins made his second error of judgment in coming to London with what was virtually a demand for independence in his pocket during a crisis for Anthony Eden and his Conservative Government which extended well beyond the immediate requirement to 'topple' Egypt's nationalist dictator Gamal Abdel Nasser or be 'humiliated' by his threatened nationalisation of the Suez Canal Company. Huggins had been monumentally tactless to demand amalgamation from Churchill in April 1944; in June 1956 he may have reckoned that vociferous Rhodesian support for Eden in his impending conflict with Nasser would earn the Federal independence prize. Huggins was wrong; Lord Home, Commonwealth Relations Secretary in a Cabinet which, when not deeply divided about 'Suez' was unanimous in fearing its consequences, made it quite clear that independence for the Federation was not only a matter for Her Majesty's Government to decide, but was not on the immediate political agenda.

Huggins – by now Lord Malvern of Rhodesia and Bexley, an exquisitely absurd conjunction of the imperial and the suburban – had made a written *démarche* to Home in March 1956, based on the nostrum: 'independence within the Commonwealth'. Huggins coupled his demands with the statement that Africans 'would never acquire more than an equal share of the partnership'. Huggins was wise to avoid interpretation of this elusive, indeed illu-

1 Hail: Lord Malvern welcomes Harold Macmillan to Salisbury, January 1960

2 Farewell: Sir Alec Douglas-Home says goodbye to Sir Roy Welensky, Downing Street, May 1964

3 Before UDI: Harold Wilson and Arthur Bottomley meet detained
African leaders, Old Sarum airport, 27 October 1965

4 After UDI: Bulawayo at dawn, 25 November 1965

sory concept: in 1953, 380 Africans were on Southern Rhodesia's common roll; in 1956, 560. Instead, Huggins stressed to Home – doubtless, in his own mind, simultaneously reassuring him – that 'Government would remain in civilised hands'. Not content with evoking the shade of Cecil Rhodes, Huggins then proceeded to tackle Home direct. Supported by Lord Llewellin (the Federation's Governor-General, a former Conservative Cabinet Minister and a kind of lesser Lyttelton), Huggins, on 14 June, argued that independence should be granted before the Labour Party was returned to power. Home did more than riposte; he delivered a political repulse to Huggins by 'advising him to win African support by devising liberal formulae for franchise citizenship'. Home underlined this repulse by making it absolutely clear that no consideration would be given to independence before a Federal constitutional review – in 1960.

Huggins cannot have enjoyed his June visit to London. On the 22nd Lennox-Boyd warned him that 'the consequence of forcing independence could be a break-up of the Federation'. Huggins replied that 'economic necessity' would prevent that. This was a reasonable reply, given all the exchanges and deals between Huggins and Conservative Ministers since 1951, but it was an inadequate one at a time when Eden's Government, when not otherwise preoccupied, was planning further constitutional changes for Northern Rhodesia and Nyasaland. These changes were designed to give Africans a genuine role in the Legislative Councils although not in the Executive sphere. Huggins had not gone to London to see the *Colonial* Secretary, to be reminded that the Federation was not only a dependency but that two of the territories were, constitutionally speaking, none of his business. But, despite Lennox-Boyd's invariable affability to visiting colonial politicians whatever their colour, Huggins was put in his place. At the end of October he resigned, his aim frustrated by what Welensky was later to call 'a gutless lot of B's'.

The received version of the Federation's history argues that conflict between London and Salisbury dates from early 1960 and the leaked reports of the Monckton constitutional review Commission. We can now see that conflict began four years earlier, and was caused not only by Huggins's lack of perception but by a combination of factors and feelings in the minds and hearts of British Cabinet Ministers which subsequently led them to regard the Federation as expendable. Welensky, on succeeding Huggins, failed to appreciate what was happening in London; he banked on 'friends' there to support his intention of so adroitly outwitting Lennox-Boyd's moral scruples and constitutional niceties that independence would come by stealth.

With all his many virtues, Sir Roy Welensky is not adroit. It is not that his tactics in the six years of a painful Federal premiership were maladroit; it is simply the case that he and Macmillan (who succeeded Eden, after the Suez debacle, in February 1957) were living in different worlds. Macmillan knew that the imperial era was over; henceforth, Britain must live by its wits. Welensky – 'fifty per cent Polish, fifty per cent Jewish, a hundred per cent British',[9] as Lyttelton had amusedly, condescendingly noted – believed that Britain, in Africa, remained omnipotent. As a kind of plenipotentiary for such a power, Welensky saw no reason why independence should not be secured. White men, everywhere, would benefit. That the two are men of vastly different temperaments – Welensky committed to plain speaking, Macmillan incapable of it – only emphasises, it does not explain, the differences which divided them as those six years saw Zimbabwe receive its first, uncovenanted bonus, the collapse of white Rhodesia's belief in the word of a British Government. The road to UDI led to Zimbabwe, however much British Governments and Rhodesian regimes mined the route. By the late 1950s the whites in London wanted, and were determined, to abandon or even break up the Federation because it thwarted their plans to preserve a British role in black Africa. By the time that whites in Salisbury consciously accepted this reality, Africans' opposition to Federation had not merely become a political process but the precursor of demands for *their* independence.

12

How Africans Resisted

Welensky and Macmillan did, unwittingly, give nascent Zimbabwe a bonus. It was to be about the only one. The study of the recent past in Central and Southern Africa has not only suffered from the myth that the British Labour Party and its broadly liberal affiliates effectively supported African opposition to Federation, but from the complementary notion that from the first there was a real political opposition to support. The truth is that Africans were opposed to Federation as 'passionately', and for the same non-political reasons, as they opposed amalgamation. Africans, although rarely given to outrage, detested the infinite varieties of discrimination practised against them, and were perfectly well able to distinguish between the fiction and the truth of 'equal rights for all civilised men'. An Afrikaner South Africa was several times worse than Huggins's Rhodesia, but the latter was bad enough. For much of the 1950s African opposition to Federation reflected the realities of life for the vast majority in Southern Rhodesia, where the Land Apportionment Act gave over 50 per cent, and that by far the best, to the white minority – most of whom, be it noted, lived in Salisbury or lesser towns; and where the franchise was rigged to exclude talent unaccompanied by means, let alone to restrict, nay deny political rights as such. But above all Africans opposed discrimination. As that high Tory Lord Blake has so justly said:

Africans were only served in shops after every White had been served. Shop assistants were themselves always white. There were separate entrances and counters for Blacks and Whites in post offices. There was rigid separatism in state schools, hospitals, hotels, restaurants, transport, swimming baths and lavatories. Our immigrant would observe, but soon find it natural, that an African was called 'boy' whether he was six, sixteen or sixty. Nor would he long be surprised that Africans could not touch European alcoholic drinks, beer, wine or spirits, but only 'Kaffir beer'.

He would also discover that Africans were governed by a rigid system of certificates and passes. An African had to have a *Certificate of Registration* which allocated him to some area that was African under the Land Apportionment Act even if he had been born in an urban location. Armed with this he could travel, but as soon as he entered an urban area he had to secure another document, either a *Current Visiting Pass* or a *Town Pass to Seek Work*. If and when he had got some sort of job he had to procure either a *Certificate of Service* or a *Certificate of Self-Employment*. The head of a family had to have a *Certificate of Occupation*. A woman, unless employed, was required to have a *Certificate of Recognition of an Approved Wife*. These documents had to be produced on demand from the police and other officials. It was fear of extension of this system to the north, which, more than anything else, made the Africans of the protectorates dig in their toes against federation.[1]

But of these human problems most whites were unaware or indifferent. 'I remarked that I had expected to see more African villages about. "No," he said. "Not near the line of rail. But there are plenty of them up and down the place. We'd be better off without them. Still . . ." He smiled and realizing by my remark that I was an immigrant [circa 1955], he added, "But you'll soon get used to them. It's just as though they weren't there." '[2] Yes, Africans not only opposed discrimination but the uncivilised white concept of 'non-person', knowing they had both an identity and a history. In the extraordinarily restrained personal accounts of men like Ndabaningi Sithole and Lawrence Vambe nothing is more striking than the establishment in the reader's mind of personal identity, totally unrelated to nationalism or 'Pan-Africanism', wholly grounded in the knowledge, 'I am a man.'

But, all that said, Africans did not oppose Federation as that verb is usually understood. In most cases during the 1950s Africans had no alternative to offer; in several critical instances of key personalities - Nyasaland's Hastings Banda, Northern Rhodesia's Kenneth Kaunda, Southern Rhodesia's Joshua Nkomo - funds covertly provided from Whitehall, not federal, sources ensured support for a British policy which was as ambiguous in 1953 as it was a decade later. (Kenya's Tom Mboya and Tanganyika's Julius Nyerere - 'an outstanding African leader' as one Secret Intelligence Service (SIS) CX Report noted in June 1959 - were amongst the first recipients of such funds, establishing a pattern which has changed little over the years.) These prospective politicians and one-party 'successor state' leaders in place (even if sometimes in gaol) were not going to blow the whistle on their paymasters (for their parties, be it stressed, not for themselves) by telling their followers 'patience, time and Her Majesty's Government are on our side'.

Other African leaders like Jasper Savanhu were ready to fall in behind Huggins and hope for a place only just below the salt. Vocal African opposition to Federation and Federal policies was thus initially confined to trades unions in the two Rhodesias; subsequently, but only when it became increasingly clear to perceptive Africans that Macmillan's Government was hedging its post-imperial bets, opposition took a definably political form in Southern Rhodesia. But only in Nyasaland's Banda was there found a demagogue who could attract both liberal and governmental support in Britain whilst enlisting it, with degrees and varieties of persuasion or coercion, from the Protectorate's embryo electorate.

If these comments seem harsh, they are based on the evidence. The earliest document in *Zimbabwe Independence Movements* dates from 1937, and is included, revealingly enough, in a section entitled 'The Period of Protest' and a chapter called 'The Politics of Reformism'. The Southern Rhodesian African National Congress's (ANC's) first 'Statement of principles, policy and programme' affirmed 'complete loyalty to the Crown'; demanded the repeal of the Land Apportionment Act; and insisted on universal suffrage. But no demand was made for breaking up the Federation, and Congress only sought 'greater independence'[3] within the Commonwealth and under British protection. Certainly, in a vague, pervasive way the progressive collapse of white imperialism in Asia and Africa did encourage Africans in the Federation to hope that circumstance, not choice, would force British Governments to abandon the shibboleth of 'self-government' and, if only in their own interest, offer national independence as a means of transforming the British Empire into a Commonwealth of many races and diverse cultures. Independence for the Gold Coast in 1957 and Nigeria in 1960 not only immediately and strongly influenced nationalist sentiment in Southern Africa, but changed attitudes in Britain to a remarkable and enduring degree. By the early 1960s, Oliver Lyttelton could converse amiably enough, as a businessman, with Ghana's Kwame Nkrumah – no longer a 'negro' but a national leader – for both to agree that there was only one thing worse than not having what you wanted. That was to have it – 'independence' in this case – and not to be able to do much with the consequences.

Lyttelton's cynicism and Nkrumah's wry acceptance of the world's inexorable severities reflected not so much a common attitude as a mutual awareness that each new African state would, in practice, pursue the national interest. The British could no longer divide and rule; they could grant independence to nations, of a sort, and do good business in the process. Much has been heard of de Gaulle's Francophone Africa, less of Macmillan's Anglophile equivalent. A great Frenchman used subterfuge to establish and maintain his neo-colonialism; a lesser Englishman did likewise, including Northern Rhodesia and Nyasaland as makeweights to Southern Rhodesia's inevitable UDI. Meetings in Nairobi during the late 1950s and early 1960s of British Colonial Office, SIS and MI5 officers (from which the Federal Intelligence and Security Bureau was, at first, deliberately excluded) stressed that 'Communism (amongst African political movements) has made no great impact'. Africans, in short, wanted to run their own affairs – with discreet support from Britain.

These meetings also discounted 'Pan-Africanism'. Yet the broad liberal groupings in Britain not only failed to discern what

Macmillan was up to – this was hardly surprising; he was the arch dissembler, in Welensky's bitter words near the end, 'as soft as butter, as sharp as a razor' – but assumed that there was an African 'consciousness' which cut across territorial frontiers, not merely tribal barriers. There was little such consciousness, partly because in many territories tribal loyalties meant, and mean, more than 'government', white – or black. But the notion of 'Pan-Africanism', artfully propagated by Africans who preferred the sympathy of English and Scottish liberals to the severities of white rule or the tensions of tribal faction, not only blurred the real issues but sowed in the ever-suspicious minds of Federal Ministers the conviction that a conspiracy was under way to supplant them with a bunch of quasi-communist blacks. A conspiracy was indeed under way from the late 1950s onwards, but its roots were in British policy, not liberal dissent or African revolt.

In considering, therefore, the nature and form of African resistance to 'a great new dominion in Central Africa', a careful distinction must be made between attitudes and actions. Unless this distinction is made, it will be impossible to appreciate why Africans conducted a political struggle in the 1960s and fought a liberation war in the 1970s. Federation certainly had much to do with Zimbabwe, but the connection must be seen as tenuous unless we appreciate how deep-seated was African antagonism to discrimination, yet how slow, and reluctant, was the transition from words to deeds. At all times the African was forced to ask whether any white man would support his struggle. The notion that British Governments and political parties might do so led to a naive belief that some white Rhodesians would do so. Yet no Southern Rhodesian cracked down more forcibly on African dissent than the missionary turned rancher-Premier, Garfield Todd.

The Capricorn Africa Society – a collection of slightly eccentric, post-1945, well-heeled immigrant settler farmers, led by the militarily dashing but politically inept Scot David Stirling – genuinely wanted to end racial discrimination. But Stirling and his soldier settlers had no belief in African independence. For these reasons no African leader pursued a more devious course than the shrewd, avuncular, hesitant Joshua Nkomo. No white man did more to remove the most odious, visible forms of discrimination that Todd's aloof, ostensibly 'right wing' successor, Edgar Whitehead, a politician even capable of considering repeal of the Land Apportionment Act - what time, in 1960, he was also pondering Macmillan's hints that the break-up of Federation must mean independence for Southern Rhodesia. When the hints had been digested, Whitehead changed a repressive security apparatus into a punitive one. African 'agitators' were chivvied, then imprisoned. Yet not until the advent of Welensky's former Federal Chief Whip Ian Smith were the political and battle lines between black and white clearly drawn.

The first four years of Federation were, by contrast, a time of hesitation and doubt, acquiescence - and incipient organised opposition. These mixed reactions came from Africans who had traditionally led - tribal chiefs, whether dominated and paid by Government or not - and from those who, knowing well that tribal affiliations played into white hands, sought to organise political movements of one sort or another which actually or ostensibly drew on wider loyalties. Almost all the 'new men' being mission-educated, there is an understandable identity of moderate dissent from white power in the approach of such bodies as Benjamin Burombo's British African Voice Association, and the City Youth League formed by four men who later became prominent nationalists: James Chikerema, George Nyandoro, Edson Sithole and Dunduza Chisiza.

Both postwar organisations were founded in Southern Rhodesia - the latter in 1955 - and reflected antagonism to discrimination and land tenure inequities rather than opposition to government as such. With the advent in 1957 of Nkomo's Southern Rhodesia ANC these early movements of non-tribal association and protest lost momentum. The years of protest ended, the period of resistance began. Nyasaland, however, benefited by Chisiza's return after he was deported from Southern Rhodesia in 1956. As Secretary-General of the Malawi Congress Party he had much to do with Banda's virtual monopoly of a newly-enfranchised electorate. Chisiza is thus an outstanding example of the point made by Glyn Jones (Nyasaland Chief Secretary at the time of Banda's release from detention in April 1960):

Young men were forced by the hut or poll tax to leave the Protectorate in search of work. In Southern Rhodesia (and South Africa) they discovered the necessity for political organisation. When they returned to Nyasaland they put their lesson into practice. They became effective political agitators.[4]

But Huggins and Todd, as Federal and Southern Rhodesia Prime Ministers respectively, took little notice of African views or susceptibilities. Huggins who, on the longer view, appears as the most odious example of mindless prejudice, was not even true to his assertion that as Africans 'advanced' – to 'civilised standards' – they would gain not only the vote but status. When the first Federal Parliament met in February 1954 Huggins refused to allow the handful of African members to appear in their traditional dress. British officials staffing the new High Commission in Salisbury had convinced themselves that 'multi-racialism' stood a chance, that 'partnership' might become a reality, that permanent power for the white man might become acceptable to Africans who became, as it were, honorary whites. Huggins brought these officials down to earth by declaring that a 'Western' Parliament required European dress. As Huggins's apologist puts it: 'Fearing that he [David Yamba] might appear in a toga, topped by a fantastic headdress, and therefore secure inordinate publicity, Huggins testily ruled that, as Parliament was based on a Western tradition, only Western dress was appropriate.'[5]

This incident may seem trivial – would the kilt, if occasionally worn by that sturdy settler Hugginsite, the Duke of Montrose, have been 'appropriate'? – but must be seen in the context not only of racialist contempt but African moderation. Five months after laying down the law on dress, Huggins, during a debate on the kind of insulting discrimination described by Blake, remarked: 'You cannot expect Europeans to form a queue with dirty people, perhaps an old umfazi [African woman] with an infant at her back, mewling and puking and making a mess of everything.' African members, who had initiated the debate, stressed that Nyasaland had never had much racialism, Northern Rhodesia was losing it – gradually but inexorably as the copperbelt and RST prospered together – yet Southern Rhodesia was determined not to change. So much for a multi-racial Federation, built on the ideal of partnership.

These now forgotten Africans, these moderate men, the Yambas, the Kakumbis, and the Chirwas, the Uncle Toms who supposedly were to inherit a portion of the white man's earth, were thus put in the intolerable position of resisting Federation because of the absolute hypocrisy of its proclaimed ideals; accepting the role of second-class citizens, and thus being treated at best with condescension by whites and, at worst, contempt by militant Africans; or embarking on a campaign to produce a radical alternative to Federation. But Huggins and Welensky were determined that, whatever woolly British minds might encourage and even allow in Northern Rhodesia and Nyasaland, Southern Rhodesia would remain a white preserve. In December 1954 Welensky clashed with RST, nominally over the growing strength of African trades unions, in reality because of their indirect role in politicising Africans from moderates acceptable to whites into militants acceptable to the British Government. Trade union leaders like Lawrence Katilungu were genuinely admired by Ronald Prain and his RST confrères. In Southern Rhodesia they would have been gaoled or deported.

Sooner or later the Katilungus would seek, or demand, a place in Northern Rhodesia's colonial Government, the Executive Council. With the Nyasaland constitution due for review in January 1955, Huggins and Welensky – at that time undisputed leaders of white thought and action in the Federation – knew that if 'liberal' trends also appeared in Southern Rhodesia all that they held as paramount and permanent would crumble into the African dust. The first federal election, held at the end of 1954, strengthened Huggins's position. He won twenty-six seats with his United Federal Party (UFP) out of the thirty-five contested. But even at this early period, Huggins faced opposition in the new House from the six African elected and three nominated white 'African interests' members. The latter, according to Huggins, were 'nursemaids'[6] to their black colleagues, teaching them virtual subversion – disguised as parliamentary opposition – rather than respect for their betters. The only sure shield for the Federation was Southern Rhodesia.

It is a further myth of a period all too easily seen in simple terms of black and white that Garfield Todd, Southern Rhodesia's Prime Minister between 1953 and 1958, was responsible for an African political consciousness awakening there to match trades unions in Northern Rhodesia and the Malawi Congress Party in Nyasaland. In a sense Todd was responsible, not because he encouraged the consciousness but because he tried to suppress it once it moved beyond the stage of moderate dissent. Todd's personal qualities of warmth, tolerance, courage, humanity – and complete conviction that he knows best – have never been in doubt. They were sufficiently strong for his white opponents to depose him in 1958. But, as Prime Minister, Todd was equivocal in his attitudes. For example, he had none of Welensky's obsessions with 'communism' as the poison which would turn African moderates into militants.

Todd, in the extremely unlikely circumstances of his becoming Federal Prime Minister, would not have put politically active Africans under constant surveillance. Todd certainly would not have assumed that British staff at the University of Rhodesia and Nyasaland – established with much fanfare in 1953 – were agents of disaffection, thus requiring the Federal Intelligence and Security Bureau to put them under surveillance also. Nevertheless, Todd's actions in declaring a state of emergency in 1954 and suppressing a strike at the Wankie colliery in 1955 reveal him as a politician determined to keep the African in his place. Before commenting further on the Federation, Northern Rhodesia and Nyasaland, some aspects of Southern Rhodesia during Todd's premiership must be summarised. At the end of those five years, and symbolised by the founding of the ANC in 1957, Zimbabwe's political consciousness had, indeed, taken root.

The disturbances in 1954 and 1955 not only presented Todd with a challenge but revealed the absurdities of a Federation where coercive power was diluted by constitutional formulae. Despite the good personal relations between RST and the African unions on the copperbelt, the latter were quite prepared to agitate for continued improvements in pay, conditions, and status. The unions' robust actions in 1954 undoubtedly influenced the men at Wankie. Yet federal authority could not readily be invoked to arbitrate a Southern Rhodesia industrial dispute. Todd chose, or was forced, to rely on the territory's security forces for crushing a strike which had political roots, and whose aftermath should have been tackled in political terms.

Todd was, of course, boxed in by the overall racial attitudes and policies of the Federal Government on one side, and his always critical Parliament on the other. It was also the case, in the mid-1950s, that although Wankie was as much an element in the Federation's economy as the copperbelt, Africans there had not shown the negotiating skill of their Northern Rhodesian colleagues. This is hardly surprising. Men kept under the harrow rarely display self-confidence and flexibility. Wankie was not Ndola. Yet a chance was missed after the miners had been forced back to work. Todd, to put the fairest construction on events, failed to stress the long-term implications of the strike. Like his colleagues, critical and otherwise, he thought that amelioration of working conditions would solve essentially political problems.

Nkomo's ANC was, therefore, an inevitable step along the road to Zimbabwe. Congress reflected resistance bred from frustration, but not yet tempered by outright and persistent coercion into the kind of opposition favoured in the later 1950s and early 1960s by Robert Mugabe – an African who did not take British cash for his movement, and the one Rhodesian African whom Macleod distrusted because he did believe, however reluctantly, that power came from the barrel of the gun. Nkomo believed, by contrast, in conciliation. 'Instead of mobilising the black masses, Nkomo and his associates gave full priority to winning support for the African cause in Britain and lining up the United Nations and friendly African and other foreign governments to pressure the British Government into intervening directly in Africa.'[7] Nkomo's flirtation with Federation preceded his recruitment by Whitehall, followed a career in social work, but tallied with a brief episode as insurance agent and auctioneer. By December 1958, when Nkomo went to Accra to represent the ANC at the first All-African Peoples' Conference, he was a man marked by ambiguity. He was in Cairo when the ANC was banned in 1959, and only returned to Southern Rhodesia after a long sojourn in London. There, for the moment, we must leave Nkomo and other incipient nationalists, because by then all in the Federation, consciously or not, were caught up in the ambiguities of Macmillan's policies.

So could Africans be said to have resisted in Southern Rhodesia during the 1950s? Despite states of emergency and the ANC's brief life, detention centres were not full as, between 1958 and 1960, they were in Nyasaland. Resistance was often rhetorical, and even then others, elsewhere, had more to say. It was Northern Rhodesia's ANC President, Harry Nkumbula, not Nkomo, who in April 1957 said to Lennox-Boyd: 'Federation is a deliberate sabotage of the African's hopes for self-government and independence within the British Commonwealth of Nations ... Federation was created to place both economic and political power in the hands of the European minorities.'[8] Nkumbula had opposed Federation from the outset, temporarily joining forces with Banda (in London) to do so. By the late 1950s Nkumbula's authority in the Northern Rhodesia ANC was decreasing, Kaunda's growing. But both men, and their ANC, presented a challenge to Federation which far outstripped that of Nkomo and other dogged but bewildered Africans in Southern Rhodesia.

Were these men bewildered because Todd appeared to sympathise with African aspirations even when he cracked down hardest on their activities? There is a grain of truth in the question, but the answer must be that Africans in Southern Rhodesia stood no chance against coercive power which was unrelated to any fundamental change in the political situation – or, to put the matter more accurately, was applied in order to serve notice on British Governments, not only on 'natives', that no fundamental change would take place. (In any case Todd fell, as it were, by his own hand. His manner, not his policy, ensured his downfall.) The prospect of real change for Africans in the Protectorates, hinted at before Macmillan's advent and cautiously, often covertly planned thereafter, served not only or so much to weaken the Federation as to convince Welensky and whites in Southern Rhodesia that they had no choice but to 'fight for their rights'. It was not until March 1962 that Welensky actually wrote these words – when drafting his 'New Plan of a Central Africa' – but they really only reflected emotions lying long and deep in the Southern Rhodesian whites' subconscious.

By the late 1950s, therefore, Federation was already beginning to fail. RST's Ronald Prain – one almost writes Rhodesia's, or even Zambia's Ronald Prain – saw Welensky in May 1959 and told him that he was withdrawing his support for Federation. Prain put the case euphemistically. He actually said that RST was withdrawing financial support from the United Federal Party, the creation of Huggins and Welensky, dominant in the Federal Parliament and the basis of the Federal Government. Prain was convinced that Africans would get, and sooner rather than later, 'complete independence under black majority government'.[9] Prain believed this would happen in Northern Rhodesia and Nyasaland. He knew that Southern Rhodesia would resist even the semblance of black rule. But, whatever happened there, the Federation was doomed. Prain did not believe any kind of economic or social amelioration would even delay the black independence process. Above all, and the real death knell to Welensky, Prain, speaking for his shareholders, did not believe an independent Northern Rhodesia would accept the appearance of power without its reality. Africans would want first to control and then own the copperbelt, the source of the Federation's revenues, not merely its economic potential. Provided negotiations were reasonably conducted, RST was prepared for nationalisation. RST's Northern Rhodesia was not the Union Minière's Congo.

Africans in Northern Rhodesia hardly needed to resist when Welensky was given a knock-out punch by Prain. Welensky had thought Prain was on his side. The punch hit Welensky in his political solar plexus. Although Welensky thereafter disputed endlessly with Lennox-Boyd and Macleod over the almost metaphysical complexities of Northern Rhodesian constitutional change he did so because there was not much else he could do. He fought to gain time. The British Government virtually ignored Southern Rhodesia until the 1961 constitutional conference, and in Nyasaland proceeded by such devious methods that Welensky felt he was fighting an opponent who hit below the belt. The former heavyweight boxing champion of Southern Rhodesia was outpointed in every round. Welensky's preoccupation with Northern Rhodesia partly reflected his loyalties to the territory, his deep distrust of Benson and his successor Sir Evelyn Hone, and his reiterated hope that if Africans were offered parity of seats in the Legislative Council they would wait whilst federal economic growth – an undoubted fact – produced tangible benefits for the masses.

Welensky can scarcely be blamed for his attitude or for the approach which he tried to adopt regarding Southern and Northern Rhodesia. But he was virtually unaware until early 1960 of the true situation in Nyasaland. On the surface, until 1958, all appeared calm in the 'colonial slum'. The Protectorate's ten thousand whites were not only sufficiently tolerant in their racial attitudes, but were split in roughly equal proportions between those who had a permanent stake, as tea planters and the like, and expatriates. The Nyasa, relatively undisturbed by tribal divisions, knew of Banda, but did so very much as a king over the water. He had been absent for nearly thirty years. *African Liberation Movements* hardly mentions Banda. He never received the accolade of a freedom fighter, because independence was handed to his country on a plate.

Yet before we turn to an examination of what Britain did when the honeymoon with Federation ended, and how Africans and whites reacted to what was really happening, a final comment is necessary on the perceptions of the Federal Government. The very notion of African 'resistance' except in the form of professional troublemakers of 'subversive elements' never crossed the collected Government mind. That Africans should resent discrimination sufficiently to organise politically when it was entrenched – which, if alleviated, merely revealed the underlying realities of white power – never occurred to men who were, in some cases, 'third and fourth generation Rhodesians' but seem to have derived their knowledge of the African mind from servants and paid chiefs. Basil de Quehen, Director-General of FISB, was tasked with penetrating African organisations. De Quehen did occasionally, deferentially, hint to Welensky that his attitude to Africans needed adjustment. But his words were ignored. Welensky and his colleagues were blind to the realities of African resistance because they also ignored Africans as people, as individuals. As the Rhodesian told the immigrant, 'It's just as though they weren't there.' But they were there all right, in the bush and the townships, at the white man's table and behind his bar. When the Macmillan Government came to tackle – or shelve – the issue of Federation, it was a conscious acceptance of this fact, of a new

Africa which could not be kept in place by white bayonets, which really decided the issue.

13

What Britain Did

One cannot discuss the later years of Federation, let alone its dissolution, without some further and more detailed reference to Harold Macmillan, the Government and Party which he led, and the times which imposed on him the necessity to sacrifice both black and white Africans in order to preserve British interests. History will find it difficult to assess Macmillan. His official biography must not be published until his death. Former colleagues, reminiscing as only Tory politicians can - jokes and chat - reveal nothing, except for one key statement: 'Macmillan wanted the Central African Federation off the Cabinet Agenda.'[1] Macmillan's lengthy, discursive - not to say rambling - autobiography is, in itself, a study in ambiguity. His verbal musings of recent years continue the process. Even the 'wind of change' speech of 3 February 1960, delivered in Cape Town and generally construed thereafter as a warning that Southern Africa's whites should mend their racialist ways, has lately been defined by Macmillan as a tribute to Afrikaner achievements - and as a hint that South Africa should have made common cause with Southern Rhodesia.[2] Before explaining why Federation's demise not only produced UDI but frustrated black nationalist endeavours for another decade, Macmillan's real intentions and decisions must be discussed, and some attempt at understanding them made.

South Africa, about to become a Republic, left the Commonwealth in May 1961. Macmillan has recorded his distress at these acts. There is no doubt he made genuine and unsparing efforts

97

to prevent the latter. The ostensible cause of departure was the South African Government's refusal unconditionally to accept diplomatic missions – High Commissions – from newly independent, black African Commonwealth members. Dr Hendrik Verwoerd, who followed the arch racialist and nationalist Johannes Strijdom as Prime Minister in 1955, had told the Commonwealth conference held at Lancaster House in May that he would receive such missions 'officially' but could not consort with them on any personal or social terms. The new, increasingly Third World Commonwealth rejected this insulting compromise. Macmillan, Macleod and Duncan Sandys (who succeeded Home as Commonwealth Relations Secretary in July 1960) did not dissent from rejection, but concentrated on stressing to Verwoerd and his Foreign Minister, and confidant, Eric Louw, the shared strategic interests of Britain and South Africa.

The Afrikaners' response, which had its roots in the past and was to affect much of the future, was a pledge of continued strategic co-operation against the menace of 'communism' – provided British Governments let white men south of the Zambeze get on with the job of entrenching apartheid. Macmillan had been consistently cool to Welensky's reiterated pleas that Britain and the Federation should draw a 'defence line' across Africa in order to keep subversive Africans north of the Zambeze. Macmillan, by his own admission, had no objection to Verwoerd and Louw drawing the line. In fact, they had already done so. On 21 March 1960 blacks were massacred at Sharpeville, on the outskirts of Johannesburg. The South African Government informed the United States Embassy in Pretoria – and Welensky – that communist 'revolutionary' agitators provoked a riot, forcing the police to open fire.

The Embassy drew its own conclusions on 31 May. They are in line with earlier messages sent to the State Department – and those sent to London by Baring and his successors. There would be outcries at Sharpeville but 'any strong move against South Africa on the part of the West could threaten the West's economic and strategic interests in that country'. So far as South Africa's coercive capacity was concerned 'the security forces should be able to contain them [protests and strikes] without difficulty'. African organisations would be deprived of funds, their members of food. Punitive action would be effective: 'A recent change in standing orders, directing police to fire at the leaders of a demonstrating mob rather than over their heads as previously, indicates that the Government is fully prepared to employ, in case of need, massive force whatever the cost in lives to South Africa's reputation overseas.'[3]

The capacity of the Union's African National Congress (which had been banned in April) to organise resistance was doubted. The Embassy did not swallow the story of communist influence. Any State Department official reading these comments could only infer that the South African Government would stamp on Africans in order to promote apartheid, and would only play the communist card if 'the West's' Governments started wringing their hands. The observations concluded with a statement from the Central Intelligence Agency (CIA) station in Pretoria which is not only perceptive, but aptly defined relationships between South Africa and Southern Rhodesia of which Macmillan was so acutely aware: 'South Africa's Whites cannot afford to make concessions to African nationalism. The fate which befell [Garfield] Todd, who with his cautious, paternalistic, middle-of-the-road approach was anything but a flaming liberal, must act as a warning to any politician.'[4]

Macmillan thus made the trade with Verwoerd in May 1961 because, well before the 'wind of change' speech, he and his advisers had come to accept – although never to make plain – that Britain's economic interests in Africa south of the Sahara could at no point or place be sustained except by a combination of diplomacy and intelligence operations. There were no strategic resources left, or available, to sustain African commitments. Policy, therefore, must be based on support, equally but *separately*, for the new or embryonic Commonwealth members of West and East Africa and for that Southern African coalition of white interests centred on Pretoria and Salisbury. In the first group, Nigeria's oil potential was a decisive factor: in the second, Britain's constitutional right to grant independence to Northern Rhodesia and Nyasaland was to prove equally decisive. Once it became clear after the Monckton Report was leaked in mid-1960 that Welensky and his colleagues would never compromise on sharing decision-making power with Africans, the Federation was sacrificed in order that Britain, no longer dividing and ruling, could divide and trade. Africans in Southern Rhodesia were sacrificed after the Federation's fate was sealed and the nod given for a UDI which would not be opposed, because it could not forcefully be deterred by a British Government.

The critical year in this process of adaptation to circumstance is 1958. A year earlier Duncan Sandys, as Minister of Defence, in publishing the annual statement had revealed that not only was Britain the proud possessor of an 'independent nuclear deterrent', but that the roles of non-nuclear forces were to be reduced. Conscription for the British armed forces was to be abolished; 'strategically mobile' forces were partially to replace garrisons; the 'East of Suez' commitments were to be retained, but Africa was mentioned essentially in the context of overall tasks and strategies. By the end of 1958 Macmillan had commissioned a Whitehall study which dealt at length with future strategic commitments. The Sandys statement was expanded by Sir Patrick Dean and his colleagues into an analysis of what could be defended, and by what means. Africa, except for a passing reference to training facilities in Kenya and emphasis on the continued importance of Simonstown for protecting the 'sea lanes' against a prospective Soviet submarine threat, was virtually ignored.

Some attention was given to staging posts at Kano and Nairobi in support of the Royal Air Force's new long-range trooping roles, but the inference was clearly drawn that the Commonwealth in Africa was not an area of strategic commitment or defence by overt means. The Report was given to Macmillan in mid-1960. The timing is significant. In 1955, when the Simonstown Agreement was made, Britain had pledged troops to defend 'Southern African' interests. But the Agreement, once rendered into Treaty form, contained reservation that it 'does not contain any substantive obligations'.[5] Although Verwoerd and Louw accepted Britain as a major arbiter of events in Africa, they drew the right conclusions from this escape clause. The South African Government, like its successors, both feared and, psychologically, welcomed isolation. In practice, Britain encouraged Afrikaner Governments to go their own way. No suggestion was made by the British Government in 1955 that the Salisbury-based Federation should move closer to South Africa. Five years later,

Louw, amongst others, was arguing privately that Southern Rhodesia should do so.

Welensky has claimed that he never received, directly or otherwise, even the gist of Sir Patrick Dean's Report nor, by the same token, and from the Federation's High Commission in London, any notion of what Macmillan was actually planning to do, whether in political or intelligence terms. It is possible. Senior Colonial Service officials serving in the Federation were on the Dean 'distribution', but Macmillan had no intention of showing his hand then, or later, to Welensky. In any event, the Federation High Commission was not an especially alert outfit, and, as we have seen, FISB as such was not automatically welcome at Conferences organised by British officials. Moreover, in 1958, Welensky still believed in an Englishman's word. That Macmillan was, in some sort, a Scot appears to have escaped Welensky's attention. He wrote to 'My dear Harold' and 'My dear Alec [Home]' as if to his equals, and was replied to in comparably Rotarian terms. Welensky should not have been fooled.

During the February 1961 constitutional conference on Southern Rhodesia Sandys told Welensky, 'Britain has lost the will to rule.'[6] Sandys, normally phlegmatic, spoke in the heat of the moment and, possibly, to deflect by the use of rhetoric Welensky's attention from what was actually at stake. This was Southern Rhodesia's destiny – white rebellion against the Crown, followed by a sanguinary racial conflict – if the Sandys formula for African majority rule in a politically credible time-scale was rejected. In reality and, collectively, neither Macmillan and his Cabinet nor Whitehall and its representatives overseas had lost any such will. But when resources diminish vanish, or are diverted to other uses, will and intention, must be related to capacity. The building of a nuclear deterrent and the abolition of conscription reflected what were essentially economy measures, although the former was certainly an expensive demonstration in political terms of the strategy of prestige. But these policy decisions, taken by a Government which undoubtedly had the will to maintain a major international role for Britain, spelled Federation's demise. If R. A. Butler, as Macmillan's Secretary of State for Central Africa in 1962 and 1963, was the Federation's undertaker, Sandys was certainly first grave-digger.

Any account, therefore, of what Britain did to preserve its interests, break up Federation and thus make inevitable UDI and guerrilla war should be dated from secret decisions taken in 1958. Two years earlier, Home and Lennox-Boyd had rebuffed Huggins's bid for independence. Britain thus remained committed to an evolutionary Federation whose progress would be reviewed by a Constitutional Commission in 1960. By 1958 the commitment remained but circumstances had changed. 'Suez' had come and gone. The advent or, at least, the beginning of post-imperial Britain, forced Macmillan to consider the impending federal constitutional review as a device for squaring his strategic circles, whereas to Welensky it was a chore which would be supportable if it accelerated the processes leading to independence. Neither Macmillan nor Welensky cared a rap for African susceptibilities, but the former was determined to have a Commission which would make the right liberal noises about racial issues, whilst the latter remained adamant that it would not be empowered to make recommendations which would cause the Federation to break up.

There were those in Welensky's Government who were shrewd or cynical enough to see what was in the wind. Although the two years preceding the appearance of the Monckton Report are significant mainly in connection with Nyasaland and Northern Rhodesia (and are so very much in that order), it is also relevant to note that several of these worldly-wise Federal Ministers did consider, from 1958 onwards, the prospects of UDI for the Federation. Welensky noted the reflections of these politicians from the self-governing Colony of Southern Rhodesia but ensured that the Federal Attorney-General poured plenty of cold water on such ideas throughout 1958 and 1959. Had not Lennox-Boyd told Welensky and his Cabinet in January 1957 that 'Her Majesty's Government was still fully supporting Federation; there could be no whittling away of this and no question of secession'?

More to the point, UDI was a recipe for economic suicide. The Federation would be isolated in 'a cold, hard world', its £113 million of sterling assets frozen by the British Government, all prospects of economic progress put in jeopardy. But the Attorney-General's office, in the course of agonising over the constitutional implications of a Unilateral Declaration of Independence (UDI), reached a conclusion which, like so much else, was rejected by Welensky because it was unpalatable. In the final analysis, Britain did have the constitutional right to decide the Federation's future, to determine above all whether any member could secede. Even to hint at UDI would change constitutional complexities from academic arguments into a live political issue. Much ink has been spilt condemning Monckton for, rather half-heartedly, referring to secession. In fact, some Federal Ministers grasped all along that secession remained the British Government's secret weapon. The possession of such a weapon made these Ministers all the more keen to opt for UDI, and damn the consequences.

It would be something of an exaggeration to say that Welensky was wholly isolated from his colleagues in the years when he wrote so pleadingly or agitatedly to Macmillan and company. Indeed, Malcolm Barrow and Julius Greenfield (the Federal Ministers for Home Affairs and Justice), who by no stretch of the imagination can be considered as other than hard-headed, were personally closer to Welensky than any other members of his Cabinet. But whilst Welensky continued to believe in the power of exhortation, Barrow, Greenfield and others of their kidney were looking down the UDI road. If the Federation failed in its independence bid, Southern Rhodesia need not do so. Either way, South Africans would not forget Rhodesians, the descendants, in terms of political pedigree if little else, of the men of the Pioneer Column and the Matabele wars. In April 1960 Louw told de Quehen, 'Rhodesians should stand firm and come along *with* the Union.'

Louw, sensing that he might get further with de Quehen than with Welensky regarding covert activities and political poker, then proposed intelligence liaison between the Union and the Federation on a 'declared' basis. Without indulging in technicalities, it may be said that such a basis indicates, or is intended to indicate, a degree of trust and co-operation between Governments which provides for intelligence to be shared – up to a point. Louw was thinking ahead, well aware that if such a liaison was established, Britain, the Union and the Federation would be acting secretly together on many important matters, not only in terms of political and strategic decisions but also in the acquisition of intelligence and the penetration of organisations known or thought to be subversive or 'revolutionary'. De Quehen replied cautiously to Louw's suggestion, because he had not yet decided what the long-term FISB liaison with SIS and MI5 should be – or, for that matter, how to reconcile federal and territorial intelligence objectives. De Quehen was looking ahead, perceiving that Welensky's trust in Macmillan and his colleagues might be shattered as events in Nyasaland and Northern Rhodesia developed. The intelligence and security services in Northern Rhodesia and Nyasaland reported to London, not to Salisbury. When – or if – Welensky woke up to realities, 'declared' liaison between Britain and the Federation might be difficult to sustain.

Welensky thus embarked on his tussle with Lennox-Boyd and Macleod over Nyasaland not only ignorant of Macmillan's intentions but insufficiently aware of what his advisers in Salisbury and their confidants in Pretoria wanted. Yet Welensky was sufficiently aware that Nyasaland's future would decide the Federation's fate to oppose vehemently any suggestion that Banda, in or out of detention, should be groomed for autocratic leadership of even a 'self-governing' territory, let alone an independent state. Welensky had few personal complaints about Lennox-Boyd, but from the first was convinced that Macleod, as he put it, 'hated his guts'. Macleod was, in fact, a poor hater, but undoubtedly did regard Welensky as tedious in his vehement assertion of white interests compared with the African politicians, whose gifts of flattery appealed to his Celtic imagination. Colonial Secretary and Federal Prime Minister were temperamentally chalk and cheese. Macleod was not averse to saying one thing whilst doing the opposite. For years Macmillan got away with this trick because, in Welensky's eyes, he was a true Briton. Macleod, a place man, was not allowed by Macmillan to demonstrate that politics is the art of the inevitable, not merely the possible.

Despite Home's chilly advice to stay at home, Welensky visited London several times in the later 1950s, supporting by face-to-face contact with these evasive Tories an epistolary bombardment which never succeeded in hitting the target. Despite the rebuff to Huggins in June 1956, Welensky remained convinced that independence for the Federation could be hastened by his advocacy. In November 1957 Welensky told Home that the Federal Government had begun to prepare for the 1960 constitutional review. Home, in reply, indicated in his usual laconic manner, that not only were such preparations premature but that it was not the Federal Government's business to make them. These visits were undoubtedly a mistake. No snob, Welensky could be duped. He reflected happily that he was the first railwayman to sleep in Windsor Castle. Pilgrimages to Hatfield House, where the Lord Salisbury of the day preached imperial sentiments, deluded Welensky into believing that Macmillan, who certainly loved a lord, would respond to so famous, so appropriate a name. But on 28 March 1957 Macmillan had sacked 'Bobbety' Salisbury from his Cabinet because he opposed plans for an independent Cyprus. Politics knows few loyalties. Macmillan had become Prime Minister in February 1957 largely because of Salisbury's influence in the Conservative Party. Welensky did not understand that Party: his High Commission of businessmen and diplomatic *arrivistes* compounded this fundamental ignorance by reporting to Welensky only what he wanted to hear.

In July 1958, after thirty years Hastings Banda returned to Nyasaland and became President of the Malawi Congress Party. Banda had chosen his moment well, although, with Whitehall still pondering whom to recruit, it might be an exaggeration to say it was chosen for him. Lennox-Boyd was still 'supporting' Federation, but had become resigned to the fact that a full-scale campaign against it and in favour of secession was under way in Nyasaland. Banda would not have returned if he had seriously believed that, over time, the campaign would fail. On 3 March 1959, however, the Governor proclaimed a state of emergency, arresting Banda and over 1,300 of his followers immediately beforehand. Intimidation and violence justified the Governor's actions, but Welensky's unwise despatch of federal security forces to Nyasaland on 21 February and his assertion of federal authority in what was a matter for the British Government provided the latter with exactly the excuse which it later sought. Banda was removed by federal order to Gwelo, in Southern Rhodesia. Welensky claimed the legal right to do so, no doubt somewhat carried away by Barrow's assertion that Whites in Nyasaland would have been massacred but for the federal crackdown, and by an atmosphere hardly conducive to consideration of cause and effect.

Whitehead had also declared a state of emergency in Southern

Rhodesia on 26 February – one which was to last beyond Zimbabwe's independence twenty-two years later. Benson in Lusaka followed suit on 10 March by banning the Northern Rhodesia ANC and arresting Kaunda. His leadership had been notable for moderation, but the establishment of Southern Rhodesia's ANC in 1957 had put all Africans who criticised Federation in an impossible position. If they counselled restraint, militants protested. If they urged opposition, the Federal Government was ready and waiting. Acting on advice Kaunda formed a new party – the United National Independence Party – thereafter to be his means of achieving Northern Rhodesia's independence in a political context designed by Macleod, the Colonial Office and Benson's subordinates.

Although Armitage and Benson insisted that they acted on their own initiative in banning and proscribing, subsequent investigation under Lennox-Boyd's authority – notably by the Devlin Commission concerning Nyasaland – revealed that the federal hand was at work in the Protectorates. For over a year Welensky had been vehemently opposed to Benson's plans for giving Africans parity, possibly a majority in Northern Rhodesia's Legislative Council, let alone seats on the Executive Council. Lennox-Boyd insisted on 'advance', but Welensky remained hostile, partly because, intermittent violence apart, Africans did behave with circumspection, robbing him of the chance to put the troops in. Nor could Welensky find comfort in Nyasaland. Devlin, reporting on 23 July 1959, dismissed the massacre plot and stated that 'Nyasaland is – no doubt temporarily – a police state where it is not safe for anyone to express approval of the policies of the Congress Party.'[7]

The battle lines between London and Salisbury had been drawn. Macleod was appointed Colonial Secretary immediately after Macmillan's impressive victory in the October 1959 General Election, three months after Devlin had reported, seven after Welensky had tried to demonstrate that, in an emergency, the Federation would act independently of the Crown, however dubious the cause and unconstitutional the acts. That same October de Quehen urged a conciliary attitude on Welensky 'now that the Tories have been returned in strength'. De Quehen, stressing that he spoke for his colleagues in FISB and elsewhere in the federal bureaucracy, and that they were 'hardly do-good-ers', urged a tolerant attitude towards Africans, promotion for the more 'advanced', and a realisation by the Federal Government that the impending Monckton Commission was intended to make a reality of 'multi-racialism' not offer a prescription for independence.

De Quehen was rebuffed. Despite cordial personal relations with Whitehall, de Quehen was neither knowledgeable nor subtle enough to tell Welensky that Macmillan's General Election success freed his hand to dismember the Federation if he wished. Two days after Nyasaland was put under a state of emergency Macmillan noted, 'It looks as if the Federation plan, although economically correct is regarded with such suspicion by "advanced" native opinion as to be politically unacceptable.' Macmillan calculated that the Conservative Party in the House of Commons would support him, but that if he supported Welensky, the Labour Party and Conservative 'do-gooders' in combination might, just possibly, dish him.[8] On 21 July Macmillan had announced that an 'Advisory Commission' on the Federation was in train. Thus was born the Monckton Commission, formally established on 24 November, its members in place throughout the Federation early in the new year.[9]

On 26 November, Macmillan wrote a 'Top Secret and Personal' letter to Welensky, which declared: 'We have no intention of making an extension of the terms [of the Monckton Commission] to include secession.' Welensky believed what Macmillan wrote, and it is natural or, at least understandable, that he should have done so. But, as events rapidly proved. Macmillan had every intention of secretly making an extension of the Monckton Commission terms to *include* secession. Indeed, the whole purpose of the Commission was the continuance of Federation provided racial conflict - which might involve Britain *in extremis* despite absence of resources to deter or contain violence - could be avoided. Since such conflict was all but unavoidable if real power throughout the Federation remained in white hands, Macmillan deliberately considered secession, and deliberately deceived Welensky about his aims.

In December 1959 Banda and most of his followers were still detained or their movements restricted. Macleod decided to release Banda. Release would simultaneously demonstrate the British Government's assertion of authority, its repudiation of federal pretensions, and a determination to back Africans who campaigned on secession. The decision had nothing to do with any consideration of independence for Nyasaland, everything to do with what, in Macmillan's judgment, was neither politically acceptable nor strategically feasible – a federation of Rhodesia and Nyasaland for which Britain was responsible. Although Macleod's biographer claims – with inside knowledge – that the decision about Banda was personal, the months preceding release on 1 April 1960 reveal a degree of co-ordination with Macmillan and Home which cannot be explained by coincidence.

Macmillan's task was to tour Africa, and be all things to all men; Home's to keep Welensky quiet or, failing that, in a state of contained rage; Macleod's to work out the implications in Nyasaland and Northern Rhodesia of releasing an African nationalist determined to bust the Federation. The Monckton Commission of good white men and true, plus a few tame Africans, had the task of justifying Macmillan's private observations on a great new dominion which had become a political liability. After the Commission had reported, a constitutional review conference was to be held in London. Thereafter, both Northern and Southern Rhodesia were due to have their constitutions revised. Thus 1960 was deliberately planned by Macmillan and his colleagues as the year which would settle the future, or fate of Central African Federation.

Macmillan's seven-week 'Commonwealth' tour of Africa between 5 January and 15 February 1960 has been the subject of various interpretations ranging from the adulatory to the derisive. We see an elder statesman bestowing the light of his countenance on the new Commonwealth; there is the elderly gentleman escaping the rigours of an English winter. The truth is more subtle. Macmillan reckoned that if he told his hosts what they wanted to hear in places as far apart as Lagos, Salisbury and Cape Town, the more obvious contradictions would be left for others to resolve. From a perspective of twenty-six years it is doubtful if Macmillan cared greatly whether his hosts responded to his words with alarm or approval. Nothing new was going to come out of Africa so far as Macmillan was concerned. Nevertheless, some faint imperial sentiment, together with a curious, exaggerated respect for House of Commons' reactions, induced Macmillan to deliver his contradictory statements with greater care than usual.

Not until 2 February did Home warn Welensky that Banda's release was being 'contemplated'. But on 12 January, in Lagos, Macmillan said: 'There is no question of forcing Nyasaland to remain in a fully independent Central African Federation.' The *Financial Times* reported Macmillan in these terms: 'Britain has made it "abundantly clear" that she will not remove her protection from Northern Rhodesia or Nyasaland until their peoples have expressly opted for Federation.' The *News Chronicle* correspondent in Lagos wrote: 'Mr Macmillan tonight made Africans a promise which will rock Sir Roy Welensky, Premier of the Central African Federation. The British Prime Minister, who will be Rhodesia's guest in five days' time, chose Lagos to slap down Welensky's demand for Commonwealth status for the Federation.' On 15 January Macmillan, still in Lagos, went further: 'Before the British Government's ultimate responsibilities over Nyasaland and Northern Rhodesia are removed, the people of the two territories will be given an opportunity to decide on whether the Federation is beneficial to them. This will be an expression of opinion that is genuinely that of the people.' One feels that Oliver Lyttelton would have thought poorly of the doctrine of paramountcy being extended, thirty years late, to the Protectorates.

Yet, as Welensky subsequently wrote of the years between 1960 and 1963, conveying in his bitter account a version of sustained British duplicity whose nature he abhorred and whose consequences he feared, Macmillan was able to delude him yet again when they met in Salisbury. Macmillan arrived on 18 January 'bland and unrepentant',[10] claiming he had been misreported in Lagos, flattering Welensky as only he knew how to do, apparently eager to engage in serious, private talk on what he loved to call 'matters of high importance'. A crowd of whites cheered Macmillan at the airport. Africans who attempted a comparable display were attacked and their placards torn down before the police 'dispersed' them.

Macmillan and Welensky met on the 19th and 20th, attended

on the second day only by Norman Brook, the British Cabinet Secretary, a veritable mine of unrevealed intelligence. Macmillan's task then, as later, was to tilt Welensky towards South Africa without appearing to do so crudely or encouraging his host to renounce Federation and publicly call for Verwoerd's help. Macmillan played on Welensky's archaic, committed imperialism, and gave no hint of his impending Cape Town speech. But Macmillan did put to Welensky the suggestion, the scintilla of an idea that independence for Southern Rhodesia would, perhaps, result from a constitutional review which revealed deep African hostility to the Federation. Whitehead and Greenfield, present at the initial exchanges, pre-empted Macmillan by hinting at UDI. Welensky clung to independence for the Federation within the decade.

Macmillan played the Rhodesians off against the Federalists; he needed to use Welensky as occasion served, above all for preventing a House of Commons accusation that Africans in Southern Rhodesia had been abandoned. What, however, Macmillan, then and later, failed to grasp, was that Welensky not only believed in Federation but, in any circumstances, was opposed to a Southern Rhodesian UDI, above all one dependent on a South African pledge of support. Although Welensky paid several visits to South Africa when he was Prime Minister, he disliked Afrikaners and rejected the notion of Southern Rhodesia being a kind of appendage to nationalist Governments in Pretoria. Welensky's imperialism was not only archaic; it was his political *raison d'être*. Therein lay his downfall.

Thus there was a meeting neither of minds nor temperaments between Macmillan and Welensky. The latter further dug a pit for himself by using Barrow in an attempt to cause alarm. Barrow described the security situation throughout the Federation in exaggerated language. He alleged that 'the Nyasaland Government' (the colonial administration) was 'pushing the Malawi Congress Party under Orton Chirwa who was, of course, legal adviser to the banned ANC'. Chirwa was a moderate African to all but the most prejudiced white. But he no longer supported Federation, and that, to Barrow, was evidence of subversion. Banda's future was not discussed, both Welensky and Barrow hoping that Macmillan would accept their version of the security situation as it stood. The banned Southern Rhodesia African National Congress had been revived on 1 January 1960 as the National Democratic Party. The key figures of later years began to emerge from the shadows, speaking out before they passed into prolonged detention.[11] A call was immediately issued for a 'one man, one vote' franchise - to which the British Government responded in equivocal language - and although the NDP expressed rather greater loyalty to the Crown than could be found in many a white Rhodesian, Barrow remained convinced that Africans were on the revolutionary march.

Welensky failed to see that Macmillan did not respond to this kind of talk, except in the sense that diatribes about African politicians in general obscured the particular issue of what to do with Banda. Macmillan was given more help with blurring the issues when Welensky, in their restricted session on the 20th, turned to security in Central and Southern Africa as a whole. Macmillan was armed with the report of a group of Foreign Office and State Department officials who had just concluded that 'there is no immediate communist threat to Africa'. Welensky said that he 'did not dissent' from this conclusion - although he did - yet riposted by urging that not only a 'defence line' be drawn across Central and Southern Africa, but that intelligence liaison be improved and developed. Welensky expressed fears over the Congo, whose imminent independence had led him to consider a plan for supporting the province of Katanga with federal troops in an emergency. (Katanga's mineral wealth, in white hands, was a prize which any African revolutionary would seek to gain.) Welensky also said that more attention should be paid to Mozambique, where nationalist movements were beginning to stir. Welensky protested to Macmillan that liaison with British officials on these issues was inadequate. Macmillan replied inimitably: 'Due to the fallibility of human memory things did somehow tend to get overlooked.'

Macmillan, by these words, expressed a kind of contempt for Welensky's gullibility. The British Government was fully aware of Katanga's importance, and was covertly active as a result. Nothing was being 'overlooked' in the liaison field. Welensky's anxieties were known. He had already begun to press for a closer relationship between the British secret services and FISB. London preferred close relations with Lusaka and Zomba, although on federal matters liaison remained personally cordial if operationally rather limited. The British High Commissions in Salisbury and Pretoria knew that de Quehen's doubts about too close a set of relationships were not shared by Welensky. *He* was not planning UDI; he just wanted SIS to open a station in Salisbury. On 30 January Welensky formally requested Home to do this. The particular reasons for Welensky's request, the fact that Home received and responded to it – up to a point – and the place of intelligence in the scheme of things require a little attention before we encounter Welensky, suspicious at last, reacting to the *démarche* of 2 February dealing with Banda and Nyasaland. Above all, at this turning point in the entire British involvement in Central and Southern Africa, one must note the pivotal role of the British High Commission in Pretoria in the acquisition and distribution of intelligence. The South African Government's liaison with Britain was not only on a 'declared' basis, but the former also co-operated with British Army intelligence throughout the entire region south of the Zambeze, including Angola and Mozambique. British regular soldiers known as Field Service Intelligence Officers (FSIOs) operated under the High Commission's cover. South Africa's departure from the Commonwealth in May 1961 made no difference to this liaison. It continues today.

In the 1950s and 1960s the British secret services (SIS and MI5) had roles which were anomalous rather than complementary. The Commonwealth as such, like the Empire before it, was primarily the responsibility of the Security Service, MI5. Tasks included acquisition of intelligence, liaison, counter-intelligence, and occasionally hostile – or what the Service called 'robust' – operations. Counter-intelligence in practice meant penetration of actually or potentially subversive political organisations. Because this penetration was often conducted with skill and imagination, the aims of nationalist politicians were known with some precision. The virtual recruitment of Mboya, Nyerere, Banda, Kaunda and Nkomo – although by SIS rather than MI5 – was substantially due to good intelligence about the kind of organisations which they actually or prospectively led. Whitehall was well aware of the fact that men of this calibre and potential leadership

5 Ian Smith prays for guidance, Geneva, October 1976

6 Margaret Thatcher seeks reassurance, February 1979

7 Talk: Kenneth Kaunda, Julius Nyerere and Samora Machel in
Lusaka, September 1976

8 War: a captured guerrilla, 1977

would only respond to overtures on behalf of their movements, not for their own benefit. Nairobi was the regional MI5 Head-quarters during these years of advancing African independence, and it was there that Security Liaison Officers (SLOs) met to plan the continued support of key figures and the training of nascent intelligence and security services.

An SLO from MI5 was also stationed in Salisbury, operating on a declared basis with FISB. In practice, this produced little in terms of co-operative effort, either within or beyond the Federation. The British South Africa Police Special Branch vied with FISB for control of counter-intelligence operations in the Federation; neither organisation had a remit to acquire external intelligence. De Quehen attempted a certain amount by way of liaison with the Portuguese authorities in Mozambique, well aware that FISB knowledge of that territory was minimal. Until the early 1960s SIS played a minor role in British Africa, confining its attention, recruitment apart, to the dependencies of other powers.

The MI5 Salisbury SLO did not engage in counter-intelligence operations against African organisations; his colleagues in Lusaka and Zomba did do so. The difference is crucial, and that there was such a fundamental difference emphasises the differing aims of British and federal policies. MI5 penetrated in order to identify African leaders, and to sustain them; the Federal Government – in practice, the BSAP – penetrated in order to weaken or destroy African political movements and, in Southern Rhodesia, to maintain absolute white power. At the time in question both the Salisbury SLO and de Quehen tended to agree that the subversive character of these movements had been greatly exaggerated. The BSAP, by contrast, collectively took a hostile attitude to Africans, to their organisations, and to anybody who had co-operative dealings with either. In Southern Rhodesia this attitude, from Federation's earliest days, was translated into the objective of destroying African nationalism. To add a further twist to a faintly bizarre spiral of factors, BSAP officers were monitoring Banda's conversations in Gwelo with a distinguished British lawyer throughout the week Macmillan spent in Salisbury.

Welensky found Banda's exchanges with Mr Dingle Foot QC

profoundly disturbing. Welensky was unaware that Foot was one of those Liberals interested in Africans whom Macleod utilised to acquire information, sound opinion and drop hints. When Welensky read the transcript, wherein the Monckton Commission's intended consideration of secession was just discernible, he immediately asked Macleod for an explanation.[12] Foot had said that he knew Monckton very well, and that he was 'certainly taking the line that he is not going to be restricted by the terms of reference'. Welensky had begun to grasp that Nyasaland's secession would not only break up the Federation but lead inevitably to Southern Rhodesia's independence, seized rather than granted. Welensky needed a reply from Macleod. He was forced to wait until his visit to London the following May. Welensky's letter of 30 January to Home was, therefore, a plea to one whom he still regarded as on 'his' side – because the latter had been remote yet apparently sympathetic – to send an intelligence officer who would really riddle out subversive elements, but do so on Britain's behalf. Indirectly, SIS was seen by Welensky as an antidote to the Monckton Commission. Welensky asked for 'the possible attachment to the Federation of an officer from C's organisation'.[13]

'C' was – is – Director-General of SIS. 'C' at the time was Sir Dick White, who was certainly thinking about Africa, but not yet prepared to accord territory south of the Zambeze much priority. The SIS Director Middle East included Africa in his fief. In early 1960, and for years thereafter, White and the DME concentrated their African efforts on the Congo and, by extension, Northern Rhodesia. Welensky, who was not in this picture at all, made it clear to Home that he wanted SIS to open a station in Salisbury in order not only that FISB could acquire external intelligence, but so that counter-intelligence operations would be conducted within and beyond the Federation. But the plea was also ignored, for five months. Even the remote yet sympathetic Home was part of an operation designed to frustrate Welensky over the central issue of Hastings Banda. On 2 February, whilst Welensky's plea about SIS was beginning its Whitehall journey, and as Macmillan and Brook put the final touches to the 'wind of change' speech, Home signalled the 'contemplated' release of Banda. The language was, of course, restrained: 'We are fully seized with the serious view which you and also Armitage and Hone [Benson's successor] take of the security risks which would attend the release of Banda in the present circumstances ... On the other hand, we do not think we can possibly contemplate maintaining the emergency in Nyasaland and keeping Banda detained for so long as that.' (Namely, until the Monckton Commission had reported.)

According to Parry, Welensky could not at first believe Home was serious. Considering that Welensky was equally dumbfounded by the 'wind of change' speech, his reply to Home on 3 February was restrained in turn. But restraint – and the nominal use of Parry to reply – apart, Welensky knew he had been gulled. Banda was to be released before Monckton had reported, not, as Welensky had repeatedly demanded (if he was to be released at all), afterwards. Banda was to be released not because he could not be detained but because Her Majesty's Government, in pursuit of their own interests, had 'contemplated' the expediency of doing so in order that he might conduct a secession campaign. Fully aroused and aware at last, Welensky replied to Home through Parry in words which do much to explain why the following three and a half years were not only those of mutual recrimination but were also, in a sense, a period of anti-climax. 2 February 1960 was really the Federation's day of execution. Those who saw this truth most quickly were best able to indulge in some contemplation of their own. None were quicker to do so than Welensky's white parliamentary associates and the Southern Rhodesia Government. Amongst the former was the Federal Government Chief Whip, Ian Smith by name. By contrast, African leaders were in the dark.

'The Prime Minister must deplore the decision which had been taken without the further consultation with him which he understood had been promised him by Mr Macmillan.' Thus Parry on 3 February. On the 9th Home made it clear to Welensky that he was not Prime Minister of even a quasi-independent state. True to form, Welensky wanted to come to London – where he would be spared criticism from disloyal parliamentary colleagues like Smith – in order to confront Macmillan and seek comfort from the Tory right wing. Home stated the case: 'I do beg most sincerely that you will not do so [come to London]. In all our considerations here of what to do in Nyasaland both Iain Macleod and I have put first and foremost the interests of the Federation.' This statement, once decoded, and in the light of 'contemplation' about Banda meant that the British Government had decided Federation was no longer viable. A 'looser association' between the territories might be possible, but a white-dominated Federation, kept in being by Rhodesian, British – or South African – bayonets, was not within the compass of Britain, *circa* 1960.

Macmillan added insult to injury a little later (the letter is undated but was sent after he returned to Britain from South Africa) by telling Welensky, 'We must have faith. I know yours is strong and undiminished. So is mine.' Welensky was forced to swallow this insult. Throughout the next six weeks he waited, helpless. On All Fools' Day, Banda was released; returned to Nyasaland in triumph; received confidences and virtual pledges of support from Macleod and the Colonial Government – the white community in general accepting the inevitable rather than seeking federal intervention – and proceeded to conduct a secession campaign with all the verbal and physical force which the well-drilled Malawi Congress Party could muster. By July Banda was in London attending a constitutional conference on Nyasaland. The conference pre-empted the Monckton Commission Report; its recommendations enfranchised 100,000 Africans and put their representatives into all but dominating positions on both the Legislative and Executive Councils. On 17 August Macleod recommended that Banda be a member of the Nyasaland Executive Council and, together with the Malawi Congress Party, be a participant in the Federation Constitutional Review Conference. Banda is not amongst Africa's liberation heroes; his subsequent career, to the present, in support of his white masters' interests is maybe one explanation; his easy ride to the top is possibly a more credible one. But whichever view one takes, Zimbabwe's real founding father is, in a sense, Hastings Banda.

In these weeks of early 1960 Welensky was totally out-manœuvred by Macmillan and his colleagues. Thus by the end of April they had no objection to Welensky visiting London. In May Welensky was told he could also have the assistance of an officer from SIS – but only, as de Quehen was told, and as he stressed to Welensky, for the acquisition of intelligence, not for

the penetration of African organisations. Whether the fact that
the officer selected was the son of a well-known Southern
Rhodesian politician was a goad or a sop to Welensky must
remain a matter of speculation. De Quehen certainly took the
appointment as an augury that SIS would not inquire too closely
into Southern Rhodesia's independence moves – as he had feared
– and redoubled his efforts at improving FISB liaison with Pretoria and Lourenço Marques. White had advised Home to confine the Salisbury SIS station's requirements to acquisition, and
to hasten slowly in liaison with the South African services. Events
and personalities overtook this sound advice. South Africa left
the Commonwealth a year later, and it was not, perhaps, a coincidence that SIS officers thereafter appointed to Pretoria sometimes made little secret of their sympathy for close relations
between the new Republic and the self-governing Colony, subsequently a rebel regime, of Southern Rhodesia.

De Quehen took comfort from the development of intelligence
liaison but, by May, had become infected with most of the suspicion which Welensky, belatedly but bitterly, had begun to entertain about Englishmen. De Quehen told Welensky that not
only must the SIS officer work closely with FISB but 'we do not
want him influenced by that crackpot Stirling. He must take his
target line from us.' In short, de Quehen feared that 'liberals'
like Stirling (with whom the nominated SIS officer had served in
the Special Air Service Regiment during the Second World War)
might have the gall to hint that UDI was in the wind. But de
Quehen was reassured by arrangement quickly made for the 'target line' to be acquisition of purely external intelligence in liaison
not only with the South African but the Portuguese authorities.
Liaison was also established between FISB and the CIA. On
16 May, Home formally approved liaison along these lines. But
neither Home nor White grasped that limitation of SIS activities
within the Federation – in practice, Southern Rhodesia – would
rob Whitehall and its masters of critical intelligence about UDI
factors in 1964 and 1965.

These early months of 1960 have been described in some detail
because they show clearly not only why and how Welensky was
dished but why a head start was given to those who saw UDI for
Southern Rhodesia as inevitable. The head start, despite the

opposition of those loyal to the Crown and the fears of those doubtful of South African support, meant that African leaders and organisations in Southern Rhodesia were, for years, uncertain about their policies or strategies. Not, of course, that they were allowed to make many moves without a succession of Prime Ministers - Todd, Whitehead, Field, Smith - cracking down hard on them. After the declaration of the state of emergency on 26 February 1959, restrictive legislation not only banned all African Congresses in the Federation and South Africa but allowed for imprisonment without trial of any person whom the Governor - in reality the Southern Rhodesian Government - alleged to be associated with events which led to such a state being declared. This blanket power, expressly and exclusively directed at Africans, and meeting with neither protest from nor the use of reserved powers by the British Government 'went far to remove from the inhabitants of Southern Rhodesia - and particularly from the "native" - that protection of the law against executive authority which has been built up by generations of struggle in Britain'.[14]

Repression split African movements, dividing members between militants and moderates. The former pondered war, the latter still hoped for British intervention. Thus were Mugabe and Nkomo divided. But the point must be made again if we are to travel the road to Zimbabwe that Macmillan's policy of 'taking the Central African Federation off the Cabinet agenda' - followed after 1965 by Harold Wilson's policy of ambiguously worded concession to Smith - delayed the start of the liberation war by at least a decade. The rapid advance of Kenya and Tanganyika towards independence, together with the British Government's determination to introduce virtual African 'self-government' into Nyasaland and Northern Rhodesia once Monckton had reported were other factors working powerfully and simultaneously in favour both of UDI and repression.

Thus Welensky's visit to London in May 1960 not only initiated a period of anti-climax which lasted until Smith declared UDI in November 1965; Macmillan, through Macleod, utilised the visit to throw a little more dust in the gulled man's eyes whilst the Monckton Commission proceeded to record African opinion throughout the length and breadth of the Federation.

On 30 May Macleod told Welensky he should not worry about Dingle Foot: 'I do not regard him as either trustworthy or efficient.' Yet Macleod and Foot knew and trusted each other, sharing a conviction that independence for Nyasaland and Northern Rhodesia must be pushed forward as rapidly as possible. Welensky also sought assurances from the British Minister of Defence (Harold Watkinson) that the Federation's pledge of troops in the event of Britain's involvement in a major war would be met by a response concerning federal security. Watkinson turned Welensky over to the Chief of the Defence Staff (Lord Mountbatten), who gave the latter no comfort at all. The Federation must look to its own moat because Britain's straitened strategic resources allowed virtually nothing for Central Africa. Welensky was urged to develop federal forces suitable for fighting guerrilla wars. In real terms, Mountbatten was referring to Southern Rhodesia's forces. No clearer hint at what the future held could have been given. Welensky did not take the hint. His Federal Government colleagues from Southern Rhodesia, far more familiar with Whitehall than he was, did reflect, and act, on the hint.

Welensky was never obtuse. But he had been gulled, was suspicious, had become bitter, and was thus unable to react to all these concerted moves except by protests and pleas, dignified or savage according to mood and provocation. Not until early 1962 did Welensky abandon all hope for the Federation, and turn his mind to a 'New Central Africa' where white Rhodesians and multi-national business would, he hoped, finally realise Rhodes's vision. Welensky spent the rest of 1960 and most of 1961 struggling to keep the Federation in being, but the combined effects of Banda's release, the Monckton Commission Report, and proposals for constitutional advance in Northern Rhodesia led him into further tactical blunders. Welensky seems to have become convinced that the overall security situation in the Protectorates was actually or prospectively so bad that if he harped on it, and again threw in the Congo for good measure, Macmillan would be forced to respond in a positive way. In June Welensky criticised Macleod's draft proposals for amending Northern Rhodesia's franchise qualifications. Welensky had already spent the better part of two years in what Dr Wood calls 'the futile Federal attempt to influence Northern Rhodesia Reform', but only in

1960 did he wake up to the fact that pressure for reform was coming from London rather than Kaunda and the copperbelt trades unions.

Welensky was incensed that the franchise qualification was to be lowered to £75 annual income, 'much lower than the lowest qualification in other systems at present in force in the Federation'. A qualification of £120 would enfranchise a maximum of 15,000 Africans; one of £75 would put 200,000 on the roll, enough to tilt the Legislative Council balance away from the whites. Welensky's fears were made all too plain; he saw Macleod as the author of franchise reform, determined to lower the qualification to £75. The tone consequently became grandiloquent. On 20 July Welensky told Macleod: 'I must ask you to refrain from doing it.' On 1 August Macleod delivered a curt rebuke. Northern Rhodesia was set on the road to both 'responsible' and 'representative' government for Africans. Despite Kaunda's detention, the banning of his Congress, and the possibility that even a British-backed United National Independence Party (UNIP) might not be a successful ploy, elections in 1959 had resulted in two safe Africans being given 'ministerial portfolios' on the Executive Council. Benson, emotional as always, and devoted to a 'traditional' Africa of chiefs and paternal British rule, had described Kaunda's Congress as 'Murder Incorporated'.[15] Home took an altogether more prosaic view of developments, and ensured mass support for UNIP. In true British fashion the alleged murderers, their party banned, nevertheless found themselves a year later being taught to hold and handle the reins of power.

Welensky, in 1960, was equally unsuccessful over the Congo, which, at independence on 1 July, immediately split into tribal factions, violently opposed to each other and, Katanga excepted, to a continued quasi-colonial white presence. Macmillan was not a city man like Lyttelton, but knew well enough what Katanga meant to the multi-national world: the province 'supplied in 1960 nearly ten per cent of the world's copper; sixty per cent of its cobalt and most of its radium, plus large quantities of zinc, industrial diamonds, germanium and other metals. Katanga produced half of the metal used in making jet engines and radar equipment in the non-communist countries.'[16] The Union

Minière du Haut Katanga, legal owner of this wealth, was the kind of multi-national Rhodes would have put together. But Macmillan - and Whitehall - had other ploys for and in Katanga; despite intelligence liaison, neither Welensky, nor Federal troops, nor FISB on the ground was welcome. When the Federal Cabinet on 12 July sought British support for 'Katangese independence', Home replied tartly two days later: 'The external movement of Federal troops would require British sanction in terms of international law'.[17] Welensky's response to this rebuke was to set about establishing Army units which would be trained for guerrilla war. Welensky had taken Mountbatten's hint. Units like the Southern Rhodesian Selous Scouts, whose commanders took a cavalier attitude to international law - and much else - thus owed their origin to Welensky's frustrations and his colleagues' UDI premonitions.

Welensky was, possibly, influenced by Whitehead's treatment of Africans during these months of seeming British gutlessness. In July 1960 eleven Africans died at the hands of the Southern Rhodesia police - the first such deaths since the Matabele War of 1896 - and when the new National Democratic Party was banned after a short six months of strenuous but ill-co-ordinated activity, Nkomo (in London) commented, 'Whitehead intends to use South African troops to quell the disturbances.'[18] This was far-fetched; in 1960 such troops were neither needed nor welcome. Southern Rhodesia security forces entered Highfield and other African townships without meeting even token resistance. The NDP's leaders - Michael Mawema, Ndabiningi Sithole, Robert Mugabe, Herbert Chitepo - could be locked up and their followers scattered without South African help. True, there were repercussions. Entrenching the police state led to the resignation of the Federal Chief Justice, Sir Robert Tredgold, the kind of genuine liberal Welensky could least afford to lose.

But, by 16 September, when Welensky received a leaked version of the Monckton Commission *Report* (published on 11 October) consideration of who his candid friends were had been quite replaced by rage. On that day Welensky told Sandys that Banda's inclusion in the Federal Review Conference would be 'intolerable'. Once Welensky grasped that the Monckton recommendations included, implicitly, the right of secession he burst forth:

I do have a closed mind on the subject of secession. As I anticipated from the beginning, the *Report* is a disaster. Its mere publication will make the continuation of federation virtually impossible. Almost without exception its recommendations play into the hands of African extremists and its philosophy of appeasement will rule out any possibility of reasonable changes being made. The secession proposals are the last straw and I consider them to be a complete breach of the understandings upon which I agree to the appointment of the Commission.

After this hotchpotch of assertion and accusation, Welensky continued: 'This is a depressing message to have to send you. But we are in the midst of events which I believe will, if not very carefully handled, lead to the end of civilised and responsible government in this part of Africa before very long. This may not seem such a disaster in Whitehall. But those of us who have made our homes and lives here have no alternative but to resist to the bitter end.' Whenever white Rhodesians mentioned 'civilised', British Ministers and their advisers knew they were rattled. For the remainder of September Welensky continued to write in these terms, not only to Sandys but to Macmillan. The latter refused to admit that the Monckton Commission had exceeded its terms of reference. On 10 October Welensky told Sandys, 'We have now come to a parting of the ways.'

Yet, in truth, the Monckton Commission certainly did not recommend secession as an alternative to Federation. Federation was thought to be viable if multi-racialism took a genuine political and social form. Indeed, the only positive recommendation was that there should be parity of African and white representation in the Federal Parliament, eventually. But the Report's reference to African opposition was stated so uncompromisingly that it blotted out all the rest:

The dislike of Federation amongst Africans in the two Northern territories is widespread, sincere, and of long standing. It is almost pathological. It is associated almost everywhere with a picture of Southern Rhodesia as a white man's country. This attitude, rather surprisingly, is adopted even by Africans who go frequently to Southern Rhodesia to work and enjoy the higher wages and standard of living available to them there ...[19]

These comments were made in a *Report* which was signed by all the members, and which was based on a search for African opinion far more thorough than anything undertaken before. In particular, what struck two of the four members who represented the Federal Government (Albert Robinson and Robert Taylor) was how ignorant whites in the Federation were of the reality of African opposition. The African opposition had been there all the time; most whites had never seen it, nor grasped that the African saw it all, and bided his time. As a result, whites destroyed themselves as leaders of an independent nation.

The period between 11 October and 5 December (when the Federal Review Conference opened) was thus one not only of growing frustration for Welensky but of increasing alienation from colleagues who accepted Federation's demise and advisers who were convinced that 'multi-racialism' should still be attempted. Whitehead remained aloof from all individuals and groups, a solitary, enigmatic figure determined to show that harsh security laws and less segregation were a prescription for Southern Rhodesia's peaceful independence. If Whitehead had succeeded in repealing the Land Apportionment Act it is just possible that Zimbabwe's independence might have been won by conciliation, not bloodshed. The Southern Rhodesian Government's second *Select Committee Report on the Resettlement of Natives* (published on 16 August 1960) was, despite its archaic title, an argument for first amending, subsequently repealing the Act. Land Reform and an end to segregation might also have allowed the two Rhodesias to link, if not to federate or associate with a 'new Central Africa'. Kaunda was determined to achieve Zambia's independence by compromise and conciliation, and was always responsive to olive branches.

But although Whitehead favoured amendment and repeal of

the Land Apportionment Act, his opponents took the chance of
the late October debate on the *Report* to state their case:

> We on this side of the House regard the Land Apportionment
> Act as the cornerstone of our society in Southern Rhodesia
> and we wish to make it very clear to this House and to the
> country that we are absolutely, utterly and entirely opposed to
> any breach of the Land Apportionment Act as suggested in
> this report of the Select Committee. In fact we find this report
> repugnant and cannot support it in any way.[20]

The immediate point at issue was *ten million* acres of unoccupied
land, reserved exclusively for Europeans. White refusal to allow
a single 'native' farm on these acres was Southern Rhodesia's
self-willed destructive device.

Welensky, his eyes fixed on London, his judgment impaired
by emotion, totally failed to support Whitehead with federal
authority when the Land Apportionment Act was debated. There
were many whites in Southern Rhodesia who knew, and said,
that unless Africans were recognised as equal and told 'you have
a place in the world on an equal basis with all other races'[21] the
rioting and violence which marked much of 1960 would, eventually, escalate to civil war. But for every white politician, official
or man in the street calling for real partnership, there were twenty
to say 'Atavistic repression [sic], it seems, is part and parcel of
the Bantu make-up, as it has been for centuries.' The Bantu,
once seen, was supposed to be, and in a crisis was treated as a
savage. The Land Apportionment Act was finally repealed, as
part of the 'Internal Settlement', in 1979. Repeal had been
bought with blood.

These central issues of race, land, treatment of one man by
another, must, in retrospect, make the Monckton Commission's
recommendations seem academic, however searching the questions and honest the answers. Broadminded, liberal beliefs stood
little chance against those who regarded the native as atavistic.
In any event, and aside from the Commission's reaffirmation of
the British Government's 'sovereign right' both to establish and
dissolve the Federation, Banda's release killed all chance for the
survival of the 'Federation of Rhodesia and Nyasaland'. Once the

Federation was doomed, any white gesture could only be seen in the light of an African future. The gestures were not made – except in a few trivial instances – and the next stage was set. Allowing Africans to use Salisbury whites' swimming pools was not going to save Federation – or the whites. The December Review Conference was, therefore, doomed before it got under way. Meeting at Lancaster House on 5 December under Sandys's chairmanship, a hopelessly bewildered Welensky and his cynical colleagues from Salisbury (Whitehead, Winston Field and William Harper) heard Banda denounce the Federation and claim the right for Nyasaland to secede. Kaunda and Nkomo, hardly at their ease in these surroundings, heard Banda speak, but were themselves silent. A week later, at Chequers, and with Macmillan trying his elder statesman role, the same gathering heard Banda repeat the Federation's death sentence. On this occasion Kaunda murmured about a 'progressive' Federation (of the two Rhodesias), but otherwise let Banda orate. The Elder of the Church of Scotland had given his fellow Africans their chance, but only Kaunda was able to take it. Nkomo knew that returning to Southern Rhodesia was simply a one-way trip to detention. His colleague – and prospective rival – Robert Mugabe was already paying the price for resisting racialism on the spot, not from the safety of London.

What Britain did in and regarding the Federation between 1958 and 1960 was thus to undermine belief in authority without providing compensation or clearly stated alternatives. By implication, alternatives were offered – to those with stout hearts and sharp swords – but the frustrated Welensky and the divided, driven Africans of Southern Rhodesia were as one in their refusal or inability to see which way the wind of change was blowing. The immediate future belonged to the Ian Smiths; they were not slow to take advantage of it.

PART FOUR
UDI

At this point I interjected and said, ' For heaven's sake, let's keep some grip on reality. It's quite possible that what the P.M. calls the will-o'-the-wisp of Rhodesian independence will be a fact long after the Labour Government is thrown out of office.'[1]

Richard Crossman, commenting on a Cabinet meeting of 6 December 1966

I am not at liberty to tell the hon. Gentlemen what the Secret Service was doing at that time [November 1963]. But it did not require a secret service to tell every newspaper in the world that goods were entering through South Africa and going to Rhodesia. Of course, this was well known. The House knew it perfectly well. What was also well known was that neither Administration was prepared to impose an economic blockade on South Africa, nor is the present Administration prepared to do that today.[2]

Edward Heath, speaking in the House of Commons, 8 November 1978

Preamble

For all but five years, from December 1960 to November 1965, the parties to Federation's establishment and dissolution engaged in a kind of slow motion political farce. By November 1959, at the latest, Macmillan, assuring Welensky of his opposition to secession and his belief in Federation, had, in fact, abandoned it.[3] In mid-1963, yet again at Victoria Falls, the bogus political experiment came to an unlamented end. As the formalities of dissolution were set in motion, Northern Rhodesia and Nyasaland completed the processes necessary for independence (granted to both territories in 1964).[4] Meanwhile, Southern Rhodesia's white politicians fought amongst themselves to secure a leader who would, with his followers, rebel from the Crown if independence was not granted on terms guaranteed to preserve apartheid.

This fight intensified as African nationalists in the territory, their movements banned, their very relative liberty threatened or lost, split into distinct, tribal factions. For all practical purposes, Nkomo's Zimbabwe African People's Union (ZAPU) and Ndabaningi Sithole's (later Mugabe's) Zimbabwe African National Union (ZANU) remained separate between 1963 and 1976, when the Patriotic Front (PF) was formed. ZANU was set up in August 1963, a month after the Victoria Falls Conference; thereafter ZANU opposed white rule, did so as a militant organisation and, potentially, as a liberation movement. The PF reflected incipient victory for that movement rather than a desire for co-operation with ZAPU. Indeed, to Joshua Nkomo, ZANU was a breakaway movement, inflaming tribal loyalties and animosities in order to destroy genuine nationalism.[5]

Welensky never accepted that, even by the late 1950s, Southern Rhodesia's UDI was probable rather than otherwise, or indeed that the end of Federation created a situation where the only alternatives to white rebellion in that territory were surrender to independence demands or strong and consistent action by the British Government in pursuit of a fundamental transfer of power to Africans. But Welensky, inhibited by his own racial beliefs and progressively disillusioned with Macmillan and his colleagues (Home, for some reason, always excepted), ceased to have political significance as the events of the 1960s unfolded. Welensky had tried, with characteristic energy, courage and honesty, to develop Federation along lines which he thought not only viable for the three territories (power for the whites, decent subsistence for the African), but acceptable to the Conservative Party of Great Britain. Welensky's failure has almost a tragic quality; he was blind to the realities seen clearly and cynically by Macmillan in London and white politicians in Salisbury.

Although these five years are as important as any in marking the long road to Zimbabwe's independence they are dealt with briefly in these pages. Ian Smith's Unilateral Declaration of Independence on 11 November 1965 was virtually inevitable once, late in 1962, Banda's Nyasaland had formally been given the right to secede from Federation, and a comparable right had been given to Northern Rhodesia early in 1963.[6] UDI became absolutely inevitable once not only Smith's Rhodesia Front Party but the mass of, often hesitant, whites grasped that rebellion would not be opposed through forceful action by Her Majesty's Government in London or by her loyal African subjects in the bush. But the importance of these five years lies not so much in the British Government's attempts in 1961 to provide Southern Rhodesia with at least the semblance of a, prospectively, multi-racial constitution, as in the belated realisation of moderate African nationalists like Nkomo, James Chikerema, and Sithole that any compromise which they might be prepared to accept would be repudiated not only by their militant opponents but also by their colleagues.[7] In 1963 it would have taken a prophet to say that the uncompromising Mugabe would be Zimbabwe's first Prime

Minister, but perhaps there was a certain inevitability nevertheless in the split between ZAPU and ZANU and the course thereafter followed by the two movements.

By the same token, although it was easy for white politicians
to claim that Duncan Sandys's 1961 constitutional proposals for
Southern Rhodesia were wrecked by Nkomo's enforced rejection
(after an initial acceptance), subsequent events clearly showed
that relatively moderate white leaders like Whitehead and Field
were also menaced by intransigent racialists, grouped round Ian
Smith. This group, strongly influenced by Afrikaner beliefs and
policies (although few of its members were from the Republic)
was as little known to Welensky and his erstwhile federal colleagues or Southern Rhodesian associates as it was to the territory's white elite, successive Governors, or the British High
Commission.

In any event, the main element in the proposals was, not the
offer of fifteen out of sixty-five seats to Africans (on a franchise
so complex as to be intelligible only to a constitutional pedant),
but that Britain should renounce its 'reserved powers', above all
to veto discriminatory legislation. Although the powers had never
been exercised, their retention, coupled with the emotional
attachment of an important minority of Southern Rhodesians to
the Crown, had prevented white rebel movements from taking
cohesive shape. Abandonment of the rights, coupled with sufficient nods and winks about independence from British Ministers, was a far more potent factor in the moves towards UDI
than white racialists' fears of African militancy. As Sandys
said, describing the residual British role as trifling, 'it was a
miracle that the nationalists had even initially accepted the constitution'.[8]

But rejection of the new constitution was inevitable once the
collective nationalist mind had digested proposals which promised Africans an eventual place at the white man's table, but well
below the salt and long after the time when the British Government had abandoned the pretence of playing any role in the
territory. Africans, so frequently supposed to lack the power of
logical thought, understood what many in Britain then, and later,
failed to grasp or accept: there was no point in a British Government urging basic change, or even insisting on it as a pre-

condition of independence, if reserved powers – implying the capacity in certain circumstances to enforce them – were abandoned as part of a bargain with white politicians in Salisbury. Thus all that the constitutional conference in February 1961 achieved was the means whereby Whitehead could make a valid claim for independence.

It is not surprising, therefore, that all white movements save the far right Dominion Party accepted the proposals, which, enshrined in a new constitution, enabled Rhodesian racialists, not moderates, to triumph at the December 1962 elections. Winston Field's Rhodesian Front, in practice dominated by Smith, and successor to the Dominion Party, used the constitution to entrench itself in power at the expense of moderate views, and to prepare for a strategy where unavoidable British rejection of outright independence demands would appear to legitimise rebellion. Hopes for peaceful African political progress were doomed. But Smith's strategy posed a crude challenge to any British Government claiming *some* interest in African rights. It would have taken bolder Prime Ministers than Harold Macmillan, Alec Home or Harold Wilson to say openly that Britain was no longer responsible, in any shape or form, for Southern Rhodesia.

Once Federation was openly scheduled for dissolution all white politicians in Southern Rhodesia pressed the British Government for the formal grant of independence. Smith's political skill lay in putting together a programme in which independence demands were linked to racialist politics. The relative moderates, by contrast, provided a tepid programme consisting of the case for independence in a country where Africans would gradually take some share in government. Such a programme made little appeal to a white electorate increasingly dominated by Afrikaner beliefs and the artisan class of postwar emigrants from Britain, whose attitude to the Crown was negative even when it was not hostile. When Smith replaced Field as Prime Minister on 13 April 1964 he packed the Cabinet with supporters who had doubts neither about their racialist politics nor their loyalties. Three days after becoming Prime Minister, Smith arrested Nkomo, exiled him to the bush, and broke up his movement.[9] In May 1965, and after a referendum in November 1964 asking, 'Are you in favour of independence based on the 1961 Constitution?' Smith won a

General Election and annihilated moderate white opinion. The Rhodesia Front won all fifty 'A' roll (white) seats.

The Dominion Party's slogan had been 'Rhodesia, first, last, and always'. This creed remained Smith's to the end. He deliberately chose Armistice Day for his declaration of independence, and made it in terms which suggested the utmost loyalty to the Crown.[10] In fact, although Smith ostensibly sought the widest measure of white co-operation, he spoke to and for Rhodesians who looked to South Africa for political inspiration, not merely economic and military support. This double challenge – to Britain's role in Southern Africa and to its Government's relations with the Republic – was to prove a more formidable problem for Harold Wilson and his successors than their verbal attempts to claim that African rights were being supported when, in reality, neither the means nor the will to sustain them existed.

Neither Alec Home, who succeeded Macmillan as Prime Minister in October 1963, nor Duncan Sandys (who remained as Commonwealth Relations Secretary) openly conceded Field's and Smith's independence demands. Indeed, as claims became more insistent and the position of Africans in Southern Rhodesia more vulnerable, these two high Tories formulated a response which, in Wilson's day, became known by the acronym NIBMAR – no independence before majority African rule. Abortive talks were held in mid-1964, but the following words, spoken by Sandys in the House of Commons on 15 November 1963, should be pondered by those who doubt that the counter-arguments were much more, then, than political rhetoric:

Southern Rhodesia, we must remember, has for over forty years enjoyed complete internal self-government. Up to the creation of the Federation she was responsible for her own defence and was represented by a High Commissioner in London. I hope that those outside who always tell us we ought to interfere and do this or that in Southern Rhodesia will realize there is not a single official or soldier in Southern Rhodesia responsible to the British Government. We have long ago accepted the principle that Parliament at Westminster does not legislate for Southern Rhodesia except at its request.[11]

Those who believe in the determination of British Governments forcibly to oppose UDI should note that Harold Wilson, in correspondence with Smith dated 29 March 1965, accepted the meaning behind the Sandys statement and, in private, extended it to a virtual surrender of Britain's constitutional responsibilities. A Conservative Government dissolved Federation, exercising an undoubted constitutional right; a Labour Government tacitly accepted UDI, failing to execute its responsibilities because insufficient resources existed to do so. But that same Conservative Government paved the way for UDI, and even a resolute Labour Government, provided with ample strategic resources, would have been faced with a major political crisis if it had attempted to contain and defeat a rebellion by the despatch and commitment of British troops. If white Southern Rhodesia chose to go its own way there was not much a British Government – especially one with at best a majority of four in the House of Commons – would do about it. Wilson rejected force, either as a deterrent to UDI or as a punitive instrument for restoring legality once it was made clear that neither course was open to him in realistic political or strategic terms.

Welensky always retained mixed feelings about Southern Rhodesia, reserving his affection for Northern Rhodesia, and disliking Ian Smith and company even more strongly than the avowed racialists of South Africa. Nevertheless, Welensky spoke and wrote habitually about Southern Rhodesia's 'civilising' mission whoever was in power there, and from early 1962 onwards made strenuous efforts to provide the territory with most of the dissolving Federation's assets. Welensky's rather cloudy ideas for 'a new Central Africa' met with a characteristically coded yet relatively positive response from R. A. Butler, whom Macmillan appointed Secretary of State for Central Africa in March 1962. Of all Macmillan's colleagues – and rivals – Butler was the most apt choice for this essentially late British Mandarin period appointment, for the ritual dismemberment of Federation, something already moribund but whose organs were capable of transplant to a live political body.

Not even Welensky really believed a new, white-dominated Central Africa of the two Rhodesias was possible in any formal sense. Although, on 1 February 1963, Welensky actually proposed a 'United Rhodesia' to Butler – 'an independent state preferably within the Commonwealth' – and deplored the notion of mere economic association, Butler's response was primarily designed to shift real assets into Southern Rhodesia as fast as possible. Aided by the fact that Banda had already taken Nyasaland along his own road, and by Kaunda's always surprising willingness to listen to other people's ideas for his country's future, Butler gave Southern Rhodesia the lion's share of the Federation's prospective economic wealth and actual military strength. Thus the potentially rebellious territory acquired an economic and, most important, a security structure incomparably more powerful than the two African territories. This structure provided the ideal base for a policy designed to keep the vast majority of Africans in their place; to offer a few of them a modest share in rising standards of living; to crush dissent by condign, forceful means.[12]

The really clever trick performed by Butler was not only to provide Southern Rhodesia with assets, but to ensure that Northern Rhodesia did not retrieve those which had been diverted across the Zambeze during Federation. During the early 1950s, Huggins succeeded in damming the Zambeze at Kariba, not at Kafue. But Southern Rhodesia had consistently benefited from revenue allocation and other forms of economic support. The matter went deep. The copperbelt was fuelled from Southern Rhodesia's Wankie collieries, no attempt having been made during Federation to develop alternative energy resources in Northern Rhodesia. Copper was exported by rail, primarily through Southern Rhodesia to Beira or Lourenço Marques on the Mozambique coast. Above all, and the most revealing example of chicanery, Kariba's switch-gear system was located in Southern Rhodesia. Butler's 'success' at the June 1963 Victoria Falls conference in arranging for Kariba to operate for the benefit of both territories was nothing more than a surrender to white demands. Nothing was done about the switch-gear system. Northern Rhodesia's copper industry was certainly prosperous in 1963, but was thus wholly dependent 'upstream' on Southern Rhodesia and 'downstream' on the international metals market, in which a black face was, and is, a rarity.

Northern Rhodesia was, in fact, a 'one crop' third-world economy, vulnerable to external pressures, whether manipulated or not, and thus always at the mercy of others. Kaunda's Zambia was, indeed, not unlike Lumumba's Congo in its utter dependence on white interests. Nationalisation of the copper industry in the late 1960s made absolutely no difference to this harsh fact. Southern Rhodesia, by contrast, has been well described in these words – exclusively from UDI-period white sources:

> For all its disappointments the Federal period was one of economic consolidation for Rhodesia. There is little doubt that Southern Rhodesia was the main long-run beneficiary ... the fiscal arrangements engineered 'a massive fiscal redistribution from Northern Rhodesia to Southern Rhodesia and Nyasaland. The removal of all trade restrictions between the three territories and the establishment of a common protective tariff [systems basically retained after dissolution of Federation] stimulated development in Southern Rhodesia but on balance was a disadvantage to the other territories'. Therefore Southern Rhodesia gained and Northern Rhodesia lost on both counts.[13]

Kenneth Kaunda has often been criticised by African militants for his failure to be one himself. Critics should remember that Kaunda has never been master in his own house, but merely the custodian of interests located in Johannesburg and the London Metal Exchange, not only in Pretoria, Washington – or Wall Street. For all Prain's good work in Northern Rhodesia, Kaunda's Zambia has been, and is, the creature of white politics and big business. For all the professions of faith in moderate black nationalism by British Governments of the time, none devised a policy for Central and Southern Africa which protected the Kaundas and the Nkomos when subject to extreme economic or political pressure. Zambia's independence in 1964 was purely political; Nkomo's relative freedom ended once Smith became Prime Minister. In considering the course of the African political struggle and subsequent guerrilla war in Southern Rhodesia, we should remember that those who struggled and fought did so to the end without the possibility of effectual support from Zambia or, until 1975, from Mozambique. Banda went his own way, and although Bechuanaland became independent Botswana in 1966 – Seretse Khama coming at last into his own – this huge territory remained wholly within the South African economic and strategic orbit.

These realities of international markets and racial politics were underlined by the civil war in the Congo. Welensky's assumption that his fears for the Congo were shared by Macmillan and his colleagues never led to a common policy, but was valid to the extent that all white interests, in Salisbury, Johannesburg, London – and Wall Street – were determined to preserve the power of Union Minière du Haut Katanga however much chaos and suffering afflicted the territory, that most artificial yet vicious of imperial conquests. Moreover, during the conflict the Congo became a proving ground for new and extended theories about the Cold War and the ability, or otherwise, of the Soviet Government to acquire a foothold in Central Africa. As has been indicated already in Part Three, neither the Foreign, nor the Colonial or the Commonwealth Office saw Soviet-backed 'Pan Africanism' as a particularly serious threat to British interests. Officials argued that the best antidote to this possible threat was the encouragement and support of moderate African nationalists, territory by territory. Within the Federation, Banda and Kaunda were duly encouraged and supported. Nkomo was told to wait and see.

The civil war in the Congo, however, raised the ante on this careful hedging of bets. The Soviet Government gave immediate backing to Patrice Lumumba, independent Congo's first Prime Minister, subsequently to Antoine Gizenga and to several other breakaway tribal leaders. Although backing was vocal rather than practical, the complexities of the situation in the huge, chaotic territory forced the British Government, using Northern Rhodesia as a convenient sanctuary, to engage in some robust covert operations so that Katanga, whether it firstly seceded from the new state or not, would remain firmly in the Western camp. With SIS also established in Salisbury – by an arresting coincidence only weeks before the Congo's independence – the British Government had in place sufficient covert resources to support efforts inside Katanga, indeed throughout the Congo. Soviet-backed tribal politicians were thwarted by various means, primarily the seizure of funds in the form of gold despatched from Moscow.

Northern Rhodesia's colonial administration provided facilities whereby the British Government learned a great deal more about events in Katanga than Lumumba and his successors in far-away Leopoldville or the hapless United Nations in New York and on the ground.[14] Most of Katanga's copper and other minerals were railed through Northern Rhodesia on their way to Beira or Lourenço Marques, and Welensky's assumption that objectives on these matters were the same in London as in Salisbury would have been entirely valid if Macmillan had evolved a coherent and consistent policy for the preservation of white interests in Central and Southern Africa as a whole. But as the SIS Director Middle East and Africa (as he became in the mid-1960s) subsequently noted 'there was no policy; there was merely a conflict of vested interests'. Welensky was quite wrong to assume that because London and Salisbury thought alike about Katanga, his intervention in the Congo would be welcome to Macmillan. Welensky was even more unwise to assume that he could take advantage of the civil war in the Congo to re-establish an effective, lasting relationship with Macmillan and his colleagues concerning either the Federation or 'a new Central Africa'. Because the British Government used Northern Rhodesia for its own purposes, it did not follow that positive policies existed or would be executed concerning either the Federation or Southern Rhodesia.

In the context of UDI and its aftermath, the civil war in the Congo is also relevant because, for the first time, a United States Administration became deeply engaged in Central and Southern Africa. Whitehall, both overtly and covertly, played a sustained, strenuous role in protecting Union Minière and thwarting Soviet-backed tribal leaders, but the Kennedy and Johnson Administrations were led, through exaggerated fears of Soviet penetration, into commitments to black nationalists and white industrial interests which were both ambiguous and contradictory. The calm appraisal of the early 1950s – and, from the US Embassy in Pretoria, until 1960 – was replaced by strong warnings of Soviet machinations. The men on the spot remained calm, but the State Department, by and large, did not. There was no panic – except, intermittently over the Congo – but a strong conviction obtained that the Cold War had come to black Africa. The papers of Mennen Williams, Kennedy's and Johnson's Assistant Secretary of State for African Affairs, the unwittingly but aptly named 'Soapy', indicate with sufficient detail the problem of balancing black political aspirations against Western strategic interests and commercial demands. But whenever Williams swayed on the tightrope, as not infrequently he did, the always formidable figures of George Ball, George McGhee and Paul Nitze were available to redress the balance. These three veteran practitioners of Super Power diplomacy were supported at all times by Dean Rusk, the Secretary of State. Rusk had little sympathy for Williams's liberal rhetoric and less for his good intentions.

Rusk and advisers of his own stripe did not see themselves as executing an obviously tough or demonstrably assertive Super Power diplomacy in order to rubbish Williams. Rusk wasn't a hawk, as the word is usually understood; Williams wasn't a dove. His Papers reveal a preoccupation with real or, more usually, alleged communist encroachments in Africa which was stronger than his critics', one moreover which betrays considerable ignorance of both colonialism and Soviet foreign policy. There was, however, a basic difference between Rusk's conviction that the imperatives of Super Power foreign policy in the period between Cold War and *détente* required the establishment in Africa of reliable surrogates and satellites – whatever the colour of their skins – and Williams's assumption that American support for African nationalist movements offered a feasible alternative to communism.

Williams told Kennedy he believed in 'Africa for the Africans'. The President replied drily, 'I don't know who else Africa should be for.' Rusk rejected Williams's rhetoric: 'One or two more Congos and we've had it.' Williams and his able deputy Wayne Fredericks may have influenced Kennedy in his decision to impose an arms embargo on South Africa, and in other ways to 'back off' from too close an overt relationship with Pretoria. Visits from the United States Navy to South African ports were curtailed; satellite-tracking operations were put in suspended animation. Yet intelligence liaison between Washington and Pretoria

was extended to include the two Defence Departments. Moreover, despite Fredericks's expert opposition (he had worked in
South Africa, unlike his confrères), American capital investment
increased throughout the 1960s. Williams was opposed to sanctions against South Africa; he remained a businessman at heart.
Much of the contradiction in American attitudes to Africa at this
time stemmed from a shared belief throughout the State Department that Soviet foreign policy was based on the doctrine of
exerting maximum pressure at all points and places where the
United States was, or might become, vulnerable in one way or
another. This belief distanced, nay separated Secretaries of State
and the Department from their British opposite numbers, and
continued to do so in following years.[15] But another explanation
for contradiction lay in a sustained conviction that 'programmes',
above all of economic and military aid, would make a real difference to African attitudes.

Gratitude for American generosity was hardly to be expected
– although Williams occasionally expressed regret at its absence
– but there was a rather naive hope that a power whose wealth
could be so abundantly spread would get recipients of it to toe
the right political and economic line. British Foreign Secretaries
and their advisers took a more detached, a more cynical view of
handouts producing such benefits. Aid was supposed to be defensible in its own right. Here was another issue, a marked difference of approach, which divided the American belief in programmes from the British struggle to meet certain minimum
strategic and economic requirements.

The civil war in the Congo thrust the United States into
a Southern Africa where neither aid nor rhetoric had much to
do with the realities of race and power. The Mennen Williams
Papers show a State Department which collectively saw Angola
and Mozambique as 'a focus of Soviet intervention', and consequently more important to the United States than the Central
African Federation. Williams and Fredericks were all but isolated
in their concern for what would happen when Federation was
dissolved. The prevailing note was struck by Kennedy, who supported nationalist movements in Angola and Mozambique, 'but
with reservations'. Williams and Fredericks opposed independence for a white-dominated Federation; Rusk and his peers

opposed more than 'self government' for Angola and Mozambique. Gradually, Williams came into line. Despite the arms embargo planned to come into force by the end of 1963, all in Washington knew that this was a gesture, not a programme. Exempted items, above all 'civil aviation' aircraft, would continue to provide South Africa with the weapons of repression.

Contradiction came to a head over South Africa. On 28 January 1963 Williams noted for Rusk: 'United States security interests in South Africa are of great importance.' Ten days earlier, Nitze had written that 'the United States wishes to continue cordial, co-operative relations in areas removed from specific racial policy questions'. The 'strained relations' between the two countries, which Williams had remarked in September 1961, had been replaced less than two years later by joint naval exercises and related activities. Williams described these, very oddly, as 'co-operations in the military field furthest removed from apartheid'. Williams continued: 'The South African Government has met our request to conduct secret military operations [in Angola] even although given no details about their nature.'

Too much should not be read into the CIA having a look at Angola nearly a decade before Henry Kissinger did so. By the early 1960s the Agency was a growth industry which few could check – even after the Bay of Pigs fiasco. Much of the CIA's influence in Washington derived from its senior members' skill in arguing that covert operations were capable of defending actual or prospective American interests without the odium of direct intervention being incurred. The argument – always suspect and often spurious – was to wear pretty thin in succeeding years, but its apparent credibility at the time led Rusk and Williams to agree on a policy towards South Africa which foreshadows much that was later framed and executed by Kissinger. Williams defended, or comforted, himself with the notion that close but covert relations might persuade the South African Government to modify apartheid in return for 'a guarantee by the United States and United Kingdom to protect South Africa'.

Rusk wasted no time on idle speculations. In late August 1963, the State Department and the CIA held a comprehensive debate on the situation in Angola, conducting a kind of war game, played along Congo lines. Williams argued that Angola's nationalists would be satisfied with 'self-determination', and should be supported. Williams made the same claim for Namibia, towards which other anxious American eyes were beginning to turn. But the war game concluded by recommending support for South Africa, whose understanding of Angolan issues was thought to be the key to averting civil war in the territory. In 1963 Namibia was left to the multi-national minerals industry; the commercial imperative was never far below the surface of American policy.

The preponderant American commercial and strategic concern for raw materials in 'safe' hands – that is, theirs – was not confined to the Congo, South Africa or Namibia. In January 1963 Welensky and J. A. Clark (the Federal Minister of Commerce and Industry) discovered that their planned export of 500 tons of cobalt to the Soviet Union had met with powerful and effective opposition from the United States. The British Government had no objection to the sale but, as Clark noted on the 29th, 'have asked us not to let the USA know this'. For once both London and Salisbury were in complete agreement. It was absurd for Washington to protest about the sale on strategic grounds when American mining companies were just about to put 600 tons of the stuff on the international market – whence some would inevitably find its way to the Soviet Union. To further illustrate inconsistency – or reveal the truth that America's business really is business, first and last – Clark also reported that American metals brokers were buying chrome from the Soviet Union at such low prices 'that the chrome producers of Southern Rhodesia face the very real risk of having to close down'.

Clark continued: 'Of course it can be argued that both America and Russia already have enough atomic weapons to obliterate mankind and that our sale of cobalt to the USSR – or our refusal to supply – would not affect the situation at all.' But that revealing comment aside, the reader will appreciate the considerable irony of a situation where Katanga, source of 60 per cent of the world's cobalt, was being kept intact in the collective Western interest while this mineral from American sources was being made available on demand. In the process, and in the jungle of international business, Washington – and Wall Street – clearly considered the Southern Rhodesian economy to be expendable.

It is hardly surprising, therefore, that one motive for UDI was to tell the world that white Southern Rhodesia was no longer a British Colony, was not an American satellite, was economically viable, and intended to remain so.

In short, the five years in question witnessed basic changes in Central and Southern African affairs, although those did not become apparent until UDI posed a challenge to the whole concept of self-determination and independence for Africans in the region. The view that UDI challenged Britain's authority and, in the process, divided the liberal sheep from the reactionary goats on the central issue of race is true enough so far as it goes, but is nevertheless inadequate and parochial. The issue was not peculiar to Southern Rhodesia, and although the subsequent liberation war there is of great historical importance because it was so nakedly racial, other states and Governments, whether directly or marginally concerned, saw the conflict in terms far removed from African rights or what Ian Smith quite accurately – and justifiably – called 'a struggle for our very lives and existence'.[16]

Beyond even the issue of race – expressed in the crudest prejudice of the 'civilised' white man versus the 'atavistic' Bantu – was the question of whether the Western world, not only Britain and the United States, should, or could, make sacrifices in pursuit of a principle. Harold Wilson was talking extraordinary nonsense when he told his Cabinet colleagues just before and after UDI that the issues were so grave that failure to resolve them could cause major international conflict in Africa. Wilson should have said that the issue was whether or not the era of decolonisation had ended and that of counter-revolution – white economic and strategic interests versus black political demands – had begun.[17] In truth, the new era had begun. Only in retrospect can we see that Wilson's and his successors' refusal to accept UDI as a *fait accompli* whilst attempting repeatedly to give Ian Smith most of what he wanted reflected an almost desperate search for compromise between de-colonisation and counter-revolution.

The Federation of Rhodesia and Nyasaland had masked the contradiction between liberal principles and reactionary practices. Federation had been seen, above all in Whitehall, as a balancing act, capable of resolving the contradiction provided nobody tugged too hard on the tightrope. When Banda tugged with all his might, a renewed choice was imposed on Britain, a new choice on the United States: to support African nationalism south of the Zambeze – and, if only by implication, to the Cape – or oppose it. The period between UDI and the 1978 'Internal Settlement' witnessed British Governments and United States' Administrations appeasing white interests between the Zambeze and the Cape, and doing so not because they lacked principles but because they could not afford to put them into practice.

If this preliminary comment on the thirteen years following UDI seems harsh it should be put in the context of a Britain impotent yet still determined to play some role in resolving the issues. Labour Governments found it easy to make a parade of principle, often, in Party terms, essential to do so. Conservative leaders and Governments wore their principles with a difference, but although rarely able to practise them did not abandon everything to their Party critics. Nothing surprised Smith and his colleagues more than British Governments' and Ministers' refusal, as it were, to throw in the towel. In the months immediately preceding UDI, Andrew Skeen, Smith's High Commissioner in London, whose views on Africans were extreme to say the least, was consistently bemused by Alec Home's refusal formally to concede the principle of Rhodesian independence except on the NIBMAR basis. Home was leader of the Conservative Party, but fully supported Wilson on all five points. As Heath's Foreign Secretary in 1971, Home again refused to consider the grant of independence by a British Government except on NIBMAR terms. (Heath simply wanted to dispose of the issue, but accepted Home's verdict that this was impossible.)

These Conservative principles may not seem very high priced given the practical fact of Southern Rhodesia's *de facto* independence, but upholding them gave a dimension to a conflict whose nature can only be appreciated in historical terms. Time, however, was not on Britain's side. Increasingly, the African leaders of the struggle in and beyond Southern Rhodesia turned away from a Britain they had been bred to believe in and towards those who would put weapons in their hands. Yet although Moscow and Peking have their place in the story of those thirteen years, ultimately effective pressure on Britain as the only state constitutionally responsible for the rebellious Colony was imposed by that multi-racial Commonwealth which had been fostered in Whitehall; Ministers also saw the new Commonwealth as an ingenious means of concocting policies of compromise, and sustaining British Governments in the retention of an international role, however limited. Before the July 1964 Commonwealth Conference in London Ian Smith was told he would not be welcome. In effect, the new Commonwealth blackballed him.

The Conference fudged the Southern Rhodesian issue, but a new element had entered Commonwealth affairs none the less. In the summer of 1965, by which time those few who acquired intelligence and knew how to assess it had grasped that UDI was a matter of not whether but when, the Commonwealth Secretariat was established in London.[18] The time appeared ripe for a consultative body. But the Commonwealth had grown in a decade from a small group of white haves into a loose collection of states, mostly coloured have nots, some twenty-five in number. The Governments of these newly independent states contained many men and women of great ability, hard-won experience, and considerable debating power. Their affection for Britain – which had educated even if it had imprisoned them – did not inhibit plain speaking. Mere consultation was not enough.

The Secretariat was immediately, uncordially disliked by Whitehall – an attitude which remains – and every kind of effort was made not merely to limit its effectiveness but to interfere with its tasks. Initially, those tasks were little more than to act as a clearing house for ideas and to promote schemes of economic and technical co-operation. But Whitehall saw clearly enough that the new Commonwealth had a Trojan horse element. Those within it would criticise Britain freely, and with increasing power to make their presence felt in economic and strategic terms, unless British Governments upheld and acted on principles of racial equality.

In Arnold Smith, first Secretary-General of what was later, and aptly, called 'the United Nations in miniature', Canada fielded a diplomat both unctuous and shrewd. The Foreign Office in particular found it difficult wholly to oppose Smith, who had begun his career in British service, had seen much of Britain in the travails of the Second World War, and had been his country's

Ambassador in Cairo and Moscow. Smith played a waiting game, and it was left to Shridath Ramphal, his Guyanese successor in 1975, to bear the full weight of Foreign Office pressure – and to see the 1979 Lusaka Commonwealth conference vindicate the African campaigns fought in the Rhodesian bush. As the Commonwealth grew in importance, Britain's roles diminished. By the mid-1970s, when the bush war in Rhodesia grew intense and diplomatic initiatives to end it were renewed, Britain retreated to the wings, or sought American assistance. Only after the Lusaka conference was a last effort made to take the centre of the stage, to settle, at last, the Rhodesian issue – in favour of counter-revolution.

Smith's Rhodesia was boycotted by the Commonwealth – and became an easy target for abuse at the United Nations – but relative isolation from much of the international community provided a strong psychological boost towards closer relations with South Africa. Rebel Colony and *herrenvolk* Republic both shared and gloried in an isolation which appeared to justify all acts and give meaning to all rhetoric about defending Christian civilisation against godless communism. Yet the nature and degree of practical South African support for the beleaguered Smith regime needs to be carefully assessed. Although at all times South African Governments held the better cards in their dealings with London and Washington over Rhodesia – as Henry Kissinger should have discovered in 1976 – the hand always included a joker: Mozambique.

South African intelligence was slow to assess either the nature or probable consequences of the nationalist struggle in Mozambique but, in liaison with SIS, it had done so by the early 1960s, long before FISB became fully aware of the situation. After UDI, Southern Rhodesia's Central Intelligence Organisation (CIO) hoped to liaise with Pretoria about Mozambique, but despite past efforts by de Quehen and Louw and the increasingly Afrikaner nature of the rebel regime, Smith and his colleagues failed to grasp the implications of the strains on Portugal's colonial army, above all, its regimental officers' progressive loss of morale from repeated tours of duty in the territory.

Until the early 1970s the Smith regime assumed that Portugal would soldier on in Mozambique indefinitely. Smith therefore dismissed Mozambique from his mind but, in doing so, also failed to understand that consistent South African support depended on his ability to further the aims of a policy in which all states beyond the Republic were seen as satellites. The satellites' task was – and is – to contain internal dissent so that it does not spread to the Republic. When, after 1975, and Mozambique's independence, the Rhodesian guerrilla war swung in favour of ZAPU/ZANU, the South African Government began to consider a black successor to Smith, one not only amenable to all-white interests concerned in Pretoria, Salisbury, London and Washington, but willing to assist in a policy of containing Mozambique.

South African support for Smith was undoubtedly vital at UDI, and it is almost certainly true to say that without prior agreement to supply Southern Rhodesia with oil products rebellion could not have occurred. But because this support was vital, South African Governments always knew when to give and when to withhold it, thus indicating the nature of an unequal relationship which, however, all too few members of the rebel regime in Salisbury fully understood. The rebels and the republicans shared the habit of deceit and double talk, and did so not only beyond the period of the 'Internal Settlement' and the end of the guerrilla war in 1979, but until Zimbabwe became independent. In one sense, moreover, relations between Salisbury and Pretoria were closest when most ambiguous. The received version of events is that Henry Kissinger put pressure on South Africa's Prime Minister, John Vorster, in September 1976, and the latter in turn forced Smith to surrender white power to an acceptable black nominee, Abel Muzorewa.

The truth is that Vorster merely persuaded Smith to drop the appearance of power whilst retaining the reality for his followers – control of Rhodesia's economy and its security forces. Smith was, apparently, sacrificed in the deal, not to please Kissinger but because he no longer served South Africa's purpose. Yet Vorster succeeded in convincing Smith that behind the façade of black rule he and his whites would retain real power. What might be called the 'Lumumba' – or Kaunda – factor came into play. But this deal, however useful to Smith at the time – because the subsequent 'Internal Settlement' pre-empted a comprehensive Anglo-American attempt at ending the war and giving recognition to the Patriotic Front – preserved the illusion that South Africa would always stand by its white brothers north of the Limpopo. In April 1980, and on the morrow of Zimbabwe's independence, South Africa decided to ignore the brothers' appeal.

Yet South African support was sufficiently strong and seemingly consistent enough for Smith to spin out negotiations with British Governments from the time he became Prime Minister until Muzorewa nominally took over control of Southern Rhodesia. The South African factor operated, moreover, in two ways, both adverse to Britain. The Republic could simultaneously support the rebel regime and remind British Governments of economic and strategic realities. Britain's partial dependence on South Africa throughout the first ten years of UDI was accentuated by mounting economic problems and a growing requirement for uranium from South-West Africa. Even if Harold Wilson had been a realist, and possessed of some negotiating skill, he would have had little chance to coerce Smith. Since the latter was indifferent to persuasion, to argument, to compromise – although Wilson and his successors offered plenty of the latter, all in the rebels' favour – the frequent and protracted 'negotiations' were simply a public relations exercise.

Whether it was Wilson in person confronting Smith on board one of Her Majesty's warships – a symbolic venue totally inappropriate for a rebel – or any one of the many emissaries despatched in well-known secrecy to Salisbury in the 1960s and 1970s, engaging in talks about talks, the facts remained the same. Smith certainly had to weigh his words with Vorster and Verwoerd; before Kissinger's 1976 excursion Smith even had reason to doubt continued South African support for white rule in Rhodesia. But, overall, the support was constant and, symbolised by South Africa's increasingly aggressive policies towards Angola and Mozambique after 1975, kept white hopes alive in Rhodesia. All these factors weighed heavily with British Governments up to, and beyond, the 1978 'Internal Settlement'.

The emissaries, whether Wilson's political adherents or from Whitehall, went to Salisbury – occasionally, in genuine secrecy, to Pretoria – from a sense of obligation or duty, not in any expectation that Smith or assorted South Africans would actually listen to them, much less respond. The political emissaries, whether Ministers or otherwise, lacked authority; those from Whitehall were sceptical. As time passed, the latter came very strongly to believe, sometimes even to minute, that Rhodesia should not just be removed from the agenda; the slate should be wiped clean, and a new relationship established with the regime in Salisbury and the Government in Pretoria. Scepticism was transmuted into conviction for various reasons, but a contributory factor was widespread dislike throughout Whitehall for Wilson's manœuvres, the claque which surrounded him, the sub-Disraelian atmosphere which he created and sustained. The great Lord Salisbury once described Dizzy's foreign policy as 'noise and splash'. Whitehall felt much the same about Wilson. Illogically, but perhaps not unnaturally, Whitehall found sense amongst the hard men in Salisbury and Pretoria. As the Foreign Office came to absorb both the Colonial and Commonwealth Relations Office, Whitehall lost its remnant of commitment to black Africa south of the Zambeze.

Thus it was left to the ragged, poorly trained and (on the whole) badly led guerrillas of ZAPU and ZANU to destroy Smith's Rhodesia and the façade built round Muzorewa. If Portugal had remained willing and able to rule Mozambique no guerrilla skills could have prevailed against the Rhodesian Security Forces (RSF). Once Mozambique became independent, and aid trickled in from 'freedom-loving' sources, the Rhodesian Security Forces were forced into a war of manpower attrition which, short of a major South African military involvement in Rhodesia, could only have one result. Once the attrition rate accelerated the regime found itself caught in a vicious circle. Intensification of the war forced more whites to spend more time in uniform; not only did the security situation deteriorate: the economy declined. As a result, emigration began to exceed immigration; those remaining in Southern Rhodesia thus spent even more time in uniform. As Lieutenant-General Walls, the RSF's Chief of Staff, said in June 1979, 'a white military victory is not on at all. It just can't come.'

The period between Mozambique's independence in June 1975 and the 'Internal Settlement' in March 1978 must be seen, therefore, as one where Britain, the United States and South Africa engaged in diplomatic manœuvres whilst the Rhodesians and Africans slugged it out on the ground. Nkomo and Mugabe, temporary allies but essentially rather bitter rivals, had gained sufficient standing from the war's intentification to participate briefly in these manœuvres – above all at the Geneva conference of October–December 1976 – but remained doubtful of their outcome. Nkomo was willing to replace Muzorewa – or any other African stooge – but Mugabe was only interested in victory. In any· event, with Nkomo's ZAPU Matabele tucked up in Zambia and Mugabe's Shona ZANU operating freely from Mozambique, the fundamental difference between the two movements could only develop. ZAPU earned an unenviable reputation in Zambia as a violent, unwelcome guest, but contributed little to the war in Rhodesia. ZANU, through its military wing ZANLA, fought a war on the ground whose intensity pushed all wider political considerations to one side.

Yet neither Nkomo nor Mugabe was fully in control of his forces; neither appreciated that the ultimate victors in the struggle would expect to be the arbiters of an independent Zimbabwe. Above all, and despite being free by the mid-1970s to observe and occasionally attend the diplomatic manœuvres, neither Nkomo nor Mugabe appreciated that at what appeared to be the turning point on the road to Zimbabwe, Britain and the United States were negotiating with South Africa on, ostensibly, an entirely separate issue – the future of South-West Africa. Separate or not, no decisive attempt was made by Britain or the United States between 1975 and 1978 to take advantage of the vicious circle in which Rhodesia's whites were caught. In particular, the British Labour Government of these years refused to commit itself wholly to recognition of the Patriotic Front. President Carter was prepared to do so; he had little to lose. Meanwhile, the war on the ground continued, and it was a bitter war because the enemies were fighting for their very existence, isolated from the diplomatic manœuvres, indeed hardly aware of them.

14

1965: Britain Impotent

If the Commonwealth and Her Majesty's Government won't have us, we have good contacts with South Africa and could work with them in defence and in economic development.

Winston Field, talking to Harold Macmillan in March 1963

The Rhodesian issue which dominated all others in the decade between UDI and Mozambique's independence in mid-1975 was whether or not Britain could have, or should have, intervened with overt or covert military force to deter, contain or crush what was in constitutional law an act of rebellion against the Crown and, in real terms, an act of racialist counter-revolution. There were few participants or commentators who actually believed that sanctions would have ended rebellion (Harold Wilson was, perhaps, the solitary exception at the decision-making level), but many believed at the time, and some believe today that British troops in Rhodesia would have done so. The issue is not disposed of by reminders that Wilson, between becoming Prime Minister on 16 October 1964 (with a majority of four in the House of Commons) and UDI on 11 November 1965, explicitly rejected recourse to military force; however, he was not explicit, then or later, on why he so gratuitously reassured Ian Smith that he had little to fear from rebellion, or so bluntly warned Rhodesia's African leaders that even his verbal support for their aspirations of majority rule was dependent on the time 'when achievement warranted it'.[1]

The answers to the intervention issue, personalities and British party politics aside, are that Britain's armed forces were inadequate in numbers and resources to deter, contain or crush UDI; and that even if intervention of one kind or another had taken place, a breakdown of law and order in the wake of collapsing white rule could not have been restored without the active support of African leaders. Even if a British Government had then pledged majority rule, such support, with ZAPU and ZANU fairly bitter rivals, could certainly not be assumed, and was not so assumed by those in Whitehall who, from mid-1963 onwards, were writing the appreciations as to whether either deterrence or containment was feasible. Whatever Wilson and his Cabinets really thought about racialism in Southern Rhodesia (with a few exceptions, there is absolutely no evidence of innate opposition, or *per contra*, sympathy for the Africans' plight, and it was this negative attitude which preserved a consensus approach in the House of Commons), no British Minister was going to commit Britain to supporting mutually antagonistic tribal leaders, none of whom, whether recruited by Whitehall or not, showed signs of being able to control his movement, let alone convey the impression of a potential national leader. This was a biased, an unfair judgment in many ways, but it conditioned the policies of all British Governments through the years of UDI. Only Bishop Abel Muzorewa, Ian Smith's creature, was given active, covert British support, although Nkomo remained convinced that it might, one day, be again accorded him.

There is little doubt, however, that a cross-bench clutch of British MPs, many African leaders, much of the Commonwealth, and virtually every Third World member of the United Nations believed Britain could have, not merely should have, 'dealt with' Ian Smith and company. This belief may have been strengthened by the rapidity and skill with which British forces tackled the East African mutinies in 1964, but, in retrospect, seems to have reflected the impotence of African critics in the face of a determined racialist regime, backed when and where it mattered, by the South African Republic and an international network of arms merchants and sanctions busters.[2] At no time during the decade (or, more specifically, between UDI and the virtual collapse of Portuguese authority in the Tete Province of Mozambique in early 1972) did the UN, the Commonwealth, or the Organisation of African Unity (OAU) prepare to arbitrate the Rhodesian issue with military force. The period saw the UN committed to 'peace-keeping' in Cyprus and Sinai (but being forced out of the latter area at President Nasser's behest in June 1967); the Commonwealth Secretariat was unable then, as it is today, to take collective military action seriously; the Organisation of African Unity, although partly responsible for the despatch of a Nigerian battalion to Tanzania in 1964 after British troops were withdrawn, did not become involved in the Rhodesian dispute until black Africa's most serious crisis of the period (the Nigerian civil war between July 1967 and January 1970) was over.

These factors, taken together, should help us to understand why the decade following UDI saw Smith's regime go from strength to strength, virtually forcing British Governments to make repeated concessions in the hopes of taking Rhodesia 'off the Cabinet agenda', and enabling attention to be concentrated on actually, or apparently, more pressing matters: membership of the European Economic Community; overall reduction of strategic commitments – but *not* the South African uranium-based 'independent nuclear deterrent'; and above all, and constantly, the British economy, whose fortunes seemed so dependent on sterling balances and the international gold market. However pusillanimous this policy of concessions may seem, and however painful were the processes whereby Rhodesia's Africans came to realise *they* would have to fight for their independence (unlike the colonies of West and East Africa, or the protectorates of Northern Rhodesia and Nyasaland), it was based at the operational level and above all other considerations, on the fact that the Royal Rhodesian Air Force (RRAF), less some transport aircraft, was given by Butler to Southern Rhodesia when the Federation was broken up in 1963.

The RRAF was virtually part of the Royal Air Force, a relationship which did not obtain, the Special Air Service Regiment (SAS) an important exception, with the British Army and the Federation's infantry and armoured-car units. Officers from the RRAF were seconded to the British Joint Planning Staffs;

squadrons participated actively in joint operations for the defence of British interests, notably concerning Kuwait in mid-1961. When Butler handed over the RRAF to Winston Field he ensured on the one hand that the 'kith and kin' factor (of which Wilson was later to make so much) meant something, and on the other that no responsible military adviser to a British Government would recommend deterrent or punitive action over UDI except by covert means.

Butler, in effect, not only ditched Britain's chances of honouring its obligations regarding paramountcy; in handing over the RRAF to Field and his successors, he also provided the Rhodesian Security Forces with their most valuable asset (mobility) for fighting the liberation war. One of Butler's advisers subsequently remarked: 'The Royal Rhodesian Air Force was seen as a white bastion on the Zambeze rather than the Limpopo.' Eventually, however, it was from south of the Limpopo that the rebel Rhodesian Air Force was to draw its strength, indeed its very means of existence.

The British Chiefs of Staff forwarded a Joint Planning Staff appreciation to the Cabinet on the eve of Federation's break-up (an item catalogued in but, significantly, missing from the Welensky Papers) which, in circumlocutory language, argued that although contingency plans for assisting in the restoration or order in Southern Rhodesia *at the request of a Government in Salisbury* should be revised, no plan should be prepared for the deterrence or containment of a unilateral declaration of independence. Doubtless, the Chiefs were influenced by Butler's 'secret and personal' message to Field of 20 April 1963 (the substance of which would have been conveyed to Lord Mountbatten, as Chief of the Defence Staff), which is referred to on p. 336, but should be cited here, 'In my letter of 9 April I affirmed the Government's acceptance in principle that Southern Rhodesia will proceed through the normal processes to independence.' So far as military appreciations were concerned, it was the fact, not the nature of independence or the means by which it was achieved which mattered.

The Chiefs, in their verbal submissions, referred to but were careful to avoid stressing the 'kith and kin' factor (whether relating to the British Army or the RAF), but left Macmillan in no doubt at all that should UDI come about it would have to be treated as a virtual *fait accompli*. These recommendations were accepted by Macmillan – and by Home and Wilson – and one is compelled to say that nobody in their position could have done otherwise. Wilson was unwise to tell Smith he had no coercive cards – revision of the contingency plans, plus the possibility of hostile covert action, might have had some effect on a potential rebel who, during his visit to London in September 1964, was 'more apprehensive than fearsome'[3] – but, by the same token, it was futile of armchair moralists and strategists to urge deterrent or punitive action when the resources for either were lacking. Resources, in real terms, were lacking in relation to possible conflict with a well-armed opponent, defending 'hearth and home', and operating on interior lines.

There is, of course, the argument, or the assumption, that the despatch of British troops to Zambia would have posed a challenge to which loyal elements in Southern Rhodesia's armed forces would have responded. Apart from the logistic problems of maintaining a force in Zambia for any length of time (of which probably too much has been made; it was the lack of readily available troops for sustained operations which added further weight to the British Chiefs of Staff's recommendations), this assumption ignores the retaliation available. Thanks also to Butler, the Smith regime controlled Zambia's economy, and there is little doubt that the victims of high-minded action by a British Labour Government would have been black, not white. There would have been no necessity for Smith to commit the RRAF's strike aircraft to operations in Zambia. All that he had to do was blockade the country, and shut out its copper exports.

In any case, the 'loyalty' assumption had little warrant. In October 1964, well before UDI, Smith had sacked senior officers whose loyalty to him was doubtful – or whose loyalty to the Crown was not in doubt. Political intelligence from the British High Commission in Salisbury was sparse and poor, but when the bran was bolted few in Whitehall could doubt that Smith had the armed forces behind him. Given that factor, covert operations, designed mainly to separate the loyal from the disloyal, were discounted once they were mooted. If Southern Rhodesia's armed forces had been overwhelmingly black in composition something might have been attempted. The black element was not large, and nothing was done. To the Foreign Office's Information Research Department and the BBC was left the doubtful honour during the early years of UDI of providing or transmitting material designed to reassure the loyal and bid them be of good cheer. There is no evidence to suggest that recourse to this 'white' propaganda, propagated unenthusiastically but conscientiously, affected events. The loyal remained so because they were, or felt, British rather than Rhodesian. Those that stayed loyal kept their heads down and hoped for better days.

When to all these elements in the situation one adds that Wilson knew, at UDI, oil-refinery capacity at Beira had been increased (in 1964) to meet an expected surge in Southern Rhodesian requirements; that oil products were also reaching Southern Rhodesia from South Africa; and that at no time was he prepared to extend British or UN sanctions to South Africa, it can be appreciated that the six years of his first two Governments (October 1964 to June 1970) can be passed over with little more than a glance at an oddity here and there.[4] Both the drama and melodrama of UDI on 11 November 1965 – Smith proclaiming 'God Save the Queen'; Wilson asking Southern Rhodesia's armed forces and Civil Servants to stay at their posts whilst all but simultaneously letting it be known that he equated rebellion with the dangers of a Third World War – have been adequately dealt with elsewhere; the flow of oil products over the Beit bridge was reported not only by the world's press but SIS, even although Whitehall and Ministers had difficulty convincing Wilson about what was actually happening.[5] Only he, and his cronies, lived in fantasy land. The absurdities of the 'quick kill' and 'weeks rather than months' – whereby sanctions would end rebellion – can be dismissed, as can further bouts of rhetoric by Smith's extreme right, equating rebellion with the defence of Christian civilisation against Godless communism.

The *Tiger* and *Fearless* talks between Wilson and Smith in December 1966 and October 1968 have been amply documented (and revealingly commented on by Wilson's closest political ally and harshest personal critic, Richard Crossman). The impotence was a fact, however little acknowledged at the time. What really matters is what happened to ZAPU and ZANU up to the advent of the Pearce Commission in January 1972, when the entire Rhodesian situation was radically transformed. The Commission, enquiring into African opinion on lines remarkably similar to the Monckton Commission in 1960, discovered – or rediscovered – that there was a majority, usually silent from fear or habit, which totally rejected Ian Smith's assertion that the (salaried) tribal chiefs, in reality creatures of the regime as they had been of lawful government, reflected a public will or consensus.

The Commission found, and reported to Prime Minister Heath, an African identity, a nationalism which, moreover, unlike the incipient variety discovered by Monckton and his team, was preparing to fight white domination, and shed blood for a cause. The Commission, collectively, was not impressed by African political leaders (Muzorewa in particular), although allowance must be made for the fact that men who have spent years in prison or in equivalent circumstances rarely do impress. But the Commission returned to London convinced that Africans would fight, whereas formerly they had submitted. The Africans in Southern Rhodesia had been politicised by repression; they had become a militant force, not merely a resistance movement. Smith and Heath did not do a deal.

When, however, Wilson went to see Smith in October 1965, Nkomo and Sithole were brought from detention for the doubtful pleasure of a meeting. Before the meeting both men were stuck in a Land Rover for five hours on the perimeter of Salisbury's New Sarum airport (an humiliation which Nkomo refers to with impressive restraint in his autobiography), and although Wilson chose to ignore this example of Smith's 'civilised' behaviour and of the 'integrity' which the Commonwealth Relations Secretary (Arthur Bottomley) attributed to him, he should have been left in little doubt about the kind of man he had to do business with. Smith humiliated and oppressed Africans (he was later to refuse Mugabe permission to bury his son) because he could afford to regard them as a beaten people. Yet throughout the liberation struggle, Africans, especially the Shona, sought comfort from the spirit of nationalism which sustained them during the Matabele war. Before UDI and during its heady days, Smith and his like sought inspiration from the slaughter meted out by their (mostly adopted) forebears during that conflict.

Eventually, the spirit of 'Chimurenga' triumphed over white emotions, and white oppression. But in objective terms, there is little doubt that for seven years at least African resistance to the post-UDI Smith regime was negligible. Kaunda's connivance in, not merely enforced compliance with, white policies compounded ZAPU's problems, but even if he had provided effective sanctuary in the 1960s, it is doubtful if an organisation led, *in absentia* or otherwise, by the essentially pacific and conciliatory Joshua Nkomo could have operated successfully against a regime which not only understood force but found South Africa willing, from 1967 onwards, to conduct long-range penetration operations into Zambia. (No protest at this penetration came from the British Government: 1967 was the year of complex negotiations for buying uranium from the new Rio Tinto Rossing mine in Namibia. In October 1967 the Suez Canal was closed as a result of the Arab-Israeli war. Oil tankers were forced to use the Cape route. Western dependence on South Africa axiomatically increased.)[6] By the late 1960s and what seemed the comparatively enlightened days of Edgar Whitehead, it was ZANU's adherents who began to ponder his words:

It is a very ancient tradition of the British people that governments should defer action against subversive movements until actual rioting or bloodshed has occurred. My government does not subscribe to this tradition. I do not think it would be exaggeration to say that the security forces have always been a little in advance of subversive elements in Southern Rhodesia. It had become evident that if these people had been allowed to continue indefinitely in these courses, disorder and probably bloodshed would be the inevitable result. Existing laws were not designed to deal with a subversive movement which had as its ultimate objective the overthrow of all existing authority; and although many prosecutions were instituted it soon became clear that completely new measures were necessary to deal effectively with the menace.[7]

Whitehead made this statement after Nkomo's ANC was banned in February 1959. There had been neither disorder nor bloodshed; there had been vigorous, concerted, politically significant opposition to the Land Apportionment Act – which, as we have seen, Whitehead was prepared to amend. But, as also recorded, he failed; thereafter, Whitehead tried to recover ground with his right wing by invoking and executing a policy of repression which was, indeed, fundamentally different from 'a very ancient tradition of the British people', especially when put to the test in Nyasaland and Northern Rhodesia. The ANC had no subversive intention; but redress of wrongs was distorted into such an intention in the minds – and emotions – of white racialists. The result, six years later, was that both ZANU and ZAPU, but only the former effectively, became convinced of a reality which Wilson could not understand, in a situation where few of his advisers were able to influence him.

In a sense, both UDI in 1965 and the reactions, such as they were, of British Governments thereafter, were irrelevant to a fight to the finish between black and white amongst the kopjies of Manicaland or along the flats of the Zambeze. Fourteen years and 20,000 lives later the fight was finished. There is ironic contrast to be found between Wilson's 'weeks not months' declaration on 11 January 1966 (at the Commonwealth Heads of Government meeting in Lagos) and the first concerted guerrilla operation of 27 April that year. Wilson responded (reluctantly) to a Commonwealth demand for mandatory sanctions against the Smith regime – what time *all* white political forces in South Africa were supporting the Southern Rhodesian rebels by supplying oil, or verbal encouragement.[8] Both sanctions and the first guerrilla operation were total failures, but the latter cast its long, bloody shadow down those fourteen years of intensifying conflict and ultimate black victory. Between November 1969 and May 1970 links were established between ZANU and Samora Machel's Front for the Liberation of Mozambique (FRELIMO) which, another decade later, virtually ensured the former's victory over ZAPU and all other parties in Zimbabwe's independence election. The link between Machel and Mugabe was also the hinge on which the war and all relating to it moved.

Much has also been written about the second 'Chimurenga', but mostly in partisan terms, whether from the black or white corner. Relatively little has been written about the nature of the war in its operational context of leadership, forces, resources and, above all, terrain (cover inside Rhodesia and sanctuary beyond it).[9] These aspects of the war will be discussed in some detail later, but stress must be laid here, and at once, on the unique nature of the racial conflict. Unlike the Portuguese in Angola and Mozambique who, in the field, progressively lost the will to fight, or British Governments responsible for Nyasaland and Northern Rhodesia, who saw no point in attempting to impose solutions, the Smith regime had absolutely no intention of making any compromise. Indeed, Smith's so-called 'Constitution' of June 1969 embodied the creed which he asserted when the October 1968 *Fearless* talks ended, inevitably, in mutual recrimination: 'There will be no majority rule in my lifetime – or in my children's.'[10]

In place of a white community ostensibly still loyal to the British Crown, Smith's 'constitution' provided for a Republic and, in most important respects, established a political, social and economic structure indistinguishable from and in some ways even more repressive than South Africa's. Although Africans could still be represented in Parliament, the franchise was keyed to income on lines which Huggins could not have bettered. A little arithmetic showed that 980 years would elapse before Africans even secured parity of representation. To consolidate white supremacy:

> The Land Apportionment Act was replaced by the Land Tenure Act which imposed new restrictions on the African population and permanently divided land on a racial basis; white and black areas in future consisted equally of 45 million acres despite the 1:20 population ratio [250,000 Europeans:4·8 million Africans]. The Act virtually made any African living in a white area, including all urban areas, a sojourner whose right to domicile and ownership there were at the discretion of the whites. It regulated the employment of Africans in urban areas and their use of schools, hospitals and hotels and provided for the eradication of 'black spots' in white areas.[11]

After a referendum, Rhodesia became a Republic on 1 March 1970. The Governor resigned – and retired to his farm. The Wilson Government gave him a gratuity of £6,000. A few months before the Republic was proclaimed, Rhodesia's two Anglican Bishops 'decided after much heart searching and widespread consultation with the clergy and laity'[12] to omit references to the Queen and Royal Family from prayers. This disloyal hierarchy proposed to offer prayers for 'those who govern this land', who were, it was hoped, to be guided by 'heavenly wisdom'. Most of Rhodesia's judges had already accepted the rebel regime; they accepted the Republic. Neither heavenly mercy nor human justice were, it appeared, to be provided for Africans who formed 90 per cent of Rhodesia's population. Yet Wilson continued to send assorted politicians, magnates, and mystery men to consult in semi-secrecy with the leader of this new *herrenvolk*.

On the ground, however, Whitehall's covert representatives accepted developments, and laid plans for operating in a political situation which appeared to be moving inexorably towards the evolution of a Pretoria–Salisbury axis. President Nixon's Henry Kissinger pushed a review (completed in Spring 1969) which was designed overtly to change US policies towards South Africa and Rhodesia from wrist-slapping condemnation to active support.[13] Once Rhodesia became a Republic the British mission in Salisbury was closed; intelligence for Whitehall was, thereafter, wholly covert, and was acquired from the Rhodesian CIO, rather than SIS or MI5. Smith won the April 1970 General Election in a landslide, taking all fifty white seats – and enlivening the proceedings, if that is the right word, by singing at one meeting an Afrikaans song whose refrain may be translated: 'Baboon, climb the hill.'[14]

The new immigrants, whose growing numbers were an unforeseen result of UDI, may not have shared all the sentiments and expressions of their scarred, 'slim', vindictive ex-fighter pilot Premier, but their rapidly acquired life-style of servants and swimming pool ensured that even if the new Republic's capacity to fight a permanent guerrilla war might decline its will to do so would never falter. There were a few wise men in Rhodesia who forecast that the Republic would eventually destroy itself in a war waged by embittered, voteless, landless, *exiled* Africans, but for many years their warnings were rejected or simply ignored. In November 1965 Smith surrounded himself with men whose open contempt for and frequently expressed neurotic hatred of Africans reduced even the most worldly wise of Wilson's and

Heath's secret emissaries to private comments notable for shock and foreboding.[15]

But the comments were also notable as expressions of impotence, because it was in this first phase of the war, from 1966 to 1972, that the regime's strength and the guerrillas' weaknesses were made all too clear. The Rhodesian Security Forces possessed the crucial advantages: a determined political leadership; an homogeneous intelligence, police and military structure, which enabled Whitehead's version of internal security to be applied rapidly and with due concentration of force; mobility; firepower; and, above all else, morale. South African security forces were active in support, specifically in regular reminders to Kaunda of the essential fragility of his economic base. In those early years the headmen and other Rhodesian Africans who acquired and provided intelligence for the RSF had little doubt who was, and would remain, master. In truth, until the final years, the morale of these informers and mercenaries did not weaken. From early 1966, moreover, the RSF's white-officered black units developed techniques of penetration and clandestine operations which ensured reliable intelligence even when village sources failed.

By contrast, neither ZAPU nor ZANU had a clear operational aim nor the leaders and human resources to attain specific objectives. The reason for these deficiencies are entirely understandable, residing mainly in the often overlooked fact that black and white Rhodesia were separate communities to a degree found nowhere else at this time of seemingly worldwide revolutionary war and guerrilla campaigns. Opportunities for acquiring intelligence, for politicising African villages and townships, for penetrating the black elements in the RSF, in short for deciding on what to concentrate, were few and scattered. When to these facts in the situation is added the imprisonment or detention of ZAPU and ZANU leaders and cadres it is not difficult to grasp that the fourteen guerrillas who attacked white farms some sixty miles from Salisbury in April and May 1966 were engaged in a leaderless, seemingly forlorn hope. To be sure, it is hard to imagine any leader of either movement actually fighting in the bush; their background and temperaments fitted them only for consolidation of tribal interests and extraction of support from sympathisers or, in the case of Moscow and Peking, opportunists. For both roles,

Nkomo, Chikerema, Sithole and Mugabe possessed particular gifts, sharpened by rivalry, developed by circumstance. But, unlike many of their co-revolutionaries elsewhere in the world, these rivals led only from the rear.

Attacks on isolated white farms continued for years to be the main guerrilla activity. After Mozambique became independent in mid-1975, a large, insecure area of such farms in Manicaland was made the 'new front'. Attacks increased in weight – and savagery – producing an invariable and, for some years, effectively crushing riposte. The utter failure of the first attacks was to be repeated many times, and for a decade. Ineffective ZANU leadership all but ensured that Tete became a liability rather than remaining as a sanctuary. The guerrilla reasoning, however, or that of assorted Plaza Toros and Russian, Chinese and Algerian advisers, was that the white Rhodesian farmer was not only an easy target but a politically important one. Isolation rendered him insecure; as the equivalent of a kulak, or Chinese proprietor, his labourers would flock to the guerrilla cause once he had perished in the flames.

This reasoning, suitable for application elsewhere, was quite inappropriate for Rhodesia, and would have been so even if guerrillas had been formidable rather than inept. White farmers knew how to shoot back, and quickly learned how to shoot first from the protection of stockades. The labourer knew that his employer represented, with a few exceptions, the best, not the worst in white Rhodesia. Unlike their voteless, landless, embittered compatriots elsewhere, labourers on white farms were reasonably contented. The boss was a man of his hands; he ran his chance with the elements, as they did. If not one of them, he was not alien, as was Ian Smith, the butcher's son from Selukwe. The labourers did not flock to the cause. When guerrillas descended to intimidation, coercion – and worse – the results were even more counter-productive. The African labourer on the white man's farm was not, and never became, a freedom fighter.

It is odd, in retrospect, that such moderately capable ZIPRA (Zimbabwe People's Revolutionary Army) and ZANLA commanders as the war produced should have taken so long to grasp that, in contrast to the classic political precepts of Mao and Che, Rhodesia demanded a new approach. This, in practice, meant developing a threat to the white agricultural economy as such through destruction of crops and livestock, forcing the RSF to disperse in an effort to control, indeed occupy territory, rather than to pounce from the sky at will. Eventually commanders like Josiah Tongogara and Rex Nhongo (ZANLA) and the almost unknown, Russian-trained ZIPRA intelligence officer Dumiso Dabengwa did learn the lesson, but they did so the hard way, long after 1972, and by rejecting not only the rhetoric of their putative leaders but the theories proffered by their political commissars. From attacks in the mid-1970s on the white economy, ZANLA moved, in default of actively politicising the mass of Tribal Trust Territories (TTT) Africans, into an onslaught on black subsistence and white administration. The resultant misery alienated many Africans from the PF. But the PF achieved its aim: the Smith (and Muzorewa) regimes were discredited because they could not protect the territories from guerrilla attack.

Between 1966 and 1972, however, Smith and his regime were impregnable, suffering only from a hubris which reflected the apparent realities of a war which was being fought between two vastly unequal opponents. Paradoxically, in view of Britain's impotence so far as ending rebellion or influencing the war was concerned, it was the Heath Government's attempt at a deal with Smith in 1971 – on the basis, be it noted, of the latter's 'constitution' – which revealed that there was a Rhodesian African nationalism which might be tapped by ZAPU and ZANU if only the means were found. It was the conjunction of this discovery with the beginning of Portugal's collapse in Mozambique which changed the balance of the war slowly but inexorably in favour of the guerrillas, forcing Britain and the United States to reconsider the implications in terms of a prospective threat to South Africa, and hence to their own regional interests.

Britain's response to developments was, as hitherto, uncertain and ambiguous; President Nixon's decisive and partisan. On 17 November 1971, he signed the Byrd Amendment. '... this piece of legislation would authorize the importation into the United States of seventy-two "strategic and critical materials" from Rhodesia, the most important being chrome, ferrochrome, and nickel'.[16] For the next five years the Nixon and Ford Administrations backed Salisbury and Pretoria to the hilt. Not until

Jimmy Carter, with his supposed concern for human rights, formed an Administration, did this backing come to be decisive in influencing the policies of the Smith regime and the Vorster Government.

15

1972: The Portuguese
Empire Collapses

In strictly chronological terms, unfolding events in the Tete
Province of Mozambique preceded the British Government's
attempts throughout 1971 to do a deal with Ian Smith, in effect
surrendering to him in the belief that he was, indeed, impregnable. There were those who thought otherwise. Not only a small
minority of white officials and soldiers in Rhodesia looked ahead
and saw Smith's destructive hubris; some in Whitehall also understood that should Machel defeat the Portuguese in Tete the
war in Mozambique would swing in FRELIMO's favour – and
ZANU would be able thereafter to strike at Smith's exposed
flank in Manicaland. But although a minority in the Joint Intelligence Committee and the Foreign Office inferred these developments, their masters did not. The end of Federation and the
advent of UDI left a large hole in British government's understanding of Southern Africa; this may be called a black hole,
because although people knew something was there, few could
argue satisfactorily about the most effective way of ensuring that
it did not produce an enormous racial explosion.

When Heath replaced Wilson in mid-1970 there was certainly
neither disposition nor intention on his part to pursue the problems of race further than Western Europe. Like all his immediate
predecessors, Heath made Britain's membership of the European
Economic Community his first foreign policy objective and, being
the man he is, was not easily or readily persuaded that Rhodesia
mattered, or existed. Heath's attempt to sidestep the issue at the

January 1971 Commonwealth conference in Singapore, plus his tactless references to South Africa's role in supporting the West's strategic and commercial interests and its need for modern arms from Britain, produced 'an unhappy and acrimonious gathering'.[1]

For the first, but by no means the last, time Britain found itself in the Commonwealth dock over Rhodesia, and only some superhuman efforts by those in the background prevented debacle. As a result of acrimony which Home (Foreign and Commonwealth Secretary) realised from experience reflected genuine anger, he visited Ian Smith the following November. Smith, in a strong position, verbally accepted moves towards eventual parity of African representation in the Rhodesian Parliament, but little else. His gesture towards Home (once this deal as the basis for 'return to legality' had been accepted by Heath) of a Commission headed by Lord Pearce was based on his conviction that Africans would do as they were told, knowing, as he said, where they were well off, better off in fact than anyone else on the subcontinent.

Confident of success, Smith made a big mistake. As with 'Monckton' twelve years before, Pearce and his fellow commissioners found Africans articulate in their views and specific in their objections. They were intimidated neither by Smith's security apparatus nor the blandishments - and threats - of the Chiefs. One should also consider the possibility, if no more, that Africans sensed that Smith's Rhodesia was not quite so impregnable as he made out. By January 1972, when Pearce arrived, the net flow of immigrants had ceased. Since 1964, 82,000 whites had arrived - but 88,000 had left. This was a trend which was to develop ominously in the years ahead. At all events, and for whatever reason, Home was forced to announce in the House of Commons on 23 May 1972 that the proposals included in the deal were not acceptable to the majority of the Rhodesian people. Pearce and his colleagues had reported unequivocally to that effect. Home added, with characteristic lack of optimism: 'The best atmosphere for constructive discussion and advance will be provided if we maintain the situation as it is today, including sanctions, until we can judge whether or not an opportunity for satisfactory settlement will occur.'[2]

In retrospect, the Pearce Commission is a curious affair.

Home's relative liberalism and residual commitment to the idea of a fair deal for Rhodesia's Africans rather than one nakedly in favour of the whites is not in doubt. Nevertheless, it is a little hard to believe that, in the words of one of Home's most senior advisers, 'Pearce was designed to make the deal with Smith fail.' If there is one issue on which all such officials involved in Rhodesia at the time agree it is the overwhelming desire of Heath and his Cabinet *finally* to remove the territory from the agenda. Indeed, another of Home's advisers also remarked to the writer that if the Pearce Commission had arrived in Rhodesia and completed its work 'before Christmas' (1971) African reactions would not have coalesced or been organised by the new African National Council – and the Front for the Liberation of Zimbabwe; the deal could have been pushed through.

Maybe. Both the ANC and the Front for the Liberation of Zimbabwe (FROLIZI – a short-lived, hardly militant, attempt to bridge the gap between ZANU and ZAPU, but, hopefully, strengthening Nkomo's and Mugabe's rivals Sithole and Chikerema in the process) operated in a hit or miss fashion, essentially confining specific political demands to 'immediate parity; majority rule in five years'. But again, maybe not. In the words of the Commission's Secretary, Sir Harold Smedley: 'We discovered an African identity.' The discovery was proved in April 1980. During the intervening nine years, both white and black nationalists sought to mould this collective identity (by persuasion, coercion and bribery) into a submissive mass. All nationalists, with the partial exception of Mugabe, failed, because none could offer the African what he desired even more than racial justice: the right to go about his own business in peace and quiet.

Despite the vast amount of time reluctantly devoted to Rhodesia in Whitehall between November 1965 and April 1980 – in order to supply successive Governments with papers which would show Britain was still 'responsible' for events there – reliable raw intelligence about the situation on the ground and especially in adjoining territories became increasingly hard to acquire. Inherent difficulties aside, Africa was a low priority intelligence area compared with, say, the Middle East. Between late 1967 and early 1970 the Nigerian civil war absorbed much time and effort. Mozambique, without exactly being *terra incognita*, tended to be dealt with too much from the military intelligence, too little from the political intelligence aspects. Not only did Whitehall collectively place great reliance on liaison with Pretoria; Washington, from July 1963, relied on the Pentagon equivalent of FSIOs to acquire intelligence and report, via the Consul-General in Lourenço Marques, to the State Department.

A generally optimistic tone prevailed in these reports, inducing Dean Rusk, his colleagues – and successors – to believe that 'self-determination' would suffice for Machel and his kind.[3] A few words off the cuff with Franco Nogueira, Salazar's amiable but hardheaded Foreign Minister, might have shed light on the realities of the Mozambique situation, but the latter rarely talked in terms to Washington and London. Until a stroke robbed him of power in 1968, Salazar told the truth about Mozambique (and Angola) only in private, and he expected his Ministers to do the same.

British and South African intelligence officers were reasonably well-informed about Mozambique in the early 1960s; their political masters then jointly came to some fairly sombre conclusions (from their point of view) as a result. But in the later 1960s the Portuguese Colonial Administration in Mozambique (as in Angola) initiated a series of reforms, which although designed only to satisfy 'self-determination' – if that – appeared to show that Africa's oldest white Empire was not yet in its dotage. South African Governments, who badly needed to believe in the effectiveness of these reforms, to which in economic terms they were also heavily committed, began to report optimistically to London and Washington. Under President Johnson the State Department balanced overall optimism with a fair degree of scepticism about these reforms – although the record shows that even the most radical survivors from Kennedy's New Frontier in Africa wanted to believe in them as an antidote to 'communist penetration' – but with the advent of Nixon and Kissinger in 1969 the National Security Council (NSC) began to fabricate America's foreign policy.

South Africa no longer suffered from 'divided co-operation'[4] with the United States, in Louw's words; the verbal, and sometimes real 'backing-off' which was noted by Pretoria during the Kennedy years was replaced by a policy of which the Byrd

Amendment was but one, if perhaps the most significant, element. As a result of this major change in the formulation and execution of US foreign policy, the view began to prevail in Washington that a 'non-Communist' Mozambique (and Angola), independent or otherwise, might survive, provided always that Pretoria's role was not only decisive but supported, without division, in the West. The collapse of Portuguese authority in Tete did more than raise the stakes in Rhodesia: the United States embarked on a Southern Africa policy thereafter based on a close, covert relationship with South Africa.

More will be said later of this 'National Security Council' policy – to be followed in most respects by Presidents Ford and Carter, not to say British Governments; but the reader should appreciate the considerable shock felt in late 1972 and early 1973 amongst South African and Western observers once the Portuguese failure to control Tete sank in. The shock was all the greater because of the reputation enjoyed by Kaulza de Arriaga, the Portuguese GOC in Mozambique. Although aptly described as an 'ultra conservative', de Arriaga, an energetic sapper, had 'established a reputation as the man who could block the guerrilla advance'.[5] He had done so, within the arguably well-intentioned but undeniably somewhat specious programmes of political and economic reform; by relying on air mobility to concentrate and strike; by the increasing use of native troops to sustain Portugal's exhausted regular officers and unwilling conscript other ranks; and, unfortunately, by a belief in his own star and vaulting ambition. But a desire, one day, to become President of Portugal had little relevance to a guerrilla war where time was not on his side. FRELIMO's commanders, however slow they were in assessing Tete's potential for inhibiting air mobility by virtue of its terrain and contiguity to relative sanctuary in a remote area of Zambia, grasped quickly enough that de Arriaga could not indefinitely sustain operations there.

Tete also bordered southern Malawi, but although no voluntary sanctuary could be expected from Hastings Banda, who was already responding to John Vorster's blandishments, relationships in 1970 had not developed to the point where South Africa's forces could be despatched to support the Portuguese.[6] Southern Malawi became, in consequence, an involuntary sanctuary, where

Banda's exiguous security forces were loath to operate against hard men. Menaced on all sides, Portuguese forces in Tete fell back on the old, discredited policy of 'protected villages', punitive sweeps - the equivalent of the disastrous 'search and destroy' operations which American forces were concurrently undertaking in Vietnam - and a vain hope that FRELIMO would revert to internal feuds rather than press home its advantages.

But, by 1972, Machel had liquidated all rivals. He consolidated control of Tete, and although the situation remained 'fluid' in Portuguese military communiqués, the political realities were reflected in lack of initiative, an ennui, all the more pervasive for its transmission by the conscript subalterns whom Salazar's successors had reluctantly sent to Mozambique because regulars had quit the field. Thus was born the Lisbon coup of 25 April 1974. The US Ambassador in Lisbon (Frank Carlucci) who, from his varied intelligence experience, should have known better, reported that communism was about to triumph in Portugal, whereas, in fact, the main effect of the coup was to hasten the process whereby the metropolitan Portuguese accepted a Government which was determined to quit Angola and Mozambique. American firms in Portugal began to 'disinvest'. In Southern Africa, the Nixon Administration started to go down the road which led to further covert operations in Angola and elsewhere.

FRELIMO in Tete destroyed a Portuguese Empire and started a Zimbabwe war. De Arriaga spent Christmas 1972 in Tete, but he did so in a fortified camp which bore more than a passing resemblance to French enclaves in Indo-China during the 1950s when the guerrillas there also destroyed an Empire. Ian Smith 'officially' proclaimed on 21 December 1972 that the war for Rhodesia had begun, following a damaging if inconclusive ZANLA attack on the Altena farm in Manicaland. One might suppose, therefore, that Smith had read developments in Tete correctly. Indeed, at least one historian, to whom this writer owes a considerable debt, implies that Smith's 'acceptance' in 1971 of the Heath/Home terms for a settlement reflected his tacit admission that unfolding events in Tete had put his regime on the defensive; the necessity was imposed on him in order to prosecute a war in defence of white interests, and with white support from far and near.[7]

From a longer perspective than was available at Zimbabwe's independence we can see that the situation in the early 1970s was more complex than this. Edward Heath's Government was certainly not aware that events in Tete marked the beginning of the end for white power in Rhodesia. Whatever deficiencies existed in the CIO concerning the implications of events in Tete, the RSF was operating there from 27 April 1970, when three members of the Rhodesian Light Infantry (RLI) were blown up by a mine. Although this setback may have checked operations for a time, sustained penetration was well under way by March 1972, and willing co-operation from the weary Portuguese ensured that the higher command in Salisbury was able to assess the new threat at its true value.

A reasoned assessment concluded that the threat was serious, but that it could be contained provided the ZANLA sanctuary in Tete was attacked as appropriate. No fears were entertained about ZAPU incursions across the Zambeze. At the beginning of 1973, an RSF appreciation noted that, 'No serious guerrilla infiltration across the Zambeze border, from Victoria Falls in the West to Chirunda in the East has taken place for three years.' For all practical purposes, this situation obtained until the end of the war. Neither ZAPU nor its military element ZIPRA succeeded in establishing an area of operations in north-west Rhodesia; the RSF riposte on Zambian targets, however brutal – as the writer can bear witness – was confined to spreading discord between Kaunda and Nkomo not, as in Mozambique, directed at the destruction of guerrilla bases and interdicting their lines of communication.

One cannot fault RSF reasoning, nor the political assessment that even ZANU would find it difficult to establish, maintain, and draw support from Africans living in 'white' Manicaland or neighbouring Tribal Trust Territories if ZANLA continued to attack the former's farmers and terrorise indiscriminately. Because so much ink has been spilt on the evils of the Smith regime there remains a tendency in some quarters to assume that all those who fought for the survival of white supremacy were bigoted fools. But although Smith's racialist claque may be so described, there were many in the RSF, the CIO, and elsewhere in the Salisbury establishment who understood Africans and assessed at its true value the rooted black objection to *force majeure* at the hands of alleged compatriots, resorts to witchcraft as a means of evoking the spirit of that earlier Chimurenga, and failure to overcome tribal faction in order to fight together in a liberation war.

Tragically – in terms of enormous human suffering – this enlightened minority lost influence as the war intensified. But as neither ZANU nor ZAPU succeeded in organising and conducting sustained urban guerrilla war, Ian Smith was able until the end to retain a hold on his electoral fiefs of Salisbury and Bulawayo. Yet Smith was psychologically unable to appreciate underlying realities, because he could not see at what point ZANLA and ZANU might politicise the mass of Africans, or at what stage Rhodesia's economy would begin to suffer in a war of attrition. When Smith said to a group of journalists on 4 December 1972, 'the security position is far more serious than it appears on the surface',[8] he was stating no more than the truth, whilst preparing his followers to swallow the painful fact that defending their elitism would in future be expensive, certainly in cash, probably in lives. But, in December 1972, Smith shared with virtually all Rhodesian whites the conviction that ultimate victory was not in doubt. Operational objectives and methods would change; the political aim would never do so.

All that said, there is also a tendency in some quarters where the issues are seen narrowly in terms of race and ideology to suppose that the Pearce Commission proved conclusively that the Rhodesian African had become politicised, and was willing to support ZANU and ZAPU (or any variety or combination of these movements) in prosecuting the liberation war. But what in fact the Commission found was an overwhelming African objection to the terms for ending rebellion in favour of a white regime which would still have, and be able indefinitely to retain, political and economic power. What Africans objected to was the Smith regime, not white authority as such. Except informally – and to an extent unavoidably – members of the Commission did not ask Africans about militant liberation movements. Members were not tasked to do so, and showed no inclination to take their remit in asking for reactions to the Heath–Home deal with Smith beyond the point of acceptance or rejection. The overwhelming rejection may have deluded some observers then, as it has since, into believing that ZAPU and ZANU had a fertile field in which to proselytise and fight. There is no evidence that either movement's leaders thought so, in terms of a common effort, despite the crucial revelation that even African members of the RSF opposed the deal.

Indeed the intensity of factionalism which developed between 1972 and the establishment of the Patriotic Front in 1976 suggests that Nkomo and his rivals put personal enmities before all other considerations. Where leaders were able or willing to address themselves to the deal – dignified by the euphemism of 'The Anglo-Rhodesian Settlement Proposals' – they strictly avoided any hint that a force more militant than the voices and views of Africans in the bush and townships would, one day, decide the issue. The impassioned letters which Sithole wrote from prison in January 1972 to Heath and Home; the lucid appeal which Nkomo then made; and the reasoned arguments of the African National Council: all concentrate on a peaceful settlement of the issue.[9] These occasionally eloquent expressions of African moderation – Mugabe being a notable absentee – may be said to represent the last time Rhodesia's Africans in durance or suffering constant harassment appealed to a British Government to act, unilaterally and responsibly. The tide was running against such men, was beginning to rise in favour of a Mugabe who believed that power came from the barrel of a gun.

What guerrilla commanders and cadres thought remains something of a mystery despite, or because of, the mythology which has developed that they were welcomed as freedom fighters whenever and wherever they appeared. Certainly the balance of the war changed slowly but remorselessly in favour of the guerrillas after 1972; certainly the findings of the Pearce Commission not only destroyed the deal – possibly to Home's private relief, in salvaging something for conscience – but forced London in conjunction with Washington and Pretoria to ponder the implications. Undeniably the findings could have – the writer, a white foreigner dare not say should have – provided ZANU and ZAPU with a programme for jointly seeking politically active support inside Rhodesia from Africans on whom hard circumstance had all but imposed a kind of nationalism. But the truth is that neither ZAPU's nor ZANU's political leaders did succeed in this endeavour, and there is not much evidence to show that they jointly attempted to build on the foundations laid by their suffering brethren herded into Smith's laager.

The years between late 1972 and Kissinger's descent on South Africa in September 1976 reveal therefore not so much successive phases as separate and sometimes nearly simultaneous developments. The war began – or intensified; ZAPU and ZANU in Lusaka and Lourenço Marques (Maputo after Mozambique's independence) quarrelled, nay fought amongst themselves; Portugal ended five hundred years of Empire; and, in consequence, that queer quintet of Vorster, Smith, Kaunda, Nkomo and Muzorewa began to circle round each other in a process which has come to be called, rather oddly, '*détente*', or, more revealingly in South Africa, 'the *détente* exercise'. All that emerged from these developments and manœuvres was that South Africa left the Afrikaner laager to strike at will in Angola, Mozambique, Zambia and Botswana. By the time Kissinger appeared on the scene he was well aware of this Southern African counter-revolution – in which, indeed, for some years the CIA had been active – and proceeded to operate accordingly.

Despite the qualifications made about ZANU's and ZANLA's credibility, 21 December 1972 remains a key date in Zimbabwe's liberation war. Six years and seven months had passed since ZANU began the liberation struggle; little had subsequently happened in Rhodesia to suggest that guerrillas had learned how to operate, let alone politicise along Mao's – or any other revolutionary's – lines. But the Altena farm attack in the Centenary area showed signs of planning in the sanctuary; reconnaissance from a lie up near the assault; a line of escape; a degree of logistic reliance on farm labour; and, above all, a capacity to make the RSF overreact. After a second attack on the 23rd, in which the RSF suffered minor casualties, Centenary was declared 'a restricted area'; and members of the territorial forces were called up 'to assist with the conduct of current operations, particularly those related to the protection of lives and property'.[10] In every essential, the purely operational pattern for the next seven years had been laid down, dictated by circumstance, terrain and, above all other factors, numbers.

ZANU's 'War Communiqué No. 1', reporting the attacks, is a ridiculous document, however much one understands the euphoria. Fifteen members of the RSF had not been killed in the first attack, nor twenty-five in the second. Thirty-one Rhodesian soldiers had not died when their lorry was (*sic*) destroyed. And so on. Nevertheless, and despite an ostentatiously held white wedding not far from the incidents on 4 January 1973 – almost symbolically, the bride was the daughter of the President of the Rhodesian Tobacco Association – both Rhodesian and South African senior intelligence, police and security forces commanders accepted that the real fight had begun. Ian Smith briefly closed the Rhodesian border with Zambia – a move which reflected awareness of Kaunda's vulnerability rather than operational requirements – but the realities of the latter were indicated in the regime's 'emergency regulation' of 15 February, 'which increased the maximum penalty for aiding guerrillas or failing to report their presence, from five to twenty years' imprisonment with hard labour'.[11]

By the end of June much of north-eastern Rhodesia was effectively under military control. Africans' freedom of movement in and out of the Tribal Trust Territories was further restricted; their relative liberty was made dependent on a stringent identification system. Both 'protected villages' and the punitive removal of those deemed unco-operative were set in train. Cash rewards up to $5,000 were offered for information 'leading to the death or capture of guerrillas'.[12] Thus the two attacks by ZANLA of December 1972 not only led the RSF to overreact in terms of manpower, but almost encouraged the regime to do so in order to show who was master. Punitive internal security decrees were accompanied by further apartheid measures. The partial social integration of the 1960s was destroyed by a regime which equated survival with segregation.

Those in the CIO and RSF – and Parliament – who had argued that ZANU's and ZAPU's resort to coercion provided opportunities for conciliation were brushed aside. Smith's 'negotiations' with African nationalists were never more than stalling exercises. A war of increasing brutality began, in which, since truth should be told, there was not much difference between varieties of white and black depravity. Rex Nhongo, who led the

Altena attack (and who, at time of writing, is Zimbabwe's Army Commander), would dissent from that statement. So would Peter Walls, who was the RSF Chief of Staff in 1972. Many guerrillas and members of the RSF fought as cleanly as a liberation war allows – which is not very much. Terrorism was selective, ostensibly – and usually – intended to act as a warning. But a civil war, revolutionary or otherwise, is a degrading business. The reality of brutality – and its relevance to the course of the conflict – should not be ignored because one side fought for racial survival and the other for racial justice, of a rough and ready kind.

Robert Mugabe and Joshua Nkomo would also dissent from these strictures, but neither, then or later, was in any position to affect events on the ground. As the real war began both leaders remained Smith's prisoners, helpless to prevent the evolution of a design in which the war's intensification was counterpointed by four of the strange quintet's comings and goings and, when those ended in failure, by a more intricate pattern wherein South Africa, Britain and the United States sought to contain African nationalism whilst appearing to legitimise it. The establishment of the Patriotic Front, and the appearance of Nkomo and Mugabe on the international stage, might suggest their belated involvement in the war. Not so. The war took its own course, whilst Nkomo in Lusaka – but all too frequently globe-trotting – and Mugabe in Maputo fought a guerrilla campaign for political ascendancy and international recognition. Between late 1972 and the onset of that crucial year 1976 there are, in chronological terms, three developments to summarise: firstly, the *détente* exercise; secondly, dissension within ZANU, ZAPU and other movements; and, thirdly, the evolution of a new London/Washington/Pretoria axis concerning the region, of which the key elements were covert American support for South African operations in pre- and post-independence Angola, and the discreet British cultivation of Abel Muzorewa in Rhodesia as an African who would accept the appearance of black power there minus its reality. But Nkomo was not wholly neglected.

The *détente* exercise, although greeted with derision by most African militants at the time – and handled with kid gloves by conservative Western commentators then and since – is important for any understanding of why London and Washington continued

to seek compromise over Rhodesia for the remainder of the 1970s.
James Callaghan (Foreign Secretary after Wilson again formed a
Government in March 1974) and Arnold Smith played a some-
what ambiguous role behind the scenes in order to convince
Vorster of the long-term implications for South Africa of the
Lisbon coup; Arnold Smith's contacts with Lisbon, Luanda and
Lourenço Marques strengthened convictions in London and
Washington that no solution to or even alleviation of the region's
assorted racial problems was possible unless Pretoria was directly
involved.[13] Angola's and Mozambique's independence required
South Africa to become a strengthened bastion of white interests.
Yet Pretoria, it was thought in these Western capitals, must offer
olive branches to 'moderate' African nationalism.

By a very real paradox, the total failure of the *détente* exercise,
occurring in early 1976 (when Smith and Nkomo broke off bilateral 'negotiations') and as Mugabe's ZANU became the undeclared front-runner in the Zimbabwe independence stakes,
brought South Africa far closer to Britain and the United States
than in the days when relationships were sustained by the Republic's uranium and gold. Between late 1974 and mid-1976,
Nkomo and Muzorewa were South Africa's nominees for a satellite role in Rhodesia should Ian Smith be forced into some kind
of compromise. The Lancaster House Conference of September
to December 1979, presided over by a British Foreign Secretary,
saw the two acquiescent Africans play the same role.

Détente was primarily an exercise by the South African Government, as advised by its intelligence and military staffs, in which
the strengths and weaknesses of the opposing forces in Rhodesia
were assessed in the light of the situation in Mozambique. In so
far as a solution was sought to the Rhodesian conflict, the South
African Government could only support Smith *plus* a Kaunda/
Nkomo axis *against* a ZANU whose leadership was being internally disputed but whose growing ability to wage a guerrilla war
was undisputed. The 'exercise' is correctly named because the
predictable failure of such an odd alliance – however much the
three Africans may have, probably did, desire it – nevertheless
enabled Pretoria to consider the next step in the light of a potential threat to the Afrikaner laager more menacing than de Arriaga's problems in Tete during 1972: independence for Angola

and Mozambique, coupled with incipient unrest in Namibia. The exercise, in short, enabled South Africa to decide its future regional policy, one which, in all essentials, was established by the mid-1970s, well before any Anglo-American 'initiatives', and which continues in full force today.

Although the details, both of the *détente* exercise and African nationalist dissensions, are complex the essential element is clear enough: *all* Rhodesian Africans save Mugabe and his power-broker Josiah Tongogara were prepared between late 1974 and early 1976 to do a deal with Ian Smith, and on terms broadly akin to, but no better than, the ANC's approaches to the Pearce Commission. Smith's failure in December 1975 to provide acceptable terms for Nkomo all but coincided with Mugabe's emergence as ZANU's leader, the one black nationalist committed to a fight to the finish. Failure of the exercise was an undoubted blow to Kaunda and Nkomo, a final one to Sithole. Failure did not bother Smith, who remained convinced until Kissinger appeared in Pretoria the following September that Vorster was still unequivocally committed to the white Rhodesian cause. Smith's characteristically black and white interpretation of events appeared correct until just before the Kissinger episode because Vorster, throughout the early months of 1976, increased his support and demonstrably took South Africa further beyond the laager. By the beginning of 1975 South African para-military forces in Rhodesia numbered over 2,000.[14]

Mugabe would probably have supplanted ZANU's founding fathers Sithole and Herbert Chitepo sooner or later, whether peacefully or violently. However, there can now be little doubt that the whole of the protracted *détente* exercise, with its odd mixture of motives, and methods, opportunism and idealism, provided Mugabe with the setting he needed to convince ZANU collectively, Machel and, belatedly, Julius Nyerere that he was the only leader who understood the underlying issues in a naked racial conflict. Nyerere, spared the close South African attentions inflicted on Kaunda and Seretse Khama, gradually emerged after the end of the *détente* exercise as the most influential African leader behind the scenes. Secure in his own power base – thanks, like Kaunda, to covert British support; personally *bien vu* with a surprisingly large number of political figures in Africa and elsewhere; persuasive in the OAU; influential in the Commonwealth: Nyerere was, between 1974 and 1980, the man for all seasons. He even balanced Moscow against Peking, a feat which Machel rarely managed, and Mugabe could only admire.

From the perspective of the mid-1980s, the chronology of the *détente* exercise and its immediate aftermath of Robert Mugabe's emergence as leader of a ZANU totally committed to the armed struggle – indeed, according to Mugabe's biographer, seeing the struggle as an end in itself – reveals the absolute futility of Kaunda's and Nkomo's efforts to achieve compromise with Vorster and Smith. Admittedly, fear and ambition usually warp judgment, but the two moderate African nationalists should have realised that even temporary success for them would inevitably have been followed by ZANU's domination of subsequent, intensified conflict. On 7 December 1974, Nkomo, Sithole, Muzorewa and Chikerema signed a 'Declaration of Unity'. They did so in their capacities, entirely nominal in every case except Nkomo, as Presidents respectively of ZAPU, ZANU, ANC and FROLIZI. The Declaration reflected pressure by Kaunda to compromise; followed acrimonious meetings in State House, Lusaka; indicated some pressure by Vorster on Smith to release his ZAPU and ZANU prisoners for the sole purpose of discovering what they would accept from their white masters; was attended by Nyerere, Machel and Seretse Khama; but was notable for the unexpected – and unwelcome – presence of Mugabe, who had been more or less mandated by his fellow inmates to accelerate a process of removing Sithole from office which had been under way for some time.

Although ejected from the Lusaka conclave of recognised nationalists, Mugabe used his time in Lusaka to some effect. Before being returned to prison, he became aware of Tongogara's plans for Chitepo's removal. This was the first critical step taken by Mugabe in his rise to power from mere Secretary-General to leader 'by acclamation', after he escaped from Rhodesia five months later and made his way to Machel. Chitepo was as vehemently opposed to negotiating with Smith as Mugabe. The revolutionary rhetoric reproduced in partisan accounts conveniently overlooks that fact, thus ignoring the reality that Chitepo, who had also formulated ZANU's strategy of protracted struggle without the benefit of travelling to Peking, simply stood in Mugabe's way. Chitepo's murder in March 1975 - following an attempt by various disaffected elements in ZANU to seize power for themselves - cannot with certainty be ascribed to anyone. Kaunda, through the device of a loaded Commission of Inquiry, implicated Tongogara and, by extension, Mugabe. These two, the Trotsky and Lenin of Zimbabwe's revolution, returned the compliment by virtually accusing Kaunda, although, oddly, not the Rhodesian Special Branch. It matters not. A militant, in *Lusaka*, had become an encumbrance, whether to moderates or other militants - who knew that the battle must be waged elsewhere.

Just six days short of a year after the Lusaka Summit Smith and Nkomo signed a 'Declaration of Intent to Negotiate a Settlement'. This was another meaningless piece of paper, which reflected the failure of a conference the preceding August organised by Vorster and Kaunda; the feud between Muzorewa and Nkomo for domination of any movement under the umbrella of the ANC willing to do a deal with Smith; the demise of FROLIZI - despite certain complex but irrelevant manœuvres designed to produce a guerrilla army uniting elements from all nationalist movements; and the virtual extinction of Sithole as a force to be reckoned with in ZANU. Never a militant, Sithole had come to believe that the armed struggle was wrong, not merely violent. Mugabe's ZANU had no place for such a man. As Smith and Nkomo continued their charade, Mugabe completed the processes whereby he secured control of ZANU and ZANLA; consolidated a secure political base in Tanzania; and acquired a relatively secure operational headquarters area in Mozambique. Machel's cautious but firm support for Mugabe was the latter's real triumph, not 'the coup from prison' of late 1974.

All these events are directly related. Apologists for Mugabe, his confidants, and ZANU as the sole repository of the true revolutionary faith have been diligent in demonstrating purity of motive, but there is plenty of evidence to show that the *détente* exercise and Nkomo's persistent readiness to compromise - not least in order to replace Muzorewa as a force *inside* Rhodesia - provided the one nationalist movement which was actually able to fight with a spurious claim to zeal and fervour. Mugabe relentlessly criticised Kaunda - a convenient way of attacking

Nkomo by implication – but neither in 1974 and 1975 nor later did he concede that it was one thing to tangle with Smith from Lusaka and quite another to fight him from the sanctuary of an independent state which was endowed with strategic assets. Moreover, Samora Machel succeeded with extraordinary skill in establishing a working relationship with Pretoria despite support from Peking, occasionally from Moscow, and always from Dar es Salaam. In that remote capital all the threads of outright and unrelenting opposition to white rule in Rhodesia were pulled together. In Lusaka, Kaunda was merely a broker for improbable deals.

Yet we cannot ignore, much less deride, Kaunda when considering developments in 1974 and 1975. These were relatively uneventful years in the liberation war as such: a marked drop in conflict throughout Manicaland – at one time no more than seventy guerrillas were operational – masked a great increase in recruits to ZANLA, whose training centres in Mozambique gradually supplanted those long established in Tanzania. The average white Rhodesian was more affected by the imposition of petrol rationing – due to interruption in crude imports after the October 1973 Arab–Israeli war, not to pressure for *détente* applied by South Africa – than the growing burden of service in the RSF or Police Reserve. But the two years in question finally separated the militant African nationalist from the moderate so far as Rhodesia was concerned. All the developments between 1976 and 1980 – and, indeed, since Zimbabwe became independent – should be seen in this context of a fundamental separation, whatever temporary alliances like the Patriotic Front were cobbled together in order to assess moves by the United States and Britain during their 'initiative' of 1977 and 1978.

Kaunda's pivotal role is reflected in the fact that at much the same time in June 1974 as he agreed to Vorster's proposal for *détente* he was in touch with Machel about the long-term implications of Mozambique's independence. Kaunda who, despite his air of ostentatious piety, remains one of the sharpest operators in the business of political survival, saw more quickly than most that an independent Mozambique would force African moderates to pre-empt ZANU militancy by acceptance of white Rhodesian 'concessions' despite the fact that these made no advance on the deal between Home and Smith three years before. Kaunda knew from Arnold Smith, who, on Callaghan's behalf, was assiduously cultivating the Junta which took power after the April 1974 Lisbon coup, that the youngish officers who comprised it would push independence for Angola and Mozambique far more quickly than either Pretoria or Salisbury appreciated. With President Nixon's Secretary of State Henry Kissinger bogged down by a CIA operation in Angola, Callaghan was able to exercise a modest degree of initiative in discovering what actually was happening at the crucial points: Lisbon, Luanda, Lourenço Marques – and Lusaka.

For the last capital, in mid-1974, read Pretoria and Salisbury. Kaunda's able emissary for special missions, Mark Chona, established a working relationship with Vorster's equivalents, Hendrik Van Den Bergh and Brand Fourie, which defied all the laws of probability.[15] Given the degree of covert political liaison between London, Pretoria and Lusaka, together with the Portuguese factors noted here, one can only record surprise at the persistence of the British Government's collective belief in a 'moderate' solution to the Rhodesian impasse. Independent Mozambique plus militant ZANU equalled Chimurenga, to the bitter end. But then, of course, British eyes were fixed firmly on South Africa. London believed, not merely desired, that Vorster and Kaunda could achieve *détente* on wholly white terms by hobbling ZANU and ZANLA – in Zambia – rather than by offering the vague hope of eventual black majority rule in Rhodesia to whichever moderate could out-manœuvre the other. But – and the central factor must be emphasised yet again – neither Mugabe's rise to power nor the realities of the guerrilla situation in Mozambique as a whole were appreciated in the white capitals. British intelligence remained extremely poor on the political side. Arnold Smith, although politically acute, was ignorant about and indifferent to the operational realities of guerrilla war. So all-white interest in 1974 and much of 1975 remained focused on that shrewd survivor, Kenneth Kaunda.

Despite a temporary revival of copper prices in early 1974 and the imminent completion of a rail link to Dar es Salaam, Zambia remained vulnerable to internal and external threats. Kaunda and Vorster – who had began corresponding in October 1968, two

years after the latter succeeded the assassinated Verwoerd – did
not meet face to face until, in August 1975, they sat in a South
African Railways dining car a mile away from the border town
of Livingstone and poised exactly half-way across the bridge over
the Zambeze. This somewhat bizarre setting for a display of
South Africa's ability to force Smith and Nkomo together ob-
scures the more material factor that Vorster and his advisers were
primarily interested in Kaunda as a moderate who could actively
assist in defeating ZAPU and ZANU, whether they operated
singly or in combination. Vorster was not disappointed in
Kaunda's readiness to hobble ZANU, and by means hardly consistent with the latter's pacific image. But, a further emphasis
which must be made, Kaunda's pressure on ZANU only drove
its survivors into Mozambique via the involuntary sanctuary of
southern Malawi. ZAPU remained in Zambia, a blister on the
body politic, not a force for ending white rule in Rhodesia.

Whether or not Chimurenga should be seen, on the black side,
in tribal terms or not, the fact remains that 80 per cent of Zimbabwe speaks Shona; that ZANU, despite significant inter- and
intra-tribal groupings, remained essentially Shona in composition, enabling it to communicate and operate with tribes in Mozambique; and that when the guerrilla campaign was effectively
re-opened in 1976, the main thrust, and the only sustained one,
came from and remained based on Mozambique. Thus Kaunda's
readiness to condone, nay to encourage so-called *détente* mainly
had the effect of driving ZANU into sanctuary and encouraging
Mugabe, impelled already by the strength of his introspective
intellect and silent demeanour, into leadership of a highly moti-
vated organisation. The motivation was opportunity rather than
ideology; between September and October 1975, Mugabe's 'coup
from prison' – as Machel had called it the preceding December –
was transformed with Tongogara's and Nhongo's support into a
movement whose guerrillas could declare: 'We the freedom fighters will do the fighting and nobody under heaven has the power
to deny us the right to die for our country.'[16] These words
should have been pondered by those who predicted victory for
Nkomo – or Muzorewa – in the 1980 independence elections.

Mugabe, the Jesuit-educated outsider (a Zezuru, like Nhongo)
had fashioned, for others to articulate, a revolutionary rhetoric

that was more powerful than the Marxist variety with which he was credited, or charged. Mugabe appealed to a national identity which, dormant but deep-seated, as both the Monckton and Pearce Commissions had discovered, enabled ZANU to politicise far more effectively than ZAPU once the war swung so far against the whites that guerrillas inside Rhodesia could become undeclared election agents. In January 1975 the OAU Liberation Committee had abandoned support for ZANU, thereafter backing the ANC in the various manifestations of Nkomo and Muzorewa; it mattered not. By late 1975, Machel was behind Mugabe, and Nyerere, the architect of change, was behind Machel. These shifts in the black balance of power were not finally cemented until September 1976, and just before the Patriotic Front was established. But from March 1975, when Mugabe, in a Salisbury township, achieved what may be aptly called a coup in an hotel, he and his principal political henchman, Edgar Tekere, moved into a position within ZANU which was almost unassailable. Nkomo, posturing in a Russian uniform, became a Lusaka-based back number, a prisoner rather than a beneficiary of *détente*, as he was to be a pawn in rather than an influence on the Anglo-American 'initiative' of succeeding years.

By the end of 1975, on all but the eve of Kissinger's African mission and the years of Anglo-American 'initiatives', the real issues were being decided on the ground. Nkomo declared with force and feeling, 'I longed for majority rule in Zimbabwe, and justice for my people. I wanted these things with as little killing as possible between white people and black people.'[17] Nkomo was not alone in that longing; he could have carried a silent majority with him. But to Vorster and Smith these words were empty rhetoric. To Mugabe the words were meaningless. That prison-hardened Jesuit had taken the violent road, eschewing rhetoric, echoing an older conviction than moderation and compromise: 'to know, to will, to dare, to be silent'.

16

1976: Kissinger Takes a Hand

The reader who has survived to this point in grappling with
détente and black nationalist rivalries should take comfort from
considering the years which followed South Africa's evolution of
a regional role backed by Britain and the United States, and
Mugabe's relentless, progressive assertion of power in ZANU.
The issues became clear at last, above all to Vorster and Nyerere.
There would be either black or white *power* in Rhodesia, whatever fudging expedients might be devised to pretend otherwise.
As a 'front-line State' President – who was not in the front line
at all – Nyerere could objectively see that the issues transcended
Rhodesia's fate or Zimbabwe's future; they embraced Southern
Africa as a whole. The *détente* exercise had produced impotence
for Kaunda, frustration for Nkomo, opportunity for Mugabe,
humiliation, as it seemed, for Muzorewa. Yet Nyerere knew well
enough that Vorster's exercise would be followed by the real
thing, an operation designed to bring Smith's Rhodesia into
South Africa's orbit in much the same way as Angola, Mozambique – and even an 'independent' Namibia. All would be en-
circled by the facts of economic power and military strength. Yet
even Nyerere might have been surprised to find that Abel
Muzorewa would in June 1979 become Rhodesia's first African
premier.

When Henry Kissinger flew to Pretoria in September 1976 on
the second of his two visits to Africa one may doubt whether he
knew or cared much about the war on the ground in Rhodesia.

He was not – and is not – a man who learns from others, or even from the briefing papers with which American Secretaries of State are so extravagantly provided. For all his undoubted intellectual gifts it is Kissinger's enormous self-confidence devoid of vanity which strikes home. Such confidence had survived Kennedy's dislike, Johnson's indifference, and the grimy embrace of the corrupt President Nixon. For a man who once remarked to the writer, 'I love power', Kissinger in office was almost uniquely capable of separating the vanities of success from the realities of achievement. In October 1973 Kissinger and the Soviet Foreign Minister Andrei Gromyko had separately prevented their respective clients, Israel and Egypt, from expanding war to the stage where direct American and Russian participation might have become unavoidable. This exercise in crisis management was followed by six months of intense diplomatic activity, culminating in the successful negotiation of a stand-off between Egypt and Israel which was, indirectly, precursor of that peace between the two countries which was the solitary foreign policy achievement of the Carter Administration.

The stand-off was almost entirely due to Kissinger's energy, determination, advocacy – and self-confidence. As an historian, of moderate distinction, he was convinced that the nation would endure as a political entity. As a nuclear strategist, of equally moderate distinction but unusual tenacity of argument, this conviction hardened into a belief that Clausewitz's dictum must be stood on its head: diplomacy was the continuation of war by other means. Nations would continue to have conflicting interests, but compromise was usually possible if the consequences of conflict were made plain. This combination of reflective power and political conviction gave Kissinger's diplomacy after the October 1973 Arab–Israeli war an impressive authority and lustre. Here, to the unbiased observer, was an American Secretary of State who neither asserted his country's power nor its enemies' designs. Kissinger and Gromyko established a relationship which was blessedly short on self-justification.

Yet despite this achievement in the resolution of one particular conflict, Kissinger remained convinced that Russia was his country's enemy, to be deterred from aggression or subversion only by armed American strength and reliable satellites. History will remember Kissinger for his achievements in the Middle East, forget – or overlook – his deceit regarding Laos and Cambodia. But these Far Eastern experiences left their mark. Kissinger's doctrine of 'linkage', whereby latent worldwide hostility between the two Super Powers would be lessened by mutual understanding about spheres of interest, was really nothing more than a coded means of saying that he wanted America's allies to do their stuff on America's behalf. Israel, Iran, even China, were links in a chain which was intended to bind these recipients of arms and other favours to Kissinger's strategic system.

Kissinger's visit to Pretoria, his meeting with Vorster, and his subsequent encounter with Smith, rightly mark an important stage on the road to Zimbabwe. The meetings led to the 'Internal Settlement' – and to Muzorewa, from June 1979, if but nominally, having an army of his own. But Kissinger's motive in coming to Pretoria had nothing to do with Rhodesia as such, much to do with white South Africa's role as America's ally. The visit had also something to do with what remained of the Anglo-American 'special relationship'. Kissinger had no formula of his own for settling the Rhodesian issue; he was content to rely on the British Government for the necessary pieces of paper.

It was the undeclared alliance between America and South Africa which sent Kissinger on his travels in 1976. The alliance had not been long in the flowering, but its postwar roots were deep; from the uranium deals of the 1950s to Kissinger's National Security Council (NSC) analysis of 1979 one can trace a certain inevitability. Angola and Mozambique's independence in 1975, which the NSC six years earlier had not foreseen, coupled with the emergency of a black nationalist movement in Namibia, led South Africa inexorably beyond the laager. It was not enough that De Beers should sell Angola's diamonds or Durban's dockers keep Maputo in business. It might not even be enough for De Beers and Rio Tinto to operate diamond and uranium mines in Namibia from behind a barricade of armed police and ruthless surveillance. South Africa's role as America's ally in a subcontinent where the Soviet Union was active in its support of nationalist movements, and where the newly independent Angola and Mozambique had allegedly 'Marxist' Governments, required that blacks could be found who would either lead break-away movements or accept puppet roles.

To Kissinger, whose activities in 1976 were to exercise a direct effect on the events of the next three years, the concept of allies and satellites was not one which admitted of much argument. This most intellectually gifted and diplomatically experienced of men was – and is – a committed chauvinist. The fact that Kissinger expressed chauvinism through scepticism about natural mutuality of interests rather than crude insistence on American power cannot disguise this truth. With Israel and Iran, both client states whose survival or prestige depended entirely on American support, Kissinger's convictions were irrelevant. It was the cash and arms which mattered. With China the possibility of a working alliance against the Soviet Union raised such momentous prospects of coercion and compromise that even Kissinger did little more than make the appropriate noises. But with South Africa, whose ruthless Governments had no direct or obvious need of the United States, Kissinger found himself in a situation of give and take which, in all essentials, he tackled by subterfuge. On his first visit to Africa in April 1976 Kissinger said he had come with an open mind. He had done nothing of the kind. He went to Africa in order to see who could be squared.

Vorster, whatever his reservations about Ian Smith, had no intention of allowing a black Government to have power in Rhodesia. A formula on the 'Parry' lines which obtained for Patrice Lumumba at the Congo's independence in 1960 would be allowable, but a black Government in Rhodesia which controlled the security apparatus, armed forces, and economy was totally unacceptable. The Rhodesian Central Intelligence Organisation was in liaison with Pretoria's Bureau of State Security (BOSS); the RSF depended for much of its operational credibility on the South African Defence Forces (SADF); the Rhodesian economy, in mineral terms, was part of a multi-national world of which Johannesburg was virtually the capital. Vorster was certainly anxious to settle the Rhodesian issue, because the 1974-5 *détente* exercise had shown its intractable nature – provided ZANU opposed compromise and ZANLA continued to fight. Therefore, Vorster was determined that Kissinger would make proposals to Smith which would keep Rhodesia's whites securely, permanently in power, whatever formula was concocted to produce 'majority rule'.

Kissinger and the CIA had made a hash of things in Angola. The Soviet Union was taking advantage of the CIA's mistake in spending a mere $28 million in the attempt at supporting a puppet. Kissinger undoubtedly had to take some direct, personal interest in Southern Africa. The 'benign neglect' of the region, which was expressly repudiated in the 1969 NSC Memorandum, had to be replaced by commitment. South Africa was needed to support such a commitment; although keen to acquire American arms by devious and covert means (Kissinger was happy to oblige), Vorster's Government was not a suppliant as were Israel and Iran. If Kissinger, with his reputation, his gift for reconciling seemingly intractable differences, could pull off a deal over Rhodesia, well and good. But it would be a deal on South Africa's terms. The London/Washington/Pretoria axis was one sustained, above all, in South Africa's interest.

What Kissinger called 'constructive ambiguity', and others have rightly defined in harsher language, was thus employed to pretend that he had forced Ian Smith to accept African majority rule in Rhodesia at the end of a two-year interim period. The truth, so strangely and widely misunderstood, is that, with candid although bilateral preliminaries (Vorster and Kissinger; Vorster and Smith), an *offer* was made to the white rebel, which he would have been a fool to refuse. The deal gave Smith's fellow whites all they needed to stay permanently in power. What Kissinger offered was, in his words, '*responsible*' majority rule, with constitutional, electoral, security and economic matters left predominantly in white hands. Such an offer, made by America's Secretary of State in pursuit of strategic objectives common to Washington and Pretoria, was the prize which Smith had always sought. His fight against 'communism' had been expressly recognised, vindicated and supported. Smith's likely departure from office as part of the offer is a mere detail, and it is fair to say that whatever one's view of him as a bigot, he was not the man to complain of his own fate if white Rhodesia's future was secured.

Yet the Kissinger–Smith exchanges have been recorded, presented, and analysed as if the latter's white power-base had been captured. Much of the misunderstanding and confusion at the time is understandable, because immediately after the Pretoria meetings Kissinger briefed Kaunda and Nyerere in words which suggested that Smith had been forced to concede power. It is doubtful whether Kaunda really believed this, but even Nyerere appears for a time to have swallowed the deception. To understand why, aside from Kissinger's tactic of deliberately giving different versions of the same exchanges in different places to different people, we must consider for a moment the position of the Southern African and Rhodesian policies (so far as they can be said to exist) of the British Government at the beginning of 1976. These policies, which formed the basis of what Kissinger consistently, and accurately, called 'the Anglo-American proposals' (for Rhodesia), also had a direct bearing on the events of the next three years.

On 3 December 1974 Harold Wilson had announced that talks would be held in 1975 with the South African Government to end the 1955 Simonstown Agreement. There was no doubt that not only the British Labour Party but a substantial section of public opinion in Britain disliked the notion of apartheid, and that there was some genuine revulsion against the practices of the Afrikaner Government. But successive British Governments had accepted the reality of South Africa's economic power and strategic importance. The Vorster *détente* exercise, and the march beyond the laager to consolidate or defend Western interests in sub-Saharan Africa, had met with no opposition by the British Government, despite the embargo on arms sales, and was sustained at many levels in Whitehall and by British missions throughout the region. The SADF Operation PROTEA, conducted intermittently throughout 1976, in which preliminary sorties were made to establish a centre of operations in southern Angola, was reported fully to SIS by the FSIOs in Pretoria.

Of Simonstown's strategic importance to Britain, as a maritime state if no longer a naval power, there could be no doubt. The decision to end the agreement was not only Wilson's characteristically coded concession to what may be loosely called his left wing, albeit one which included the Cabinet Minister responsible for buying Namibia's uranium. Such a concession also reflected both waning powers and disillusionment (Wilson was to resign in April 1976, having been Prime Minister, on and off, for eight years), and a growing, if unacknowledged awareness that Britain's capacity for independent action in Southern Africa – or anywhere else – was rapidly disappearing. Pressure from the Commonwealth and the United Nations for Britain to be seen to be doing something to oppose South Africa – and remain committed to defeating the Rhodesian rebellion – may be advanced as an excuse for ending the Simonstown Agreement, but it is not one which convinces for a moment. Ending the agreement (in 1975) put no British pressure on South Africa; it merely increased the South African Government's determination to extend its strategic horizons and develop an arms industry – prospectively in concert with the United States and the 'ABC' countries, Argentina, Brazil and Chile. When Kissinger first met Vorster on 23 June 1976 they discussed Namibia and South Africa's regional role, on land and sea. The two politicians did not talk much about Rhodesia, to them a relatively minor issue.

By another paradox, but one which is far more apparent than real, British gestures against South Africa in the mid-1970s served only to strengthen the latter's capacity to arbitrate issues in Southern Africa as a whole. But, in any case, even if the gestures were not futile, they disguised – all too successfully for some – the probes which James Callaghan (Wilson's Foreign Secretary) was making in 1975 and the early months of 1976 with the objective of persuading moderate African opinion to accept a formula for majority rule in Rhodesia.[1] The formula, which was privately accepted by Muzorewa – henceforth the principal recipient of British favours – was that which, in all essentials, Henry Kissinger presented to Ian Smith in September 1976.

The preceding March, Smith had rejected the formula, stating afterwards that 'not in a thousand years' would he accept majority rule. Smith's talks with Nkomo, on much the same formula as Callaghan's, broke down on 19 March. Callaghan's formula was openly presented only three days later. It is one thing, however, to reject an offer from a Government which lacks power of implementation, and another to accept one from an Administration which has. It must not be forgotten that if Smith had been unwise enough to reject 'the Anglo-American proposals' – as financially underwritten by the US Treasury and strategically backed by South Africa – he would have been abandoned by

Vorster. There were others in Rhodesia besides Smith who knew where their country's military power came from, and knew also that 50 per cent of Rhodesia's defence bill was paid by South Africa. After a major RSF operation in Mozambique during August, Smith had been crudely reminded of these facts.

Throughout 1975 Callaghan had spoken of Rhodesia as 'a matter of honour, of Britain redeeming its promises'.[2] Once he became Prime Minister, he adopted a less hyperbolic tone. His successor at the Foreign Office, Anthony Crosland, avoided hyperbole altogether. Although the result of Kissinger's April exchanges with Crosland before he set off on his African journeys 'bore the clear imprint of British policy',[3] it was also made plain that 'the Government's approach to the problem of Rhodesia was understandably cautious'. The caution is understandable, but for a better grasp of why it was so one must consider some of the tactical problems which faced Kissinger as he prepared to conciliate black presidents and white power at virtually one and the same time.

Callaghan and Kissinger enjoyed each other's company – and guile; Crosland enjoyed the guile, but did not appreciate its effects. The new Foreign Secretary may have liked Kissinger's constructive ambiguity as an exercise in versatility, but although inexperienced in diplomacy he temperamentally disliked guile when it reached the point where confusion resulted. Yet Crosland had no choice but to act as Kissinger's confederate in a policy which was designed to offer black nationalism the appearance of power whilst preserving the reality of it for Rhodesia's whites. Crosland had not wanted to become Foreign Secretary, despite the post's Cabinet seniority. An unusually serious and clear-sighted politician, with an intellect considerably more powerful than Kissinger's, Crosland concealed a rather sombre perception of power behind an elegant demeanour and a consistent detachment from Prime Minister and colleagues in Cabinet.

What, in effect, Kissinger had to do was offer Smith a deal which African states would also accept, subsequently putting pressure on the nationalists whom they backed to do the same. The Front Line States (Angola, Botswana, Mozambique, Tanzania and Zambia), a loose coalition of states determined not to accept UDI, needed to be convinced that Kissinger had changed Smith's outlook. Kissinger had to be guileful – up to a point.

193

Whether he went beyond that point must be a matter of opinion. Despite all that has been written on this period and these participants, the only substantial difference between the British Cabinet and the American Secretary of State was Ian Smith. Callaghan and his colleagues wanted to see the back of a man who had consistently out-manœuvred British Governments. Kissinger merely saw Smith as a piece on the South African chessboard. Crosland, a newcomer to Rhodesia, was mainly anxious to get a move on. If Kissinger could succeed with Smith where Callaghan had failed, well and good. But Crosland had no illusions about the fact that this apparent success might well be vitiated once Africans realised what they had accepted. Crosland kept his doubts to himself and only ensured that he would not become politically lost in the Rhodesian maze.

Kissinger, therefore, departed on his first African visit with a brief which encapsulated British policy over Rhodesia: get acceptance of majority rule from Smith; with this in your pocket get the co-operation of the Front Line States' Presidents, and specifically Nyerere and Kaunda, so that through them, a black leader will emerge who is willing to accept that majority rule – in a short space of time – and power are not the same. Lest this policy be thought either cynical or futile, it should be stressed that there was a fairly widespread belief in Whitehall that if Smith could be persuaded to accept majority rule much else would follow. Acceptance of majority rule was seen as a catalyst, changing all existing elements in the situation, possibly producing a cease-fire and some kind of power-sharing formula. All was negotiable – except ZANU's terms for surrender of white power. Machel, who articulated Mugabe's thoughts, said of the Anglo-American proposals: 'You see in Zimbabwe today we have an armed struggle, that is the secondary school. When it becomes a revolutionary struggle, that is the University, and Dr Kissinger is coming to close the University before they can get there.'[4]

Whitehall's suppositions not only rejected Mugabe – who was not susceptible to Kaunda's blandishments, and would not be subjected to Nyerere's – but assumed that Vorster was so anxious to knock some compromise into Smith that he would support a policy which might lead to 'power-sharing' in Rhodesia. But by the time Kissinger reached Pretoria in September he had experienced two long sessions with Vorster which, although conducted in the somewhat improbable venues of Bordenmais (Bavaria) and Zurich, left him in no doubt that the South African Government had a clear and consistent perception both of its Southern African strategy in general and its Rhodesian one in particular. Moreover, although Kissinger's reputation had preceded him to Africa, his country's failure (in South African eyes) to stick to the Angolan breakaway leaders Holden Roberto and Jonas Savimbi virtually forced Vorster to demand what were the extents and limits of American concessions to black aspirations. It was one thing for Vorster to exercise *détente* on Kaunda; as has been well said – and attributed to Kissinger – 'When you have them by the balls their hearts and minds follow.' But Kissinger represented a country which consistently declared its detestation of apartheid, and also supported black aspirations when they did not conflict with American interests. Kissinger, arriving in Lusaka on 27 April, had, *inter alia*, called for black majority rule in Rhodesia; some mistakenly drew the inference that majority rule meant black power. Five months later in Pretoria, on 19 September, face to face with Smith, Kissinger turned that call into an ostensibly realistic offer no sane white Rhodesian could refuse.

This rather fundamental *démarche* was, of course, the 'Anglo-American proposals' in terms, but the concessions to Smith – specifically the addition of 'responsible' to 'majority rule' – reflected Vorster's insistence on relating Rhodesia to other Southern African issues. There was one place where the United States and South Africa could agree – or clash: Namibia. The overall strategic and economic importance of this formerly mandated territory (which the Union of South Africa had occupied and the Republic had then dominated with tacit American approval) hardly needed to be stressed by Vorster when he first met Kissinger. But stress was nevertheless laid on the fact that although America's need for uranium had diminished, Namibia's overall mineral resources, together with its geographical place in Southern Africa, imposed on Washington and Pretoria the absolute necessity to think and act as one.[5]

If Kissinger offered black nationalists genuine majority rule for Rhodesia, comparable demands would be made elsewhere, above all in Namibia. The Callaghan formula suggested that majority rule would be only a façade, but Vorster needed to be sure that Kissinger would not allow it to become a reality. The importance of the meetings in Bordenmais and Zurich lay quite simply in the fact that *Vorster* shaped the course of ostensibly Anglo-American diplomacy. The fruits, the extremely sour fruits, of these exchanges between two hard men were not to be tasted until, in 1978 and 1979, Cyrus Vance and David Owen tried to sweeten the UN's stance on Namibia, supported by the covert presentation of a formula which, as elsewhere, would have left real power effectively in white hands. But the seeds of an understanding between Washington, Pretoria – and London – were sown in that agreeable Bavarian location of Bordenmais.

The events of 1976, culminating with the farce of a conference on Rhodesia in, of all places, Geneva, can be best perceived therefore as a continuation of Vorster's 'beyond the laager' *détente* exercise, one developed with active British and American support. South Africa provided the framework in which offers were made and a farce performed. The framework was strengthened and extended to the point where the Owen-Vance initiatives which made the diplomatic news from early in 1977 onwards were essentially a response to the facts of South Africa's power. The initiative was also weakened by the unadmitted fact that the British Government wanted a settlement in Rhodesia whilst the 'born again' President Carter hoped to preside at the restoration of human rights.

Immediately after Smith's acceptance of the Anglo-American South African proposals he reported to the regime in terms which justified his public statement in Salisbury on 24 September that 'further changes are not negotiable'.[6] There is no doubt of the shock which white Rhodesians felt when they discovered that 'good old Smithy' had shrunk 'not in a thousand years' to two years in a matter of seven months. But within days, and aided by continued success in breaking up guerrilla groups in the eastern operational areas, most Rhodesians adjusted to what appeared another of good old Smithy's slim escapes from South Africa's clasp and the odious interference of London and Washington. By the mid-1970s a mood, hard to define or describe, had gripped white Rhodesia. Net emigration could no longer be disguised; the economy was beginning to crack, not only from the effects of emigration and call-up, but as the world slid into 'recession'.

In Rhodesia '1976 was a record year for bankruptcies',[7] an unsurprising fact for a country whose citizen-manned armed forces had increased by 60 per cent in two years, but a sign of the times none the less. Although Machel's closure of the Mozambique-Rhodesia border on 3 March 1976 was matched by greater use of the Beitbridge rail link with South Africa, this switch of import and export routes only underlined the Smith regime's dependence on Vorster and his Ministers. Yet although several of Smith's colleagues to left and right were restive, the average white Rhodesian continued to live as though slaughtering 'terrs' was some kind of safari. As Smith became himself again after the trying but encouraging weekend in Pretoria he turned increasingly for comfort and reassurance to his 'Foreign Minister', P. K. Van der Byl. The latter, all too frequently in these years seen stalking in and out of the Cavalry Club in Piccadilly, provided Smith with psychological support. Van der Byl's remarks about 'kaffirs' matched Skeen's on the eve of UDI. When Smith and Van der Byl met Mugabe in Geneva even the most hardened commentator found it difficult to stomach Smith's contempt and Van der Byl's loathing for the one African they could not buy or propitiate.

Kissinger made it clear to Callaghan and Crosland as he passed through London on the way back to Washington that his job was done. The majority rule offer had been accepted by Smith; it had apparently been accepted by the Front Line States. Now the great man had other work to do – or not, if President Ford lost the November presidential election. What the British Government must do was to convene a conference at which parties concerned in a Rhodesian settlement would fix the details and put flesh on the bones of the Pretoria proposals. The Foreign Office which, after Kissinger's meetings had, with unconscious irony, called Smith's acceptance of the offer 'a victory for realism and common sense'[8] began to see that an enormous toad lay under the stone so deftly placed by the departing Secretary of State.

Whitehall's detestation of Smith did not blind its members (by 1976) to wry acceptance of his peculiar talents. The Foreign

Office collectively knew what Smith meant about 'no further changes'. A conference attended by an intransigent Smith and the savagely divided Africans who opposed, and fought, him would be a hopeless affair. Such a conference, with the British Foreign Secretary as Chairman, would put the British Government in the African dock, would see that tedious jury of UN and Commonwealth once again indulging in jaundiced reactions to displays of impotence. For some years, and despite the enormous amount of time which Whitehall had given to Rhodesia since UDI, British Governments had managed to stay in the background. Throughout much of 1976 Dr Kissinger had taken charge. Now he had gone to fresh fields of endeavour, leaving Britain to reconcile the probably irreconcilable.

The Front Line States' meeting in Dar es Salaam on 6 September had been studied with painful care in London. Whilst Kissinger, the *deus ex machina*, had descended on Africa, junior Foreign Office Ministers and other emissaries had done their best to assist in the process of softening up – or bamboozling – African Presidents whose support for Nkomo and Mugabe governed how the war in Rhodesia was fought. By 1976 Nkomo's ZAPU and ZIPRA were irrelevant to the war as such but remained an unavoidable element in any common front against Smith. Muzorewa, finally sundered from Nkomo, was thought, correctly, to have a following only in Rhodesia itself. Neither Nkomo nor Mugabe realised that Muzorewa was now the wild card which London, however reluctantly, hoped to play. From October 1975 Kaunda had begun to hedge his bets between Nkomo and Muzorewa; the Lusaka bellwether had been turned into an oracle by men in Whitehall determined to keep Mugabe out of the running. If the two antagonists, soon to become protagonists, had known about these ploys Nkomo would have been furious, Mugabe indifferent. In truth, of the three only Mugabe saw the issue clearly: 'What is required is the total destruction of Smith's army and its immediate replacement by ZANU forces ... we shouldn't worry about the Kissinger–British proposals. They can put in any puppet Government they want, but a puppet Government cannot contain us.'[9]

Nyerere took Mugabe's points, but also saw too much of the wider picture to accept ZANU and ZANLA as the only pieces on the board. Nyerere's habit of cryptic, occasionally tart asides suggests he suspected that Muzorewa, 'his little Bishop', might do a deal with Smith and cash in on the 'Kissinger-British' proposals. The purpose of the meeting in Dar es Salaam was to form a united front so that the proposals would be made genuinely acceptable if hardly palatable to African nationalism as a whole. Nyerere, who rarely bothered himself with details, also put some faith in the catalytic effect of 'majority rule in two years' so eagerly advanced by the Foreign Office. If Nkomo and Mugabe could form a front, to contest the details rather than the principle of a Rhodesian settlement on the basis of majority rule, much might develop. Like all his front-line colleagues Nyerere never wavered in his support for a genuinely independent Zimbabwe. But, like all of them, he was utterly sick of the war and hardly less so of the endless quarrels between men who should have shared a common cause.

When, however, the Kissinger deal became public, Nyerere and Kaunda realised they had been deceived. 'Majority rule' was seen to be no more than a formula for denying power to black nationalism. Meeting in Lusaka on 25 September the Front Line States' Presidents protested at the deal. But they did not utterly reject it, a concession to compromise which gained no plaudits from London. For, as has been well said 'Kissinger had made it impossible for any black African leader to refuse to assist in the American endeavour to bring about majority rule.'[10] The Presidents were caught in a dilemma partly of their own making. Something more concrete than protest was needed if Smith was not to escape yet again. The Lusaka meeting produced, on 9 October, the Patriotic Front, whereby Nkomo and Mugabe pledged themselves to a united stand in any negotiations with Ian Smith.

The received version of events has it that the PF pledged opposition to the proposals as they stood – or, to put the matters in terms, so far as agreed versions of them had been published. Certainly PF spokesmen were able to indulge in their penchant for rhetoric. But the PF decided to attend a conference under British chairmanship, and one can hardly suppose that hard-pressed men would traipse off to what has been well called 'one of the most expensive cities in the world'[11] for the doubtful pleasure of demonstrating *their* intransigence. As a matter of fact, it was Muzorewa who spoke out most vehemently against the proposals at the Geneva conference. This is hardly surprising. Muzorewa was about to climb into bed with Ian Smith: a note of defiance sounded better than one of mere protest.

Not much imagination is needed, therefore, to understand why the Geneva conference (28 October to adjournment on 14 December) was a farce. The venue was absurd – the British Government could not distance itself from the issues by finding a fancy location. The participants had no common ground, however much Nkomo and Muzorewa were privately, and separately, willing to accept the proposals as they stood. Smith, in the eyes of most of his supporters, had conceded quite enough. A conference could only settle details ambiguously formulated in the offer made to him in Pretoria. Mugabe came to learn, to be insulted by Smith, to be supported by Nhongo and Tongogara, whom Kaunda released from prison for the occasion. The conference was a farce because Callaghan, Kissinger and Vorster had been too clever. As has also been well said: 'Although he [Kissinger] had achieved the "conceptual breakthrough" by ignoring the complexities of the conflict he ensured the eventual failure of the mission.'[12]

But perhaps above all other factors the conference was a farce because Britain's Foreign Secretary did not take the Chair. Crosland's refusal to become deeply involved in Rhodesia is understandable, all the more so as he was supported by Callaghan and the Cabinet. But Crosland's refusal of responsibility is inexcusable; all the excuses which were made for limited involvement, ranging from the demands of the 'Cod War' with Iceland to attendance on the Queen during her 'Centennial' visit to the United States, only reveal the depths to which a British Government had sunk in its refusal to take up the black man's burden. It seems not to have occurred to those advising Crosland that even hardened operators like Nyerere retained some faith in Britain, some belief in the words as well as the actions of the British Government. Crosland's refusal to attend the Geneva conference marks the nadir of British policy over Rhodesia.

In Crosland's place went Ivor Richard, Britain's Ambassador to the United Nations. There, the large, affable Richard was a perfectly acceptable representative of a former colonial power.

But Richard was unconvincing in any role but that of Government spokesman. The idea of this former Junior Minister successfully imposing his will even on the conduct let alone the substance of a conference comprising incompatible, nay warring figures, revealed as few other factors could the real intentions of James Callaghan and his Cabinet. It would be too much to say that once Mugabe and Tongogara had stated their case in Geneva Callaghan was resigned to failure. But success, either for acceptance of the proposals *tout court* or for compromise on details, would have imposed responsibilities on the British Government which, unilaterally, Callaghan had no intention of incurring or executing. Callaghan was determined to have American support, somewhere and somehow, for resolving the Rhodesian issue. No such support was possible during or in the immediate aftermath of an American presidential election.

The Geneva farce thus led, by an inexorable logic once the rhetorically idealistic Jimmy Carter replaced Gerald Ford in the White House, to a situation where the 'Anglo-American' proposals were revived. But revival reflected a Southern African, not a Rhodesian, situation, one which the South African Government arbitrated, and in which Britain and the United States played subordinate parts. Revival also masked the evolution of a trade on Namibia and Rhodesia which, by comparison, reduced the Kissinger exercise of 1976 to a mere display of wheeling and dealing. With the collapse of the Geneva conference after all participants had said their piece, re-stated their positions, and retired to fight or intrigue, the stage was cleared for serious business: Vorster's South Africa playing the dominant role in a drama which provided Carter's Secretary of State and Britain's Foreign Secretary with little more than walk-on parts. The centre of the stage was occupied by Namibia. Backstage Ian Smith and Abel Muzorewa concluded a little theatrical business, interrupted but never halted by the Anglo-American 'initiative'. In the meantime, the war dragged on. Mugabe was the only African nationalist who gained from Geneva. He had become *primus inter pares* with Nkomo. In the process he had realised that the man he had to beat was Abel Muzorewa. This discovery was significantly to affect ZANU strategy throughout the length and breadth of Rhodesia in the years to come.

17

1977: Anglo-American Initiatives and the 'Internal Settlement'

The Geneva conference had one decisive effect on events. Despite a palpable reluctance to become involved in direct, conference negotiations with the contestants, the British Government had been forced to return to the Rhodesian stage, there to play an humiliating role without the direct support of the United States. Callaghan was determined that this humiliation would not be repeated. When Carter became President in February 1977 and at once spoke up as a champion of the oppressed, an opportunity for reviving the Anglo-American approach to Rhodesia seemed to be on the cards. When Vice-President Mondale met Vorster in Vienna on 19 and 20 May 1977 he embarked on some very high-minded rhetoric. But the substance of the talks, as it had been with Vorster and Kissinger a year earlier, was Namibia.

Thus when Carter came out of the clouds and examined the Southern African terrain even he was forced to accept that any American initiative there would have to concentrate on Namibia.[1] The South African Government was, in any case, insistent that Namibia's future must be discussed with its American ally; a new, 'progressive' President presented challenges to a Government already sufficiently preoccupied by an incipient guerrilla war in Namibia, backed by Angola. Of equal concern to Pretoria was the fact that the United Nations was about to put Namibia high on its agenda. Carter had appointed a black, Andrew Young, as his Ambassador to the UN, and another, Donald McHenry, as his Deputy. These moves were not lost on Vorster. Yet it is doubtful if Vorster took Carter seriously. Asked about the new President the day following his election Vorster replied: 'It's a question of wondering rather than worrying.'[2]

The immediate, not the approximate effect of these shifts in American politics and the Southern African scene was that the Anglo-American initiative could not be confined to Rhodesia. Moreover, Britain's role was not merely subordinate to America's; Rhodesian affairs became subordinate to Namibian. It was too much to expect that Crosland's successor, the quite excessively self-confident 38-year-old David Owen, a young man in a hurry, would understand these realities until the Rhodesian 'initiative' had changed into an Anglo-American Southern African policy. But the realities were present from the outset of the initiative, and were to affect all that followed until Callaghan's Government was defeated in the General Election of May 1979. In the meantime the Rhodesian 'Internal Settlement' consummated the September 1976 agreement between Kissinger and Ian Smith. On 1 June 1979, following agreement with Smith in March 1978 that the latter should step down, Abel Muzorewa became 'Zimbabwe Rhodesia's' first – and last – black Premier.

After experiencing an election in which 'supporters' of the Internal Settlement were forced to the polls and opponents of it beaten up, Muzorewa found himself presiding over a Cabinet where all key portfolios were held by Smith's colleagues; Parliament reflected a 'constitution' whose blocking mechanisms included the adventitious addition of a second chamber Senate, empowered to entrench white power indefinitely. The RSF, police, and all other elements in the security structure remained in white hands. Not more than twenty Africans, for example, were commissioned army officers in a force which, at full mobilisation, numbered nearly 100,000, by 1979 predominantly black. Despite apparent land reform, none was undertaken. 'De-segregation' had been cosmetic. The war continued, unabated.

In considering the respective positions of the contending Southern African Governments, regimes, movements, factions – and individuals – the increasing problems of the Front Line States, and the unenviable equivocations of a British Government all too dependent on official advice and covert activities, something must be said of the Carter Administration as such. Once said, the strategy and tactics of Carter's extremely disingenuous Southern African policy, and its effect on Rhodesia, can be seen as consistent with what the United States had done in relation to the region since 1945, at least. We may as well begin with Mondale's formal statement after his May 1977 meeting with Vorster:

There has been a transformation in American society of which we are very proud. It affects not only our domestic life, but our foreign policy as well. We cannot accept, let alone defend, the governments that reject the basic principle of full human rights, economic opportunity and political participation for all its peoples regardless of race ... I made it clear [to Vorster] that without evident progress that provides full political participation and an end to discrimination, the pressure of international events would require us to take actions based on our policy and to the detriment of the constructive relations we would prefer with South Africa ... We hope that South Africa will review the implications of our policy and the changed circumstances which it creates. We hope that the South Africans will not rely on any illusions that the United States will in the end intervene to save South Africa from the policies it is pursuing, for we will not do so.[3]

Save for the stage army of the good, nobody in Britain would have come out with this sort of stuff, certainly not in 1977. But although the statement is simply flatulence, it cannot so easily be dismissed. Cyrus Vance, the new Secretary of State, chose to believe that Vorster was 'bitter'[4] about Mondale's words. This is unlikely. Kissinger had already pledged 'majority rule' for Rhodesia; 'one man, one vote', which Mondale declared to be the sense of his words, was merely another, and equally meaningless formula in relation to the real issue of who ran the country. Vorster could not possibly have supposed that Mondale intended the formula to apply to South Africa. The Government's position on what it called 'citizenship' was perfectly clear: no African had the vote, and no foreign power could give him one. So far as Namibia was concerned, Vorster and Mondale, as shortly became apparent, set in motion a method of determining the independence which left real power in South African hands. Finally, if

Mondale thought that Vorster cared a damn about 'human rights', the murder of Steve Biko on 12 September 1977, following a major police onslaught on African political movements, should have, belatedly, brought him to his senses.

Yet Mondale's words need analysis because they reflected a strain of moral conviction, not mere moralising, in the American public character of which, at the time, Jimmy Carter was only the most obvious expression. For Carter, 'South Africa was Georgia writ large.' Even the hard-headed trio of Young, McHenry and Richard Moose (Assistant Under-Secretary for African Affairs, and a veteran of the Mennen Williams years) was occasionally responsive to a high moral tone; the two blacks were, indeed, not unaware of the effect of their advent at the UN on opinion in the General Assembly and throughout the African continent. In McHenry's view, their appointment by Carter 'gave us a two year honeymoon with the Organisation of African Unity and the Front Line States'. Anthony Lake, whom Carter appointed to run the Policy Planning Department at Foggy Bottom, really did believe that fine words buttered parsnips, and reminded the President regularly of this great moral imperative. But Lake was the author of a book on the Byrd Amendment and related matters, and genuinely thought all would be different with a Democrat in the White House.

Carter came into office believing that he was to be a President who would not only disprove his predecessor's assertion that '*Détente* with the Soviet Union is dead',[5] but prove that the Kissinger doctrine of linkage was false. On these two points Carter was initially joined by Vance, who, in writing a personal pre-election appreciation for Carter in October 1976, argued that 'US/Soviet issues will not be permitted to dominate our foreign policy.' Vance had been Kennedy's Secretary of the Army and Deputy to McNamara under Johnson; he was the most experienced member of the new Administration. A Wall Street lawyer who affected the tweeds and style usually associated with East Coast Anglophiles, Vance was notably more relaxed about dealing with the Soviet Union – in Africa, or anywhere else – than Carter's totally unestablishment National Security Adviser, Zbigniew Brezinski. During the October 1962 Cuba missile crisis, Brezinski had advocated the bombing of these sites; he continued in this hawkish vein throughout succeeding years of very moderate academic distinction.

Brezinski, much disliked by many in the Carter team, was a xenophobe rather than a hawk. Suspicion of Russia was entirely understandable given his Polish origins, but coloured recommendations so darkly that Carter became assailed by two fundamentally conflicting sets of policy options. Brezinski, it is true, spared relatively little time for Southern Africa, apart from jibes at Britain's 'Foreign Ministers' and a jaundiced belief that Vance took 'an excessively benign view of Soviet and Cuban penetration'.[6] Nevertheless, conflict within the Administration imposed hard choices on Carter. He could either accept Vance's appreciation and deal with Southern Africa, and its component parts, *sui generis*, or he could follow Brezinski's line.

In practice, Carter followed the line all the way, but he covered this route to what his successor's advisers have called 'constructive engagement' with South Africa by the kind of rhetoric which Mondale produced after the Vienna meeting with Vorster. Over Rhodesia Carter spread a thicker cover, and more confusion, by identifying himself with the Patriotic Front. This identification concealed, for a time, his real intentions concerning Namibia; even Nyerere temporarily believed that Carter's declared support for the Front indicated comparable backing for the South-West Africa People's Organisation (SWAPO), led, more or less, by the exiled Sam Njomo. In the event, Carter succeeded only in ruining the 'Initiative' – neither Callaghan nor Owen accepted the Patriotic Front as parties to a settlement of the Rhodesian issue in any terms which included Robert Mugabe – and thereby complicated relations with Vorster and his successor P. W. Botha. Nor did Carter's apparent sympathy for SWAPO – expressed, in practice, by Young in the UN General Assembly – elicit support from Owen. In his view 'SWAPO was no bunch of angels'. If Owen had said Njomo and his lieutenants were incompetent he would have been nearer the mark.

Writing in mid-1982, retired from the cares of office, Vance rather blew this cover. 'We recognised that identifying the United States with the cause of majority rule was the best way to prevent Soviet and Cuban exploitation of Southern Africa.'[7] This was essentially the Mennen Williams formulation of the 1960s, 'majority rule' being merely an updated version of 'self-determination'. In the Kennedy and Johnson years, however, the Soviet penetration of Africa was both uncertain and unsuccessful, and no surrogate save the extremely unenthusiastic German Democratic Republic was available for the kind of covert operations which seem inseparable from a major power's attempts to influence matters in far-off countries of which they know little. By the mid-1970s much was changed. The Soviet Union was still uncertain and often unsuccessful in its penetration of Africa, but had established a presence, of sorts, in the Horn. Aid, of very variable quality and quantity, was provided for liberation movements and their armed forces. ZIPRA, for example, formed an armoured brigade; Soviet tanks, Soviet artillery. Varieties of missiles were also added to ZIPRA's order of battle. These toys served only to demonstrate that Nkomo and his colleagues had ceased to think in realistic terms about guerrilla war.

The Cubans in Angola, however, were another matter. Neither Kissinger's diplomatic sleight of hand in Pretoria nor the operations of the CIA in Angola had dislodged a foreign body whose military credibility was slight but whose capacity, simply in being Cuban, for inflaming American emotions must never be underestimated. Carter, for all his high-minded talk, was a stump politician who needed Congress. He needed a Congress whose collective suspicions about Fidel Castro and his expeditionary forces in Africa not only mirrored much in middle America, but whose overall attitude to the Soviet Union was, by 1977, not far short of Gerald Ford's. *Détente* was dying, if not dead, because America was not the self-confident country of the 1960s. Vietnam and Watergate took a toll whose side effects included an awfully muddled set of notions inside President Carter's head as to what was actually happening in Southern Africa. The President's perceptions were not strengthened by the activities of Congressmen and pressure groups who were actively sympathetic to John Vorster and Ian Smith.

Fortunately for the maintenance of some kind of balance in the conduct of the Administration's Southern African policy, McHenry and Moose were a pair of professionals who could utilise intelligence about what was actually happening on the ground. United States intelligence operations in Southern Africa had been characterised in the 1960s by optimism over Mozambique and in the 1970s by half-hearted support of anti-Government forces in independent Angola. Elsewhere, South Africa told its own tale; Rhodesia was low priority. From the time of Carter's election, and not coincidentally, the State Department, seeking in any case to exercise some better late than never control over the CIA, started to concentrate on the acquisition of reliable raw intelligence about the situation in Rhodesia, and the revision of some long-held American beliefs about the West's economic dependence on South Africa.

This is not the place for a disquisition on relations between the State Department and the CIA; the latter's well-established role until the Carter years, as a kind of alternative Government, subject to few presidential or congressional restraints; or the serious disagreements within the Agency between those who argued that acquiring intelligence should take priority and those who asserted that a combination of counter-intelligence (or penetration) and patently hostile if ostensibly covert operations best served America's interests. But the growing congressional concern with the CIA's activities in the aftermath of Vietnam and Watergate is relevant to any account of Southern Africa in the mid-1970s. Something of an upheaval occurred in the Agency at this time. One effect was that Station Officers and their agents in Southern Africa, together with the Defence Department's Military Liaison Officers, concentrated on acquisition rather than penetration. These operations were co-ordinated with US diplomatic missions and the State Department, whose Bureau of Intelligence and Research had for long provided reliable material on political and economic matters. Early in 1978 a US 'liaison office' was established in Salisbury, not in recognition of the impending 'Internal Settlement' by the US Administration but as an indication that events in Southern Africa were reaching the stage where a definable American presence on the ground in Rhodesia was deemed essential.

Moose and, by extension, McHenry were thus provided with good raw intelligence on what was actually happening in Rhodesia and South Africa, and came to firm conclusions and recommendations as a result. Mugabe's wing of the Patriotic

Front would attain in measurable time its twin objectives of defeating the RSF in a guerrilla war of attrition, and of politicising for its own ends Africans in the eastern operational areas. It was, therefore, in the interests of the United States, if not the Anglo-American 'initiative', to regard Smith's (and Muzorewa's) Rhodesia as expendable. South Africa's raw materials, with the exception of chrome and chromite, were no longer 'strategically vital' to the United States. Moreover, in the United States, uranium oxide had been stockpiled, as had precious metals for periods considered long enough to force South Africa to its economic knees.[8] Congressmen like Jesse Helms (accepted as powerful in his North Carolina fief but thought to be insignificant internationally), who spoke up for Smith and Vorster as champions of Christian civilisation and gallant opponents of godless communism, should be put firmly in their place. This intelligence assessment was, as we shall see, largely ignored or rejected, but the fact must be recorded that Carter and Vance were provided with it.

Callaghan and Owen were not so provided. Cledwyn Hughes, an old colleague of Callaghan's with a long experience of fruitless missions to Smith, remarked at the time that 'we had to rely a great deal on our advisers'. This gnomic utterance reflects not so much the truth that British Governments are greatly dependent on Whitehall and overseas missions in the formulation and execution of foreign policy as the fact that over Rhodesia they simply had to listen to the experts. Unfortunately, the expertise was vitiated not only by an enormous collective Whitehall wish to be shot of Rhodesia, but by lack of reliable raw intelligence about the situation there. Both MI5 and SI5 perforce relied on agents whose intelligence was distorted by their prejudices if white and the desire to produce something if black. The net result was low grade, unreliable material. Both MI5 and SI5 additionally chose to rely also on the CIO. Obviously no liaison as such could be maintained with the intelligence service of a rebel regime. History must also record, however, that Kenneth Flower, the CIO's Director-General, was as frequently in London during these years as Pieter Van der Byl. After the collapse of the 1976 Geneva conference, both men marked their card for Muzorewa. Whitehall did the same.

The British Government's intention to play the Muzorewa card has been noted in connection with the mish-mash of views and fears which characterised all preliminaries to the Geneva conference. Yet hopes were retained in London and in Kaunda's Lusaka that Nkomo could still play some role in reaching a settlement of the Rhodesia issue by the expedient of including all interested parties save Mugabe in negotiations. The logic of the 'Kissinger–British' proposals (as Mugabe so neatly defined them) led to a Geneva conference in which only ZANU and ZANLA revealed effective intransigence. Neither the ANC nor 'The Bishop' had an army; ZIPRA, by 1976, had become an incubus to Kaunda and a joke to the RSF. A guerrilla army which sits in barracks and messes its officers apart from their men is not a serious fighting proposition.

By extension, and after the advent of a US Administration trapped by its rhetoric into a continued search for settlement, an 'all-party' approach was widely seen as one which excluded those who demanded sole power and repudiated power sharing. Even Nyerere, as the most experienced and articulate of the Front Line States' Presidents, was driven to concede that the issue of who should control independent Rhodesia's (or Zimbabwe's) security forces might need compromise at some point. Nyerere had little time for Nkomo, but he saw quite clearly that if ZAPU accepted joint control of an independent Rhodesia's armed forces Mugabe might be isolated.

It is in this context of who controlled what in the Rhodesian security forces' structure that Nyerere's August 1977 visit to Carter in Washington should be seen. The visit was a more important event in the leapfrog of 'initiatives' and the 'Internal Settlement' than Owen's and Vance's activities, and is also one which must be considered in the wider Southern African context. In the early months of 1977 Nyerere had watched Owen enter the fray with characteristic assurance and also, one must admit, with a verve long absent from the conduct of Britain's Rhodesian and South African policies. Owen fully shared Callaghan's insistence on an Anglo-American initiative or none; indeed, Owen was so strongly pro-American in his entire approach that it took him some time to realise that Vance's amiable assent to his various propositions was not necessarily reflected in the acts of a

President whose rhetoric was a façade for domestic political calculation.

Callaghan and Owen paid the then customary visit to an incumbent President in March 1977. Carter was set to repeal the Byrd Amendment; the time seemed propitious for floating a plan which appealed to Callaghan and Owen because it would further dilute British responsibilities.[9] Smith was already known to be developing his own, post-Geneva notion of a settlement, one based on 'majority rule' – but also grounded in continued Rhodesian control of the security forces. Should Smith succeed, using Muzorewa and Nkomo, singly or in rivalry, and with such figures from the immediate or recent past as Sithole and Chikerema available as bargaining counters, political opinion in Britain and in the United States might demand acceptance of so seemingly reasonable a solution. But Owen knew that such a settlement would not only be rejected by the Front Line States but by the United Nations and the Commonwealth. Nyerere had not neglected his peers in this most cumbrous yet symbolically potent organisation. A reliable source noted at the time that Commonwealth opinion, so far as it could be given substance and form, had shifted 'towards approval of the guerrilla campaign'.[10] In plain English these words indicated approval of the intransigent Mugabe, not the malleable Nkomo.

Owen hoped to bridge the gap – between an embattled Smith and a Patriotic Front supposedly united in its rejection of the 'Kissinger-British' proposals – by devising an interim British administration for Rhodesia. For a period of six months or so a 'Resident Commissioner' would assume absolute power in the colony, during which time all parties anxious for a cease-fire and reconciliation, a return to legality as the essential preliminary to the grant of independence, and participation in a constitutional conference, would seek a solution to the crucial security forces issue by relying on an outside armed force to keep the peace. An 'international force', a UN force, or a Commonwealth force (Owen was always vague on details of composition) would inject a neutral, objective element into Rhodesia's ravaged, racially riven society. Six months' relative calm might, in Owen's view, enable compromise to be reached on the security forces issue.

Elements of both the RSF and ZANLA/ZIPRA could, perhaps, form the basis of a new, multi-racial army.

That a 'monitoring force' did, in December 1979, deploy throughout Rhodesia is less a tribute to Owen's foresight (although he should be given credit for genuine initiative) than a reflection of the fact that a further extension of Anglo-American endeavours led to the Commonwealth's belated but comprehensive involvement in an issue where British Governments had always, and understandably, tried to placate the whites and mollify the blacks. In March 1977, however, Owen hoped that the new idea of interim British administration and an impartial 'peace-keeping' force would, when backed by the United States, bring all but Mugabe to the negotiating table. A successful result would be an independent Rhodesia (or Zimbabwe); a Commonwealth member; a state with 'majority rule' – and hence a black Government, of sorts. The levers of power – the security forces, the Civil Service, the economy – might perhaps be pulled by black hands but they would be firmly guided by white ones. At no time in his two years as Foreign Secretary did Owen envisage, believe in, or support an independent Zimbabwe whose armed forces would be based on and primarily composed of ZANLA and ZIPRA.

There were four reasons why Owen failed, and indeed had failed by mid-summer 1977 so comprehensively in pushing the idea as it stood that an experienced chronicler of these events is constrained to say: 'It was probably from this point (July 1977) that the Anglo-American initiative was doomed.'[11] At the time Nkomo could neither be severed nor even divided from Mugabe in any terms which offered him a place in the scheme of things. Secondly, Smith opposed any further concessions, as he saw them, to what had been agreed with Kissinger, and was hostile to the notion of an interim British administration. Smith's opposition to British proposals was always aggravated by class consciousness. He took particular exception to the idea of a retired Chief of the Defence Staff (Field-Marshal Lord Carver) being appointed Resident Commissioner. This was a unilateral act which Owen could painlessly perform and Carver public spiritedly accept. But it may be noted as an example of human cussedness if in matters of life and death that Carver caused much annoyance to Smith by turning up at New Sarum airport in uniform (at intervals throughout 1977 and 1978), a clumsy reminder that the latter saw the former not only as a rebel but one to be taught a lesson. Carver's erstwhile colleague and commander designate of the 'international force', the diplomatically experienced Indian General Prem Chand, wisely reflected realities by accompanying him *en civil*.

Smith's intransigence was fortified by winning a General Election (31 August 1977) whose campaign was, necessarily, devoted to the issue of finally settling Rhodesia's affairs on the basis of 'majority rule', but internally, without outside interference. But this second reason why the Owen idea was doomed from the outset gained strength from Vorster's declared opposition at the time, and subsequently, to any negotiations which diluted white control of Rhodesia's security forces. Vorster not only made his views clear to Owen and Vance; he pressed them on Carter. In doing so Vorster reminded all concerned of South Africa's power to arbitrate the region's affairs. By doing so he enabled those concerned to see, if not necessarily in every case to appreciate or accept, that the fourth reason why Owen's Rhodesia failed was Carter's refusal to force it through against South African opposition when he was primarily concerned to do a deal with Vorster on Namibia.

On 2 July Vance, speaking to, of all audiences, the National Association for the Advancement of Coloured People in St Louis, said, 'We cannot impose solutions in Southern Africa. We cannot dictate terms to any of the parties; our leverage is limited.' This statement was certainly coded. Considerable leverage was available to Carter if he had chosen to use it. Restriction of American capital investment in South Africa; a vigorous effort to plug the holes in the official arms embargo; ending intelligence liaison. South Africa, not the United States, would have suffered if Carter had matched his deeds to Mondale's words. Such leverage would not have changed South Africa's internal policies, but could well have given negotiations over Namibia an overdue element of reality. The South African Government had no intention of finally relinquishing control of the territory but, given growing strains on SADF formations committed there, could possibly have taken a less intransigent – or disingenuous – line when, in

August 1978, the Security Council produced a report which recommended independence elections under UN supervision. But by October 1978 Carter was writing personally to P.W. Botha in terms which emphasised that 'the United States wanted to have "normal" relations with South Africa ... the tone of the language used was a far cry from that of the Administration at the Vienna meeting between Vice-President Mondale and Prime Minister Vorster eighteen months earlier.'[12]

In observing the leapfrog of these two years it is essential to realise that Owen's and Vance's periodic visits to Dar es Salaam, Lusaka and Salisbury were not only preliminary but subordinate to arriving in Pretoria for discussions about Namibia. A cynic would say that Vance came along for the first stage of the ride to ensure that Owen accompanied him on the second, the important stage. But there is truth here. Carter did not need Callaghan over Namibia as Callaghan needed him over Rhodesia. But Carter needed to secure wide support outside the United States for a deal with South Africa over Namibia. Chronology is important in this connection. The UN had been discussing Namibia for many years; but from the time Kissinger first met Vorster early in 1976, it was United States policy to pre-empt the UN in its more ambitious plans for the formerly mandated territory by constructing the basis of a deal remarkably akin to that which Owen eventually proposed for Rhodesia.[13]

When Callaghan and Owen arrived in Washington during March 1977 they found that Namibia, not Rhodesia, was Carter's Southern African priority. There and then was born the idea of a five-nation 'Contact Group' on Namibia (the United States, Britain, Canada, France and the Federal German Republic), whose unavowed purpose was to ride herd on a United Nations General Assembly which, at intervals in the late 1960s and early 1970s, had declared SWAPO 'the sole authentic representative of the Namibian people pending independence and elections'.[14] South African Governments totally rejected this opinion; fought SWAPO's military force PLAN (People's Liberation Army of Namibia) ruthlessly and effectively by attacking its Angolan bases at will; and, from the time of the 'Turnhalle' Conference in Windhoek during August 1976, set in train a process markedly similar to Smith's 'Internal Settlement'.

The March 1977 meetings in Washington must be seen as a process whereby Owen tried to pre-empt Smith before the latter's 'Internal Settlement' became a virtual *fait accompli*; where Carter and Vance hedged their bets on the 'Anglo-American' initiative for Rhodesia even before opposition to it – in the terms of Owen's idea – coalesced and hardened; and where President and Secretary of State, putting Namibia first, sought British support for a scheme which would bridge the gap between UN-backed, SWAPO-dominated independence and an 'Internal Settlement' which would meet South Africa's assorted needs – but whose acceptance by the United States would destroy Carter's credibility as champion of human rights. Carter's support for these rights was a bit like Gladstone's over the Bulgarian Agitations in 1876 – fervent condemnation of Turkish atrocities but continued backing of the Sublime Porte. The Contact Group was the machinery for Carter's deal with Vorster over the future of a territory where, although apartheid was not practised so rigorously as in the Republic, Africans were not even second-class citizens. They were the helots, and the 'Turnhalle' Conference, dominated by the white 'South-Westers' and attended by acquiescent tribal leaders who feared SWAPO's Ovambo-dominated objectives, intended that they should remain so. The 'Contact Group's' function was, like the Anglo-American 'initiative' over Rhodesia, to bridge gaps between two entrenched positions.

Nyerere watched these manœuvres with growing concern. Tanzania's immunity from attack by South Africa or Rhodesia (although Smith never entirely rejected this option) enabled Nyerere to look ahead. This was a privilege denied his harassed or embattled colleagues amongst the Front Line States. They could only react to events and, increasingly, bend to South Africa's will. Nyerere, from his Dar es Salaam eyrie, saw that even a British Labour Government might come close enough to accepting a Rhodesian 'Internal Settlement' for a Conservative successor to do so entirely. Callaghan's Government only succeeded in retaining sanctions against Rhodesia by narrow majorities in the House of Commons. The elections in April 1979 from which Muzorewa, like a black rabbit from a white conjuror's hat, emerged as 'Zimbabwe-Rhodesia's' first black Premier – one at which, all too revealingly, 'There was no register of black voters'

– nevertheless had an effect which 'the British and American Governments could not ignore'.[15] Nyerere could look ahead, and was determined to render the 'Internal Settlement' null and void.

Nyerere was less directly concerned with Namibia – the hapless Kaunda was involuntary host to SWAPO's UN-backed 'Institutes', and Agostinho Neto in Luanda endured the unwelcome presence of PLAN – but commitment to a cause, pride and a certain belief in his persuasive powers took Nyerere to Washington in August 1977. His objective was to use those powers on that verbal idealist, Jimmy Carter. By August 1977 there had been much criss-crossing of the African continent by assorted luminaries. President Podgorny and Fidel Castro had been and gone, attracting more attention than Cyrus Vance and David Owen in their April journeys. Young was eloquent at the UN; McHenry embroiled in the Contact Group; the RSF continued to wreak havoc in Mozambique, the SADF in Angola. It was time for Nyerere to act.

Over Rhodesia, Nyerere succeeded – temporarily. Over Namibia Nyerere failed, completely. Carter 'accepted' that the PF (or Mugabe) determination to arbitrate the Rhodesian security forces issue was the key to an internationally recognised solution. But Carter performed this act of acceptance unaware of South African objections and indifferent to British rejection of Mugabe. Some would argue that Carter accepted the State Department's intelligence assessments about the RSF and ZANLA. But Carter's subsequent actions reveal no such acceptance; although the State Department's response to Muzorewa's apotheosis in March 1978 was 'adamant', and officials declared 'the Settlement is totally inadequate'[16] (an opinion which Vance appears personally to have shared), Carter was intermittently responsive to suggestions that Ian Smith's black rabbit could become a useful pet.

Despite the State Department's opposition to Muzorewa (as a natural loser), Vance writes that 'The President cautioned me and Andy Young neither to support nor reject outright the March 3 Agreement.'[17] On 14 March 1978 the United States and Britain abstained on a General Assembly Resolution condemning the 'Internal Settlement'. *Lifting* sanctions against Rhodesia was never far from Carter's mind; as the 1978 mid-term Congressional elections approached his further about-turn seemed not unlikely. Nyerere had tried to look ahead, especially as Mugabe had his own battles to fight. Carter's responses are understandable given his ignorance, but his August 1977 volte-face over the Patriotic Front – in reality Mugabe's ZANU – only complicated an issue which had already driven experienced men to distraction.

In effect, therefore, Nyerere overplayed his hand, persuaded Carter to a commitment which wrecked Owen's 'interim administration' proposals (published on 1 September), and did so even before opposition to them from Mugabe, Smith and Vorster had hardened. When Carter's private pledge to Nyerere was intercepted a few weeks later by those who badly needed to know its contents,

> it was understood to affirm that the new Zimbabwe National Army would be 'based on the liberation armies', a reference to the guerrilla forces under the command of Mr Mugabe and Mr Nkomo. The White Paper [Owen's, of 1 September] had used a carefully chosen and neutral form of words on this point – that the Zimbabwe Army would 'in due course replace all existing armed forces in Rhodesia', which left open the precise way in which the army of the future independent Zimbabwe should be formed.[18]

One must have some sympathy for Carter. When Nyerere, for example, insisted in Washington that Rhodesia's police should be under African control, the President immediately assented. Police were, after all – police. That the 'police' in question was the BSAP, Smith's praetorian guard, just would have escaped the notice of a President who, in any case, did have other, larger international issues to contend with.

The Carter–Nyerere accord, to give it more status perhaps than it deserves, virtually forced Owen during the following twelve months into a ploy which had rarely been absent from British thoughts but which had lost credibility: the use of Joshua Nkomo. In August 1977 Nkomo, with support from the usual British operators, met Ian Smith at Kaunda's State House; exactly a year later he repeated the exercise, once again by courtesy of MI5 – and the CIO. During that year, Smith and Muzorewa consummated the 'Internal Settlement', and all the further travels and travails of Owen and Vance to Dar es Salaam and points south proved to be no more than an ineffectual verbal protest at a situation which only Nyerere and Mugabe were prepared to contest. It was an article of faith with Whitehall that no negotiations, 'secret' or otherwise, could or would be held with Mugabe, alone. There was little enthusiasm for talks with the Patriotic Front, alone. But once Carter and Nyerere had precipitated the failure of Owen's proposals, Nkomo was given one more chance to perform the difficult act of isolating Mugabe by conciliating Smith.

Whitehall recognised that the breach between Nkomo and Muzorewa was complete so far as influence within Rhodesia and control of the ANC was concerned. Even low-grade agents could produce plenty of intelligence on that score. Indeed, the services of these agents were hardly required; rows between the two rivals for the white men's favours lost nothing in the telling. But what Whitehall needed was a bridge between the Smith–Muzorewa camp and that part of the Patriotic Front which saw some merit in accepting the 'Internal Settlement'. If Nkomo could bridge that gap, doubtless a place could be found for him in an independent Rhodesia – or Zimbabwe – which would be accepted by white men south of the Zambeze and only opposed by black men who could not compromise with force of circumstance.

Vance remarks of this period, in his usual Ivy League prose, that 'Owen had referred to a long-standing British interest in promoting an accommodation between Smith and Nkomo.'[19] 'Accommodation' is good, especially as Vance respected Moose's strong objection to both Muzorewa and Nkomo. ZAPU's leader was not a natural loser, but in the opinion of Americans on the ground he was, by 1977, a spent force. Nevertheless, Vance made no attempt to dissuade Owen from playing the Nkomo card yet again. When, in March 1978, the 'Internal Settlement' came about – after a futile conference arranged by Owen in Malta during February at which the two factions comprising the Patriotic Front were given a last chance to act in unison – Vance noted with a detachment comparable to his earlier comment: 'David Owen ... was increasingly drawn toward the idea of building upon the Internal Settlement.'[20]

A British observer puts the case in similar terms: 'In London,

David Owen was tempted to support it.'[21] In London, yes; in Dar es Salaam, no; In Lusaka, maybe; in Pretoria? Inside the laager the British Foreign Secretary, like the American Secretary of State, spoke softly, carrying no stick, large or small. 'David was deeply concerned with the interaction of the Rhodesia and Namibia negotiations. The contact group, he argued, should not push the Namibia negotiations with South Africa so hard that Pretoria withdrew from the process. If they did, the Western powers would have no means for avoiding sanctions and our strategy for dealing with the more urgent Rhodesian issue could be damaged.'[22] That seems about right – if one accepts that South Africa dealt its cards more shrewdly than Britain or the United States, and that Owen was, rather desperately, trying to keep the Rhodesian 'initiative' alive.

The Nkomo ploy failed because even a Rhodesia-weary White-hall could hardly succeed with Muzorewa *and* Nkomo, especially as, by the late 1970s, the latter had lost most of his credibility. He had tried to be all things to all men. A guerrilla war destroys the moderates. Muzorewa found his natural place as the white man's stooge; Mugabe's ZANLA fought on. There was no place for Nkomo to go. British political intelligence on Rhodesia was consistently inadequate. That it should be poor on Nkomo in person, who was resident in Lusaka and accessible at all times, must be put down to a combination of factors of which a kind of intellectual ennui about Rhodesia was not the least.

By March 1978 Owen and his advisers had few cards left. The 'Internal Settlement' was a fact, and although Nkomo was dealt again in August 1978, no hopes were entertained that he would turn up trumps. On 3 September ZIPRA shot down a Rhodesian Airlines Viscount with one of those ingenious Russian heat-seeking missiles. The survivors of the crash were massacred. Nkomo initially treated this particular tragedy as an episode in war. After that he *was* a spent force so far as a place in Owen's version of the 'Internal Settlement' might be found. In October Ian Smith, with Muzorewa in tow, visited the United States as the guest of assorted well-wishers and representatives of vested interests. Vance saw no reason to deny either the white survivor or the black *arriviste* a visa. One can see his point.

Owen's frustrations – and temptations – are aptly summarised in the views attributed to him by Vance. The United States was locked into Southern Africa because of Carter's rhetoric and, to a considerable extent, genuine anger in the United Nations at South Africa's policy over Namibia. But Britain remained trapped in the region because, in seeking American support for compromise over Rhodesia, it became involved in Namibia. American interest in Rhodesia rapidly cooled in 1978, even although the war there moved inexorably in favour of ZANLA. But American interest in Namibia increased; Owen found that he had become a junior partner in American policy, not the leader of 'Anglo-American' initiatives.

Britain's interest in Namibia was certainly strong, given Rio Tinto's uranium mine at Rossing, but it was essentially a reflection of the long-standing relationship with South Africa. No British Foreign Secretary or Whitehall official spoke or minuted, publicly or privately, about South Africa in relation to 'communism'. What had been agreed at intelligence conferences in the 1950s remained a reasoned assessment twenty years later: South Africa was important to Britain because it supplied vital materials, not because it was a barrier to communism. When Vance, unbuttoned, occasionally suggested to Owen that their two countries should consider sanctions against South Africa, the latter's reaction was a sharp and vehement protest. The United States could afford to make such gestures – they were never more than that; Britain could not. The economic and strategic imperatives of the 1950s also remained.

South Africa as a barrier to communism was, however, an assertion which no American Secretary of State could simply brush aside. To Vance, the political imperatives so painfully pondered by Mennen Williams and so wholeheartedly accepted by his advisers remained valid. They were valid for Carter and, as the 1978 Congressional elections drew near, the non-committal remarks about Namibia made to Nyerere the preceding August hardened into a policy which, in the event, succeeded in antagonising Congress without appeasing South Africa. Carter did genuinely desire to be seen as a champion of the oppressed. The chosen forum for expressing support was the General Assembly of the United Nations. Carter also wanted to be re-elected President of the United States in November 1980. He needed Congress;

he also needed to appear a strong upholder of American interests in the world. One forum for expressing those interests was the UN Security Council. Three permanent members of the Council (the United States, Britain and France) were members of the 'Contact Group' on Namibia. Given these imperatives, Carter and Vance had one, real, undeclared Namibia policy: appeasement of South Africa.

Namibia – as yet still wholly within South Africa's grip, a territory by 1978 with no readily definable legal status – may be regarded as peripheral, or a mere by-path on the road to Zimbabwe. This view is wrong. This brief history will neither recount nor analyse in detail the events of 1978 and 1979 in relation to Namibia, but the fact remains that the activities of the Contact Group and, in particular, those of the UN Commission on Namibia are directly relevant to the leverage – as Vance, in another sense, would undoubtedly have put it – which South Africa could exert on negotiations about Rhodesia. Owen's caution, as quoted on p. 219, indicates that he came to realise that if Britain and the United States were to get some kind of deal on Rhodesia the active assistance of South Africa was essential. But there was a price to be paid for such assistance. To the extent that Vorster and, after September 1978, P. K. Botha were prepared to help behind the scenes with an internationally acceptable version of the 'Internal Settlement', they demanded an Anglo-American approach to Namibia which was, to say the least, in South Africa's favour.

As has been narrated already, neither Vance nor Owen had any innate desire to put pressure on Namibia. But, broadly speaking, the United Nations was determined to end Namibia's false status, its total dependence on South Africa, and to take all steps possible to prepare the ground for genuine independence. There were, however, officials in the UN Secretariat and amongst the Commission on Namibia who deplored the General Assembly's blank cheque support of SWAPO. The latter's inability to operate effectively as a nationalist movement, and PLAN's lack of credibility as a guerrilla force – despite the strains imposed on the SADF and the South African economy – led to doubts in the Secretariat about a successful outcome of independence negotiations. One indication of doubt which resided even in Julius

Nyerere's breast as to the overall effectiveness of SWAPO, a movement which he was pledged to support, is indicated by the fact that, in May 1978, after his failure with Carter in August 1977 to urge strong and rapid action on Namibia, he released from house arrest in Dar es Salaam one Andreas Shipanga. This erstwhile colleague of Njomo's was returned, rather like a wrongly addressed parcel, to Windhoek. There, under the watchful eye of the Administrator-General, Mr Justice Steyn, Shipanga proceeded to establish a rival to Njomo's SWAPO, the oddly named SWAPO-D (for Democracy). Shipanga, an articulate, even a commanding figure (Njomo is a cipher), came to play a role in Namibia's convoluted affairs not dissimilar to Nkomo – or Muzorewa – concerning Rhodesia.

Nyerere's act in releasing Shipanga must be understood in a context where he not only saw South Africa's leverage power very clearly but believed that some compromise over Namibia could lead to a settlement in Rhodesia – the Kissinger deal in reverse, as it were. After more than a decade of unequal struggle even the philosophical and resilient Nyerere can be forgiven for losing some of his perception. Nothing better illustrates South Africa's capacity – or determination – to go its own way virtually immune from international, let alone regional, pressure than the events of 1978. Neither Vorster nor Botha did, in fact, put pressure on Smith. In Namibia, Shipanga was simply used to thwart Njomo, and as a useful but minor device to further harass and obstruct the UN in its various works.

When, therefore, the UN Commission produced a report on 29 August 1978 which recommended elections on the issue of Namibia's independence, only an optimist would have supposed that South Africa was going to co-operate in a scheme whereby a force of some 7,500 (the United Nations Transitional Assistance Group [UNTAG] for Namibia) would replace all but 1,500 SADF. Although the Report ducked various crucial issues, notably the future of Walvis Bay and the control of Namibia's uranium and diamond mines, it was, as the writer can attest, an overtly honest attempt to establish the security bases of an independence process. But behind this façade of a UN Report which the Security Council approved and the General Assembly welcomed, a covert scheme had been concocted. The Foreign

Office was privately to call this scheme the 'Non-Plan for Namibia'. But, whatever title one gives to a piece of chicanery, it is a fact which no amount of official denial can remove that UNTAG's first commander designate (the Austrian Major-General Hannes Philipp) and the GOC 'South-West Africa' (Major-General Janie Geldenhuys) did, in early 1978, produce a plan which was intended to exclude SWAPO from an independence election.

The substance of the plan lies on the writer's desk at this moment. The 'military interpretation and operational implementation' details of the plan were designed to ensure that SWAPO, hoping to return its members to Namibia (much as ZANLA and ZAPU sought to do in the 1980 Rhodesia independence election), would be effectively shut out by the concerted deployment of SADF and UNTAG. The election would last for four, not seven months, as the 29 August 1978 Report had proposed. South African troops and police would not be confined to one or more 'bases' but allowed an operational role denied to SWAPO. Again, one finds striking resemblances to the 'Assembly Places' plan which formed a key element in the 1980 Rhodesian elections. No mere coincidence provides an explanation. The plans to exclude SWAPO and the Patriotic Front were both made in Pretoria.

It is possible that South Africa's effective rejection of the August 1978 UN Commission proposals for Namibia, and the Government's intention to use the 'Non-Plan' as a basis for 'negotiation', would have been less uncompromising if Vorster had not resigned then in a flurry of scandal. Vorster had shown apparent flexibility on both Rhodesia and Namibia. The several journeys which Vance and Owen made to Pretoria in 1977 and 1978 were ultimately futile, but Vorster always asked them back. With the advent of P. K. Botha (the former Defence Minister) and the appointment of 'Pik' Botha as Foreign Minister the Southern African sky darkened. The two Bothas, and their Cabinet colleagues, are men of the inflexible type, indifferent alike to confrontation or compromise. Smith's Rhodesia was assured of survival by the Bothas; the 'Anglo-Americans', the UN, and the Contact Group were assured of a frigid reception in that bastion of white power and Afrikaner zeal, Pretoria.

PART FIVE
The Triumph of Robert Mugabe

'Independence is not negotiable.'

Robert Mugabe, speaking at a ZANU rally, 31 August 1977

Preamble

On 3 May 1979 Margaret Thatcher won a General Election for the Conservative Party and became Britain's first woman Prime Minister. Her decisive victory over a divided and dispirited Labour Party set in train a domestic programme which she intended to be matched by a comparable tone of chauvinism and xenophobia in the execution of foreign policy. Well before May 1979 Mrs Thatcher had made quite clear her support for the Rhodesian 'Internal Settlement', and had indicated, although in slightly less positive language, her intention to recognise Zimbabwe-Rhodesia as an independent, sovereign state once she became Prime Minister.

Until early August and virtually the conclusion of the Commonwealth Heads of Government meeting in Lusaka, Mrs Thatcher remained convinced that the 'Internal Settlement', possibly with some minor modifications here and there, was not only a solution to Rhodesia's problems which all races could accept but one which would, at last, remove the NIBMAR issue from the British Cabinet agenda. This personal, rather than Prime Ministerial conviction, was based not only on loyalties and prejudices which were immune to reason and persuasion, but reflected profound ignorance about what was actually happening, on the ground, in Rhodesia. This ignorance was common to several of Mrs Thatcher's advisers; indeed, her prejudices, although innate, were also quite widely shared. She, newly come to office, must also be forgiven for ignorance about the wider Southern African picture. The days when Duncan Sandys briefed Arthur Bottomley were long past. David Owen had little to tell Lord Carrington, the new Foreign Secretary.

Before narrating, therefore, the thirteen months between May 1979 and April 1980, some attention must be paid to the war which the 'Internal Settlement' had failed to stop. One fact alone will almost suffice to emphasise the cost rather than the purpose of the war. By early 1978, white Rhodesia's population had decreased by a fifth, from emigration, since UDI; this social leukaemia had accelerated rapidly from the mid-1970s; since then insufficient immigrants had arrived to check a terminal condition.[1] The 'Internal Settlement' could not cure this wasting, prospectively fatal disease. By the time the Settlement was cobbled together Mugabe and his lieutenants were sufficiently confident of ultimate victory to mount operations in Rhodesia's eastern areas which so committed the RSF and all elements supporting it that, as a 'second front', urban guerrilla war became a feasible option. David Owen, Cyrus Vance and assorted diplomats trundled to and fro in 1978; ZANU and ZANLA ignored this charade; they deployed their forces throughout the eastern areas with the aim not merely of drawing the RSF away from the white urban strongholds, but of establishing a political base impregnable to policies of compromise and conciliation.

It was precisely this double objective, whose attainment was sought just as the definable inability of the RSF to contain guerrillas – let alone 'end' the war – was publicly admitted, which gives the eastern area operations their particular importance. The operations are important not only in the context of a protracted guerrilla war, but for our understanding of what was at stake in Lusaka and at the subsequent Lancaster House conference. The situation in eastern Rhodesia governed the tactics of all engaged or involved in the independence election between December 1979 and March 1980. The operations, and above all their political attributes, can also explain the course of events in Zimbabwe since independence. In 1979 Mugabe established a power base in eastern Rhodesia from which he could not be dislodged; which gave him strength to counter the last-ditch manœuvres of London and Salisbury after the Lusaka meeting; and which, since independence, has enabled him to free punitive resources for the purpose of subduing Nkomo's followers in the west and south.

From the moment the Altena farm was attacked in April 1972, all those responsible for the conduct of operations in Salisbury realised that the war would be won or lost in the area bounded by Centenary, Nyamapanda, Umtali, Mount Selinda, Rusape. The essential characteristics of this area, and their importance to ZANLA after Mozambique became independent in 1975, have been described. Stress has been laid on the fact that despite geographical and political advantages, ZANLA repeatedly failed to make good use of opportunities, indeed not only misused them but alienated natural allies or supporters in the Tribal Trust Territories. Comparable stress has been laid on the Rhodesian regime's collective failure to win support from Africans whose loyalties were abused by guerrillas skilled neither in warfare nor persuasive indoctrination.

Much of the regime's failure can be explained by the racial intolerance and arrogance of Smith's claque – to which the police, the RSF higher command and staff, together with the CIO and many able, devoted administrators in remote areas rarely gained entry, and then only to hear abuse for any attempt to win tribal loyalties. But some of the failure must be attributed to the nature of the war – void of decisive events, so governed by the asymmetrical factors of morale and numbers that even major RSF strikes into Mozambique and Zambia came to be seen as sideshows, mounted for political purposes and executed by troops whose savagery met a psychological need rather than an operational requirement. Between April 1972 and the 'Internal Settlement' of March 1978 the war in the eastern areas remained one of attrition. Acute observers saw this war move steadily in favour of ZANU; manpower strains on the RSF became so great that by the time of the settlement black troops predominated in most police and army units.[2] But until March 1978 only a prophet would have predicted a decisive shift in the campaign.

When, however, Muzorewa became 'Zimbabwe-Rhodesia's' Premier-elect, Mugabe realised that what he had perceived at the 1976 Geneva conference had to be given form and substance. Whatever contempt Mugabe might feel for, and occasionally express about Muzorewa, the settlement posed a challenge to

ZANU and ZANLA which had to be met by a bold riposte. Mugabe, in 1978, took the decision to *install* the two movements he jointly dominated throughout Rhodesia's eastern areas, not merely to raid there with the aim of politicising by coercion or intensifying strains on the RSF and local administration caused by a strategy of total economic war. Certainly this war was savage enough: by the time of the settlement, half a million cattle, valued at £30 million, had been destroyed, or had died from disease. The deaths were due to loss of veterinary services, reflecting destruction of an administrative structure inimical to black farmers and ultimately disastrous to white. This was the war whose cost to the Rhodesian economy by 1979 was estimated at £500,000 a day, a fourfold increase in four years; in 1978, the Gross Domestic Product fell by 7 per cent, accentuating unemployment to Africans in cities and townships. Thus are urban guerrillas bred.

But it was the decision to put ZANU into the eastern areas which forced the RSF into a strategy of widespread, quasi-static deployment, and thus destroyed its hitherto successful tactics based on mobility and concentration. Arguably, if the RSF had ignored ZANU's political threat, and had stuck to its successful tactics of attacking ZANLA concentrations, overall support for Mugabe would have remained dependent on intimidation. Attacks on ZANLA, however, had been supported by bombing operations against targets in Mozambique, aimed at destruction of supplies rather than guerrillas and their families. By the time of the settlement the Rhodesian Air Force was down to four worn-out operational Canberra light bombers, and the South African Government had nothing comparable in its own armoury which readily, or with prudence, could be spared. Moreover, the settlement was such a bogus compromise that neither Smith nor Muzorewa could wholly afford to ignore ZANU's political threat. The RSF became committed to an ultimately hopeless strategy of occupying territory in eastern Rhodesia in the attempt to deny ZANU the opportunity of doing so.

Statistics tell the tale more effectively than disquisitions on politics and tactics. In 1972, the RSF was a well-trained and disciplined force of no more than 6,000, including reserves. Thanks to R. A. Butler's division of the Federation's military spoils and the support of South African Governments, this small force was well able to utilise intelligence provided by tribal Chiefs and those dependent on them to mount and execute decisive, economical operations. Guerrilla columns were observed and tracked; dispersing, they were attacked by helicopter-borne troops, supported at short range by fixed-wing strike and transport aircraft. Unopposed Canberra operations on targets in Mozambique posed constant threats to ZANLA columns in the eastern areas. Lines of communication were interdicted; guerrillas' families were killed. Not surprisingly, ZANLA morale fluctuated; increasing numbers in the field simply meant more guerrillas killed in relation to the number deployed. 'The armed forces of Rhodesia won virtually every battle they ever fought against the guerrilla armies . . .'[3]

Of complementary importance to this ability of the RSF to deploy and strike at will was the strength, composition and roles of the British South Africa Police. This, the senior element in Rhodesia's security forces, was also, in 1972, the largest: some 8,000, including 2,000 Africans, excluding reservists. The BSAP, as a gendarmerie, maintained the Whitehead version of internal security (as quoted and discussed on p. 158), but, intermittent repression apart, was undoubtedly respected by Africans. Competition to join the BSAP was strong, and the Africans who served therein were loyal to their superiors rather than the white man's Rhodesia. A force of such calibre, tasked to maintain security in Salisbury, Bulawayo, the African townships and other main urban centres, released the RSF to fight a bush war ruthlessly and economically. Although both the RSF and the BSAP relied on commando-type, covert operations, and counter-insurgency units, no unit was allowed to operate independently of a Combined Operations Headquarters. The CIO co-ordinated intelligence with fair success, and drew heavily on the RSF's Radio Intercept Services, which monitored the usually insecure guerrilla traffic. Commanders and their staffs, although unavoidably dependent on a rebel regime for favours and promotion, were sufficiently cohesive in experience and objectives for standards of recruitment, training and discipline to be maintained. Senior officers supported or opposed Smith's apartheid version of Rhodesia but agreed in operational intentions and methods.

No guerrilla force, whoever led it, was likely to prevail against such a combination of confidence and competence without a fundamental change in the political situation. Mozambique's independence was such a change, of which Mugabe was the ultimate beneficiary. In the interim, and particularly after the mid-1970s, the RSF and BSAP were expanded so rapidly to meet a given threat – rather than one which increased in intensity month by month or even year by year – that by the time of the April 1979 General Election 100,000 men and women were mobilised to ensure that Abel Muzorewa became the white man's first black Premier. During these seven critical years – April 1972 to April 1979 – armed guerrilla forces in the field grew from a few hundred to some 10,000. All save 2,000 of this number was ZANLA. We can ignore ZIPRA's heavily armed but virtually immobile battalions and tank squadrons. These remained in Zambia. Their compatriots in the field had occasional success, but the pattern of RSF operational deployment reveals that ZIPRA was not seen as a serious threat to the survival of the laager. ZIPRA's ineffectiveness and the fluctuating relationship between Nkomo and Muzorewa produced one significant result: by 1978 there was a widespread assumption in Salisbury, Pretoria – and London – that Nkomo had lost his political base in 'Zimbabwe-Rhodesia' to Muzorewa and his 'United Africa National Council'. This assumption was proved to be wholly false during the 1980 Independence Election, but the calculations and manœuvres in and between Salisbury, Pretoria and London during 1979 were substantially governed by it.

One might suppose that a roughly approximate increase in RSF and PF numbers, with the kill ratio moving always in the former's favour, would indicate an attrition war of almost indefinite duration. But, to complete the quotation on p. 231, '... yet they lost the war'. White Rhodesia lost the war, and had lost it *by* April 1979, because in seeking to counter the combined ZANLA–ZANU threat the regime not only dissipated numbers throughout the eastern areas but did so with forces which increasingly lacked morale, cohesion and basic operational effectiveness. Seven-fold expansion might still have held Mugabe's combined guerrilla forces in check if standards of recruitment, training and discipline had been maintained; if 'Combined Operations' orders had reflected the clear command which creates – and maintains

- control; and, of course, if the 'Internal Settlement' had not been a bogus affair.

White Rhodesia's security establishment lost two battles with Smith and those about him during the seven years. Senior administrators, intelligence officers, police and soldiers who believed in genuine progress for the African and, above all, a humane if severe security policy in the eastern areas were removed or sidetracked. When expansion became unavoidable, those who argued for maintenance of standards and, above all, co-ordination of operations, were ignored. Both reserve and special forces multiplied and proliferated, private armies became laws, or lawless unto themselves. This unco-ordinated expansion produced two other results, both indicative of progressive loss of grip by Smith. Hurriedly trained men, posted to expanded or newly-raised units, were packed off to HURRICANE, THRASHER, REPULSE, there to sit tight or swan rather aimlessly to and fro as their commanders sought to deny ZANU influence in these emotively named areas. These units were augmented by the Guard Force and the Rhodesia Defence Regiment, whose poor calibre and low morale merely invited the contempt of those whom they were supposed to protect. As Map 1 (p. 234) indicates, regular units were concentrated in and about the main white strongholds in preparation for an urban guerrilla war which, in serious terms, never materialised. The white farmer – never among Ian Smith's constituents – was left to his fate as his labourers came, at last, under ZANU's merciless sway. The white artisan was provided with a palace guard. The largest estates, however, notably those owned by foreign companies, continued to be guarded by detachments of regular troops, and suffered comparatively little from guerrilla attacks.

Special forces became not only a means of vindictive, merely punitive operations but, after March 1978, were joined by black troops serving under Muzorewa's banner. The so-called *Pfumo reVahnu* ('Spear of the People') became, if it were possible, more feared and hated than the Rhodesian Special Air Service, the Grey and Selous Scouts. Although these regiments stemmed from the British Ministry of Defence's suggestion in the late 1950s that the Federation should augment its forces with units trained for irregular operations, they degenerated into *banditti*

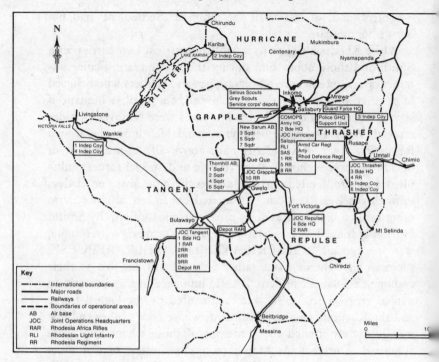

Map 1   The Deployment of the Rhodesian Security Forces in the Late 1970s

when the war reached the decisive stage in 1978. A Combined Operations Headquarters, already sufficiently taxed to provide manpower and then train it to a basic standard, was forced to arbitrate quarrels amongst the commanders of these private armies as to who should be allowed to organise slaughter of 'terrs', and in which particular area of Rhodesia, Mozambique, Zambia – or Botswana.

The overall result of attempting to contain the situation in the eastern areas with poorly trained troops whilst concentrating the best trained in the least threatened areas was twofold: the eastern areas became Mugabe territory, where guerrilla warfare was virtually replaced by political indoctrination.[4] By early 1979, ZANU and its village *pungwes* (political meetings) had 'mobilised the masses'. The *mujibas* (village boys) provided ZANLA with eyes and ears; the village as such became a sanctuary to both ZANU and ZANLA elements which none of the units or odds and ends which Combined Operations Headquarters committed was likely to penetrate or destroy. But, and it is important to note, this transformation from the mid-1970s had been caused as much by deterioration in the calibre of the Rhodesian Security Forces as improvement in overall ZANU/ZANLA skills. By 1979 the balance had tilted so far against the RSF that even the helicopter-borne COIN (counter-insurgency) units were being out-manœuvred tactically by guerrilla groups which had come to know territory, and consider it as their own.

Territory west of Salisbury became a Tom Tiddler's ground, where Rhodesia's increasingly disparate security forces, private armies and auxiliaries conducted their own campaigns and vendettas. Throughout and beyond a country under siege, varieties of white mercenary, whose recruitment and despatch owed not a little to the CIO's liaison (official or not) with other intelligence services, stiffened and sometimes provided the motive for operations haphazard in nature and negative in effect. The seven years war had become, in General Walls's words, 'a no win war'. In default of success in the east, the RSF allowed the special forces virtually a free hand to raid into Zambia and Botswana. During April 1979, as Muzorewa assumed the title 'Prime Minister of Zimbabwe-Rhodesia', attacks were mounted on ZAPU's headquarters in Lusaka and a house sheltering members of that battered organisation in Botswana's Francistown. Neither operation affected the course of the war.

After 31 May 1979, Ian Smith's last day as a rebel Premier, PF forces were no longer referred to in Combined Operations war communiqués as 'Communist Terrorists'. They simply became 'Terrorists'. This clumsy shift in nomenclature, from the inaccurate to the imprecise, reveals that at no time did Walls, as 'Commander of the Rhodesian Armed Forces', understand the fundamental issues. He knew that the war could not be 'won'; he could not accept that the die had been cast. To complete the quotation of pp. 231 and 232:

The story of the Rhodesian armed forces during the civil war is one of tactical brilliance and strategic ineptitude. Rarely in military history have such thinly stretched troops, hampered by chronic manpower, training, equipment, and financial constraints achieved such consistent success against enemy forces which enjoyed the tactical and strategic initiative for most of the war, and often reached numerical parity in the field. But the Rhodesian obsession with successful tactics created a fatal blindness to the strategic imperatives of a protracted revolutionary war such as the guerrillas were waging.

The strategic imperative in one sense was to provide Africans, above all in the eastern Tribal Trust Territories, with security against the combination of intimidation and dialectic at which, eventually, ZANLA and ZANU excelled. Walls and his staff understood this imperative well enough, but they failed to act on their understanding because, for them, men like Tongogara and Nhongo remained – terrorists. Neither intellectually, imaginatively, nor practically could Walls bring himself to embark on a strategy which would have deployed the best-trained and disciplined RSF units throughout the eastern areas, their task being to support a policy and programme of genuine land reform, racial justice, and security. The real dimension of 'a protracted revolutionary war' was simply beyond Peter Walls, as a white regular soldier of limited capacities – and a belief, shared with Ian Smith, that, *in extremis*, South Africa and 'the West' would come to Rhodesia's aid.

General Walls put his not wholly unreasonable belief to the proof at Lancaster House. To that protracted trial of strength and the preliminary meeting of the Commonwealth in Lusaka we must now turn.

18

1979: Lusaka and Lancaster House

The delegations from forty-two Commonwealth countries who met in Lusaka between 1 and 8 August 1979 represented approximately a third of the United Nations and, which is more to the point, included twelve African nations whose independence from British rule had been so singular an achievement of Conservative Governments in the late 1950s and early 1960s. The delegations met just two months after a General Election in 'Zimbabwe-Rhodesia' which a former Conservative Colonial Secretary, Alan Lennox-Boyd, had declared to be 'fairly conducted and above reproach'.[1] The British Liberal Party had also sent observers to the election. Their opinion was that the whole process was nothing more than 'a gigantic confidence trick'. Given the circumstances in which the election took place, the latter opinion, or assessment, may be regarded as accurate, that of the Boyd Commission as no more than political ammunition – for Mrs Thatcher to use at will. There was a widespread feeling that she would do so.

There was undoubtedly a general belief amongst many Commonwealth representatives assembling in Lusaka before the meeting that although some amendment to the 'Internal Settlement' would be recommended – above all, removal of the 'blocking mechanism' to constitutional change – Rhodesia's independence might well be granted on terms essentially favourable to white interests. The Commonwealth as such had progressed in little more than a decade from a white man's club gradually, and reluctantly, admitting black and coloured members, to a loose coalition of Third World pressure groups. This coalition, by 1979, was determined to regard Britain as no more than one amongst many, in no sense *primus inter pares*. But the Commonwealth had changed in several ways which made nonsense of the simple liberal assumption that it would never allow Rhodesia's UDI to be legitimised. Giants of the 1960s like Pandit Nehru and Kwame Nkrumah had left the stage; African members had suffered more than the birth pangs of independence. Kenyatta and Nyerere dominated East Africa; Banda was omnipotent in Malawi; Kaunda walked his tightrope with unique skill in Zambia. But West Africa had endured coups and civil war. Nigeria, the giant, had recovered from civil war, but its overall influence on Commonwealth affairs was hard to assess. National self-interest appeared to dominate policy, not only in Africa but amongst the many new members, whose individual needs were great, influence slight, and interest in Rhodesia little more than rhetorical.

The white Commonwealth had also changed. Canada's Pierre Trudeau had expounded liberal themes for nearly a decade as Prime Minister. In May 1979 he lost a General Election; his successor, Joe Clark, was an unknown quantity. Australia's Prime Minister, Malcolm Fraser, cast physically in the mould of an English landowner, was nevertheless thought to look with favour on the *petit bourgeois* creed of Margaret Thatcher. New Zealand's Robert Muldoon made no secret of his support for Ian Smith, or admiration for P. W. Botha. By 1979 South Africa had become the dominant force in the region; Botha's pleasure at Mrs Thatcher's advent was essentially a reminder that he intended her Ministers to recognise the fact. The writer arrived in Johannesburg, *en route* for Windhoek, three days after Mrs Thatcher's victory. The warmth of his reception was, he was assured, no more than was due to any Englishman arriving at such a propitious moment.

But there was not only doubt, change and expectation in the Commonwealth. The Front Line States – whose non-Commonwealth members, Angola and Mozambique, sent strong observer teams to Lusaka – had suffered greatly from seven years of brutal civil war in Rhodesia. These two countries not only contended with internal strife, maintained by South Africa, but, in providing sanctuary for guerrilla forces, were targets for both military and economic reprisal. Zambia had suffered in ways earlier, and easily, described; Kaunda's tightrope, like much of his food, was provided by assorted white interests. Botswana suffered little by comparison with its neighbours, but refugee camps for ZAPU members and supporters forced Seretse Khama to walk with care. His country's new-found riches in diamonds had come too late to give it stature amongst the Front Line States. By 1979 Seretse was an ailing, ageing man, whose presence in Lusaka was a reminder only of the past. Nyerere remained the pivotal figure amongst his fellow Presidents, but in 1979 even he, troubled by the collapse of economic experiment at home and by a certain inner *accidie*, was not quite the figure who, five years earlier, had backed Mugabe to win against all odds.

Yet, curiously – or inevitably – it was just the widespread belief amongst Commonwealth representatives that Mrs Thatcher would seize the moment to recognise 'Zimbabwe–Rhodesia' which united opposition against her so strongly. In Lusaka she was faced with her first real challenge as Prime Minister. Contrary to a widespread – and carefully propagated – version of events, Mrs Thatcher did not arrive in Lusaka prepared to listen before talking. She arrived aware of the extent of the Commonwealth's opposition to her declared policies, and only after three days of the most intense pressure did she capitulate to a scarcely veiled threat that, if Her Majesty's Government granted recognition to 'Zimbabwe–Rhodesia', Britain would be expelled from the Commonwealth. The carefully staged public relations campaign after the meeting by Mrs Thatcher's Private Office to the effect that it was her initiatives which prevented deadlock on Rhodesia was mounted in order to camouflage the fact of this capitulation.

The campaign was executed by tactics intended to give the impression that although the 'Internal Settlement' constitution was defective in certain respects, this could be remedied at a conference designed primarily to place Muzorewa in an unassailable position *vis-à-vis* Mugabe at any 'independence' election which would then be held. At intervals in July Ministers in the House of Commons had made quite clear that Muzorewa satisfied all 'conditions of legality'. Consultations with Muzorewa were then in train. The plan was to 'bring Rhodesia to legal independence on a basis which we believe to be acceptable to the international community'.[2] Although that plan was destroyed by the Lusaka meeting, the British Government tried by every means to resurrect it at Lancaster House. The Commonwealth Prime Ministers and others, who had put such pressure on their colleague, ignored this campaign; they knew that much conference fighting lay ahead, and did not intend to waste their ammunition.

The pressure which was applied between 31 July and 2 August was the product or synthesis of three separate elements: firstly, the war; secondly, Malcolm Fraser, Julius Nyerere and Michael Manley; and thirdly, Lords Carrington and Harlech, and their relationship to the Nigerian Government. Despite, or because of, the April General Election in Rhodesia, the war continued unabated; casualties increased dramatically as PF forces came into the open to fight RSF troops which lacked the skills of regular units. ZIPRA belatedly played a part, negligible by contrast with ZANLA, but significant in emphasising Muzorewa's inability to do more than pose as 'Prime Minister'. Tongogara and Nhongo began to plan and mount operations aimed at encircling Salisbury, and interdicting Rhodesia's supply routes from South Africa. By the time Commonwealth representatives assembled in Lusaka 95 per cent of Rhodesia was under martial law. Mrs Thatcher was ignorant of ZANU's successes – and, revealingly, she lumped all elements in the PF together as 'terrorists', referring to them as such openly, habitually and contemptuously – but she did accept that the Settlement was, indeed, defective.

Fraser, Nyerere and Manley had nothing in common except a conviction, derived from different sources and by different routes, that the Commonwealth would not indefinitely accept, and might not survive, 'Zimbabwe-Rhodesia's' continued existence, let alone its recognition. Only Nyerere had a clear idea of the detailed issues at stake, or of the rivalries between Nkomo and Mugabe. Only Nyerere openly backed Mugabe. Strictly speaking only Manley could be described as a Liberal, but over several years of Commonwealth co-operation he had come not merely to like the aloof and moody Fraser but to influence him. Fraser underwent that rare experience for a politician; conversion to a principle. Manley, as Nyerere's disciple (a man for whom 'charismatic' is not, for once, an absurd description), thus brought

Defiance: (*right*) African women
march to detention, April 1964

Acquiescence: Ndabaningi Sithole
welcomes the Salisbury Agreement
15 February 1978

11 Stalling: David Owen (*left*), Don Jamieson, Canada's Minister for External Affairs (*centre front*) and Pik Botha (*right front*), Pretoria, 1978

12 Dealing: Lord Carrington signing the Lancaster House Agreement, 21 December 1979, flanked by Archbishop Muzorewa, Sir Ian Gilmour, Joshua Nkomo and Robert Mugabe

together an internationally-known Front Line States President and a white Commonwealth Prime Minister blessed with one critical qualification: he was liked and respected by Lord Carrington, Mrs Thatcher's Foreign Secretary. There is no easy or obvious explanation why Nyerere, Fraser and Manley should have come together, or proved so formidable in combination. It is a fact of history that they openly co-operated, and were formidable, indeed irresistible, in their strategy and tactics. Kenneth Kaunda, as Chairman of the Lusaka meeting, made a fourth in this pressure group, to the extent that his co-operation was essential and his experience invaluable.

Carrington had given a fair amount of thought to Rhodesia when in opposition; although personally almost – not wholly – indifferent to the country's fate, he had spent too much of his thirty years in politics acquiring intelligence of what actually happens in the world to ignore the dangers of Mrs Thatcher approving the 'Internal Settlement'. Carrington warned her not to commit either the Conservative Party or a British Government to more than anodyne statements. She ignored these warnings without wholly rejecting them, but countered by asserting – in Canberra, on 1 July – that 'it would be difficult' for a Conservative Government to resist a call from its backbenchers for the abandonment of sanctions. What in fact Mrs Thatcher meant was that her Conservative Government would abandon them. She represented, and took pride in the fact that her Party, her Government, knew nothing and cared less about the tradition of *noblesse oblige* which her predecessors had applied, with very varying degrees of conviction and success, to the affairs of Colonies and Protectorates. In another revealing comment during the Lusaka meeting Mrs Thatcher told her fellow Prime Ministers that the peasants of the Third World would eat better if they worked harder.

Peter Carrington did not belong to this new Conservatism, this 'I'm all right Jack' creed, which had taken Mrs Thatcher by manœuvre to leadership of the Party in February 1975 and then, by genuine public acclaim, to the top of the greasy pole in May 1979. Carrington could be cynical enough, but ministerial service dating back to the mid-1950s was a poor preparation for subscribing to the new Conservative creed. Two years as High Commissioner in Australia taught Carrington nothing about the Third World, but broadened an intelligence susceptible to impressions and curious to absorb them. After becoming Foreign Secretary Carrington pre-empted Mrs Thatcher by sending one of his own totem to sound African opinion. Lord Harlech went on his travels; in short order he reported that this opinion was unanimous. The Rhodesian General Election had not only been bogus, or rigged; the Settlement as such unwittingly but brutally reminded all who enjoyed genuine independence that the white man in Rhodesia remained in power. By the time Carrington sat down to think seriously about Lusaka he had privately decided that the Settlement must be scrapped, not merely rectified. This was a stark conclusion, reached without enthusiasm, indeed with a wry awareness that the Government of which he was the most senior member had not been able to remove Rhodesia from the Cabinet agenda. Nearly fourteen years after UDI, Britain's imperial responsibility remained. Carrington did not flinch from discharging it.

Much credit is due to Carrington's courage and clarity of perception. Although determined to back Muzorewa he never faltered in his assessment of what had to be done, at Lusaka, and thereafter. But there was another and most potent reason for Carrington's assessment: Nigeria. At intervals between May and July the Chairman of British Petroleum and the Chairman of the Committee of Managing Directors of Royal-Dutch Shell (David Steel and Michael Pocock) saw Carrington and warned him that Shell-BP in Nigeria would be expropriated if Britain recognised the 'Internal Settlement'. Warnings from such a source could not be ignored, and although Carrington is more resistant to threats than most politicians, he knew that Steel and Pocock were under great pressure. Nigerian Governments had for many years taken a stand over Rhodesia; Ministers had played a go-between role. Of more immediate importance was Britain's trade with black Africa's most populous country. This trade was thrice that with South Africa. Nigeria, as the newest member of the Commonwealth, had led the campaign for South Africa's virtual expulsion in 1961. Eighteen years later the same imperatives were operating. Carrington sensed that only acceptance of Lusaka's demand for a fresh start would prevent another expulsion. That fate avoided, time would be gained for a difficult but not impossible operation: a Rhodesian independence election, on a new constitution – which Muzorewa would still win, somehow.

Carrington, in seeking to redeem the old NIBMAR pledges whilst denying a militant, allegedly Marxist, Robert Mugabe the fruits of victory, knew he faced stiffer problems than any challenge which Lusaka could pose. No help, in any practical sense, could be expected from the United States. Meeting Vance in London on 21 May, Carrington quickly realised that although Carter would probably continue to resist Congressional and pressure group demands for the abandonment of sanctions against Rhodesia, no positive support would be given to Britain. 'Initiatives' were over. The United States had played its hand. There was no royal flush of success. Other places in the world – notably Iran – required attention. Carrington gained little from meeting Vance. He did, however, emulate the Secretary of State in one particular. Carrington sent a middle-rank Foreign Office official to Salisbury in the belief that he might pick something up. Unfortunately, what he acquired was that which the CIO chose to provide: Muzorewa had a genuine constituency, but it was under threat. Carrington had nothing with which to convince his Prime Minister that the Lusaka meeting might be difficult. He knew she was stubborn; confident in her conviction of being right she might prove resistant to pressure. Carrington left for Lusaka with what can best be described as foreboding.

Mrs Thatcher arrived in Lusaka at 2300 hours on Tuesday 31 July determined that 'terrorists' should play no part in Rhodesia, ignorant of the realities, but increasingly aware of the forces being mustered against her. Mrs Thatcher had already found Carrington an equal rather than a subordinate, but could see no reason why her particular style of hectoring obstinacy should not prevail. To most of those already in Lusaka Mrs Thatcher was an unknown quantity. A meeting of Front Line States Presidents, Ministers and officials which began in State House during the early evening of the 31st failed to concert tactics; much time was spent in speculation. What was Mrs Thatcher really like? What would she do? It was odd to hear men scarred by their independence struggles discussing a British

Prime Minister, *circa* 1979, odder to be asked by one Angolan: 'What is this Commonwealth? Can we join it?' Kaunda, prospective host in his own capital to a Commonwealth of which he is justly and genuinely proud, told all present that the auspices were favourable. Kaunda found few takers.

The entire atmosphere on the eve of the meeting was, indeed, heavy with uncertainty. The security situation was hardly reassuring. ZIPRA's levies in and about Lusaka had rendered the suburbs of that pleasant colonial town vulnerable to pillage, and worse. The Zambian army, a force both exiguous and inefficient, manned road blocks. ZIPRA drove through them. The Rhodesian Air Force had been further reduced, but could still drop bombs on very visible targets like camps – and hospitals. Most patients in Lusaka's surgical wards were ZIPRA, a maimed and melancholy crowd. The Queen's presence accentuated fears, despite her invariable calm. The Zambian Security Service had been judiciously augmented from Britain, Australia and Singapore. Security for the meeting was tight, but imperfections were easy to discover, and exploit. There were folk in Lusaka during those days whom the CIO would have gladly picked up or kept under surveillance. ZAPU was playing at home, and observers could move at will, but ZANU representatives, present at Kaunda's invitation and Nyerere's insistence, presented a rather attractive target to those who, like Peter Walls, began to see what was in the wind.

That cool winter evening of 31 July was thus one of expectation and some apprehension. The moments following Mrs Thatcher's arrival did nothing to ease the atmosphere. Despite strong-arm attempts by security men of various colours and sizes, she was hustled by representatives of the over-enthusiastic Zambian media into a VIP lounge. Forty minutes later Britain's Prime Minister emerged shaken, fighting tears, much distressed. She had been subject to the grilling a hostile witness might get at a murder trial. Understandably, Mrs Thatcher had not liked the experience. Forgivably, she declared at one brief moment when self-control nearly faltered that she would return to London – 'tonight!' Characteristically, for physical courage is hers in abundance, the following morning saw her cool, implacable – or seemingly so. Yet the nerve-shaking experience in a small, hot, packed VIP lounge at midnight may have had some bearing on what followed.

Shridath Ramphal, as Commonwealth Secretary-General, did not, as he hoped, play a key role in organising pressure against Mrs Thatcher. Carrington took, and kept, an irrational aversion to Ramphal; perforce, the latter had to be all things to all men, a role not consonant with speaking and acting tough. Carrington, no enemy to plain speaking, failed to understand Ramphal's personality and methods. But the meeting's agenda was in Ramphal's hands, and his decision to defer plenary discussion of Rhodesia for two clear days after the opening was a tactical decision of great importance. The decision was made in mid-July, giving time for Fraser and Manley to concert tactics. Nyerere was to act as spokesman, in plenary and unreported conclaves, for an agreed objective: a completely fresh start on Rhodesia.

If Mrs Thatcher accepted, at once, that the April election in Rhodesia had only intensified the war, and declared that a completely new Commonwealth initiative was essential no pressure would be applied. If however, she was obdurate, pressure would be applied in the two days between the opening speeches and the 3 August session on Rhodesia. Whatever Mrs Thatcher's reactions, the week-end of 4–5 August would be devoted to further private discussion. If Mrs Thatcher had been conciliatory, or had succumbed to pressure, this week-end would be devoted to planning the next moves, and to a certain amount of public face-saving on her behalf. If, however, she remained obdurate until the eve of this week-end, pressure would be applied in greater measure. There was absolutely no wish or intention to humiliate an untried Prime Minister. There was every intention of removing Rhodesia, at last, from the Commonwealth agenda by persuading or forcing the new Prime Minister to seize the moment for decisive action.

The Government's statement in the House of Commons on 11 July certainly was not construed as conciliatory. Worse might have been expected, but by the time Mrs Thatcher had stepped down the steps of the Royal Air Force VC10 on 31 July Nyerere and his confrères knew that the next two days would be critical. No direct confrontation would be attempted; Carrington would bear the message; accept our demands, or take the consequences. Nyerere's role was more personal, and subtle. He was to point out to Mrs Thatcher the utter horror and futility of the war, acting on the premise that even her stony heart might be touched, somewhere. After Kaunda had opened the meeting, Nyerere spoke, and was followed by Mrs Thatcher. The writer, sitting next to Mrs Sally Mugabe, will not easily forget that cool, slight figure, impassive, alert, sceptical, watching the representative of an alien culture. One formidable woman observed another. There was no comment from Mrs Mugabe when Mrs Thatcher sat down, merely a slight contraction about the eyes and mouth. Another battle in Zimbabwe's long war was about to begin.

In an address governed equally by moderation and certainty Nyerere said:

Rhodesia is dominated by a racial minority: it is in law a British colony. And in pursuing its policy of decolonisation, Britain has - except in two cases - consistently transferred power to an elected government with a democratic constitution - what ever has happened thereafter. Most of us are here because of that policy, and whatever our other differences we are united in its support. I believe that no member of the Commonwealth is willing to acquiesce in the creation of another South Africa. That was the product of an earlier phase of British decolonisation, and is now an object-lesson of the dangers of failing to transfer power firmly to the mass of the people.

Since the last meeting of the Commonwealth Heads of State and Government in 1977 there has been a political change in Rhodesia. There are now a majority of black faces in the Salisbury Parliament. There is now a black Prime Minister and a black President. This colour change follows elections on what purported to be a one-person one-vote basis, and 64 per cent of the electorate, as estimated by the Smith Regime, is said to have voted.

Whether one believes the election process itself to have been 'free and fair' depends upon whether one believes free elections are possible on a battle-field when they are organised by one of the contending Armies - and perhaps upon whether one believes the Boyd Report or the Chitnes and Paley Reports! But whatever the truth about the freedom of people to take part in, or to boycott, the election, all of us here know that the constitution of what now calls itself Zimbabwe–Rhodesia is the real issue.

It is not necessary for me to argue the case for saying that that Constitution is undemocratic. The Secretary-General's Report summarises the position very well, and I do not need to repeat it. Not only were those fighting against the Rebel Regime excluded from both the preparation of the Constitution and participation in the so-called elections. Even more important, the 'constitution' does not involve a real transfer of power from the minority to the majority because the levers of government power are put beyond the reach of the Cabinet and retained by the Minority Community. The change, although very visible, is thus more cosmetic than real. Consequently it does nothing to bring the war to an end. Instead, the war against Zambia, Mozambique, and the Freedom Fighters continues as before; the Liberation Forces have neither political nor military reason to lay down their arms; and Africa does not have any reason to urge the Freedom Fighters to stop the armed struggle.

My hope is that the Commonwealth can, at this Meeting, reach a Consensus on action which can bring the war to an end by establishing a democratic government in Rhodesia. We can do this if we all act purposefully in accordance with modern Commonwealth traditions, and if we co-operate to get the Rhodesians over this last hurdle.

Our first requirement in Rhodesia, therefore, is a democratic constitution. The second requirement is that the Government formed under such a constitution should be chosen through free and fair elections. It is not possible just to introduce a new constitution and to co-opt representatives of the external nationalists into the Salisbury government structure. For we have to make everyone feel involved, and committed to working on the basis of the new constitution. The only hope of this happening is if the people themselves can express their opinion about all those who are contending for governmental power.

We have to recognise, however, that free and fair elections

in Rhodesia are only possible if there is a Cease Fire, and if they are internationally organised and supervised. I hope the Commonwealth and all its members would be able and willing to play a part in this process, and to assist the responsible power – Britain – both in the election supervision and in the interim arrangements which internationally supervised elections presuppose.

These two conditions – a democratic constitution and internationally supervised elections – are essential if the war in Rhodesia is to be brought to an end quickly and by means other than military victory. My third proposal, which I make with some diffidence, is intended to make these two easier to implement; it has no other purpose than that.

Bishop Muzorewa and Ian Smith are at the moment taking a very hard line, and refusing to face up to the need for major constitutional changes. They are doing so because they believe that sanctions will come to an end, and recognition will be forthcoming, on the present constitutional basis or after a few more cosmetic changes. We have to make them realise that this will not happen, and that the only way to get sanctions lifted is to accept a democratic constitution and internationally supervised elections. For lifting sanctions on any basis less than this would be a betrayal of all the principles of justice which this Commonwealth tries to stand for. It would also be an announcement to the whole world – including its racialists and tyrants – that justice can be defied with impunity as far as the Commonwealth is concerned.

Certainly the war would not be brought to an end by the lifting of sanctions against Rhodesia before a democratically elected Government has been brought into existence. The only effect of such an action would be to make the war more prolonged, more racialist, and more internationalised. For if we fail to provide this alternative of a real transfer of power through international action, then the war will continue until the nationalists have won – however long it takes.

Nyerere's words have been given *in extenso* because he expressed, as no other Commonwealth representative except Kaunda could, the principles at stake. Fraser spoke, more briefly, more forcefully, but it was Nyerere who sounded the call to action. Mrs Thatcher, in reply, merely said: 'I am grateful to all those who have given their advice ... I shall listen with the greatest attention at this meeting ... ' The aim for Zimbabwe must be genuine majority rule, and to the attainment of that objective the British Government would, and the meeting should, bend all its energies. Mrs Thatcher did not say the constitution should be scrapped; or that, following a cease-fire, and the return of the PF and exiled Africans, all in Zimbabwe would be entitled to vote at an independence election based on an entirely new constitution resulting from a conference at which Britain would assume, at last, responsibility for Rhodesia's independence. If Mrs Thatcher had spoken in these terms, however ambiguously, room would have been found for manœuvre. She did not offer room: for the next thirty-six hours the pressure was applied.

Carrington was the pivot on which all manœuvres turned. He was in a difficult, possibly a dangerous mood. A few hours before the meeting opened Shell-BP in Nigeria had been expropriated. Carrington had ignored the warning as imminent, believing it to be merely prospective, a means of applying pressure on Mrs Thatcher at an opportune moment, not during a crisis. Carrington lost his temper – a fairly frequent, understandable, but damaging occurrence during these days and hours – when Nigeria's Commissioner for External Affairs, Major-General Adefope, almost discourteously dismissed the expropriation. Carrington's temper was not improved when Mrs Thatcher rebuked him in front of journalists. In truth, Prime Minister and Foreign Secretary were under great strain. The latter knew what was at stake; Adefope merely shrugged and said he had to see the Queen when Carrington furiously declared to him that expropriating Shell-BP would not affect British policy on Rhodesia. That policy was being fashioned, at last, but not by the British Government. By Thursday evening Mrs Thatcher had come to accept that she might be deaf to persuasion but was not able to withstand the kind of pressure which was being exerted on her.

But Mrs Thatcher continued to seek escape. Later that Thursday she told Carrington that her statement at the following day's discussion on Rhodesia would indicate an intention to meet the demands summarised in these pages. But she declined to be specific, and made it plain she preferred to speak extempore. Carrington knew this would not work for a moment. No escape, no ambiguity remained possible. Sir Anthony Duff, the senior Deputy Under-Secretary of State at the Foreign Office, who, through Mrs Thatcher's Private Office, had also taken soundings amongst careful observers of the scene, decided to *write* her statement (see Appendix A, pp. 314-17). Duff sat up much of the night to do so. The writer feels entitled to record one factor, of some relevance. He, with others, was asked by a member of the Private Office if an extempore statement would suffice. 'No, and whilst you're about it, and whatever the number of copies to be run off, double them.' On Friday he said 'Good morning' to the Foreign Office typist who had spent the small hours running off four hundred copies of Duff's statement. She was not best pleased.

The factor might seem trivial, were it not that immediate attempts were made, at Mrs Thatcher's insistence, to pretend that nothing very significant had occurred. Despite the statement's unambiguous meaning and the meeting's outright support for it, correspondents in Lusaka were told that any conference 'to bring Rhodesia to legal independence on a basis which the Commonwealth and the international community as a whole will find acceptable' would amend rather than scrap the 'Internal Settlement' constitution. Duff had been unambiguous, but he had written a statement in Mandarin none the less. He knew 'that woman', as the Private Office, privately, called her, would find difficulty in openly admitting defeat. A little subtlety here and there would help. Mrs Thatcher certainly read the statement, at speed – in two and a half minutes. Her head was bent over the paper; her voice, for once, lacked its usual timbre. Defeat had been unpleasant, but Duff's skill enabled the public relations campaign to get under way.

The week-end of 4 and 5 August was thus spent by the Prime Ministers of Australia, Britain, Jamaica, together with the Presidents of Tanzania and Zambia, in planning a conference, to be held at Lancaster House, where Mrs Thatcher's pledge would be redeemed. General Adefope attended this State House conclave, by virtue of economic muscle, hardly by invitation. Balancing the requirement to act quickly before temporary *rapprochement* vanished against the need for a breathing space, Carrington proposed mid-September. Invitations were to be issued on the basis of 'come one, come all'. The rebel Smith would be invited, as would his colleague in complicity, Bishop Muzorewa. The leaders of the Patriotic Front, who had not rebelled against the Crown, were invited, as were figures from the past, fringe politicians, representatives of minority interests. President Carter welcomed the conference, calling it 'a significant step forward'.[3] Muzorewa showed his white master's hand in declaring that 'it was an insult to the electorate and to the Government of this country to suggest that the elections [of April 1979] meant absolutely nothing and that we have to start all over again'. Robert Mugabe, speaking as the Lusaka meeting ended – and on the sixteenth anniversary of ZANU's establishment – asserted that little reliance could be put on the goodwill of a British Government 'after it had pronounced itself in alliance with the illegitimate and wholly unrepresentative Smith-Muzorewa regime'.[4] Mugabe demanded the disbandment of the RSF and its replacement by 'Liberation forces'. Nkomo confined his reactions to praise for the PF in wringing concessions from the British Government. That note of relative moderation aside, the auspices for the conference were not exactly favourable.

Carrington knew that even a successful public relations campaign would give him little time to organise a conference at which the PF would be present in force and in its own right, Muzorewa attending only by courtesy of Ian Smith. Carrington calculated the odds. The Lusaka meeting had certainly provided Carrington with evidence of war-weariness by the Front Line States and, in particular, of Nyerere's determination to put some pressure on Mugabe in order that Britain's belated, brief resumption of direct responsibility for Rhodesia would be preceded by a cease-fire. The new constitution must reserve some role for Zimbabwe's whites; no independence election could be held if the PF was allowed to move around Rhodesia at will, resorting to intimidation for getting its vote out. So much Nyerere was prepared to concede. He also urged Mugabe to start negotiating in a conciliatory rather than a militant mood. (Nyerere personally ignored Nkomo in making these diplomatic overtures to Carrington. Kaunda would exert some influence on ZAPU's leader, but Nyerere believed that any role for the latter would be strictly subordinate to Mugabe. The PF would remain in being for just so long as it suited ZANU to confront Muzorewa with all the 'freedom fighters' available.)

Despite Nyerere's co-operation – up to a point – Carrington knew that the odds were heavily against this last-chance, last-ditch conference achieving compromise. What, in essentials, was there to compromise about? The war had forced Ian Smith to make some gestures. The war had given ZANU a political, not merely a military constituency inside Rhodesia. The Lusaka meeting had, in one sense, merely emphasised these facts, whilst clarifying the real issue: whose hands would be on Zimbabwe's levers of power? Any Lancaster House conference which failed to settle that issue would be a waste of time. Mrs Thatcher, in accepting defeat over recognition of the 'Internal Settlement', had, in no real sense, lived to fight another day. In accepting that 'it is our constitutional responsibility to grant legal independence on that basis [genuine black majority rule] and that only Britain can do it' Mrs Thatcher had forced the Government which she led to *choose*: to support the PF or Muzorewa. However much this full-dress final conference might seek to strike and hold the balance fairly, there was no place in an independent Zimbabwe for a militant ZANU led by the Jesuit-educated Robert Mugabe and a white-dominated 'United Africa National Council' (UANC) whose titular leader was the evangelical Bishop Abel Muzorewa.

When Carrington approved Duff's statement on the morning of 3 August he accepted a responsibility – as Chairman-elect of the forthcoming conference – for either allowing the PF to make the running with full Commonwealth backing or, whilst conceding defeat on constitutional issues, elsewhere thwarting it by all legitimate, or illegitimate, means. The key element in the conference would not be the constitution, or even a cease-fire as such (implementing it would be another matter). The constitution, whatever wrangles occurred over the fine print, would only give real power to whoever won the election. The key element in the conference would be a programme for holding the independence election in a country the size of France; ravaged by war; where contending armies represented political allegiance; in which civil administration beyond the main urban centres was little more than the gallant endeavours of exhausted survivors. Whoever dominated *that* situation would win the election.

Carrington and his advisers were convinced that this appreciation was correct. So, in a sense, it was, but it was fatally weakened by an assessment, based on poor intelligence, that Muzorewa, as figurehead for white interests, could win an independence election if the odds were loaded heavily against the PF in general and ZANU in particular. The Foreign Office, collectively advising Carrington on Rhodesia – but in one form of liaison or another, heavily dependent on the South African intelligence services and the CIO – drew a distinction between Muzorewa the man and Muzorewa the creature of white interests. It was agreed on all hands that, in conference terms, Muzorewa would be no match for Mugabe. There, Muzorewa would need all the help he could be given. But there remained this delusion that in Rhodesia, and if the PF was hobbled, Muzorewa could win an election and emerge as a Prime Minister from whom international recognition could no longer be withheld.[5]

The logic of this Foreign Office assessment about Muzorewa led to there being two conferences in London between 10 September and 21 December. At Lancaster House, where the fate of so many of Britain's dependencies had been decided, Carrington presided over the arguments of angry men, embittered men, idealists, pragmatists, stooges, the disillusioned, the opportunist. Behind the scenes, in Whitehall offices and private houses, by telephone call and coded telex, another conference took place, in which the participants were diplomats and soldiers, intelligence officers and, very much up to a point, Commonwealth High Commissioners, Shridath Ramphal and the Commonwealth Secretariat. The first conference has been widely discussed and carefully analysed. Phrases like 'game plan', 'first-class solution', and 'second-best option' have been used to describe Carrington's tactics; much ink has been spilt on rivalries and intrigues. Material produced for and debated in the plenary sessions will keep constitutional lawyers happy for many a year. Some attention will be paid to these factors and developments in the following pages. But, in all essentials, what mattered during these three months and eleven days was whether white Rhodesia and its South African allies would come to the British Government's support in devising a plan to hobble the PF when the election fighting started in earnest. Whites in Southern Africa did their duty as they saw it; the PF went into the independence election hobbled – and divided. Division reflected Mugabe's belief that ZANU could dispense with ZAPU. But both ZANU and ZAPU faced Rhodesian forces whose disbandment had not occurred, and whose operational deployment had been accepted by Carrington despite Nkomo's and Mugabe's vehement protests. Yet hope remained and, on Mugabe's part, proved to be justified.

Between 8 August and 10 September Carrington found time to consider the implications of hobbling the PF, but Mugabe was granted the opportunity to make what proved to be, in the outcome, a crucial step in the assertion of black power. Mugabe and Nkomo, albeit prodded and pushed from various quarters, agreed not only to work as one at Lancaster House, but to stick to a consistent line over all issues and every detail. Nyerere had warned Mugabe that he should neither underrate Carrington's skill nor the collective ability of Whitehall's constitutional draftsmen. The PF would appear together, but they must learn to negotiate together. If the PF failed to stand together, its two elements would fail separately. Nyerere was well aware that a residual British option would be dividing the PF by offering Nkomo concessions – or prospective roles – which Mugabe would reject. In the immediate aftermath of the Lusaka meeting Nyerere had left Nkomo to Kaunda's devices. By the eve of Lancaster House Nyerere had realised that Nkomo was essential to Mugabe – until an agreement was signed.

Nyerere and his fellow Front Line States Presidents did not find Mugabe easy to train for this supreme test of political leadership. In no more than four years Mugabe had emerged from obscurity to notoriety. Working with Nkomo did not appeal. There were men and women in ZANU who saw no need for compromise, detested Nkomo, opposed the whole idea of the PF. Fortunately for Mugabe he not only had learned to listen during his years of struggle; he could reflect. Mugabe arrived in London early in September accompanied by a mostly militant retinue, in which Josiah Tongogara was, in both senses, the only man of real stature. But Mugabe brought his own thoughts. He was ignorant of what was already developing behind the Whitehall scenes; he disliked London; the idea of negotiating rather than campaigning set up a psychological barrier; above all, he regarded Nkomo as an encumbrance. But Mugabe kept his head; closed ranks with Nkomo; came to respect Carrington – who returned the compliment of one essentially honest, clear-sighted man to another. Mugabe came to London hoping for a quick result – as, for the same reason but in total opposition, did Carrington. The two antagonists were forced to endure a marathon, a factor in events which proved decisive.

By early September Carrington knew that the respite granted him after the Lusaka meeting was exhausted. The logic to which he was committed drove him to urge his momentum on all concerned once the conference opened. The Muzorewa delegation, including 'Ian Douglas Smith' – and given protocol precedence over the PF – was a shaky coalition; although the ubiquitous – but unlisted – Ken Flower, and the scarcely less active Air-Vice-Marshal Hawkins – 'Zimbabwe-Rhodesia's diplomatic representative to the Republic of South Africa' – were necessary links in a chain being forged behind the scenes, Carrington feared that Muzorewa's nerve would crack if the conference was prolonged. Despite his outburst after the Lusaka meeting, Muzorewa ostentatiously aligned himself with the British Government's assorted proposals at the start of the conference. Yet after a few days his petulance, varied with boasts of political power and electoral prowess, revealed underlying tension. Smith shrugged his shoulders, and went off to watch Rugby football. Walls spent much of his time in the South African Embassy.

Most commentators who covered the Lancaster House conference assert that Carrington's tactics were based on an assumption that the PF would reject the British Government's proposals on the constitution; a cease-fire; and election arrangements. The PF would walk out of the conference, enabling Carrington to push through change with Muzorewa's reluctant assent. An election would be held at which Muzorewa would triumph. There is no warrant for this assertion. A second election 'success' for Muzorewa on this basis would not end the war. As the final conference arrangements were made, few could deny that ZANLA was moving around much of Rhodesia, striking at will, and effectively. Carrington's tactical aim at the conference was to reach *agreement* with all parties as quickly as possible to a cease-fire and electoral arrangements which would, nevertheless, hobble the PF. He spoke repeatedly on 'not accepting the possibility of failure'.

Carrington correctly assessed the pressure being put on Mugabe by Nyerere and his fellow Presidents to accept compromise at Lancaster House and run his chance at the ensuing election. But if negotiating were spun out over the constitution, not only might Muzorewa walk out but Mugabe would start to fight in his corner about the cease-fire and the election. With every day that passed, the nominal Foreign Office proposals for a cease-fire – which were, in fact, a South African plan for Assembly Places to which PF forces were to be confined – would be examined more closely. The plan would be criticised by the PF. Of equal, possibly greater importance, the plan would be scrutinised by those given the invidious, certainly dangerous, possibly humiliating task of ensuring that the cease-fire stood some chance of being observed. Another crucial element in Carrington's tactics was to oppose the idea of cease-fire observers. They might see too much.

Carrington's besetting weakness – or great virtue – as a politician is his candour. From the outset he made little secret, in public or private, of his determination to get a move on: the reasons for hoping to do so were not that hard to discern, especially by those who knew what was happening in two places which the Foreign Office tended to leave out of its calculations: the Ministry of Defence and the Commonwealth Secretariat. But Carrington, despite the all but inexorable logic of electoral calculation, which put him in the hands of General Walls and his South African comrades in arms, was trapped in a situation of even greater complexity, and as the conference weeks slowly passed, of mounting tension. No more than the Patriotic Front, the Front Line States and, despite rhetoric, the Smith–Muzorewa team, could Carrington afford failure.

More clearly, more bitterly, more cynically than most of his ministerial colleagues, Carrington realised that as between forcing the pace to the point of breakdown and accepting procrastinating arguments in order to achieve compromise he had little choice but to accept the latter. The Lusaka meeting had put Britain back in the dock; if the Lancaster House conference failed, the verdict would be 'guilty'. Wisely, no doubt, Mrs Thatcher distanced herself from Rhodesia after the Lusaka meeting, unwittingly expressing the old Staff College dictum: 'always reinforce strength; never reinforce weakness'. But she did not distance herself entirely from the Southern African scene. Carrington was provided with a Deputy in the person of Ian Gilmour, the Lord Privy Seal, a lymphatic Minister, with a propensity to suggest that the Conference was an exercise in *sauve qui peut*. The Foreign Office team was collectively governed by considerations which reflected Carrington's cynicism and Gilmour's pessimism: dislike of, but respect for Robert Mugabe; tolerant acceptance of Joshua Nkomo; contempt for, but unremitting support for Abel Muzorewa; irritation with Shridath Ramphal, to which, by late October, was added intense vexation with the Ministry of Defence, specifically the army's intelligence and operations branches. General Walls, by contrast, was, as he remained throughout the months culminating in Zimbabwe's independence, guide, philosopher and, to at least one Foreign Office official, friend.

The PF delegations, variously preoccupied, did not fully understand Carrington's invidious position. By the same token, they did not understand the specific reason for Carrington's verbal exhortations to press on. The two delegations knew that Walls was in London, but can be forgiven for failing to know precisely what he was doing. The two delegations were penetrated with relative ease; no such weapon was available to the PF. The plan for fourteen Assembly Places (APs) into which the PF was to be herded and corralled under the guns of the RSF was put, in detail, to the British Government by Walls before the conference opened, and developed in unambiguous detail as it struggled through the opening sessions.[6] Yet with each week that passed complete secrecy became more difficult to maintain. The Walls plan, as originally conceived and supported by the British Government, would have been executed solely by the RSF. But as some inkling of the plan became known, the PF, and others, began to see the necessity of fighting the Carrington timetable all the way, not only to secure compromise on the British Government's constitutional, cease-fire and election proposals, but in order to flush the Chairman from his covert.

In a sense, therefore, Carrington lost his battle in the first half of the conference. He had originally hoped the entire affair would be over in a month. In mid-October the delegations were still arguing about constitutional details. These arguments were hardly academic, but all present in Lancaster House – with the possible exception, and for psychological reasons, of Ian Smith and Bishop Muzorewa – knew that whatever was finally devised would ensure not merely 'a genuine black majority rule' but, in removing white-controlled 'blocking mechanisms', would also enable that majority to have, or take, control of the levers of power; the armed forces; the bureaucracy (and judiciary); maybe the economy. The importance to Carrington of keeping Muzorewa in play, of ensuring he did not walk out of Lancaster House, can hardly be exaggerated.

The PF's original objections to the white Zimbabwe community retaining twenty seats in a Parliament of one hundred were, doubtless, genuine enough, but were not very substantial. But, substantial or not, wrangles about this, and other elements in the constitution continued for six weeks. Carrington's temper grew noticeably short; he made the first of several threats to apply the closure. This bluff was called; the wrangles continued, but Mugabe told Carrington privately that he accepted the British version of the constitution despite his personal wish for an 'Executive-type Presidency', in effect consolidation, not separation of powers. By 19 October compromise on the constitution had been reached. White Zimbabwe was given twenty seats; the realities of the whole business – cease-fire and election – were from then onwards the only subjects of conspiracy and debate.

From the outset, the PF wanted discussion about the two key issues to be held concurrently with debate on the Constitution. Both Nkomo and Mugabe disliked Carrington's 'constitution first' tactics. Balked of such plenary discussion – fortunately for African interests, as events turned out – the PF started to take counsel on how the cease-fire would be implemented and, above all, observed or 'monitored'. An impending UN Secretariat sponsored meeting in Geneva, where, at *South African* insistence, an enlarged role for UNTAG was up for barter, may have had some influence on the PF. The revised plan for UNTAG, devised by South Africans but discussed with such military advisers as the Contact Group could muster, called for it to be deployed in a 'de-militarised zone' along the border between Angola and Namibia. UNTAG's task would be to deter SWAPO from entering Namibia; SADF's to train its guns on SWAPO, corralled inside the country – and, in a very particular sense, confined to camp.[7] By September 1979 ZANLA's Tongogara and ZIPRA's Dumiso Dabengwa had, from various sources, been given a reasonably accurate account of South Africa's plans to use UNTAG for its own purposes. Tongogara was not slow to insist to his PF comrades in London that they must avoid the trap set for SWAPO: not only Rhodesia's cease-fire but Zimbabwe's independence election must be monitored on terms which would *not* favour white interests.

Tongogara – who was to be killed in somewhat ambiguous circumstances on 26 December 1979 – not only had the common African capacity to have a pretty shrewd idea of what the white man was thinking; uninterested in constitutional minutiae, he began to do some thinking on his own account. The great respect in which Tongogara came to be held by the military members of Britain's last, briefest, imperial administration was not only due to his character and capacities. Respect was given to a guerrilla soldier who had sat down and considered what was actually involved in establishing and maintaining a cease-fire. From the opening days of the Lancaster House conference the PF delegations began to ventilate ideas for a force to observe the cease-fire and monitor the election. In London, Nkomo had no adviser comparable to Tongogara. Perforce the PF delegations came to treat the guerrilla giant as their mentor.

If an atom of real goodwill had prevailed at Lancaster House it is possible that Carrington might have responded diplomatically to these ideas. He was captive, not merely privy to Walls's Assembly Places plan, and could reckon on a wholly antagonistic PF reaction once it was formally proposed. Some conciliatory murmurs by Carrington about observers and monitors might have allayed PF fears, might even have helped to accelerate the conference tempo. His immediate, overt hostility to a monitoring force may have reflected disdain for the grandiose, impracticable versions of Tongogara's thoughts which Nkomo and Mugabe circulated, but also undoubtedly was a half-hidden admission that the PF, entitled by the Lusaka meeting to a square deal on the cease-fire, was about to be dealt a raw one. The PF's suggestion for a UN (or Commonwealth) force of 10,000, empowered to enforce a cease-fire, was easy to dismiss; no member of either the UN or the Commonwealth would commit troops to such a perilous venture, even on the unlikely supposition of the Rhodesian rebel regime actually laying down its arms. But Carrington's riposte that the British bobby could do the job suggested not so much disdain for the impracticable as apprehension about what lay ahead.

From 22 October, however, when Zimbabwe's constitution was, more or less, settled the cease-fire issue came out in the open. By this date the conference had acquired a life and a momentum totally different from that envisaged by Carrington six weeks earlier. The PF delegations were holding together, arguing shrewdly, alleviating the occasional outburst by some discreet backstairs diplomacy. The 'Salisbury delegation' as the Foreign Office chose to call the rebels, was becoming collectively shrill in tone, individually given to gloom, or contrivance. Smith had even stopped bothering to patronise Muzorewa. The latter, in his Carlton House hotel suite, was a caged rabbit. Flower, Hawkins – and Walls – were busy; for the rest, a stumbling effort was made to protest simultaneously for the record at Carrington's concessions to the Patriotic Front and privately accept that he was doing his utmost to ensure that a rebel regime was returned to power and acknowledged as legitimate. On one occasion Carrington, swallowing hard, praised Muzorewa for his 'courageous and positive decision' to contest another election despite 'the position established last April'; on another, reference was made, when agreement on British rule was reached, to the Bishop's willingness 'to hand over authority to a British Governor'; on a third occasion, the Salisbury Delegation's 'considerable sacrifices' were praised. Carrington was forced to put some heart into Muzorewa; in doing so, he gave much of the game away.

Carrington's grudging admission on 22 October that the cease-fire might be 'observed' by a military force of *three hundred* is a key date in the real conference which was being held behind the scenes. Quite simply, matters were going badly for Carrington; the Assembly Places plan had to be sprung at some point; an absolute refusal to consider any kind of impartial military presence, to be deployed once a cease-fire was agreed and a timetable for it coming into force was established, might well have seen the conference break down far more comprehensively than, to some observers, seemed likely over the constitution. But there was a more potent reason than conference tactics for Carrington's partial concession on 22 October; before narrating the remainder of both the Lancaster House and the real conference, a final comment must be made on the war. By October 1979 even Mrs Thatcher, in reading the SIS daily reports, would have known that ZANLA was on the offensive, whereas the Rhodesian armed forces were reduced to punitive operations by what was left of the Air Force's strike aircraft, regular units and the special forces.

In early September 1979 a ZANLA group of a dozen 'cadres' (approximately one hundred men, less *mujibas* and other forms of support) actually mounted a major ambush against BSAP Reserve units who were attempting to prevent interdiction of the oil supply route between Beitbridge and Fort Victoria. Not only was the ambush successful in its own terms, despite a Police Reserve Air Wing aircraft spotting for ZANLA movements; the fire fight which developed demonstrated that the guerrillas were so confident of success that they sat tight, breaking up BSAP rushes, before dispersing at will. The Police Anti-Terrorist Unit (PATU) squads which attempted to support these rushes were reduced to slaughtering cattle in a nearby Kraal. The ZANLA group, operating in a REPULSE sector previously thought to be relatively secure, scored two important successes: a white anti-guerrilla force had been worsted on terms favourable to its weapons and reconnaissance strength; and brutal retaliation against the Kraalhead strengthened ZANU's hand for the electoral battles which lay ahead.

Incidents of this type multiplied in the last three months of the war, and it is in the context of a sustained and expanding guerrilla offensive that the last major attempt by General Walls's commanders to tilt the balance should be seen. The presence of SADF in 'Company Strength' south and north of Beitbridge had not deterred ZANLA interdiction operations. Bishop Muzorewa's Government was still in white hands; Combined Operations Headquarters continued to direct the war. Resort to an unusual form of psychological warfare was decided upon. On 26 September a small force of Rhodesian Light Infantry and Selous Scouts assaulted the main ZANLA training camp in Mozambique, New Chimio. The original Combined Operations Headquarters' intention had been to demonstrate to all assembled at Lancaster House that ZANLA was no longer a mere guerrilla movement but a Soviet-backed army, which threatened the stability of an independent Zimbabwe.

This rather unusual strategic intention was justified by good political intelligence on the scale of New Chimio and the presence of German Democratic Republic 'advisers', active in manning anti-aircraft defences. Operational intelligence, however, was not of the same quality. When the RLI and Selous Scouts assault parties went in, they encountered some 6,000 ZANLA, not only well able to defend the camp but defeat the impending major attack. Perforce, the surviving Canberras were bombed up and sent on their way. What was intended as a limited operation led to a mass slaughter. Three thousand guerrillas were killed. Such a result was not exactly what the Combined Operations Headquarters (COH) had intended; ZANLA's operational credibility had been damaged, not destroyed; ZANU had been given an unexpected bonus; Mugabe in London was not slow to remind the world what Bishop Muzorewa's Government was really like.

White Rhodesia could still fight, but its survival no longer depended on political will or military skill but the rescue operation which the British Government was mounting at Lancaster House. On 11 October, the Canberras made almost their last appearance on the scene when they bombed bridges in Mozambique, totally severing Zambia's links with Beira. The following day a ground attack was made in northern Zambia which had the effect of disrupting traffic on the Tanzam railway. The objective in both cases was also political: to force Kaunda to put pressure on the PF at Lancaster House. Unlike the New Chimio operation, the political intention was justified by the victim's reaction. Kaunda came to London in early November to plead with the PF not to worsen Zambia's plight by further argument about the cease-fire. But by the time Kaunda appeared in London, the real conference had also developed a momentum which not only enabled the PF delegations, as advised by Tongogara, to make some concessions, but forced Carrington and his Foreign Office advisers to fight a battle on two fronts.

Once Carrington had conceded that the cease-fire in Rhodesia should be 'observed', and that a British role would predominate, the Directorate of Military Operations (DMO) in the Ministry of Defence started to ask some awkward questions. Where were these observers to come from? What were they supposed to observe? Where? (The Assembly Places had already been marked up on maps ready to be issued at a suitable point in the conference, but, officially, no decisions on this score had been taken.) Under whose authority would these observers operate? With whom would they liaise? By whom in Rhodesia supported – or moved? No information had been given to the DMO. Carrington could dismiss the PF call for a UN or Commonwealth force easily enough; men of his own stripe, however, were a different proposition. In order to understand why Carrington's 300-strong group of 'observers' expanded in two months, until it was established as a Commonwealth *monitoring* force of 1,548 which acquired significant characteristics of its own, we must compare what happened on the stage with what took place in the wings. There are crucial differences between what was publicly said – or eventually agreed – and what was won by soldiers determined to commit their men only when certain basic conditions had been met.

A résumé of the main stages between 22 October and 21 December is unavoidable at this point. Virtually all the conference statements, proposals and rebuttals were either by the British Government (BG) or the Patriotic Front (PF). On 2 November, BG reiterated that 'the pre-independence arrangements' after agreement had been reached at Lancaster House would be in the hands of a duly appointed Governor. But a cease-fire must be negotiated *at* the conference. Individual Commonwealth representatives would be allowed to 'observe' the independence election. (Ramphal had already pressed, unsuccessfully, for a Commonwealth Observer *Group*.) On 9 November, and following reports from Australia and New Zealand, Gilmour unwisely and inaccurately said, 'We have always said we were going to have the cease-fire observed *and monitored* [writer's italics] ... the cease-fire has to be observed or monitored and you can't have a cease-fire without it. Obviously it is for discussion how many people there should be, where they should be, and so forth.' On 10 November, BG rejected the PF's request for a two-month period to bring the cease-fire into effect. On 10 November, Kaunda, on behalf of the PF, asked that the cease-fire be *enforced*. No means was specified. Nobody took much notice of Kaunda.

On 13 November, Carrington spoke in the House of Lords on the second reading of the Southern Rhodesia Bill. *Inter alia*, and introducing a Bill designed to give Rhodesia legal independence after an election, Carrington reiterated that the Governor alone would rule, although he would be advised by, amongst other bodies, a Cease-fire Commission. Sanctions would lapse 'with the arrival of a British Governor and acceptance of his authority'. This reference to sanctions came in a passage where Carrington deliberately mentioned that 'the Salisbury Delegation have accepted the British Government's constitutional proposals' – but said nothing about the PF. Carrington, in referring to the Cease-fire Commission, said,

> the military commanders of both sides would be represented, under the Chairmanship of the Governor's Military Adviser. The forces on both sides would be equally responsible to the Governor for the observance of the cease-fire and would come under his authority. In addition, in conjunction with some other Commonwealth Governments, we are prepared to establish a monitoring force to help reassure all parties that the observance of the cease-fire will be impartially assessed *and controlled* [writer's italics] ... It will not however be an intervention force which could find itself in conflict with the parties. I would pay tribute to the Governments of Australia, New Zealand, and Fiji, all of whom have announced they are prepared to contribute to such a force.

The same day, a PF statement accused BG of jumping the gun by giving the Second Reading to the Southern Rhodesia Bill before agreement on all points had been reached in Lancaster House. Lifting sanctions was Carrington's hidden weapon to force concessions from the PF; the latter was determined to unmask it, knowing 'sanctions' to be a word uniting all shades of

Commonwealth opinion and practice. BG riposted immediately by taking up other issues contested by the PF: there would not be a register of electors – an indirect reference to the nature and conduct of the April election; there would not be a six-month, but a two-month election campaign. These points were reasserted on the 14th; on the 16th, BG produced the first *démarche* on the cease-fire proposals: seven to ten days would be allowed for a cease-fire 'to come into effect'. We are reaching the crux; the PF had ceased to be Carrington's main adversary. On 20 November, BG rejected the PF's demand for 'demarcation areas' in a cease-fire agreement; rejected the notion of an enforcement role for the monitoring force; added Kenya to the participants; and reassured the Salisbury Delegation that 'all Patriotic Front forces at present inside Rhodesia will assemble during the run-down to the cease-fire at places determined *in advance* [writer's italics] at this Conference'. (Not, be it noted, by those publicly participating in it.)

On 22 November 'proposals on Cease-fire Arrangements' were tabled by Carrington. The Assembly Places (or Points, as they were called officially) plan was out in the open after many weeks of gestation. But although the plan was Walls's in essentials, above all in the location of the APs, which he (and General Magnus Malan in Pretoria) decided in conformity with his assessment of the very varying ZANLA and ZIPRA threats compared to the strength and deployment of the Rhodesian Security Forces, it had been amended in two crucial respects: Carrington's acceptance of a monitoring force, and his concept of a Cease-fire Commission under sole British authority, but with 'representatives of both sides' sitting on it. Whitehall arguments about the force continued unabated during late November, but it is necessary to establish at this point in the narrative that Walls's original plan had been based on the premise that the RSF would control the APs in terms of access to them and egress from them.

Walls was to have most of his plan retained by Carrington, above all in the distinction made between PF forces, which were to be confined to the APs, and the RSF, which was, for all practical purposes, to remain operationally deployed. The 22 November proposals, however, gave virtually equal weight, in the composition and strength of monitoring 'teams', as they were designated, to both RSF and PF. But due to the battle being fought between the Foreign Office and the Ministry of Defence, Carrington found himself trying to explain the role of the monitoring force mostly in terms of the PF, much less in relation to the RSF. The neurotically suspicious Salisbury Delegation wanted something better than explanations.

Few should have been surprised, therefore, when an increasingly intemperate Walls said publicly on British television (23 November), one day after his plan, as amended, had been tabled at the conference: 'If PF forces move from the APs, we will shoot them.' Dr Mundewarara (Muzorewa's Deputy) repeated this threat with gratuitous venom at a press conference on the 26th, adding that no elements of the RSF, or Air Force, would be stood down. These two outbursts gave more of the game away. Walls primarily wanted the APs in order to deter PF forces from leaving the bush, thus justifying RSF claims that they were not prepared to observe a cease-fire. But PF forces which did risk ambush from the RSF *en route* to the APs, would thereafter not only have been kept in them coercively but would be threatened with attack if they tried to leave. Carrington's partial amendment reflected pressure imposed on his advisers by the Ministry of Defence. All involved in planning the Monitoring Force at the purely military level were adamant that monitoring of movements and control of APs must exclude all elements of the RSF.

But few were aware of this Whitehall battle. High Commissions were not directly involved in the planning stages. Yet rumours abounded. Malcolm Fraser immediately asked Carrington about the implications of the outbursts by Walls and Mundewarara for the security of the Monitoring Force. Fraser had already been driven to state in the Australian Parliament on 22 November that 'In the event of any serious breakdown of law and order in Rhodesia in which the lives of Australian personnel could be at risk, they would be immediately withdrawn after appropriate advice to the British Government.' Carrington could provide no assurances. Fraser decided to give the Commanding Officer of the Australian contingent strict, personal orders not to place himself under the command of the Governor's Military Adviser, who was also to command the Monitoring Force. This absurd inhibition was to have unfortunate consequences, which were only overcome when Colonel Kevin Cole decided to ignore it.

Between 23 and 26 November the PF delegations made a reasoned reply to the nominally British proposals. In effect, the proposals were accepted. The reply reiterated PF arguments that two months would be necessary for the cease-fire to come into effect, alleging that distance, disruption of communications, and the general state of the country precluded a shorter period. A case was made that RSF Special Forces and the auxiliaries should be stood down. But the delegations dropped their demand for disbandment of the RSF, and accepted that the cease-fire would only be monitored, not enforced. Members of the delegations, Tongogara excepted, were still in the dark about the battle being waged in Whitehall, but Mugabe was slowly coming to understand that a Monitoring Force of reasonable size might, unwittingly, provide protection to PF forces who made for and stayed put in the APs. The PF delegation's reply to the AP proposals asked for equality of status with the RSF. Both should be regarded as 'forces of the Crown' once the cease-fire came into effect and the authority of the British Governor was accepted. Carrington was reluctant to accept this request; Walls drew a distinction between the 'recognised' – military definable by unit and position – RSF and the guerrilla forces. By November 1979 this distinction had worn thin. Equality of status was granted, a concession which had a crucial effect on Monitoring Force relations with PF liaison officers.

Carrington's advisers were much influenced by Walls's belief that relatively few guerrillas would make their way to the APs. These advisers can be collectively forgiven for their ignorance of guerrilla war, and the difficulties and dangers associated with monitoring a cease-fire. Poor intelligence about the situation in Rhodesia was, however, no longer an excuse for the resistance which, until 28 November, was made to the persistent demands of the Directorate of Military Operations for clarification about the objectives, methods and intentions of the force. A mood of unprecedented hostility developed in Whitehall. From 5 November, when Major-General John Acland was nominated Military Adviser, the DMO, and others in the Ministry of Defence, began to define an aim for the Monitoring Force which ran directly counter to all that Walls had in mind.

Given that there was to be a Monitoring Force, of sorts, the first requirement was to insist on a minimum strength. Outright, indeed outspoken opposition to a token figure of three hundred led to an appreciation that the minimum acceptable strength, whatever tasks might be carried out, was the equivalent of a reinforced battalion group. The DMO took the Staff College 'worst case' principle to heart. If the cease-fire in Rhodesia was either disregarded or comprehensively broke down, the Force, scattered all over the country, would be in acute danger. Provision must be made for evacuating sub-units – or 'teams' – and concentrating at New Sarum, the air head for all arriving troops. Rhodesia's 'international airport' would, if necessary, be held and defended by the Monitoring Force until such time as it was airlifted to friendly territory. Despite overtures from Pretoria – and, indeed, Walls in person – that territory did not include the Republic of South Africa.

Carrington began to give ground behind the scenes once he realised that serving British officers of the rank of Major-General were prepared to insist on minimum requirements being met even at risk to their own careers. By 15 November Brigadier John Learmont, later to be appointed Deputy Force Commander, had received a warning order to plan Operation AGILA, as it was to be called, in detail. The battle for numbers was intensifying, but with Commonwealth Governments anxious to participate (although the Foreign Office continued to keep High Commissions in London lamentably short of essential information about detailed cease-fire proposals), the minimum manpower requirement was in sight of being met. Learmont sent a reconnaissance team to Rhodesia on 22 November; at the exact moment when Carrington, Walls, Fraser and Mundewarara were embroiled in complicity and misunderstandings, Acland and Learmont were getting to grips with reality. The reconnaissance team's report provided not only an appreciation of logistic requirements – one in stark contrast with the reassurances made by Walls in London – but an intelligence summary somewhat different from descriptions of the situation on the ground put out by the Foreign Office. The RSF would provide little logistic support; short-range airlift capacity in the monitoring force must be increased. Breakdown of civil administration in rural districts meant that the force would need a signals element much larger than originally planned. The battle for numbers was renewed. In the event, no fewer than forty-four headquarters and units (or the equivalent) of the British Army, the Royal Marines and the Royal Air Force were called on to make up the numbers.

Towards the end of November Acland and his staff had begun to contemplate approaching Tongogara. Walls had objected to 'equality of status'; he opposed consultation with the PF on implementation of the cease-fire. Walls understood well enough that if the PF delegation came to regard the Monitoring Force as both impartial (in reporting incidents), and its teams as effective in controlling the APs, guerrillas might arrive at the latter in great numbers. If, and this *is* the crux, the force established really good relations with PF liaison officers, the guerrillas' march to rendezvous (RV) and thence to APs would take place in an orderly manner. The RSF, although not the special forces, might find it difficult to justify attacks on ZIPRA or ZANLA. Walls began to see, but not to accept, that a well-balanced, disciplined, properly provided and supported monitoring force would enable the cease-fire to stick, not collapse. If the cease-fire held, the independence election would not be the victory for Muzorewa so many in Salisbury – and London – had predicted.

The Force Commander and his staff had won the battle for men; initial reconnaissance had yielded much; relations with Tongogara were in train. But the twists and turns of the Whitehall battle were not over. The Force would be monitoring, not controlling Assembly Places, and, on paper, the headquarters of RSF formations. The 'British' proposals for the cease-fire envisaged no more than 'a week to ten days' for it to 'come into effect'. This time-scale was subsequently defined as 'one plus seven days'. This absurd time-scale, one should note, was to start once agreement was reached at Lancaster House. Troops were to depart immediately. Eight days later, they were to be in position at APs. Even before Learmont's reconnaissance party had reported, he and Acland knew that it would be physically impossible for the Force to be fully operational, and deployed to the RVs and APs, on such a time-scale. Acland made it plain that he would refuse to attempt deployment in eight days. Even assuming ideal road and flying conditions – and summer rain in Zimbabwe can be torrential – the process of deployment from arrival at airhead to arrival at over a hundred designated locations would take a minimum of three days. Deployment to RSF headquarters would be relatively easy; to RVs and APs fraught with difficulty and danger. Walls, once he accepted the Monitoring Force as a *fait accompli*, saw this difference as reassuring. Acland found it quite unacceptable, and said so, frequently and forcefully.

A BG paper of 28 November, full of the usual circumlocutions, masked an important shift of emphasis towards a clearly defined aim for the Monitoring Force: the DMO insisted that all 'locations' must be monitored on the principle that all lawful forces would stand fast once the cease-fire was in operation. At this late stage of the conference Carrington had made only two open concessions to the PF – on equality of status in terms of what constituted 'lawful' forces, and concerning 'equal representation' on the Cease-fire Commission – but was giving ground behind the scenes. Carrington was also again threatening to apply the closure by lifting sanctions – and despatching the nominated Governor (Christopher Soames) to Salisbury. Procrastination and argument, whether publicly or privately conducted, obviously had to end at some point. Perhaps for these reasons, the 28 November paper, which was made available simultaneously with one by the PF, appeared merely to restate the 'British' position on some essential points. These were ostensibly confined to the cease-fire; in reality, all points were directly relevant to the Monitoring Force's role in attempting to implement it. The PF openly dropped its demands for disbandment of the RSF; the AP plan was accepted, *faute de mieux*. Tongogara knew that the conference would collapse if the PF totally opposed the plan.

Despite these concessions, the BG paper stressed that a distinction must be drawn between the RSF and the PF: 'The Rhodesian forces are identified and their locations are known. That is what we mean when we talk about them monitored *from their existing company bases* [italicised in original]. The Patriotic Front forces are not identified and will have to be identified if an effective cease-fire is to come into operation.' Elsewhere in the paper the 'coming into effect' time-scale was reiterated. The quoted passage and the time-scale were the cause of a really intense Whitehall argument between 28 November and 8 December, when the Monitoring Force advance party left for Salisbury. Throughout these ten days British Government spokesmen insisted that the distinction so carefully drawn by Walls must remain the basis of the cease-fire proposals. Officially, the same intransigence prevailed over the time-scale. On 30 November, a Foreign Office spokesman gave more of the game away when he stated that no Rhodesian Air Force aircraft, strike or transport, would be grounded. There was a case for transport aircraft to remain operational; there was none for strike aircraft to do so. Outwardly, all seemed to be going the way Walls wanted.

But, by late November and early December, the Ministry of Defence and Tongogara were asking the same questions. One officer in the Ministry noted: 'Tongogara is really asking our questions openly.' In the first week of December all those most critical of the British Government's subjection to Walls's dictates united to make quite clear what would be the effect of the Monitoring Force accepting them. The substance of their views can be expressed as follows:

(i) (a) The Rhodesian forces will remain operationally deployed.

(b) The PF forces will be removed to 'assembly points'; they will be regarded as 'lawful' but of no practical value in upholding the Governor's authority, because they lack the necessary 'formed units', as the statement 28 November defines the Rhodesian forces.

(c) The Rhodesian forces will be monitored from 'company bases'. Nothing is said about monitoring the Rhodesian forces in an operational context where units and sub-units *move*.

(d) The PF forces will be confined to the 'assembly points'. They will not move.

(ii) There is, however, another point which must be made, of equal, perhaps of complementary importance to those made above. The assertions about the characteristics of the Rhodesian forces ignore the composition and tactics of special and auxiliary units. Indeed the assertions ignore the fact that even the 'identified' Rhodesian forces operate from locations known only to their commanders. A guerrilla war can only be fought intelligently if the 'formed units' adopt guerrilla tactics. Secrecy and deception are essential elements in Rhodesian forces' strategy and tactics. It is true that the PF forces elude identification, by location or unit. But, to an increasing extent, this factor applies, or should be applied, to the Rhodesian forces. Neither the Rhodesian nor the PF forces, as now established, are suitable instruments to express the Governor's authority.

(iii) It is in the context of the above points that the British delegation's other main argument must be seen:

A cease-fire to be established in 'seven days'. Any forces not complying with the cease-fire thereafter will be considered 'unlawful'. Setting aside the necessity to deploy the monitoring force *before* the cease-fire becomes effective, it will be simple, in terms of communications, for the Rhodesian forces to comply; impossible for the PF forces to do so. A very large proportion of PF forces is likely to be 'unlawful' on this time-scale.

The net result of these representations will only be appreciated when Chapter 19 is reached. But Acland's advance party would not have left for Salisbury if agreement had not been wrung from Carrington that the RSF must stand fast once the cease-fire had come into effect; on 11 December, and after more Whitehall argument, Carrington stated: 'In further refining our cease-fire proposals I would like to make it clear from the onset that there can be no question of surrender by either side.' Carrington, in dealing with the coming into effect and implementation of the cease-fire, added: 'In the circumstances prevailing in Rhodesia it will not be sufficient for the Governor to instruct the forces which have accepted his authority simply to cease firing and remain in their present positions. A cease-fire in these circumstances would have no chance of being preserved *and a Monitoring Force could not be deployed* [writer's italics].'

13 Hearts and minds: Assembly Point ROMEO, January 1980

14 At home with his people: Joshua Nkomo in Makokoba market place, Bulawayo, June 1980

15 Robert Mugabe's apotheosis, Kutama, 7 June 1980

Carrington went further. After dealing with the composition and tasks of the Monitoring Force, he said:

We have next to consider the arrangements under which the forces will disengage and the monitoring force will be deployed. We cannot arrange for the simultaneous deployment of monitoring teams to both sides, because the Patriotic Front forces are diffused and will not, at the outset of the process, be identified to the monitoring force. The Rhodesian forces will make the first move by (a) accepting the Governor's authority and agreeing to comply with his directions; (b) the monitoring teams allocated to the Rhodesian forces will then be deployed through their command structure down to company base level; (c) on cease-fire day the Rhodesian forces will disengage from the Patriotic Front forces by moving into the close vicinity of bases to permit the Patriotic Front to assemble their forces.

It will then be for the Patriotic Front to assemble their forces via rendezvous points to assembly places at which they can be monitored. The process of assembly will be continuous. For this purpose, it will be necessary for the Patriotic Front, under the auspices of the monitoring force, to send representatives to each of the rendezvous points. The Patriotic Front forces will make their way with their arms and equipment to the rendezvous point, where they will be under the authority of their own Commanders. From these they will move to their assembly places in transport which will be provided for them, with their arms and equipment and under their own command. This movement will take place under the auspices of the monitoring force, who will be in direct communication with the teams attached to the Rhodesian forces so that each side can be informed of the other's movements and there can be no misunderstanding of each other's intentions.

Carrington's statement concluded on this aspect of the initial stages of the cease-fire:

By the time the assembly process is complete we shall have reached a point at which the forces which have accepted the

Governor's authority are known and identified; the opposing forces have been separated from each other; and monitoring teams are located with the forces of both sides so that their maintenance of the cease-fire can be observed.

The dice were still loaded against the Patriotic Front – above all, in the location of APs – but if Carrington's statement of 11 December is compared with the 22 and 28 November proposals some fundamental improvements in security for the guerrilla forces can be discerned. Relatively greater security for guerrillas meant some degree of security for the monitoring force. Confining the RSF to headquarters and the 'company base level' would not effectively change operational deployment, but would limit movement. The admission that PF forces could, and would, be 'identified' further denied the RSF opportunities to claim that 'unidentified' guerrillas should be dealt with because they might be breaching the cease-fire. Above all, the two-stage process whereby PF forces were to move to RVs and then be moved to APs not only promised further security to guerrillas and offered a good chance of effective liaison with the Monitoring Force, but in practice extended the 'coming into effect' period by several days. That hard-won, tacit, barely conceded concession gave more reassurance to Acland and Learmont than any other. On 11 December agreement was announced in principle on the cease-fire. Formal agreement on all matters was still eleven days away, but on the 11th Christopher Soames flew to Salisbury as Governor of Southern Rhodesia. As a prominent Conservative, close to Carrington, Soames's appointment was purely political. A man of strong opinions, Soames frequently surprised both his supporters and his critics in the coming months. Sanctions were lifted. Of greater importance Acland, Learmont and most of their staff were given what Acland called the first small miracle: eighteen seats on the aircraft.

The reader may well feel that undue attention has been given to the evolution and establishment of the Monitoring Force. Chapter 19 will show why the Commonwealth Monitoring Force (or CMF, as it will now be called) was not only essential for maintaining the cease-fire but played a crucial role in the whole election process. But space had also to be given to the CMF as an issue which reflected how the British Government tried to stage-manage the Lancaster House conference, and what it hoped to achieve in Rhodesia thereafter. Little either of stage-management or expectation was found between 11 and 21 December, but this further delay in reaching agreement provided additional time for the CMF to become operational. Troops had been on 24 hours' notice since 3 December, and if all loose ends had been tied up by then, the airlift would have started on the 12th. Delays at Lancaster House postponed the airlift until the 22nd. Acland and his staff gained a valuable ten days in which to prepare for an operation which was to be unique in the Commonwealth experience.

Whilst Acland and Learmont tackled the situation on the ground, in London Carrington sought to end a conference which had not turned out as planned. On 13 December Carrington circulated documents for initialling by leaders of the delegations; on the 15th he was still asking for a reply. Not until the 21st, and after several final rhetorical flourishes and denunciations, was formal agreement reached. The new constitution and all the 'Pre-Independence Arrangements' were approved. A second small miracle will be found in 'Annex 2/E' of the Lancaster House Agreement:

> With effect from 2400 hours on 21 December 1979 all movement by personnel of the Patriotic Front armed forces into Rhodesia and all cross-border military activity by the Rhodesian forces will cease ... With effect from 2400 hours on 28 December 1979 all hostilities in Rhodesia will cease ... The parties recognise that disengagement of the forces will be essential to an effective cease-fire and the deployment of the monitoring force. At 2400 hours on 28 December 1979, the Rhodesian armed forces, under the directions of the Governor, will therefore disengage to enable the Patriotic Front forces inside Rhodesia to begin the process of assembly ... Movement to assembly places will be completed by 2400 hours on 4 January 1980.

In practice, therefore, the 'coming into effect' arrangements, the CMF deployment, and the PF forces 'assembly' were given a fourteen-day time-scale, 21 December to 4 January. This period had always been reckoned by the DMO as the absolute minimum in which any deployment could take place. Determination, professional skill and foresight on the one hand combined with last-minute miscalculations and concessions on the other to give the CMF – and the PF forces – the bare minimum which they needed to make a reality of the cease-fire. Many in the CMF and PF wondered what Walls would do next, and how much luck would be needed in the weeks ahead. They were to need a great deal of it.

19

1980: Election and Independence

The last stage of a journey which began when the Union flag was raised in Salisbury eighty-eight years before proved to be even more arduous for genuine black nationalism than the war of second Chimurenga. By the time Christopher Soames, literally and figuratively a Governor *sans des plumes*, landed at New Sarum on 12 December the independence election campaign was being waged by whites convinced that, with British and South African help, they could repeat their success of the previous April. Soames, accompanied by a small staff, amongst whom his Foreign Office Political Adviser, Robin Renwick, was not the least influential, drove to Government House. Once again, the Union flag was hauled to the masthead. This time, however, there was no twenty-one gun salute, and no Captain Hoste of the Pioneer Column to record that another jewel had been added to the British Crown. Soames arrived almost furtively in his VC10, knowing that the real election business would be carried out behind the scenes. Renwick quickly strengthened a relationship with Walls which had started at Lancaster House.

Whites running Muzorewa - perhaps the metaphor of an electric hare is more telling than the conjuror's rabbit - had warrant for their conviction. The Lancaster House conference had certainly not gone quite as planned in London, Salisbury and Pretoria, above all in the establishment of the CMF. But the very intensity of effort by Carrington personally and the Foreign Office collectively to hobble the PF proved beyond reasonable doubt that full support from the British Government would be given to white interests, and would continue throughout a two-month election campaign in which 'no holds barred' might serve as a slogan for all parties. Carrington's 'first-class solution' of a second electoral victory for Muzorewa would lead to a situation in which the country's affairs remained firmly in white hands, even if black gloves were worn as a gesture to the new constitution which all at Lancaster House had, finally, accepted. Mugabe's determination to dissolve the PF despite – or because of – Nkomo's vehement objections, and to fight the election from his Shona stronghold in the east also encouraged many whites in the hope that Muzorewa's South African financed UANC would come home a clear winner.

Before embarking on this final stage the reader should be warned that one of the few really objective accounts of what actually happened during the election will be drawn on rather heavily in preference to published secondary sources or even personal recollection and recorded, unattributable comment. Most accounts of the election, many admirable in themselves, which appeared in 1980 or thereabouts concentrate on how the parties attempted to win, how they competed, why they quarrelled. Very little attention was given to what the British Government, not only as represented by the Governor but by many lesser lights (some, indeed, well hidden), actually did to thwart ZANU (Patriotic Front) – as Mugabe's election party was so clumsily designated – by all legitimate, and illegitimate means.

Yet in the solid volume entitled *Southern Rhodesia Elections; February 1980; the Report of the Commonwealth Observer Group* will be found virtually all the facts which the reader needs to convince him that the culmination of those eighty-eight years saw a British Government as actively engaged in the promotion of white interests as was its predecessor when the Pioneer Column and five troops of the British South Africa Company's Police marched from Kimberley on 6 May 1891. Maybe there was a certain inevitability in such a culmination, certainly a Marxist would think so; doubtless Mugabe from his corner and Smith and Walls from theirs did see the issues in terms of a final trial of racial strength.

There was nothing inevitable, however, in the establishment

of the Commonwealth Observer Group (COG). Carrington opposed the very idea of such a group, endowed with collective Commonwealth authority, providing, as it were, an imprimatur for the independence election (or issuing a fiat declaring it null and void) even more strongly than he contested the notion of a Commonwealth Monitoring Force. We must pause, retrace our steps to Lancaster House for a moment, to note that Carrington was more comprehensively defeated over the establishment of the COG than he was concerning the CMF. Defeat reflected argument on all the issues which the Commonwealth as such, but Nyerere, Fraser and Manley in concert, had raised and settled at the Lusaka Meeting. Above all, the establishment of the COG ensured that Britain, in Rhodesia, would be *watched*, not by individuals doubtless estimable yet, alone, helpless; but by a formidable body of experience, collectively capable of questioning electoral practices, whoever engaged in them.

From the outset of the Lancaster House conference Carrington, by the manner no less than the substance of his opposition to an election observer group, had thrown down a gage to Shridath Ramphal which the latter was not slow to pick up. Nyerere's speech at the opening of the Lusaka Meeting had not only implicitly suggested such a group but explicitly called for the Commonwealth 'to assist the responsible power – Britain – both in the election supervision and in the interim arrangements which internationally supervised elections presuppose'. In the aftermath of Mrs Thatcher's written capitulation two days later Nyerere and members of his pressure group were too wise, or too conscious of further battles, to insist on terms as outlined above. But, in allowing the British Government a virtually free hand in organising and running the Lancaster House conference, Nyerere was determined to see a Commonwealth Observer Group established, composed of men whose experience would tell them where to look, and whose collective authority would compel answers to awkward questions from the most reluctant official. Fraser and Manley were relatively indifferent about the need for an observer *group* – the former, indeed, preferring that the Australian Government rest on its Lusaka laurels – but Nyerere was adamant. He had not supported Mugabe through the wilderness to see him defeated in sight of the promised land.

Nyerere's determination was given additional strength by a factor which was appreciated only by those familiar with Rhodesian realities. The election as such, as a piece of bureaucratic organisation, would have to be conducted by a Rhodesian Civil Service, overwhelmingly white, of varying loyalties, not necessarily to white interests, but prima facie more likely to be so than not. If the election had been 'internationally supervised' these Civil Servants could, to a considerable degree, have been replaced by officials drawn from the United Nations, or other sources. How such strangers, even if skilled, experienced and impartial, would have coped with a Rhodesia torn by seven years of civil war is a moot point. Setting it aside, Nyerere's concession that Britain would have responsibility for the election but would use the Rhodesian Civil Service for executing that responsibility – and much else besides – only made him the more determined that an observer group was essential to see that justice, however rough and ready, was done.

Carrington, for his part and precisely because he appreciated so clearly the power of Smith's Muzorewa, the RSF, and the Rhodesian Civil Service in combination, was equally determined that no observer group would be established. He was successful in Lancaster House plenary and in the corridors, but he reckoned without Ramphal's own determination, and he dismissed the role of a body known as the Commonwealth Committee on Southern Africa. This Committee, an offshoot of the UDI Sanctions Lobby, included Commonwealth High Commissioners, or their representatives, but was dominated by Ramphal. He saw the Committee as an antidote, and prospectively something more, to a Whitehall policy regarding Southern Africa which was favourable to white interests, indifferent – at best – to black. The Committee, which essentially reflected the growth of a Commonwealth consensus on Rhodesia, met weekly during the Lancaster House Conference, pressing for the observer group's establishment, and subjecting the Foreign Office representative, John Graham, to a hard time.[1]

Until 23 November, Carrington had successfully resisted all efforts to establish the group. At the Southern Africa Committee's meeting that day, however, Ramphal threw down *his* gage. In a long, well-argued statement (Appendix B, pp. 318–25), made after conducting some backstairs Commonwealth diplomacy of his own, Ramphal insisted that the Lusaka 'Accord' had provided for Commonwealth observation of the election, and that without this process the latter could not be declared valid. Ramphal, in effect, knowing well that he spoke for the Commonwealth as a whole (whatever individual reservations or, *pace* Fraser, changes of mood might have occurred in three months of Lancaster House brinkmanship), asserted that Britain would only have discharged its final responsibility for Rhodesia when forty-one other sovereign states said so. Ramphal went further: 'As I indicated to Commonwealth Heads of Government on 19 November, it was my understanding that what was envisaged at Lusaka was a collective role for "Commonwealth observers" rather than separate roles for "observers from Commonwealth countries".'

Ramphal said, in conclusion: 'It is important that the Commonwealth does not falter at this stage.' Ramphal knew that Carrington was exerting maximum pressure to prevent the COG's establishment. By 23 November he had invited 'each Commonwealth Government to send observers to the Rhodesian election (at their own expense)',[2] and he had done so because, as the *Financial Times* reported on 13 December: 'Carrington maintained that whatever the Commonwealth governments might have thought they collectively agreed in Lusaka ... a Commonwealth Observer Group of the type suggested by Mr Ramphal could undermine the flexibility of Lord Soames ... as he tries to juggle with the complexities of an election while trying to maintain a cease-fire.' And, as the *Washington Post* remarked on 21 December, 'It is Britain which must, in the end, be the sole judge of voting.'

Yet it was on 13 December, just as the well-informed *Financial Times* was, reluctantly, stating a case for Carrington, that he agreed to the COG on the lines of the Lusaka 'Accord' – as interpreted by Ramphal. The meeting of the Southern Africa Committee on 23 November had been acrimonious – in the sense that Carrington, as represented by Graham, was told in unambiguous language that an observer group there must be. In the following three weeks, during which Carrington gave ground on the CMF issues and the cease-fire time-table, he was subjected to pressure from a large number of those forty-one sovereign Governments. Carrington succumbed – but not before it had been accepted by all participants in the Lancaster House conference that the election would be conducted, administratively, by the Rhodesian Civil Service, and that the Governor would use its members to run Britain's last Colony. Another moot point is whether agreement would have been reached at Lancaster House on 21 December if this horse-trade of COG for agreement on the use of the Rhodesian Civil Service had not taken place. In the writer's opinion, and from his experience of these singular three months, agreement required the trade to be made.[3]

The COG was, therefore – and finally – established by due process of bargaining. Ramphal had his moment of triumph – after enduring much sour criticism from various quarters favourably disposed to Carrington and white Rhodesia – when, on 13 December, he gave the COG its terms of reference. Although given within the context of the Southern Africa Committee, the terms were marked by a very personal commitment to a Commonwealth-supervised independence election. Ramphal also wrote the COG's terms of reference, of which the critical paragraph stated: 'The Group's function will be to ascertain in their impartial judgement, whether, in the context of the Lusaka accord and the Lancaster House Conference, the elections were free and fair.' The Commonwealth, not Britain, would deliver the verdict. Ramphal also chose the eleven observers; the 13 December meeting, indeed, recorded that he 'appointed' them. The immensely experienced Rajeshwar Dayal from India was appointed Chairman, and he was supported by a strong team, a kind of Commonwealth first eleven of Mandarins, from Australia, Bangladesh, Barbados, Canada, Ghana, Jamaica, Nigeria, Papua New Guinea, Sierra Leone and Sri Lanka.[4] Nkomo and Mugabe went hobbled into the independence election, but there is no doubt that the CMF and the COG provided an unexpected, formidable means of giving them an unsporting chance.

The 13 December meeting also established 'operational requirements' for the COG, designed to leave Soames and the Rhodesian Administration in no doubt that observation of the election would be made in fulfilment of the Lusaka Accord and Lancaster House Agreement and not when electoral authorities saw fit or could find no way of preventing it. The COG was to observe, comment on – or complain about – 'every aspect of the electoral campaign'. This remit was interpreted very widely indeed; what it meant, crudely, was that for two months the COG would have the authority to poke its nose into every aspect of Rhodesian affairs, black and white. As the 'operational requirements' put it: 'In order to carry out their functions, the Observer Group will have complete freedom of movement and access to all parts of the country and the right of inquiry into every aspect of the electoral process.' Stiff terms were also established for the right not to see but be seen; to ensure the Governor's co-operation – rather than vice versa; and to be supported in terms of staff. 'Suitable ground and air transport; radios for two-way communication; accommodation facilities; office equipment.'

In short, the COG took its collective self with the utmost seriousness, well aware that any other approach would have rendered it immediately vulnerable to the delays and denials with which any bureaucracy is well equipped. Dayal had been around for a long time, and knew, from the Congo civil war and other crises, what he had let himself in for. In the Congo Dayal, as Dag Hammarskjöld's head of mission, had not only been put in an invidious position because he had not been given clear directives, but also from being unable to tell that man of mystery what was happening through lack of adequate communications. It was at Dayal's insistence that the COG only left for Rhodesia on 24 January – one month and five days before the final day of the poll on 29 February – once its directives had been clearly established and the means of complying with them provided. Circumstances were to prove Dayal's caution totally justified. The COG, investigating thoroughly and reporting much which caused its members disquiet, only overcame difficulties because it was a thoroughly professional show. At no time, or point, did the Rhodesian Civil Service welcome the COG's presence, let alone its activities.[5]

The advent and establishment of the COG and the CMF have been described in detail because it was upon these two bodies that the election's success – as a political event and an administrative process – ultimately depended. The CMF, by its bearing, courage and resolution, kept the peace, or as much as a ravaged land could expect. The COG ensured that, whatever malpractices occurred amongst the parties and elsewhere, the poll itself was conducted with scrupulous fairness and, as Dayal's final *Report* to Ramphal justly stated 'with great good humour'. Although this comment was made specifically about the African poll, it is indicative of the COG's perceptions as a whole. Indeed, the final *Report* is an unintentional, indirect tribute to the Rhodesia which was coming to an end and the Zimbabwe which was, at last, about to receive its birthright. The conscientious white official and the patient black voter are recorded impartially but imaginatively in the pages of the *Report*, which is not a mere summary of events – and malpractices – it is a narrative recording historic change.

Good humour notwithstanding, these last stages were arduous, and not only for the followers of Robert Mugabe, Joshua Nkomo and Abel Muzorewa. Peril stalked the CMF, aware at every moment of day and night that the RSF was ready to pounce; some members of ZANLA and ZIPRA were trigger-happy or bloody-minded; the special forces were itching to act as *agents provocateurs*. Every day, somebody was killed. The COG, if not deliberately thwarted by Soames and his administration, contended with a natural but oppressive reluctance to provide active encouragement and support. The COG, as something more than a watchdog, much more of a jury, was ranged in the white Rhodesian mind with Nkomo and Mugabe, and was treated accordingly. Soames kept his thoughts about the COG to himself. His replies to Dayal's courteous complaints and requests are amiable, but mostly negative. Soames fought in his corner also; he did not want to be told what, and what not to do. By contrast, relations between the CMF and the COG rapidly became cordial. Dayal, Acland, their colleagues and comrades, were all suspect in white Rhodesian eyes. Adversity makes strange bedfellows: so does a marked feeling that one is not welcome, indeed that one is not only a damn nuisance, but is letting the side down.[6] On at least one, important, occasion a soldier and an observer were swiftly able to refute an allegation about intimidation. The refutation was accepted by Soames – reluctantly – but Walls neither forgot nor forgave.

The last stages, therefore, will be narrated mainly in terms of what the CMF and COG experienced, not what Soames did or politicians said. A supremely self-confident Mugabe's triumphant return to Salisbury on 27 January; Nkomo's retreat upon his Bulawayo stronghold; Muzorewa's aerial circus; Walls's preparations for a coup should Mugabe win after all – these comings and goings have been told before, by partisans and serious observers. But to see the election through the eyes of men both impartial and actively engaged should give us a wide perspective. We begin with the CMF, if only because the nature of its deployment and the multiple tasks eventually imposed on it provide further evidence of the fact that neither monitoring nor 'control' in the literal sense was possible. This fact is starkly underlined by the following comment from the COG *Report* (referred to subsequently as COGR):

In our view this number [CMF's 1,548 men] might have been sufficient had the Rhodesian Security Forces been confined to their company bases, but in fact they were not. Indeed, throughout the campaign we witnessed a high level of activity by the Security Forces in many parts of the country, and more often than not there were no members of the Cease-fire Monitoring Group [sic] in sight. Numerous camps were monitored only on an occasional basis, and the monitoring did not extend to the activities of the Security Forces when on duty away from their bases.[7]

Despite the concessions wrung from Carrington – in reality, from Walls – the CMF, in being tasked to monitor both the Rhodesian and PF armed forces, found that as the various headquarters and so-called 'company bases' of the former outnumbered the Assembly Places and RVs by nearly three to one, the same proportion of monitoring teams had to be allotted. Given the CMF's unavoidably long 'tail', these proportions reduced the size of teams deployed to some APs to no more than seventeen. Moreover, the Lancaster House Agreement, in belatedly removing some of the imbalance between the recognition accorded the RSF and denied the PF forces, ignored the former's many categories of reserves. Together with comparable resources available to the BSAP, full mobilisation – requested by Walls, conceded by Soames – ensured that nearly 100,000 men were, as in the April 1979 election, available as 'forces of the Crown'. A fully mobilised BSAP alone numbered 46,000 men, and when the Special and Auxiliary forces are added to such numbers it can be readily appreciated that 'confined to company bases' was a mere form of words, masking an operational deployment which was *not* affected by the cease-fire agreement. These factors must be carefully borne in mind when we come to the central election issue: intimidation, actual and alleged.

The Lancaster House Agreement, in putting the entire Rhodesian Administration nominally at Soames's disposal, also gave the BSAP responsibility for 'law and order'. As no discussion took place on whether this responsibility was to be executed by British or Rhodesian methods, the Governor's authority was supported as the BSAP's Commander and senior officers saw fit. By the time Acland and Learmont had established their concept of operations (16 December) they could see very clearly what lay ahead. In addition to, or as a lurid reflection of the problems summarised above, Walls's hostility to Acland personally and to the CMF collectively was an indication of what its members might expect in the weeks to come. Lack of numbers (except for self-defence at New Sarum) and the disproportion between numerous RSF locations and APs would preclude the CMF from monitoring armed men who operated beyond the former, most of whom believed they were serving Smith's Muzorewa, not Carrington's Lord Soames. But lack of numbers, accentuated by the deployment factor, emphasised the extreme risk which CMF teams deployed to RVs and APs would be taking. A handful of strangers would plunge into the bush to 'monitor' an unknown number of well-armed guerrillas. Those who came to the RVs and APs would present a challenge; those who remained outside, a threat.

With several honourable exceptions – CMF headquarters noted 'one or two good brigade commanders' – most of Walls's subordinates stressed to Acland and Learmont that their men would be 'taken out' the first night, 'even if we were lucky enough to have got them there in the first place'. The CMF Commander and his Deputy, however, realised that if deployment did succeed, an even greater threat might come from a frustrated RSF, determined one way or another to prevent the PF forces assembling or to attack them once hobbled in sixteen well-defined locations. Acland and Learmont, therefore, took three decisions which were to affect the entire course of the election campaign. Unavoidably preoccupied as they also were with administrative tasks of unique complexity, Acland and Learmont decided to go beyond the strict ambit of the Lancaster House Agreement and seek the closest co-operation with the PF liaison officers (PFLOs). These LOs would not only accompany CMF teams to RVs and APs, but stay in the latter. Indeed, it was on the LOs' persuasions that movement of PF forces to RVs and APs would depend. It could well be said that the single most useful item of equipment which CMF teams took to APs was not their Clansman VRC321 or PRC320 radios but loud hailers.

Secondly, Acland and Learmont decided to deploy the CMF openly, by road where possible, by air where not. Thirdly, and most crucial, the CMF would not simply monitor the APs: it would *protect* those who came to them. By the exercise of a kind of moral value judgment, the decision was thus taken to turn an obvious numerical weakness into a potential liaison asset. Discipline, intelligence and, above all, courage, would be deployed to convince the PF forces that not only had they nothing to fear from the CMF: they should put their trust in its scattered teams and their limited weaponry. To that end, Acland's overworked staff also ensured that all troops arriving at New Sarum were thoroughly briefed. This briefing, obvious requirements apart (but only possible due to the pragmatic extension of the time allowed for the cease-fire to come into effect), enabled one requirement to be rammed home: 'You will observe and report on whoever engages in intimidation or breaches the cease-fire.' The CMF would not be solely committed to static locations; it would have eyes and ears.

In taking the third decision – which, although following logically from the others, did not lessen the risks or shorten the odds – Acland and Learmont took two sensible precautions. Provision was made for reinforcing the CMF from the United Kingdom prior to evacuation if the cease-fire comprehensively failed; although the Lancaster House Agreement limited the CMF teams to 'personal arms', Acland ensured that a sufficient number of general-purpose machine guns (GPMGs) supported the teams at the APs for any trouble from PF forces to be quelled in short order. By agreement, these forces were to bring their own weapons with them. As events turned out, 'weapons' came to include some reasonably heavy metal. Tongogara understood Acland's decisions, and precautions. So did Tongogara's ZIPRA opposite number, Lookout Masuku, and his comrade Dumiso Dabengwa. In Acland's opinion, these three guerrillas did more to ensure that the PF forces assembled and the cease-fire held – more or less – than any others in Rhodesia during the election. Shortly after Tongogara and Masuku arrived in Salisbury to serve on the Cease-fire Commission (21 December) Acland and Learmont began to feel that the CMF would prove Walls wrong. The airlift began on 22 December. The United States belatedly came back into the act. The British troops were flown in by the US Air Force.[8] On 26 December, deployment commenced to the RSF locations, the twenty-three RVs and sixteen APs.

The spirit of this journey to the interior, in drenching rain and across terrain liberally strewn with mines and all overt evidence of war, was in odd contrast to that of Government House. A few hundred mostly very young men were embarking on a version of 'aid to the civil power' for which neither the British experience in Northern Ireland nor the Fijians' with the UN in Lebanon provided much guidance. Senior officers could draw on experience covering the full gamut of Britain's retreat from Empire, but for the soldiers lurching to and fro over pot-holed roads or being thrown about inside C130s their one resource was fortitude. Fortunately, in Kevin Cole, Arthur Songa Songa, Jack Munyao and David Moloney the British troops' Commonwealth compatriots had commanders who supported Acland to the hilt in both the decisions and the risks which he had taken.

A Puma helicopter struck a power line a hundred miles north of Salisbury on 29 December, killing the Royal Air Force crew and three members of the CMF, but apart from those casualties, all teams reached their locations intact. Weapons, vehicles, radios (and loud hailers), powerful lamps, flags, armbands, rations (and the modern equivalent of beads and glass) for the PF: tea, sugar, salt, jam, biscuits, hard tack, cigarettes – all were necessary. But the only vital element was morale, for the PFLOs even more than the CMF. If the PFLOs and their senior officers, the 'Lieutenant-Colonel Commissioners', had not trusted their new-found CMF compatriots, had not walked into the bush to re-assure apprehensive comrades (one white soldier can look much like another), the entire operation could well have been a sanguin-ary failure.

Tension was acute in the first days of the cease-fire, and inci-dents were only contained by courage and imagination. But, by the end of the first week, 12,147 armed PF guerrillas had sought the protection of RVs and APs. This wholesale rebuttal of Walls's successive assumptions – that the PF forces would not come in; or, if they did, the CMF would be unable to handle them – encouraged Acland personally to request from Soames a two-day extension of the fourteen-day 'implementation' period. Acland argued, 'You cannot cut off the supply of human beings as one turns off water in a tap'; that many guerrillas were seeking RVs in good faith; but were unavoidably delayed in reaching them. Two days' grace would clear the bush of many armed men, and, moreover, enable the move from RVs to APs to be made in good order. Acland knew by 5 January, when the RV phase was due to end, that CMF security – his first responsibility – depended on PF forces being in the APs, not the bush.

Acland succeeded in his request. By 9 January 20,364 guerrillas had assembled, and the APs were beginning to acquire a strange life of their own, one almost of immunity from the strife and strain still endemic throughout Rhodesia. Yet, had those guerril-las not come in, Rhodesia would have experienced more than strife and strain. The war would have continued; there would have been no cease-fire, no election, no solution. But, at this point in the final stage, we must return to Government House and the troubled spirits of Christopher Soames and those about him. Acland's request was granted, but more from one Etonian – and guardsman – to another than from conviction. Soames's advisers – accredited from Whitehall, potent if Rhodesian – re-mained convinced that Muzorewa would still be brought in the winner, but were forced to concede that, as with Lancaster House, phase one of the election campaign had not gone in his favour. Mugabe had returned, but was disporting, not disgracing himself. PF forces had assembled, protected by the CMF, although menaced by the RSF. Thousands of ZANLA guerrillas remained in the bush – few ZIPRA – but Walls's 'game plan' had failed. Soames, a purely political Governor, might strive to appear impartial as phase one ended and the cease-fire came into effect, but could not but be aware that the white Rhodesian establishment – on which he depended for basic administration, the maintenance of 'law and order', and the details of conducting the election – was still capable of springing a surprise.

Soames's conduct as Governor has been held up to a critical light by some partisans; here, one need not more than emphasise the difficulties of his position before turning to the second phase, which covers most of January and early February. This phase was marked, *inter alia*, by the COG's arrival, and was characterised by the central issues of intimidation; Soames's response to predominantly white Rhodesian allegations of its frequency and nature; evidence that many allegations reflected not only hostility and bias by the Administration but attempts to dislodge ZANU from Mugabe's eastern fief and the Fort Victoria area. We must also consider Walls's second phase and penultimate attempts to save the day: by refusing to provision PF forces in the APs in the hopes that they would break out and could be attacked; and by appealing to Mrs Thatcher.

There is no doubt that ZANU and ZANLA, whether in combination or as, ostensibly, separate movements did engage in intimidation – forceful, dire threats to simple folk of what would happen to them if they did not vote for Mugabe. Verbal threats were accompanied by strong-arm coercion. There is no point in beating about the bush on this issue: *all* foreign observers, whether in groups or operating as individuals, produced convincing evidence of ZANU/ZANLA intimidation, extending throughout the entire eastern areas of Rhodesia, from Mukimbura to Chiredzi and even the South African occupied confines of Beitbridge. The evidence is all the more compelling in coming from observers who inclined to think ZANU the party best fitted to form an independent Zimbabwe Government.[9]

ZANLA's penetration of these areas; ZANU's subsequent politicisation of them; and the establishment of a new fief for Mugabe in the Victoria Province have already been described. Given tribal factors, the course of the war, and events since the Lusaka meeting it would have been odd if Mugabe and his henchmen had not reacted to the support which the British Government gave Muzorewa by consolidating their own electoral domination in the eastern areas. Given the Shona population predominance over the Ndebele, plus the curious Lancaster House decision to follow precedent established in April 1979 and arrange polling for the African parties in large 'Electoral Districts' rather than constituencies, it became almost axiomatic that Mugabe would use all legitimate, or illegitimate, means to establish total ZANU domination throughout Rhodesia's eastern areas.

Intimidation is inexcusable, but was inevitable in a Rhodesian independence election dominated by the legacy of prolonged civil war and the policies which the British Government and the Smith-Muzorewa regime attempted to concoct and execute between April and December 1979. In the interests of history, all that concerns us here is intimidation, and whether or not much of it was provoked or accentuated by Soames's Rhodesian Administration, supported by the armed and security forces, regular, reserve, special – and otherwise. ZANU(PF), by early January, and after only a fortnight of official campaigning was drawing large crowds and rapidly shortening electoral punters' odds. Could ZANU(PF), briefly legitimised as a political party by Soames's fiat, be proscribed for illegal, intimidatory acts?

This was the question which concentrated white Rhodesian minds in Salisbury as phase one ended with the cease-fire more or less a going concern. As we reach the penultimate phase or stage in the long, bloody road to Zimbabwe it is essential to recall the stakes for which the parties were contending. For old-stagers like Chikerema and Sithole, campaigning gamely but forlornly, it was the journey rather than the arrival which mattered. For Nkomo, home in Matabeleland after prolonged exile, it was, perhaps, enough to know he would not be humiliated. Muzorewa's hopes were dependent on white support. It was he who had to fight for survival against the one African who had not compromised, who had declared that 'independence is not negotiable'. Could Mugabe still be defeated – by fair means, or foul?

Two attempts on Mugabe's life were made between 6 and 10 February. Up to this point, and despite some ugly confrontations between CMF teams and RSF units in the vicinity of APs, few white Rhodesians or members of Soames's civilian staff were disposed to believe that Mugabe would actually win outright. Every time this possibility flickered into the collective Government House mind – CMF headquarters was not above suggesting it – the reassuring thought of a hung election revived hopes. Soames was empowered to choose a Prime Minister; a Muzo-rewa–Nkomo coalition, ousting Mugabe, attracted few punters but reflected a belief that even if the little Bishop could not be brought home as an outright winner the judges could disqualify his only rival. The 'Ministry of Home Affairs' card was marked; UANC, thirty-four seats; ZANU(PF), twenty-six; PF, twenty. But marking cards was not enough. Soames had not only allowed mobilisation of Rhodesia's police and military reserves; on 7 January, he 'approved the deployment of security forces to assist the police in suppressing the wave of lawlessness sweeping the country following the withdrawal of security forces under the Cease-fire Agreement'.[10]

There was no such wave, as the BSAP, *after* the Election, admitted. The cease-fire was holding, more or less, despite intermittent tension at the APs and the occasional misunderstanding between CMF teams and PF forces. Moreover, as we have seen, the security forces as such had not been withdrawn, to company bases, or anywhere else. Soames committed Walls's troops – and ignored the possibility of deploying PF forces who had 'assembled' despite the fact that in complying with the cease-fire they were also 'forces of the Crown' – partly because, at Acland's personal insistence, South Africans had withdrawn from north of Beitbridge, but primarily in order to commit the RSF, BSAP and Auxiliaries in the eastern half of Rhodesia. ZANLA was still at large in Manicaland; Soames's concession to Walls is at least understandable.

The evidence for this deployment, of the intimidation which these forces engaged in, and of the growing hostility amongst Soames's Rhodesian Administration to ZANU(PF) from this time onwards is clear from COGR and other sources. Soames administered law as devised by white Rhodesians for their benefit during the 'Emergency'. Understandably, Soames renewed the Emergency period but, in doing so, was provided with an administrative and security instrument intended to be draconian so far as uncompromising African nationalists were concerned. Soames, however, did not actually administer this law; the Rhodesian bureaucracy – in effect a police-state apparatus – did so. Some wilder members of the white Rhodesian establishment and the special forces planned covert operations designed to discredit ZANU; that such operations took place is hardly a matter of doubt. Nor is there much doubt that Walls's aim was to have the Mashonaland East, Manicaland and Victoria provinces declared proscribed areas, in which no election campaigning by ZANU(PF) would be allowed; to have ZANU(PF) candidates disqualified; and to have the entire area put under the punitive authority of the 'Zimbabwe-Rhodesia Government' – which, in terms of 'Ministries' and the like, continued in being – rather than left to the discretion of a Governor who might, just, see more than one point of view.

Before turning to these matters – of which a direct conflict of evidence between Walls and Acland on the extent and level of intimidation is the key factor – the second-phase tasks of the CMF should be mentioned. These tasks bear directly on the final phases. Once the first days' acute anxiety at the APs had been replaced by a realisation that most of the PF forces in the bush would assemble, team commanders had to accept and act on the uncomfortable fact that their charges were hungry, in many cases sick, in all but a few instances in urgent need of shelter, clothing, even plates from which to eat. Acland and his staff were not alone in grasping the dangers of this situation. Even the most stolid young English private soldier gazing at these tired, bewildered men knew instinctively that if, having found sanctuary, they were not 'provisioned', a mass breakout was likely. Well-armed men would make for areas where food might be found, degenerating into the terrorists whom so many had dubbed them already. The cease-fire would collapse; the election would be destroyed.

Learmont's administrative instructions provided for one week's provisioning of PF forces, on basic scales. He had been assured that the Rhodesian Department of Social Affairs would then execute this and related tasks. By January 1980, however, such departments functioned on a mere 'care and maintenance basis'.

All requests were referred to higher authority, in or about Government House. Let one close observer take up the tale: 'A call went out to Walls and the "Rhodesian" Government. The answer was a firm refusal. General Walls said, "No, we don't have anything available."'[11] This was not true, as both earlier and later events clearly proved. But Acland and Learmont had not brought 1,500 men eight thousand miles, or more, and dispatched them to all parts of Rhodesia to accept defeat on this score. Drawing a blank cheque on the British taxpayer, the CMF's Administration and Quartering Staff 'indented' on a large scale: meat from South Africa; shirts from Hong Kong; mugs, plates, 'irons' from wherever they could be found, the local economy if available, the world market if not; blankets, tents, pots and pans – 'the logistic support for a field army of 22,000' in Learmont's dispassionate words. Water was provided – by great ingenuity, muscle, and soldiers driving on dirt tracks through a hostile bush from dams or boreholes to APs. Medical aid was given, to the extent indeed that a local health service developed not only in but around the APs.

There was no mass breakout. Indeed, even Combined Operations Headquarters (COH – or COMOPS as it was designated by some) in its daily, totally unauthorised communiqués could neither suggest that the APs were insecure nor that the intermittent guerrilla casualties occurring in them reflected anything more than poor weapons' training and sorely tried nerves. The guerrillas in the APs knew they were safe; indeed, many could hardly believe their luck. Yet, even although another white Rhodesian card had been called, the arrival of the COG on 24 January all but coincided with a wave of 'incidents' which, whether fomented or not, forced Soames to consider whether he was to be Governor in fact or by courtesy of a regime lately in rebellion against the Crown.

In early February the Cease-fire Commission reported that since its first meeting of 2 January 220 allegations of breaches had been submitted for investigation, and of these 128 had been considered. Three were agreed as incitements to break the cease-fire by the security forces and 84 other cases attributed as follows: ZANLA, 37 breaches; *ZANLA area of operations*, 20 [writer's italics]; ZIPRA, 9 breaches; ZIPRA area of operations, 3; Auxiliaries, 1; Bandits armed with PF-type weapons, 5; unattributable, 9.[12]

The Cease-fire Commission, strictly speaking, dealt only with incidents involving armed forces, whereas the Election Commission was concerned, amongst a host of other matters, with intimidation calculated to affect the election campaign. The wholly Rhodesian National Election Directorate was responsible for electoral and policy arrangements as such. In reality, breaches of the cease-fire and intimidation were two sides of the same coin; sensibly, the COG accepted this reality, and its *Report* draws on the evidence presented and allegations made to both bodies in assessing to what extent intimidation in the narrow sense affected the poll.

Two important factors were nevertheless neglected by the COG in considering evidence of cease-fire breaches. Most of the complaints were made by the security forces; which, in being deployed – and 'identified' – were not only easily able to incite, or commit breaches, but to be discovered in the act. The CMF was committed to monitoring the RSF; given the latter's continued deployment, operational necessity, accentuated by the hostility which many of its members expressed towards Acland's troops, forced these monitoring 'company bases' and the like to move about the country, to observe and report. By late January not a few senior members of the CMF were convinced that even if the deployed reserve elements of the BSAP and RSF were exercising some restraint, the Special Forces and, in particular, the Auxiliaries had been let off the leash in order that the 'ZANLA area of operations' – the electorally critical Mashonaland East, Manicaland and Victoria Provinces – would be reoccupied. By Mugabe's own admission, up to 4,000 ZANLA remained in this eastern area; by impartial observation, ZANU(PF) resorted to intimidation, and worse, in the area on which the election result depended.

A case can easily be made for intimidation by ZANLA and ZANU alone. The Governor's sources – courtesy of COMOPs, not General Acland as his Military Adviser – showed the spread and level of intimidation; other sources provided circumstantial evidence of who was mainly responsible for it. But if one then turns to COGR – where intelligence provided by the CMF plays a central role – a very different picture emerges. Chapter 3 of the *Report* provides a detailed account of intimidation, its causes and effects, above all in the three provinces which were so bitterly contested between ZANU(PF) and Muzorewa's security apparatus – rather than between the former and its party rivals. The *Report* stresses that the course of war and, above all, the breakdown of so much tribal and white administration, had created a vacuum which ZANU and ZANLA filled. As the Election Commissioner (Sir John Boynton) remarked: 'There was a high degree of commitment to one political party.'[13] Given that factor – all the more compelling in coming from a source with whom Dayal and his fellow observers occasionally clashed – the return of Special Forces and Auxiliaries to the three eastern provinces becomes significant. COGR also reiterates: 'A major departure from the Lancaster House Agreement was the failure by the Rhodesian Security Forces to disengage to the degree contemplated.'[14]

We can now begin to see that intimidation in these areas wore different aspects according to political allegiance. The *Report* is clear in stating: 'It is our view that intimidation by the guerrillas was by no means as widespread or as brutal as official spokesmen claimed. It is also hard to judge where the line was being drawn between political activism and intimidatory behaviour.'[15] The *Report* stresses: 'This view was borne out by members of the Commonwealth Monitoring Force in different Provinces, with whom we spoke, by some British Election Supervisors, and also by a number of missionaries, amongst others.' The CMF, engaging in its own active observation, noted 'that the bulk of ZANLA outside the Assembly Places were in fact unarmed and living among the people with their weapons cached'. And further: 'In Victoria Province we were told that after the cease-fire the Security Forces had deliberately interposed themselves between areas with known concentrations of guerrillas and the Assembly Places, thus deterring them from coming forward.' CMF made similar comments on Auxiliaries whom, in Manicaland, they observed with particular care; in one instance, a vigilant Monitor succeeded in having an Auxiliary Unit commander replaced, another charged with rape. Intimidation can take various forms.

The CMF intelligence summaries and maps came to differ progressively from those issued, without Soames's authority, from 'COMOPs'. In GRAPPLE, Monitors' reports even succeeded in reducing the number of casualties inflicted by the RSF for real, or alleged, breaches of the curfew. But in THRASHER and REPULSE, Monitors were so thin on the ground that the CMF was reduced to marking its maps as evidence of a situation which would have been relatively secure but for the Auxiliaries' activities. Muzorewa's assertions that legitimate political activity was prevented by ZANLA and ZANU(PF) intimidation is belied by the fact that all parties held meetings freely throughout the allegedly most dangerous areas. Indeed, Mugabe's rivals held more meetings than he did. Boynton's observation provides one explanation for this apparent paradox, but the more material factor is that, by mid-February, Soames had partly met Walls's demands. Acting on an ordinance which he made on 5 February, Soames made up one part of his mind. ZANU(PF) was not proscribed, but on the 15th its Treasurer, Enos Nkala, was disqualified from campaigning and three days later, on the 18th, the Party was prohibited 'from holding meetings in certain parts of the Chiredzi District'.

Nkala's offence was that he had, allegedly, declared the war would continue if ZANU(PF) was defeated at the polls. Rhodesia Front candidates, speaking in similar vein – indeed invoking South African aid – were not suspended. Prohibition on meetings was, ostensibly, based on the high level of insecurity and intimidation in the area. The COG noted: 'The Governor's decision was interesting, insofar as the areas proscribed did not in our view (nor, incidentally, in the view of the British Election Supervisors) constitute the areas of greatest threat to a free and fair poll.' And, the clincher: 'The end result of his [the Governor's] actions in respect of Triangle and Hippo Valley [the Chiredzi District] was to afford greater electioneering opportunities to all the other parties in a predominantly ZANU(PF) area.'[16]

In the foreground of COGR are not only arm-twisting ZANLA but the RSF at large and an equally wild bunch of Auxiliaries, particularly given to shooting up villages likely to be centres of ZANU(PF) influence. Assaults on schoolmasters –

natural allies of a radical movement - were reported regularly but fruitlessly to higher authority. The British 'TV Eye' programme asserted that 'thirty thousand auxiliaries in Rhodesia have been under orders to show the flag in the African villages', and gave a detailed, on-the-spot account of how Muzorewa's particular flag was shown - assisted by leaflet-dropping operations from a Rhodesian Air Force C-47. Soames consistently refused to accept evidence of initimidation by Auxiliaries, 'claimed that they were essential in maintaining law and order', and, on 12 February, did no more than 'remind them of their duties'.[17] In the background of COGR, therefore, we can see the real instruments of power, as exercised by those who were nominally under the authority of the Queen's representative. These instruments had been designed to maintain white supremacy; between 12 December 1979 and 27 February 1980 they were used 'to enable the Administration to control every facet of political activity'.[18] Even the guidance material distributed by the National Election Directorate (NED) declared:

You all remember the elections held in April 1979. That was the first occasion in the history of Zimbabwe-Rhodesia that all men and women were entitled to vote. Throughout the country many people voted, not because voting is compulsory, but because they knew that their votes would produce a black majority-rule government, thus taking the initial steps towards international recognition. The British Government noted this development, and in response to its invitation, representatives of all political parties of Zimbabwe-Rhodesia attended a conference at Lancaster House in London.[19]

This ingenious distortion of the facts was intended to suggest the legitimacy of Muzorewa's 'Zimbabwe-Rhodesia' Government. Soames allowed such material to be distributed. It is hardly surprising, therefore, that COGR states austerely: 'Freedom of expression was liable to marked restriction [supported by censorship which was applied with consistent bias]; freedom of assembly was the subject of licence and control; freedom of movement was subject to restraint through arbitrary detention, and in many parts of the country was restricted by curfews.' Soames was supported, if that be the word, not only by an Election Commissioner but by a Police Adviser, Sir James Haughton. Neither Soames, the Deputy Governor (Sir Anthony Duff) nor Haughton questioned the Administration's interpretation of white Rhodesian legislation; indeed none of these eminent gentlemen knew who was detained, why, or for how long. But a check by the COG of police records revealed that most detainees were members of ZANU; and that arrests of key party officials were made up to polling day.

The COG was, in general, impressed with the impartiality and conscientiousness of the NED; the efforts made to ensure that voters not only knew their rights but could vote in reasonable conditions; and with arrangements made for a poll free from personation and other forms of corruption. The light touch is rare in COGR but in the midst of an election fraught with every kind of difficulty, and in which the eligibility of anyone over eighteen was hard to determine, an observer found time to note urbanely: 'One Presiding Officer in Gwanda found it necessary to inspect the teeth of those of whose age he was uncertain. Another in Que Que, found bust measurements to be of assistance.'[20] But the light touch is rare because the overall record is of an Administration which applied the letter of emergency legislation, not the spirit of an independence election. Police reservists played an unconscionable role in election procedures; District Commissioners saw terrorists in men calling themselves party candidates; above all, observers sensed that even a hung election would not satisfy all whites. An incautious member of the NED said to one (unofficial) observer, 'The conduct of the polling will be the most efficient and fair ever held, and after that we will kick the hell out of them.'[21] During the poll one Presiding Officer said 'he was sick and tired of having to assist all those illiterate blacks who are going to take over the country'.

Men living under great strain do and say odd things. Rhodesia's whites who, without exception, dominated and, indeed, manned the Administration at all but the lowest levels, were very tired, and in many cases emotionally exhausted by change from the euphoria of the early 1970s to the conscious or tacit acceptance of defeat. Hatred of Mugabe and all his works is understandable, but this mood is recorded in order to emphasise the strenuous effort made to hobble him and how little Soames did to prevent it. The refugee issue most aptly illustrates this truth. The Lancaster House Agreement provided for the return of refugees from Mozambique, Zambia and Botswana. The numbers estimated as existing in these three countries were 160,000, 45,000, 23,000. The numbers game can be played another way: ZANU, 160,000; ZAPU, 68,000. Obviously, this division blurs tribal distinctions and splinter party affiliations, but is substantially confirmed by the writer's own experience in visiting refugee camps.

Returning such numbers made demands on the Rhodesian Administration, neighbouring countries, the United Nations High Commission for Refugees (UNHCR) and the International Red Cross. UNHCR, under the energetic direction of the Australian Nicholas Morris, was given prime responsibility for moving refugees to the Rhodesian border. There, the CMF searched refugees for weapons, but full screening was carried out by Rhodesian officials and police, who were given complete discretion to refuse entry to any refugee whom they considered unsuitable. By 15 February, the Administration refused to accept any more. Approximately 18,000 had returned from Botswana, but only 4,200 from Zambia, and 7,300 from Mozambique. After representations by the COG to Duff, a further 5,000 from all three countries were returned but, by 25 February, the closure was applied. This act was necessary if polling was to take place in an orderly manner. There was no inevitability, however, about restricting refugee return from Mozambique to less than 5 per cent of the total.

The UNHCR and other bodies were collectively convinced that, with goodwill and maximum co-operation, more refugees could have been returned. 'The limiting factor was the policy adopted by the Rhodesian Authorities.'[22] This policy was supported by Soames and Duff, who refused to accept that adult males returning from Mozambique had a prima facie right to be considered as voters and should not be considered as actual or potential guerrillas. The COG visited border areas and saw the situation on the ground; the Governor relied on what 'his' Administration told him. The reader must judge for himself, but the facts are as recorded, and it is difficult to acquit Soames of listening when he should have decided for himself, taking as read the word of advisers who did not even assume impartiality or hoping, above all, that the card marked 'Muzorewa' could be dealt, at last.

Yet Soames did not lose his head, nor was his capacity to make the crucial decisions disturbed by the siren voices of partisan advisers. Electioneering continued. Despite the situation described in these pages, whites and Africans went to the polls in the third and fourth week of February 1980. Soames neither called off the Election nor allowed ZANU(PF) to be so hobbled that its members could not campaign at all. Despite a free-for-all concerning election expenses which gave Muzorewa a distinct publicity advantage, Mugabe – and Nkomo – made maximum use of the media. But Mugabe knew where his real strength lay, and in which areas he should concentrate his manpower resources. As with other issues, the reader must judge whether intimidation was a decisive factor in the three provinces where the white Rhodesian Administration and ZANU(PF) fought to regain or maintain their position. In the writer's opinion, intimidation was practised about equally by both main contestants; the names given to the practices differed; the motives were the same. These practices affected the campaign, not the result.

Mugabe and the two movements which he controlled had established a position in the eastern and south-eastern areas, and elsewhere in Rhodesia, which was far stronger than most people at the centre of affairs, white or African, realised. Observers and Monitors assessed the strength of this position accurately; Soames and his entourage did not. One reason why Acland, Dayal and their compatriots were less than absolutely welcome at Government House was their role as commentators on the situation, a kind of Greek chorus whom many tried to ignore or repudiate. Soames went through a bad quarter of an hour hearing such emphatically contrasted views, but he took Rhodesia to the polls nevertheless. In weather more suitable for an English election, and with 571 British policemen at the polling stations as 'Assistant Election Supervisors' providing not only an imaginative touch of reassurance but a reminder of Carrington's 'monitoring' notions in the now-distant days of Lancaster House, an estimated

93·6 per cent of those Africans eligible to vote did so. The result: ZANU(PF), 57 seats (62·992 of the poll); PF, 20 seats (24·113); UANC, 3 seats (8·227). The rest, nowhere. Smith's Rhodesian Front won all 20 white seats. The one really valid comment:

> My general conclusion is that, in the Rhodesian context ... described, the elections were in general a reflection of the wishes of the people, though in no sense free from intimidation and pressure. However my view is that in the country as a whole the degree of intimidation and pressure was not so great as to invalidate the overall results of the poll.[23]

Mugabe had won a famous victory, and many hastened to congratulate him, in Zimbabwe and elsewhere. Soames, who had met Mugabe privately on 26 February to plan reconciliation if ZANU(PF) won outright, was generous with his words to his new Prime Minister. Mrs Thatcher was a notable absentee from those sending personal congratulations. Nkomo took his defeat like a man; Muzorewa was packed back into the white man's box. Much of white Rhodesia awoke to reality, at last. But Smith, whose Rhodesia Front had won all twenty white seats, retired to his farm, never more to be Cincinnatus. Smith, however, left in Salisbury one henchman who juggled with defeat. General Walls had telephoned Mrs Thatcher from Pretoria during the election's final days, when even he could see what was going to happen. She had 'asked the participants of the Lancaster House Conference to communicate with her as necessary'.[24] There is no record of any other 'participant' making such long-distance calls. Walls contacted Mrs Thatcher again after the election, and 'pressed the British to declare null and void the elections that swept Prime Minister Mugabe to power'.

Even this last-ditch appeal from the white Rhodesian laager had its faintly bizarre aspect. Mugabe's eve-of-poll confidence led him to offer Walls command of Zimbabwe's armed forces. Partly due to CMF efforts, initial moves had been made to train and integrate RSF and PF units. Mugabe, with the instinct of a natural winner, offered Walls a double option: to pre-empt a white coup; to make a fresh start. Mugabe needed Walls, above all because he feared a South African riposte to his victory. Machel was at Mugabe's elbow at this critical moment, and advised him to make the offer. Flower, and others of his kidney, also looked ahead and provided Mugabe with advice. In retrospect, Walls's call to Mrs Thatcher can be seen as a pair of questions: Will you disown Mugabe? What should I do? Mrs Thatcher declined to help, verbally, or otherwise. Walls looked about him; he accepted Mugabe's offer. There was no coup and, in February 1980, South Africa stayed its hand. Rex Nhongo, who had led the Altena Farm raid which began it all, found himself transmogrified into a Major-General in the new army. Few acts could have had greater symbolic significance.

Thus Mugabe, portrayed so widely as a Marxist Machiavelli, emerged in a burst of reconciliation and goodwill. He asked Soames to stay as Governor until independence had been formally proclaimed. The CMF was also asked to remain, but Acland and his men, although keen to finish what they had begun, had been summoned home. A campaign medal was awarded: red, white and blue: 'The Rhodesia Medal 1980'. Most of us will think the men earned it. Acland and his staff left a legacy of goodwill which did much to help the painful process of adjustment between men lately striving to kill each other. A British army training team arrived in Zimbabwe as the CMF departed.

Elsewhere, the real reconciliation got under way – clearing mines, reopening schools, cleaning boreholes and cattle dips. Sheer necessity, aided by a certain white Rhodesian quality of resilience – one insufficiently appreciated by the international stage army of the good throughout the years of UDI – gave the exhausted land the appearance of waking up after a long nightmare. The white exodus also accelerated, but many farmers began to reckon up the odds, and decided to stay. The formal declaration of independence on 18 April 1980, the Prince of Wales in attendance, the immaculate turn-out on parade briefly recapturing an older, simpler world, seemed to herald a new country. But, for the present, all paused. The road to Zimbabwe had been a long one.

20

Postscript

'Southern Africa is becoming the new battleground in the
conflict between the oppressed and the oppressor, and all our
enemies are pinned together in an international colonialist conspiracy whose aim is to maintain the status quo in our region.'

Oliver Tambo, President of the South African ANC, quoted
in James Barber, 'Zimbabwe's Southern African Setting', *From
Rhodesia to Zimbabwe* (1980)

On the surface, the most singular aspect of Zimbabwe's four
years of independence is its survival as an African state, ruled –
and not merely governed 'responsibly' or otherwise – by a
majority which has vested its Government with genuine political
power. Robert Mugabe remains Prime Minister; his ZANU dominates the political scene; Joshua Nkomo resides, intermittently,
in the country – and retains more political liberty than most
outright opponents of Governments in a newly independent state
are allowed. But few black or white observers, in or beyond
Zimbabwe, would put money on Nkomo's chances of ousting
Mugabe.

There is much violence, although also intermittent; the
security situation is, more or less, in hand; white emigration
continues; avoidable – and unavoidable – administrative incom-
petence is rife at certain levels; drought can recur; most of the
ills which affect Third World countries at the hands of a 'free

market', multi-national system afflict Zimbabwe. Yet the country not only survives but is a going concern. Foreign investment is virtually nil, because profits cannot be remitted, but Britain and the United States continue to provide aid. The aid does not exactly flow, and is provided on a basis which reveals that independent Zimbabwe is, in many ways, as much captive to foreign interference as in its ostensibly dependent or aggressively rebellious years. But the British Military Advisory Training Team (BMATT) remains as one clear indication that the legacy of goodwill left by John Acland and his compatriots has not been entirely dissipated.

Zimbabwe, in fact, and if one looks beneath the surface, has changed from Smith's Rhodesia mainly in the change from war to peace. The long road to freedom – as many, perhaps most Zimbabweans would inarticulately define the word – has been accomplished. The South African political map has been partially redrawn. Recently introduced cosmetic changes give Indians and 'coloureds' limited participation in the white political process. But Africans remain totally excluded. Each year, over a hundred Africans are hanged at Pretoria's maximum security prison for conviction on charges of high treason and the like. Yet Africans are denied the vote in a state against which they are, supposedly, conspiring. This Hobbesian or Orwellian condition was accentuated in March 1985, when the worst riots since Sharpeville and Soweto broke out in eastern Cape Province. For the first time Africans who, for whatever reason, acquiesce in Afrikanerdom, were attacked by their militant brethren. Prime Minister Botha predictably called the riots 'communist inspired', and told the outside world in general and the United States in particular that South Africa needed no advice on how to run its affairs. A judicial inquiry into the riots severely criticised the police and, by extension, the Government. Meanwhile, units of the SADF and other, less easily definable, groups extended their operations to Botswana, again penetrated deep into Angola, harassed the Machel Government in Mozambique, and reminded President Kaunda in Lusaka that the South African Government's arm was long indeed.

The Namibia issue remains alive; in June 1985, Botha introduced – or, to be specific, re-introduced – limited 'self-government' for the territory. Carefully selected internal party leaders, Andreas Shipanga among them, were given office and fat salaries on the understanding that all key matters – economic policy directed at continued private ownership of mineral resources, security and external affairs – would remain under Pretoria's control. The 'constructive engagement' with South Africa, which the Reagan Administration has pursued since 1981, was again exposed. South African Governments do not engage constructively with US Administrations which support an 'anti-communist' line but which allow Congress to move towards recommending sanctions and 'disinvestment', and does nothing to rebuke populist politicians – Senator Edward Kennedy only the most prominent – who seek to mobilise the black American vote in attacks on apartheid. The most telling comment of the futility of Reagan's 'constructive engagement' (positively supported by only one member of the Contact Group on Namibia, namely Britain) was made by the *Financial Times* on 4 July 1985:

> Throughout this period there is scant evidence that the West's cautious diplomacy has had deterrent or constructive effect. Mrs Thatcher has set her face against disinvestment and economic sanctions. But unless she comes up with an alternative strategy, co-ordinated with European Governments, which signals that patience with Pretoria is running out, she will find her corner very difficult to defend.

However, despite suffering in Namibia, a territory supposedly under UN jurisdiction, the South African ANC cherishes some hopes for the future because Mugabe won an independence election in February 1980 despite all the forces arrayed against him. But Southern Africa's economic map has not changed at all. Nothing indicates this fact more clearly than continued white occupation of land in Zimbabwe. If Rhodes, Jameson and their fellow shareholders in the Chartered Company could return to Zimbabwe they would find that land is still preferred to niggers.

The Western press, especially the 'liberal' newspapers, have devoted a good deal of space to Mugabe's real or alleged misdeeds since April 1980. Moralising has been abundant, and easy, about violence in Matabeleland and the arrest, imprisonment, probable torture, trial, acquittal and re-arrest of white Zimbabwe Air Force (ZAF) officers between July and September 1983. But the central issue of land, its ownership and utilisation, is not only unsolved, but is also largely ignored by those so ready to throw stones at a young nation. At the time of independence, only some twenty Africans had been able to buy farms owned or occupied by Europeans. The situation has not drastically changed during the past four years.

The really critical issue of land utilisation was fudged during the final years of UDI by enforced white emigration. Abandoned farms, above all in the areas where ZANLA and ZANU gained so great an ascendancy, masked the fact that, from the time when white settlers first occupied tribal lands, they had farmed only a proportion of them. But because apartheid was practised from the first, Africans were 're-settled' on poor, overcrowded land. The Lancaster House conference's constitution for Zimbabwe – which all participants, finally, accepted – expressly justified both this pattern of land settlement and the various Acts of the Southern Rhodesian Government and rebel regime which attempted to give seizure, alienation and misuse legal authority. In the constitution section 'Freedom from Deprivation of Property', the 'right' to own land is 'to be amended only by a unanimous vote in the House of Assembly and by not less than two-thirds of the members of the Senate for a period of ten years'.

The July 1985 General Election, which the Government won decisively after the poll period had been doubled, was partly influenced by Mugabe's pledge the preceding March not to amend the Lancaster House constitution until 1990 at the earliest. Mugabe's commitment to a one-party state is well known; adherence to the Lancaster House constitution is an absolute bar to attainment of the consolidation of one party – in reality, one tribal grouping – in power. But not only is the constitution a barrier to one-party rule; it denies any fundamental change in the pattern of land ownership, except in terms which are clearly beyond Zimbabwe's financial resources.

Those who believe Zimbabwe's independence was, finally, the end of the road should read this from Zimbabwe's constitution:

Every person will be protected from having his property compulsorily acquired except when the acquisition is in the interest of ... the development or utilisation of that ... property in such a manner as to promote the public benefit or, in the case of under-utilised land, settlement of land for agricultural purposes. When property is wanted for one of these purposes, its acquisition will be lawful only on condition that the law provides for the prompt payment of adequate compensation and, where compensation is contested, that a court order be obtained. A person whose property is so acquired will be guaranteed the right of access to the High Court to determine the amount of compensation ... Compensation will, within a reasonable time, be remittable to any country outside Zimbabwe, free from any deduction, tax or charge in respect of its remission.

Whitehall's draftsmen had, indeed, displayed their skill, not in precision of language but in a combination of restrictive provisions and vague phrases. An expert comment should be pondered:

There is no definition of under-utilised land, though presumably it includes unused land as well. There is no precise definition of 'adequate compensation', 'prompt payment', or 'reasonable time to be remittable'. In addition, the section does not state who precisely is to decide whether the land is needed for the promotion of the 'public benefit', although it is significant that it omits reference to the *government* deciding that the land is required for the public benefit, so suggesting that there is some 'objective' test of whether land be acquired for the benefit of the public. It appears that most of these problems of definition and interpretation are to be settled by the High Court, whose role in land settlement becomes critical.[1]

But even supposing that the High Court of Zimbabwe had decided in the last four years that the public would benefit from compulsory acquisition, there is no foreign exchange in the Government's kitty from which 'remittable' payment can be made. '... the total cost of acquiring 75 per cent of European land at current prices would be R$733 million or £480 million at current exchange rates ... this money would have to be obtained in either loans or grants from abroad ... the British Foreign Secretary has argued that "the costs would be ... well beyond the capacity of any individual donor country"'.[2] These words, although written four years ago, are cruelly relevant today. Indeed, they gain in force from changes in exchange rates, and, of far greater potency, the determination of Britain and the United States to 'aid' only those countries which respect free-market commercial imperatives and other, apparent, hallmarks of the Western political and economic system.

As with Zambia, a good case can be made that the white, 'commercial' farmers in Zimbabwe must be left undisturbed to produce, efficiently, 50 per cent of the country's food, for domestic consumption and, in good seasons, for export. But this argument has nothing to do with, and cannot justify the continued possession of under-utilised or unused land. Over 80 per cent of Zimbabwe's African population lives in rural areas. Four-fifths of Zimbabwe is agricultural land, albeit of greatly varying quality. Despite belated UDI legislation, nearly 50 per cent of this land is owned by Europeans, the largest farms and ranches being in the hands of major foreign companies like Lonrho and Liebigs.

African farms are, with some few exceptions, unproductive smallholdings. Yet in 1976, at least 7 per cent of European-owned land was not used at all. Similar percentages applied to under-utilised land. Two years later, as the war spread, the figure had risen to nearly 20. Post-war recovery has not materially altered the situation. African squatters on under-utilised or unused land and the Government's intermittent efforts at land settlement by offering abandoned farms through lotteries have not even dented the bastions of white commercial and economic interests in Zimbabwe. Nor have the Government's promises about land settlement silenced protest; land hunger increases; with all that is thereby implied for Zimbabwe's security and eventual prosperity. A competent army would be hard-pressed to maintain security if the hunger is not appeased; a tribal army could not do so.

Facts and figures have not been given in order to justify the wrongs which Mugabe's Government has undoubtedly committed. The information is given because it remains fundamental to any understanding of the problems which Mugabe and his ex-'freedom fighter' Ministers, both ZANU and ZAPU, have faced in trying to curb the natural, the justified, hunger for land of millions of their fellow citizens. The facts and figures provide the only objective framework in which specific events and developments in Zimbabwe since April 1980 can be appreciated. Mugabe knows that his only alternative to accepting the counter-revolutionary provisions of the Lancaster House constitution is to repudiate them by compulsory acquisition without compensation. Should that happen, all aid from Britain and the United States would cease. Mugabe might then, perforce, turn to the Soviet Union or China. South Africa would certainly not accept an African neighbour on these terms. Samora Machel, who still influences Mugabe, understands these realities. Although there is sometimes a rhetorical element in South African assertions of its anti-communism, the consequences of a Mugabe volte-face are fairly predictable.

It is in this context that the British Government's determination to hobble Mugabe in his political – or foreign policy – choices, not merely over his domestic aspirations, requires comment. Mugabe almost ostentatiously ignored Soviet expressions of goodwill when Zimbabwe became independent. Moscow, therefore, used its North Korean satellite in an attempt to establish a foothold in Harare. A North Korean delegation arrived, uninvited, in Harare shortly after independence with offers of military aid, above all at the training level. Mugabe said 'no thanks'. Undeterred, another delegation appeared. At this point, an understandably irritated Mugabe had the courtesy rather than the wit to seek counsel from the British High Commission and the United States Embassy. In those late Carter days of doubt and despair, the Embassy was loath to interfere. Mugabe, however, was personally welcome. He was advised, courteously, that the North Koreans would only cause trouble. But the British High Commission virtually told Mugabe not to accept a North Korean military training team. If Mugabe wanted communists, he must dispense with BMATT.

Stung, Mugabe rejected this 'advice'. The North Koreans were invited. The High Commission's bluff was called: BMATT remained. The rest we know: the so-called 5 Brigade of ex-ZANLA troops which the North Koreans trained by methods appropriate only to a police state; the havoc which these roughs inflicted on black and white in Matabeleland during much of 1982 and 1983 with the obvious intention of destroying Nkomo as a political force; the odium which Mugabe incurred; his dismissal of the North Koreans in August 1982; their determined reappearance; final repudiation by Mugabe as he turned increasingly to BMATT; the uneasy calm of the last eighteen months; a large question mark over Zimbabwe's future. A senior member of the US Embassy in Harare during the 'North Korean' episode has publicly stated that Zimbabwe is a 'success',[3] but behind this simple assertion lies not only all the terms on which the country continues to receive aid from the West, but the shadow of a South Africa determined to keep Mugabe in his place. Other Western diplomats in Harare interpret 'success' in terms which suggest that they believe Mugabe knows his place: to do what Britain and South Africa want him to do.

No reader of these pages will be surprised to learn that all CIO files were despatched from Salisbury to Pretoria immediately the result of the February 1980 election was known. The fact would be trivial, were it not that the sabotage inflicted on the Zimbabwe Air Force at intervals during 1982 has been traced by knowledgeable and relatively objective observers to South African sources. By the same token, Nkomo's possible involvement in plots to overthrow Mugabe and his Government appear to have a strong South African connection. So, at least, was the burden of Mugabe's comments on Nkomo at the time. During the critical years of 1982 and 1983 when, after an uncertain start, genuine multiracial integration of the Zimbabwe army became a real possibility, those opposed to Mugabe – from whatever cause – realised that they must either accept his domination of the internal political scene, or try to replace him by a leader wholly subservient to white interests.

Whatever the provocation, there is no doubt that Mugabe made a serious error of judgment in accepting a North Korean training team in 1980 and, above all, in allowing his most partisan colleagues to fashion a Praetorian Guard from '5 Brigade'. This was a mistake which is commonly made by men in a position of apparent power but real vulnerability. If one is frustrated in the execution of fundamental change – land ownership and use in Mugabe's case – and moreover believes oneself threatened, it is natural to swear that some personal authority will be retained, by whatever means. Mugabe has not allowed Moscow to establish a bridgehead in Harare, but he did give his enemies a weapon when he succumbed to pride after being put in his place by a diplomat representing white interests. Once these human factors are grasped, we can appreciate that the sabotage of ZAF aircraft in June and July 1982; the alleged complicity of white officers; and the discovery of a large cache of arms and ammunition near one of Nkomo's farms in January 1982 – followed in March 1983 by his flight to London, as always by courtesy of Lonrho – cannot be seen in isolation from pressure on Mugabe which could develop into a coup against him. Nkomo's return to Zimbabwe in August 1983 suggests a prospective, not an imminent coup; Nkomo's day may be done, Mugabe's dilemmas remain.

Sabotage virtually destroyed the ZAF's strike aircraft. In effect, these aircraft were replaced by the British Government in 1983, but during these years Mugabe could not but believe that white interests and Ndebele resentment would coalesce into a deliberate attempt to overthrow him. Whether release of the white ZAF officers in September 1983 saved Mugabe's skin is a question which only Pretoria – and London – can answer. The course of events between June 1982 and September 1983 was not only marked by violence in Matabeleland which suggested a vengeful streak in Mugabe, but by insistent demands from quarters favourable to the accused officers that they be given a fair trial. Despite a virtual admission of sabotage by one of the accused in open court – not after actual, or alleged torture – the officers were acquitted. Their release after re-arrest reflected a barely disguised insistence by the British Government that if Mugabe wanted economic aid he had better do as he was told.

So is Zimbabwe a success? Has the long march achieved so much? Or is Zimbabwe, *circa* 1985, yet another example of South Africa's power to mount and execute a counter-revolution? During the last four years, South Africa has strengthened its grip on Angola and Mozambique.[4] Botswana's economic survival remains in the hands of De Beers. Namibia's independence continues to be discussed, mainly by Washington and Pretoria, in exchanges notable only for President Reagan's desire for 'constructive engagement' with a white racial system which treats Africans as creatures or non-persons. Opposition to apartheid may become vocal in America and potent during presidential elections. But white South Africa is a power not easily shaken or even disturbed by what the outside world says. In the meantime, Zimbabwe survives. The objective of genuine independence has still not been attained. The landless of 1980 are landless still. *A luta continua.*

Appendix A

Mrs Thatcher's Speech to Commonwealth Heads of Government, 3 August 1979

But I imagine that it is on the question of Rhodesia that my colleagues will wish me to speak; and I therefore propose to confine my own intervention to that subject.

The problem of Rhodesia has hung over the Commonwealth for many years. The present trouble began in 1965 when the then Rhodesian government made the illegal declaration of independence. This was followed by years in which the efforts of successive British governments to achieve a settlement based on the wishes of a majority of the people of Rhodesia were frustrated, years in which the political rights of the majority were denied. Then came the war which has brought great hardship and suffering both inside Rhodesia and in neighbouring countries.

What began as a struggle between the white minority and the black majority has more recently taken on a very different dimension. There is now an African President, an African Prime Minister and an African majority in Parliament. There have been elections in which for the first time the African majority have been able to elect the leaders of the government. There are those who seem to believe that the world should simply go on treating Bishop Muzorewa as if he were Mr Smith. But the change that

315

has taken place in Rhodesia cannot be dismissed as of no consequence.

It is the British Government's view that we must use the
opportunity created by the changes which have taken place in
Rhodesia to see if we can now find the solution which has eluded
us for so long, and to bring an end to the war.

We owe it to the people of Rhodesia to do all we can, all of
us, to help all of them, to resolve their political differences peacefully rather than by force.

I simply do not believe that there is anything now dividing the
people of Rhodesia which is worth the use of the bomb and the
gun to kill and maim men, women and children by the thousand,
or which can justify the misery of the hundreds of thousands in
refugee camps.

In the changes that have now taken place we surely have the
basis from which to try to develop a solution which will command
general international acceptance.

As you know, on the British Government's behalf, Lord Harlech saw the Heads of Government of seven African states and
also Mr Mugabe and representatives of Mr Nkomo.

Richard Luce saw the governments of a further five African
countries. We have also been in touch with all our other Commonwealth friends as well as with our European Community partners and the United States. The consultations we have had so
far have been of great value to the Government in helping to
identify what the solution should be. I should like to take this
opportunity to thank personally all those Heads of Government
here today who have helped us in this way.

From our consultations certain common factors emerge clearly.
The strongest is the view that the constitution under which
Bishop Muzorewa has come to power is defective in certain im-
portant respects.

I refer of course to the provisions which make it possible for
the white minority to block, in the Parliament, constitutional
changes that would be unwelcome to them.

This is a valid criticism – such a blocking mechanism has not
appeared in any other independence constitution agreed to by the
British Parliament.

The principle that there should be some guaranteed representation for minority communities during a certain minimum period following the transfer of power on independence is not new - and I think we all recognise the importance to Rhodesia of encouraging the European minority to remain and to continue to play a useful part in the life of the community.

But that is a very different matter from enabling them to block all change.

The other main criticism of the constitution relating to the composition and powers of the various service commissions is also valid. It is clearly wrong that the government should not have adequate control over certain senior appointments.

Those consulted also considered it essential that the search for a solution should involve the present external parties, so that their supporters outside the country might return home in peace and play their full part in political life.

Lastly, in considering the consultations we have had so far, I have been impressed by the general conviction that any solution of the Rhodesia problem must derive its authority from Britain as the responsible colonial power.

The international community has lost few opportunities to remind us that it is Britain's constitutional responsibility to bring Rhodesia to legal independence on a basis of justice and democracy fully comparable with the arrangements we have made for the independence of other countries.

We accept that responsibility and have every intention of discharging it honourably.

Mr Chairman, as I mentioned earlier, the consultations we have had with our Commonwealth partners over the last two months, and indeed with many other governments, have been most helpful. We have looked forward to this meeting as an important stage in that process of consultation before we decide our policy and initiate what we all profoundly hope will be the final approach to a solution.

I look forward very much to hearing any further views of colleagues here; but you will have gathered that we think we can begin to see the form that an attempt at a solution ought to take.

Let me therefore, before this debate continues, make certain points about the British position quite clear.

(i) the British Government are wholly committed to genuine black majority rule in Rhodesia;

(ii) we accept that it is our constitutional responsibility to grant legal independence on that basis and that only Britain can do it;

(iii) we accept that our objective must be to establish that independence on the basis of a constitution comparable with the constitutions we have agreed with other countries;

(iv) we are deeply conscious of the urgent need to bring peace to the people of Rhodesia and her neighbours; we will therefore present our proposals as quickly as possible to all the parties, and at the same time call on them to cease hostilities and move forward with us to a settlement.

Our aim is, as I stated it during our opening session, to bring Rhodesia to legal independence on a basis which the Commonwealth and the international community as a whole will find acceptable.

I believe that we now have a chance to achieve this, and we must take it.

Appendix B

Shridath Ramphal's Statement at the Commonwealth Committee on Southern Africa, 23 November 1979

The Commonwealth Secretary-General, Mr Shridath Ramphal, made the following statement today:

In all that we have been doing these past weeks in our informal consultations and meetings of this Committee we have been working collectively as the Commonwealth; and we have been doing so in support of the lasting settlement in Rhodesia which *Commonwealth* action in Lusaka made possible. The Commonwealth role, as your involvement testifies and as 14 years of Commonwealth pre-occupation attests, is not a marginal one. Major burdens are borne by the British Government and by Commonwealth African Front Line States; but many other Commonwealth Governments have played immensely helpful roles as well. The Commonwealth, as this week's developments confirm, will need to continue these contributions if the promise of a lasting settlement which the Commonwealth made to the world in Lusaka is to be brought nearer to fulfilment.

But apart from general support for the post-Lusaka procedures which Commonwealth Governments accept as natural responsibilities, there was one particular Commonwealth role for which the Lusaka Agreement provided specifically. It is about that role

319

that we are meeting today in this Committee. It is, I am sure, no secret from any of you that of all the important elements of the nine-point plan which Heads of Government agreed on, and which we have been calling the 'Lusaka Accord', none was more important than point seven in which Heads of Government:

> acknowledged that the government formed under such an independence constitution must be chosen through free and fair elections properly supervised under British Government authority, *and with Commonwealth observers.*

I am sure also that I do not need to stress the importance which Heads of Government attached to this Commonwealth observer role in relation to the elections. It is quite clear that it is of immense importance as confidence-building machinery in relation to the parties to the elections. But it is also of major importance to Commonwealth Governments generally who have made a major political investment in the procedures for achieving and implementing a lasting settlement. And I venture to think it is of much significance to the wider international community.

The second point I should make is that this is a Commonwealth role that everyone should be encouraged to see in wholly helpful and constructive terms. The elections should mark the real end of the Rhodesian problem that has bedevilled African, Commonwealth and international affairs for so long. They should be the prelude to Zimbabwe's independence and the assumption of its long-deferred place as a member of the Commonwealth and of the international community. A Commonwealth observer role which assists in confirming the validity of those elections will be a seal of assurance of great importance to Zimbabwe's future.

The third point is that we should not be confused over the questions to be settled. There is, for example, no significant (if any) disagreement over the essential elements of paragraphs 1–3 of the Outline for the Commonwealth observer role that I have circulated as the Secretariat's preliminary ideas. I believe the British Government accepts that Commonwealth observers must be in a position to satisfy the Commonwealth as a whole that the election is free and fair and that the British Government has effectively carried out its responsibility in relation to them. There is no disagreement that there should be no restrictions on the movement of the observers and that every effort should be made by all concerned to facilitate their tasks. There is no disagreement that the observers should not limit their activities merely to the events during the days on which polling takes place but must be able to observe the election campaign as a whole. There is no disagreement that the responsibility for the organisation and conduct of the election will rest with the Governor and his staff who will have the responsibility for ensuring, with the assistance of the Elections Commission, that the elections have been free and fair and that allegations of unfair practice have been properly investigated and remedied. And there is no doubt whatever that the Governor and his staff will wish to co-operate in full with the Commonwealth observers. None of these, I believe, certainly I hope, are matters of any controversy or difference within this Committee or between Commonwealth Governments.

Nor do I believe that in the spirit that has always inspired Commonwealth arrangements, there should be any problem over formalities, or, speaking for the Secretariat, any institutional *amour propre* inhibiting our working out practicable arrangements for the establishment of the group of Commonwealth observers or their functioning. Certainly, the Secretariat is not seeking a role in this matter for its own sake.

But there is an important matter of principle for Commonwealth Governments to determine and therefore, for this Committee to make recommendations on to them. In some respects it is not an issue of any great complexity; and, indeed, it was never one on which I entertained any doubt or expected any difference of view. It is simply this: when Commonwealth leaders in Lusaka agreed to give their support to the plan leading to free and fair elections 'with Commonwealth observers', did they envisage anything other than a collective observer role for the Commonwealth? As I indicated in my message to Commonwealth Heads of Government on 19 November, it was my understanding that what was envisaged at Lusaka was a collective role for 'Commonwealth observers' rather than separate roles for 'observers from Commonwealth countries'.

I said in that message that this understanding was 'in line with normal practice'. We have not had many occasions on which there have been Commonwealth observer roles for elections or for referenda; but there have been a few. The last one - a Commonwealth observer role at the referendum on the future of Gibraltar - was in 1967, and it was one of some international significance. Before Gibraltar, there were Commonwealth roles in relation to elections in Guyana (in 1964) and in Mauritius (in 1967). On all these occasions the observers were organised as a team: a group of observers reporting as a group - sometimes with reservations on the part of one or more member - but always on the basis of a collective role.

And, of course, there have been many occasions on which elections or plebiscites or referenda have been conducted around the world with 'United Nations observers': in Togoland, in the Cameroons, in Western Samoa, in Ruanda Burundi, in Saba and Sarawak, in Equatorial Guinea, in West Irian, in Papua New Guinea, in Djibuti and, only this month, in the New Hebrides. On all of those occasions, 'United Nations observers' were not merely observers coming from countries who were members of the United Nations but a collective United Nations team organised at the request of member countries by the United Nations and reporting to member countries through the United Nations. To our knowledge - which may not, admittedly, be complete - if some comparable procedure is not followed in Rhodesia this would be the first occasion on which a Commonwealth or United Nations 'observer role' is not discharged in a collective manner by an observer team established on what has now come to be standard lines.

That is essentially the question; is the Commonwealth role in observing the elections in Rhodesia prior to Zimbabwe's independence to be a normal collective role or an abnormal non-collective one? Of course, if it is not to be a collective role it will not be a 'Commonwealth' role in the true sense of the word.

The British Government has already indicated an intention to invite all Commonwealth countries to send observers at their own expense to the elections; and it may be that some Commonwealth countries will wish to avail themselves of this separate opportunity to observe the elections in a purely national context. That would not, of course, exclude the collective role of Commonwealth observers which I believe was generally envisaged at

Lusaka, or even preclude the participation in that collective group of countries availing themselves separately of the British invitation.

I should not conceal from you, however, the implications of dealing with this matter otherwise than in a collective manner. The Commonwealth, as this crowded table testifies, has 42 members; it is, I would have thought, wholly unrealistic to expect all 42 countries to participate in the process of observing the elections. For one thing the overwhelming majority of our member-states would find it an immense financial burden to send personnel to Rhodesia for what could be as long as eight weeks or more; and yet, in the absence of a collective Commonwealth role or the separate acceptance of those financial burdens, most member countries would be excluded altogether from the process. Those countries who could easily afford to send observers and are prepared to do so on a separate national basis will go on their own behalf to advise their own governments. They will not go as Commonwealth observers merely because they are joined in Rhodesia by three or four – or six or seven – other sets of observers, each of them observing the elections on behalf of their own governments.

And, of course, at the end of the day what will result is not a collective view of Commonwealth observers, with or without reservation or dissent, but so many separate reports to separate capitals. In the place of a single collective assertion that (as we all must hope would be the case) the elections were freely and fairly conducted and the new Government of whatever Party, validly elected to take the country to independence – and Commonwealth membership; instead of that collective authentication which would be the consummation of Commonwealth efforts in Lusaka, there would be a series of different reports to different Governments – *quot homines, tot sententiae*. The invitation to divisiveness could not be clearer. Yet it will be a time when the Commonwealth need most to maximise its unity. I do not believe that this is what Commonwealth leaders in general envisaged at Lusaka.

But, quite apart from the basic issue of principle, there are a number of operational reasons which suggest that individual observer teams will not be able to function in as comprehensive and effective a manner as a collective group, and, therefore, not be able to contribute as fully to the process of confidence building which is so vital:

- A collective group would establish a presence within the country as soon as practicable after the cease-fire comes into effect; individual teams will go to Zimbabwe in a more haphazard manner.
- A collective group will be able to establish its presence not only in Salisbury but also in each of the provincial or district headquarters; individual teams will not be able to do so.
- A collective group, with adequate and specialised supporting staff, will be able to observe whether the various instrumentalities of Government - including the media, the police and relevant Departments of the Government - both in Salisbury and in the provinces have maintained strict impartiality during the whole process of the election campaign. Individual teams with limited numbers will hardly be able to do so.
- A collective group, whose presence and personnel will be widely advertised through the media, will be able to play a constructive role in a manner that individual teams will not.
- A collective group will be in a far better position to receive complaints from parties and individuals about all aspects of the electoral process, to look into these complaints and, where necessary, bring them to the notice of the Election Council or the Governor - than individual teams will be able to do.
- A collective group will be able to maintain close liaison with the Governor, the Election Council, the Cease-fire Commission and the cease-fire monitoring force and all the political parties; individual teams will not.
- As the elections will be held without registration of voters, critical questions of eligibility will arise on polling day at hundreds of polling stations throughout the country. A collective group backed by substantial supporting staff will be able to observe, in a manner that individual teams will simply find impossible, how polling officers discharge their responsibilities.

– Last but not least, a collective group, without derogating in any way from the executive authority of the administering power, will be able to use its good offices and offer judicious advice to smooth out difficulties as and when they occur in a manner that individual teams will not.

For all these reasons, the observer role of a collective group is bound to be immeasurably more effective and their report is bound to carry incomparably greater weight with the people of Zimbabwe, Commonwealth Governments as a whole, and the wider international community.

I have stated all this at some length because it is important that the Commonwealth does not falter at this stage. In my message to Commonwealth leaders I referred to President Kaunda's proposals for the Commonwealth observer team – which reflected my own understandings. In response to that message, I have since heard from a number of Heads of Government, all of whom, with the exception of the Prime Minister of New Zealand, have indicated that that was their understanding also. In the end, it is a matter for Commonwealth Governments collectively to decide.

One final matter. For my own part, my colleagues and I in the Secretariat have not been immune from sniping by certain sections of the press in this country with charges of partisanship whenever it has become necessary to take a stand on principle. It has been so from the first days of this Committee when, as the Sanctions Committee in the early days of UDI, my predecessor faced the same wrath. It has been so on sanctions breaking, on the deficiencies of the internal settlement constitution and the elections that followed or, more recently, on the 'second-class option'. History has already vindicated some of those stands. The immediate knocks are unwarranted; but they are an occupational hazard we must accept. What would be wrong, would be to be deflected from principle because of them. The Commonwealth collectively has played an honourable role throughout the chequered history of the Rhodesia problem. It is essential that we should sustain that record now.

It is in that spirit that I have put forward for the consideration of Governments the proposals that are before you, and invite your particular consideration of the essential issue of a collective Commonwealth observer role at the elections – quite apart from any other roles that Governments may wish to play.

Notes

Part One: 1890-1945

1 RAISING THE FLAG

1 D. M. Schreuder, *The Scramble for Southern Africa, 1877-1895* (Cambridge University Press, 1980), p. 257.
2 Robert Blake, *History of Rhodesia* (Eyre Methuen, 1977), p. 53.
3 Colonial Office List, 1920, p. 370.
4 Schreuder, *Scramble for Southern Africa*, p. 258.
5 For an honest account of atrocities, black *and* white, see Frank W. Sykes, *With Plumer in Matabeleland* (Constable, 1897). To their great credit, certain Southern Rhodesians were responsible for this book being republished, in Bulawayo, in 1972.
6 Schreuder, *Scramble for Southern Africa*, p. 258.
7 Ibid.
8 A. P. Thornton, *For the File on Empire* (Macmillan, 1968), p. 12.
9 Quoted in Schreuder, *Scramble for Southern Africa*, p. 261. Harcourt also remarked: 'Mr Rhodes is a very reasonable man. He only wants two things. Give him Protection and give him Slavery and he will be perfectly satisfied.' Rosebery, as Prime Minister in 1894-5, was a 'Liberal Imperialist', and saw no reason to thwart Empire on the cheap.
10 C. 7555, p. 41.

Notes

2 THE SOUTH AFRICAN WAR – AND AFTER

1 Ronald Hyam, *The Failure of South African Expansion, 1908-1948* (Macmillan, 1972), p. 1.
2 A. P. Thornton, *The Imperial Idea and Its Enemies* (Macmillan, 1963), pp. 138-9.
3 Ibid.
4 Thornton, *For the File on Empire*, p. 42 – quoting Smuts from his published letters, etc.

3 SOUTHERN RHODESIA: QUIS CUSTODIET?

1 Blake, *History of Rhodesia*, p. 115.
2 Ibid.
3 Ibid., p. 144.
4 The full details of the Chartered Company's sale – or, technically, expropriation of its assets – in Southern Rhodesia are extremely complex. Sale in the Colony was not actually completed until 1933. The figure quoted in the text represents the final settlement for Southern Rhodesia, not an exact figure for specific assets at a particular time. The Company's assets in Northern Rhodesia were wholly exempt. The Company, in 1923, retained four million acres of land in Southern Rhodesia; over two million in Northern Rhodesia; *plus* (*Annual Register*, 1923, p. 279): 'a half interest in land in North-Western Rhodesia for a period of forty years'. It was the latter which became Northern Rhodesia's copperbelt, from which the British South Africa Company subsequently gained greatly, and for which it was handsomely compensated in the 1960s.

4 THE SELF-GOVERNING COLONY

1 Blake, *History of Rhodesia*, p. 187.
2 *Rhodesia-Nyasaland Royal Commission Report*, 1939, Cmd. 5949, p. 15. The members of the Commission were, in addition to Bledisloe (a former Governor-General of New Zealand), Patrick Ashley Cooper, Ernest Evans, Thomas Fitzgerald, W. H. Mainwaring, and Ian Orr-Ewing. A financial expert, a former Colonial administrator, and three MPs

329

(Conservative, Labour, Liberal) did not make for a particularly distinguished group, but their individual views – broadly in favour of closer *association* by the territories – coalesce on the central issue of British responsibility towards the majority African population.

3 Ibid., p. 16.
4 W. H. Morris-Jones and Dennis Austin (eds), *From Rhodesia to Zimbabwe* (Frank Cass, 1980), p. 7.
5 L. H. Gann and M. Gelfand, *Huggins of Rhodesia* (George Allen & Unwin, 1964), p. 100.
6 Blake, *History of Rhodesia*, p. 226.

Part Two: From World War to Federation

N. B. British ministerial statements are from Cabinet Papers in the Public Record Office, unless otherwise stated.

5 THE SCENE

1 Two points about Rhodesian (and other African) troops' contribution should be noted. At the conclusion of the Ethiopian campaign, the South African Government put pressure on Churchill 'to play down the victory of mainly non-white troops [including units of the Indian army] over a largely white [Italian] army', Douglas Dodds-Parker, *Setting Europe Ablaze* (Springwood Books, 1984), p. 73. African troops from Northern and Southern Rhodesia who fought in Burma with the 11th East African Division were denied the home leave scheme instituted for their white officers and NCOs. In consequence all white officers from Northern Rhodesia refused to take advantage of the scheme; those from Southern Rhodesia did so (private information).
2 W. R. Louis, *Imperialism at Bay, 1941–5* (Oxford University Press, 1977), discusses Smuts and South West Africa in several passages. For the long-time American interest in the territory, not confined to the Truman Administration, see Andrew J. Crozier, 'The Establishment of the Mandates System, 1919–25', *Journal of Contemporary History*, July 1979. See also *Foreign Relations of the United States* (1946), vol. v. Note also: 'President Roosevelt, in line with his New

Deal coalition, was actually more hostile to British imperialism than Soviet communism', P. Duignan and L. H. Gann, *The United States and Africa: a History* (Cambridge University Press and Hoover Institution, 1984), p. 284. The clear exception to this US policy was Central and Southern Africa between 1945 and 1980; although the men on the spot thought, and acted, differently.

3 Lord Harlech – then High Commissioner in Pretoria – made a similar comment. See Charles Douglas-Home, *Evelyn Baring* (Collins, 1978), p. 111.

4 Britain's nineteenth-century roles in Central and Southern Africa have been dealt with extensively, but perhaps the most valuable account is by Schreuder, *Scramble for Southern Africa.*

5 James Barber, *South Africa's Foreign Policy, 1945-70* (Oxford University Press, 1973), p. 36.

6 Despatch to State Department, 30 January 1951. *Foreign Relations of the United States* (1951), vol. V, p. 1,427.

6 SOUTHERN RHODESIA – AND LONDON

1 Cabinet Papers (CP) 90 (44) 3.

2 Prosser Gifford and W. R. Louis (eds), *The Transfer of Power in Africa* (Yale University Press, 1982), pp. 42, 50.

7 MONEY AND MEASURES

1 Sir Ronald Prain, *Reflections on an Era* (Metal Bulletin Books, 1981), gives a favourable picture of Oppenheimer's views. In discussion with Sir Ronald, however, a somewhat different picture emerged. Lyttelton's comment was derived from Sir Hugh Fraser.

2 Quoted on p. 171 of Dr J. R. T. Wood, *The Welensky Papers: A History of the Federation of Rhodesia and Nyasaland* (Graham Publishing, Durban; Rex Collings, London, 1984).

3 J. A. Cross, *Lord Swinton* (Oxford University Press, 1982), p. 275.

4 Background information from Sir Hugh Parry; Wood, *Welensky Papers*, p. 118, for quotation.

5 Wood, *Welensky Papers*, p. 198.

6　Lord Blake's Introduction to Wood, *Welensky Papers*, p. 28. John Buchan's comment occurs in *Prester John*. The writer knew Cohen in the 1950s. A succinct account of Baxter was also provided by Sir Hugh Fraser.

7　Gifford and Louis (eds), *Transfer of Power in Africa*, p. 394. The direct attribution is, in fact, to Ronald Robinson, but Gifford's essay provides the charitable explanation.

8　Nyasaland became 'a Protectorate administered by the Foreign Office in February 1891', consummating Lord Salisbury's plan to shut Portugal out of the lakes region. Little economic development took place in the territory, mainly because neither Rhodes nor the British South Africa Company saw potential there.

8　TRIBAL FEELINGS

1　Douglas-Home, *Evelyn Baring*, p. 214.

2　CP 40 (50) 138.

3　Egeland's comment is included in a Commonwealth Relations Office telegram to Baring of 2 July 1949. Dominions Office (DO) 35/443. Most files on the issue remain closed.

9　ENTER AMERICA

1　*Foreign Relations of the United States* (1950), vol. v, pp. 1,506-11.

2　*Foreign Relations of the United States* (1951), vol. v, p. 1,227.

3　US Consul-General in Johannesburg to State Department, 19 April 1951. *Foreign Relations of the United States* (1951), vol. v, p. 442.

4　Ibid.

10　VICTORIA FALLS, 1951

1　*Annual Register* (1951).

2　Private information.

3　Memoranda of 3 May and 25 July 1951. CP 45 (51) 109.

4　Rhodes's comment is given on p. 27 of Richard Gibson, *African Liberation Movements* (Oxford University Press, 1972).

Part Three: The Central African Federation, 1953–63

N.B. British ministerial statements and comments by others at official gatherings are from Cabinet Papers in the Public Record Office, or from the Welensky Papers in the Bodleian Library, unless otherwise stated. Sir Roy Welensky's letters, comments, etc., are from the Welensky Papers, or from interviews with the author on 1 March and 10 June 1983.

11 WHAT THE WHITES WANTED

1 CP 48 (51) 110.
2 Ibid.
3 CP 57 (52) 445.
4 David Harrison, *The White Tribe of Africa* (BBC, 1981), p. 45.
5 Barber, p. 62.
6 Interview with Sir Hugh Parry, 26 July 1983.
7 Reference to Huggins and the Franchise will be found in James Barber, *Rhodesia: the Road to Rebellion* (Oxford University Press, 1967), p. 11.
8 Harry Franklin, *Unholy Wedlock: the Failure of the Central African Federation* (London, 1963), p. 75.
9 Oliver Lyttelton, *Memoirs* (Bodley Head, 1962), p. 391.

12 HOW AFRICANS RESISTED

1 Blake, *History of Rhodesia*, pp. 281–2.
2 William Rayner, *The Tribe and Its Successors* (Faber, 1962), p. 212.
3 Christopher Nyangoni and Gideon Nyandoro (eds), *Zimbabwe Independence Movements* (Rex Collings, 1979).
4 Interview with Sir Glyn Jones, 20 September 1983.
5 Quoted on pp. 405 and 419 of Wood, *Welensky Papers*.
6 On Huggins and 'nursemaids' see L.H. Gann and M. Gelfand, *Huggins of Rhodesia*, p. 231.
7 Gibson, *African Liberation Movements*, p. 157.
8 Ndabaningi Sithole, *African Nationalism* (Oxford University Press, 1961), p. 42.

9   Prain, *Reflections on an Era*, p. 138.

13 WHAT BRITAIN DID

1   Nigel Fisher, *Iain Macleod* (André Deutsch, 1973), p. 169.
2   Macmillan's gloss on the 'wind of change' speech may be found in the *Listener* (21 Oct 1983).
3   Diplomatic Archives, Washington, State Department Research and Analysis Reports, Box 1R 8274.
4   Ibid.
5   Barber, *South Africa's Foreign Policy*, p. 86.
6   For Sandys's remark, the author relies on an interview (20 July 1983) with one who was present, Sir David Scott, as well as both Welensky interviews.
7   Blake, *History of Rhodesia*, p. 325.
8   Blake, ibid., p. 326, shows how sensitive Macmillan was to House of Commons' reactions both before and after the 1959 General Election. The Labour Party's refusal to nominate members for the Monckton Commission complicated matters, because it left Opposition MPs free to criticise Macmillan in a political atmosphere which Blake summarised aptly enough: 'It seems odd today that such a question [Federation] should appear to either side as being capable of swinging an election. Bloody and brutal occurrences all over the world, not least within the United Kingdom itself, have hardened our hearts and blunted our susceptibilities. The consequences of independence in many black African States have sadly tarnished the nationalist cause. In those days the "liberal" outlook was more idealistic and the "liberal" conscience was more tender.'
       Memories were also fresh of the Mau Mau rebellion in Kenya, whose containment, all other factors apart, put a considerable strain on Britain's military manpower resources. It was the combination of Central African Federation as a real political issue and manpower as a genuine strategic factor which led Macmillan into ambiguities which were pronounced even for him.
9   The Monckton Commission's members were:
    The Rt Hon. Viscount Monckton of Brenchley, KCMG, KCVO, MC, QC (Chairman)

Sir Donald MacGillivray, GCMG, MBE (Vice-Chairman)

From the United Kingdom
Sir Charles Arden-Clarke, GCMG
The Rt Hon. Lord Crathorne, TD
Mr Aidan Crawley, MBE
The Rt Hon. Sir Lionel Heald, QC, MP
Mrs Elspeth Huxley, JP
Professor D. T. Jack, CBE
The Rt Hon. Hugh Molson, MP
The Rt Hon. Lord Shawcross, QC
The Rt Rev. R. H. W. Shepherd, DD, D Litt

From Australia
Mr F. G. Menzies, CBE

From Canada
Professor D. G. Creighton, DLitt, LL D

From the Federation of Rhodesia and Nyasaland
Mr H. G. Habanyama
Mr A. E. P. Robinson
Sir Victor Robinson, CBE, QC
Mr R. M. Taylor, CBE

From Southern Rhodesia
The Hon. Mr Justice T. H. W. Beadle, CMG, OBE
The Hon. Mr G. Ellman-Brown, CMG, OBE
Chief Simon Sigola

From Northern Rhodesia
Mr Woodrow Cross, MBE
Mr L. C. Katilungu
Mr W. H. McCleland, CBE, JP

From Nyasaland
Mr W. M. Chirwa
Mr E. K. Gondwe, BEM
Mr G. G. S. J. Hadlow, CBE, JP

On 4 June 1960 Lord Shawcross was compelled to resign on medical advice. At the request of the Prime Minister he agreed to make his services available to the Commission for consultation and advice.

The five UK Conservatives (Monckton, Crathorne, Crawley, Heald, Molson) were well to the left of their Party. The Colonial Service members (MacGillivray and Arden-Clarke) were undoubtedly strong supporters of genuine independence for territories. In effect, Southern Rhodesia's Beadle and Ellman-Brown were in a hopeless minority position. The Africans were content, on the whole, to let the 'liberal' Whites make the running on their behalf. The Federation's and Northern Rhodesia's officials took a broadly similar attitude.

10 For Macmillan in Lagos and in Salisbury 'bland and unrepentant', etc., see Wood, *Welensky Papers*, p. 731 *et seq*. The meetings in Salisbury are given a pro-Welensky gloss in Wood. The Bodleian material is a more reliable source, and is used for citation.

11 For the Southern Rhodesia National Democratic Party, see Nyangoni and Nyandoro, *Zimbabwe Independence Movements*, p. 21.

12 Wood, *Welensky Papers*, p. 737, for the Gwelo transcript. Foot was closely connected with the liberal, UK-based Africa Bureau, on which Macleod relied greatly for detailed background intelligence of African independence movements. Unlike some liberal organisations, the Africa Bureau was never troubled by the attentions of the security services or the Metropolitan Police Special Branch.

13 Strictly speaking, Welensky should have made his SIS request to Selwyn Lloyd. As Foreign Secretary he was nominally responsible for SIS. But Home, apart from the fact that Selwyn Lloyd would have been told eventually, had a pivotal Whitehall position, as a Commonwealth Relations Secretary who fielded Welensky's outbursts calmly. Home, therefore, discussed Welensky's request with the SIS Director Middle East, who made the appropriate responses.

14 James Barber, *Rhodesia: the Road to Rebellion* (Oxford University Press, 1967), pp. 18-19, quoting Philip Mason.

15 For Benson's remarks, see Prain, *Reflections on an Era*, p. 143.

16 Katanga's wealth is described in B. Chakravorty, *The Congo Operations, 1960-3* (Indian Defence Ministry, 1976), p. 9.

17 For Home, see Wood, *Welensky Papers*, p. 798.
18 For Nkomo, see ibid., p. 802.
19 The Commission's comments are given in Elaine Windrich, *The Rhodesian Problem: a Documentary Record, 1923-1973* (Routledge & Kegan Paul, 1975), p. 33.
20 Barber, *Rhodesia: the Road to Rebellion*, p. 48; the speaker was Wynn Starling, a Dominion Party member.
21 The liberal sentiment was expressed by Dr M. I. Hirsch, of the United Federal Party. The views on the 'atavistic' Bantu were expressed by Starling.

Part Four: UDI

N.B. Correspondence etc. with Sir Roy Welensky is from his Papers in the Bodleian Library, Oxford.

PREAMBLE

1 Richard Crossman, *The Diaries of a Cabinet Minister*, vol. II (Hamish Hamilton and Jonathan Cape, 1976), p. 153.
2 *H. C. Deb.* 957, col. 999.
3 As more fully explained on p. 107, Macmillan wrote a 'Top Secret and Personal' letter to Welensky on 26 November 1959, saying: 'We have no intention of making an extension of the Terms [of the Monckton Commission] to include secession.' Welensky kept one copy of this letter which, early in 1963, he sent to the Lord Chancellor (Dilhorne), hoping for a repudiation of the British Government's authority to dissolve the Federation. On 1 March Dilhorne replied: 'Both your message and the Prime Minister's reply [i.e. of 26 November 1959] relate to the functions of the Monckton Commission and neither of them seems to me to have any bearing on the question whether in 1953 pledges were given not to legislate without the consent of the four Governments and also guarantees of the permanency of the Federation.' Dilhorne's letter, together with the comments of the *Federation*'s law officers (see Part Three, pp. 102-3), and Lord Blake's comments in his Introduction to Wood, *Welensky Papers*, should finally dispose of an issue which troubled

Sir Roy more than any other: the prerogatives of the Crown or, in real terms, the constitutional authority of the British Government.

4 Nyasaland became independent on 6 July 1964; Northern Rhodesia on 24 October 1964.

5 ZANU/ZAPU disagreements are handled subjectively in most accounts including – understandably – Nkomo's (*The Story of My Life*, Methuen, 1984). For a more detached account see James Barber, *Rhodesia: the Road to Rebellion* (Oxford, 1977), pp. 197–203. ZANU, one should note in view of the reputation accorded it by the Smith regime, succeeded in writing a programme in 1963 whose opening statement was, in fact, moderate in tone if strong in intention – 'To establish a nationalist, democratic, socialist and Pan-African Republic within the fraternity of African states and the British Commonwealth.'

6 Smith rebelled on 'Armistice Day' – the date when the First World War ended in 1918 – in order to achieve the utmost emotional impact.

7 Nkomo has always claimed that he never accepted the 1961 constitutional proposals. But Barber, *Rhodesia*, pp. 81–2, quotes chapter and verse to show that, briefly, he certainly did. On the proposals as such see also: Windrich, *The Rhodesian Problem*.

8 Sandys is quoted on p. 32 of Martin Meredith, *The Past Is Another Country: Rhodesia, 1890–1979* (André Deutsch, 1979).

9 Mugabe had been in detention since September 1962; under arrest since December 1963. Both Nkomo and Mugabe were, in effect, out of action for a decade.

10 Smith's declaration and broadcast of 11 November 1965 – two extraordinary examples of propaganda – are given in full in Windrich, *The Rhodesian Problem*, pp. 210 ff.

11 Barber, *Rhodesia*, p. 77. The statement should be read in connection with R. A. Butler's 'Secret and Personal' letter to Field of 20 April 1963. 'In my letter of 9 April I affirmed the Government's acceptance in principle that Southern Rhodesia will proceed through the normal processes to independence, and we have never suggested that a conference was necessary to agree to the principle of independence.' This latter did not necessarily preclude defence of African rights.

12 Ideas for association of one form or another between the two
    Rhodesias continued in circulation until March 1963, when
    Welensky was in London for his final, forlorn hope of saving
    Federation. He met Butler on the 26th but then, finally
    realising he had been abandoned, turned on Macmillan four
    days later, saying that to eat lunch with him 'would stick in
    my throat'.

13 G. M. E. Leistner, *Rhodesia: Economic Structure and Change*
    (The Africa Institute of South Africa, Pretoria, 1976), p. 19;
    and also quoting: A. Hazlewood (ed.), *African Integration
    and Disintegration* (Oxford University Press, 1967), p. 249.

14 The Northern Rhodesian Central Intelligence Committee
    co-ordinated these operations in the Congo, which also in-
    volved the British intelligence and security services, but *not*
    the Federal Intelligence and Security Bureau. There was
    liaison in Salisbury, but at the Northern Rhodesian end of
    this complex chain of operations a careful distinction was
    drawn by London and Lusaka between intervention in Ka-
    tanga and support for the African nationalist party in the
    Protectorate which would most effectively gain and retain
    power. Both the Federal and the Southern Rhodesian
    Governments observed with growing hostility – but com-
    parable impotence – this combined operation to back Nu-
    kulumba and then, when he failed to satisfy the British
    requirement, Kaunda in order that he should achieve a dom-
    inating position. The manœuvres after the 1959 elections for
    the Legislative Council, whereby Kaunda effectively sup-
    planted Nukulumba, reflected this covert British interven-
    tion. But the manœuvres, and the subsequent grant of in-
    dependence to Northern Rhodesia, probably had the effect
    of hastening Southern Rhodesia's UDI.

15 After Kenya became independent in 1963, the MI5 station
    in Nairobi reported: 'At once the sky was black with aircraft
    from Bulgaria, North Korea and other Soviet bloc countries.
    Within a few weeks, the new [Kenya] Government had
    stated: "We don't want these people." '

16 Smith is quoted on p. 119 of Andrew Skeen, *Prelude to
    Independence* (Nasionale Boekhandel, Cape Town, 1966).

17 The Crossman *Diaries* give ample evidence, even if causti-
    cally presented, of Wilson's fantasies.

18 In Northern Rhodesia, contingency planning for meeting
    the effects of UDI began in February 1965. (Mennen
    Williams noted as early as 15 November *1961* that the
    United States would not be able to help an independent
    Zambia in an 'emergency'. Williams was referring to the
    possibility of Southern Rhodesia's UDI. On 20 April 1964
    Williams noted: 'The British are concerned but not alarmed'
    at the possibility of UDI.) Perhaps dimly aware of what was
    impending, the final communiqué of the Commonwealth
    Heads of Government meeting (London 17–25 June 1965)
    stated that the NIBMAR issue should be settled by 'a col-
    lective Commonwealth decision'. A year earlier reference
    had been made to Britain's 'sole responsibility'.

14 BRITAIN IMPOTENT

1   Martin Loney, *Rhodesia: White Racism and Imperial Re-
    sponse* (Penguin, 1975), p. 134. Wilson also 'spoke very
    plainly to the Africans [in February 1965]. I told them they
    should work the 1961 constitution ... unlike other African
    leaders, the African nationalists [in Southern Rhodesia] have
    never fought an election and have never tried to show their
    ability to govern.' See also Robert C. Good, *The Inter-
    national Politics of the Rhodesian Rebellion* (Faber & Faber,
    1973), passim. Good was US Ambassador in Lusaka when
    UDI occurred, and well able to observe and assess.
2   In January and February 1964, British troops were sent at
    short notice to quell mutinies in the former King's African
    Rifles battalions of the newly independent Kenya, Tanzania
    and Uganda. Within weeks the mutinies had been sup-
    pressed and order restored. The issues, in terms of man-
    power, logistics, and actual or potential opposition to British
    troops, were completely different to those obtaining to
    Southern Rhodesia.
3   *Annual Register* (1964), p. 32.
4   For specific reference to Wilson, South Africa and sanctions,
    see Loney, *Rhodesia*, and Crossman, *Diaries*, vol. II. On
    11 February 1965 Lord Rhodes (Parliamentary Under Secre-
    tary to the Board of Trade) said in the House of Lords: 'We
    are proud to trade with South Africa, make no mistake about

that.' So far as oil was concerned, the major oil companies knew in the late 1960s that refined products were reaching Rhodesia from their subsidiaries in South Africa, but felt no obligation to curtail the traffic.

5 On 16 November Wilson even referred to 'the danger of a Chinese or Soviet military intervention in Rhodesia'. Loney, *Rhodesia*, p. 146.

6 A detailed account of South African penetration is given by Christopher Coker, 'South Africa: a New Military Role in Southern Africa, 1969–82', *Survival* (International Institute for Strategic Studies, March/April 1983). See also Garrick Utley, *Globalism or Regionalism? United States Policy Towards Southern Africa* (IISS Adelphi Paper no. 154, 1979–80). Utley, from personal experience and exceptionally good sources, shows how little US policy has changed over the years – and how South African Governments benefited from the realisation that Britain could not, and the United States would not, seek to influence affairs in the region. Most American studies, by contrast with Utley, try to show that South Africa's strategic relevance to 'Western' policies must govern Administration thinking, *or* that 'moral' influence will ameliorate racial practices. A useful analysis of the 'Cape route' is by J. E. Spence, *The Strategic Significance of Southern Africa* (Royal United Service Institution, 1970).

7 David Smith and Colin Simpson, *Mugabe* (Sphere Books, 1981), p. 36.

8 The mandatory sanctions were confined to the import of oil products and the export of tobacco.

9 Outstanding exceptions to most accounts of the Rhodesian civil war – or the Zimbabwe Liberation war – are: Paul L. Moorcraft and Peter McLaughlin, *Chimorenga!: the War in Rhodesia, 1965–1980* (Sygma/Collins, 1982), and Thomas Arbuckle, 'Rhodesian Bush War Strategies and Tactics; an Assessment', *RUSI Journal*, 1979, vol. 1, pp. 27–34. All three writers experienced, or observed the war at first hand, but have achieved impressive objectivity in concentrating on operational issues. A most revealing account of how some white Rhodesians saw, and experienced, the war is in Ron Reid Daly, *Selous Scouts: Top Secret War* (Galago, 1982).

10 Meredith, *The Past Is Another Country*, p. 62.

11 Ibid., p. 63.
12 For reference to the Rhodesian Anglican hierarchy, see *Annual Register* (1969), p. 7.
13 National Security Study Memorandum 39 was leaked so widely that it is fair to conclude that a substantial number of State Department, and other, officials in Washington did genuinely oppose the Nixon–Kissinger policy on South Africa.
14 Meredith, *The Past Is Another Country*, p. 65.
15 One of Wilson's emissaries, after meeting P. K. Van der Byl, compared him to Dorian Gray, the inference being that the truth would emerge at last.
16 Anthony Lake, *The 'Tar Baby' Option: American Policy Towards Southern Rhodesia* (Columbia University Press, 1976), p. 98.

15   THE PORTUGUESE EMPIRE COLLAPSES

1 *Annual Report* (1971), p. 4.
2 Home may have been partly influenced by Foreign Office officials transferred from the Colonial and Commonwealth Relations Offices when these departments were closed in the late 1960s. Lord Pearce, a Lord of Appeal, was joined by Lord Harlech (a former Ambassador to Washington and Foreign Office Minister), Sir Maurice Dormon and Sir Glyn Jones, both former colonial Governors. Lord Blake in his, generally sympathetic, history of White Rhodesia, states: 'The Pearce Report is one of the most interesting documents to have appeared on Rhodesia in the last decade ... it throws a great deal of light on Rhodesian society and politics. Nor can there be any serious doubt about the validity of its main conclusions. The Africans, after years of silent observation of the Rhodesian Front attitudes towards them, its hatred of their political aspirations, its determination to suppress them, at last had a chance to get their own back. No one could henceforth believe that Smith governed with African support, or on any other basis than *force majeure*.' Blake, *History of Rhodesia*, p. 405.
3 The reports in question may be found (summarised) in the Mennen Williams Papers. The writer saw a good deal of

Nogueira in the 1960s, and has also had the advantage of discussion with George Ball who, on President Johnson's behalf, corresponded with Salazar about the future of Angola and Mozambique. Salazar privately conceded that 'self-determination' would not suffice – a point also made to London in July 1962 by the British Embassy in Lisbon, after its Military Attaché had returned from a visit to the two territories; he noted the poor morale of the Portuguese Colonial forces. The writer observed related factors in Portugal at the time of the 1974 coup.

4   Louw's comment was repeated some time between October and December 1961 to Williams by the South African Ambassador in Washington, W. C. Naude. The Mennen Williams Paper is undated, forming part of a batch of notes sent to George McGhee, and mostly concerned with US satellite tracking stations in, and the sale – or boycott – of military equipment to, the republic.

5   *Journal of the Royal United Services Institute*, June 1984, p. 39.

6   Vorster and Banda first met, in Malawi, in May 1970.

7   The writer's dissent from Meredith's arguments is also based partly on a closer study of events from the British Government's perspectives.

8   David Martin and Phyllis Johnson, *The Struggle for Zimbabwe* (Faber & Faber, 1982 edn), p. 3.

9   The letters, etc., will be found in Nyangoni and Nyandoro (eds), *Zimbabwe Independence Movements*, pp. 201–24.

10 Kees Maxey, *The Fight for Zimbabwe* (Rex Collings, 1975), p. 114.

11 Ibid., p. 128.

12 Ibid., p. 133.

13 Arnold Smith had for some time cultivated relations with Mario Soares, leader of the Portuguese Socialist Party and, as Foreign Minister in a 'coalition Government' after the Lisbon coup, responsible for negotiations with Angolan and Mozambiquean leaders.

14 South African forces in Rhodesia were 'rotated' to make identification difficult: numbers were occasionally reduced so that Vorster could remind Smith of his dependence; a 'final' withdrawal took place in August 1975, but the key element

in South Africa's support for white Rhodesia – helicopters, pilots, and ground crews – remained until just before Kissinger's September 1976 visit to Pretoria. Subsequently, the Rhodesian Air Force acquired its own helicopter element, although many pilots were South African. Intelligence liaison remained close, and staff officers from the South African Defence Forces were all but openly seconded to RSF Headquarters.

15 Van den Burgh, as a serving police Brigadier-General, was Director of the Bureau of State Security. Behind a deceptively 'liberal', even Anglophile manner, he was one of the hardest men in Vorster's entourage. Fourie was a senior member of the Foreign Service – lately Permanent Secretary – with a clear grasp of his country's weaknesses, not only its strength.

16 Martin and Johnson, *The Struggle for Zimbabwe*, p. 200.

17 Nkomo, *The Story of My Life*, p. 158.

16 1976: KISSINGER TAKES A HAND

1 The US Treasury was prepared to provide funds to compensate white Rhodesian farmers should a Rhodesian 'black majority Government' expropriate land. This was unlikely, but Kissinger's whole approach to Smith was based on covert conciliation, overt *diktat*.

2 *Annual Register* (1975), p. 45.

3 *Annual Register* (1976), p. 41.

4 Martin and Johnson, *The Struggle for Zimbabwe*, p. viii.

5 The writer's *International Peacekeeping* (Penguin, 1981) contains a detailed account of the US interest in Namibia, dating back to the immediate aftermath of the First World War, and the subsequent 'multi-national' growth of the American minerals industry.

6 Smith stressed – after explaining that the white-dominated Council of State would be 'the supreme body' which would appoint the Council of Ministers and devise a constitution – that 'it will be a majority-rule constitution and this is expressly laid down in the proposals. My own position on majority rule is well known. I have stated in public many times, and I believe I echo the views of the majority of both

black and white Rhodesians, when I say that we support majority rule, provided it is responsible rule.' The 'Parry' principle was thus brought up to date.

7 Meredith, *The Past Is Another Country*, p. 207.
8 Ibid., p. 264.
9 Smith and Simpson, *Mugabe*, p. 92.
10 Meredith, *The Past Is Another Country*, p. 222.
11 Ibid., p. 274.
12 Ibid., p. 256.

17 1977: ANGLO-AMERICAN INITIATIVES AND THE 'INTERNAL SETTLEMENT'

1 J. E. Spence ('Detente in Southern Africa; An Interim Judgement', *International Affairs*, January 1977, p. 9) argues that elements of a US-South African deal on Rhodesia and Namibia were initiated by Kissinger. The deal as such, however, took place during the Carter Administration.
2 *South African Digest*, 12 November 1976, p. 1.
3 Utley, *Globalism or Regionalism?*, pp. 4b-5a.
4 Cyrus Vance, *Hard Choices* (Simon & Schuster, 1983), p. 265.
5 *Annual Register* (1976), Chronology, 1 March 1976.
6 Zbigniew Brezinski, *Power and Principle* (Weidenfeld & Nicolson, 1983), p. 141.
7 Vance, *Hard Choices*, p. 257.
8 The State Department's assessments of raw materials were not shared by the South African Government. See, for example, W. C. J. Van Rensburg and D. A. Pretorius, *South Africa's Strategic Minerals* (Valiant Publishers, Johannesburg, 1977). The sub-title - *Pieces on a Continental Chessboard* - reveals the theme: if the US and the rest of the 'free world' lose access to South Africa's raw materials, the Soviet Union will gain it. The assertion is somewhat ironic in view of the fact that amongst the most regular visitors to South Africa's ports are vessels of the Soviet Merchant Marine.
9 The Amendment was repealed by Congress in March.
10 The Commonwealth Heads of Government Meeting marked a distinct shift in policy towards approval of the Rhodesian guerrilla campaign. In its final communiqué it noted that 'the armed struggle has become complementary to other efforts,

including a negotiated settlement'.

11 Meredith, *The Past Is Another Country*, p. 300.

12 Utley, *Globalism or Regionalism?*, p. 22b. Vorster resigned on 20 September 1978.

13 The one British attempt to put some pressure on South Africa concerning Namibia had bizarre overtones. The Shah of Iran, whose country supplied virtually all South Africa's crude oil – and hence Rhodesia's products – was a shareholder in Rio Tinto Zinc, thanks to the latter's interest in Iran's uranium potential. RTZ's Rossing uranium mine in Namibia was, indirectly, one source of the Shah's revenues. The British Government, at intervals in 1977 and 1978, persuaded the Shah to sell his RTZ shares for a sum which would also compensate him for loss of crude exports to South Africa. The British Government calculated that loss of such crude would induce a conciliatory mood in Pretoria. The Shah negotiated the sale; exports of crude continued; Pretoria remained obdurate.

14 Gwendolen M. Carter and Patrick O'Meara (eds), *Southern Africa* (Macmillan, 1979), p. 155.

15 Meredith, *The Past Is Another Country*, p. 359.

16 Utley, *Globalism or Regionalism?*, p. 11b.

17 Vance, *Hard Choices*, p. 285.

18 David Scott, *Ambassador in Black and White* (Weidenfeld & Nicolson, 1981), p. 206.

19 Vance, *Hard Choices*, p. 268.

20 Ibid., p. 287.

21 Meredith, *The Past Is Another Country*, p. 332.

22 Vance, *Hard Choices*, p. 283.

Part Five: The Triumph of Robert Mugabe

N.B. Quotations are given as appropriate from Lancaster House papers, as made available by the Foreign Office or Conference delegations.

PREAMBLE

1 For a detailed analysis of emigration etc. see Morris-Jones, *From Rhodesia to Zimbabwe*, pp. 118 ff.

2 Conscription of the African population for military service was often considered by the regime, but not implemented until January 1979. But Africans refused the call-up, and no effort was made to enforce it. A third of all whites eligible for military service also refused.

3 Moorcraft and McLaughlin, *Chimorenga!*, p. 40.

4 By April 1979, the eastern areas had lost 80 per cent of white farmers through exodus; in 1978–9, 4,290 guerrillas were killed – but so were 408 members of the security forces. This attrition might appear in favour of the whites: it was not, because of population disparities combined with emigration.

18 1979: LUSAKA AND LANCASTER HOUSE

1 Martin and Johnson, *The Struggle for Rhodesia*, p. 301.

2 *H. C. Deb.*, 11 July.

3 Henry Wiseman and Alastair M. Taylor, *From Rhodesia to Zimbabwe* (Pergamon Press, 1981), p. 4.

4 Ibid., p. 5.

5 In the writer's presence, on 8 November, Carrington conceded that 'we don't know the situation on the ground'.

6 When the Assembly Places plan surfaced at the Conference, *fifteen* were proposed. A round number was part of a rather feeble attempt to disguise the plan's source. Subsequently, and at Ministry of Defence insistence, sixteen APs were agreed. The Ministry, disliking the concept, insisted nevertheless that guerrillas should be given the maximum chance to assemble.

7 The writer took three days off from Lancaster House to observe the Geneva meeting.

19 1980: ELECTION AND INDEPENDENCE

1 Graham, together with Stephen Low, the US Ambassador in Lusaka, had been responsible for much of the background consultation and negotiation during the Owen–Vance 'Initiative' of 1977–8.

2 Wiseman and Taylor, *From Rhodesia to Zimbabwe*, p. 74.

3 The relevant passages concerning the COG in this and

succeeding pages are drawn from the COG *Report*; page references are only given in particular instances.

4 Dayal had been India's Foreign Minister, Permanent Representative at the UN, Ambassador to France, etc.

5 In addition to the COG, the British, and several other Governments (in and outside the Commonwealth) sent observers. The British team was 'advised to report directly to Lord Soames' (*Financial Times*, 12 December 1979). There were also teams from British and other political parties and movements interested in Rhodesia. The UN and the OAU also sent groups. Altogether 'there were approximately 223 accredited observers ...' (Wiseman and Taylor, *From Rhodesia to Zimbabwe*, p. 73), plus many individuals, and over 700 journalists. Never has an election been so comprehensively watched and reported. But *only* the COG represented the Commonwealth as such, and thus reflected both the letter and the spirit of the Lusaka meeting.

6 Some white Rhodesians took particular exception to the Fijians, despite – or because of – their bearing, discipline and restraint.

7 COGR/3/25.

8 The USAF flew from RAF stations in the UK to Salisbury via Akrotiri (Cyprus) and Nairobi. But an alternative route was required for emergencies, and perforce this was via Ascension Island and South African Air Force bases in Namibia. This enforced, if partial, dependence on South Africa had no particular political overtones, but added greatly to Acland's anxieties.

9 The view of observers concerning the incidence and location, rather than the nature of intimidation, is given not only in COGR, but in Wiseman and Taylor, *From Rhodesia to Zimbabwe*, p. 28.

10 *Herald* (Salisbury), 8 January 1980.

11 Wiseman and Taylor, *From Rhodesia to Zimbabwe*, p. 55. The former observed the situation on the ground. The RSF could certainly have provisioned the APs and provided 'services'. To take one example: a tented camp had been built by the RSF to cater for the CMF on arrival in Rhodesia.

12 *Herald*, 2 February 1980.

13 COGR/4/71.

347

14 COGR/3/30.
15 COGR/3/31.
16 COGR/3/40.
17 COGR/Annex 19.
18 COGR/3/16.
19 COGR/Annex 35.
20 COGR/3/67.
21 Wiseman and Taylor, *From Rhodesia to Zimbabwe*, p. 33.
22 COGR/3/23.
23 Sir John Boynton, quoted in COGR/3/71.
24 Wiseman and Taylor, *From Rhodesia to Zimbabwe*, p. 38.

20 POSTSCRIPT

1   Morris-Jones (ed), *From Rhodesia to Zimbabwe* p. 10.
2   Ibid., p. 11.
3   Jeffrey Davidow, 'Zimbabwe Is a Success', *Foreign Policy*, Winter 1982–3. One should note that, according to this source: '[Zimbabwe] possesses two-thirds of the world's known reserves of metallurgical grade chromite [and] is the world's second largest producer of chrome . . .'
4   BMATT's assistance to the Zimbabwe Army has enabled the latter to improve sufficiently in operational terms for units to aid Machel in his continued fight against South African backed rebel movements. Assistance by BMATT to Machel's forces has also been directly, discreetly provided. 'Aid' can still take unexpected forms.

Index

1 With a few unavoidable or obvious exceptions, individuals' titles and ranks are given as held at the time of the events described.
2 For abbreviations used see pp. xiii-xiv.

349